D0952588

FAITH OF OUR MOTHERS

FAITH OF OUR MOTHERS

The Stories of Presidential Mothers from
Mary Washington to Barbara Bush

Harold I. Gullan

William B. Eerdmans Publishing Company
Grand Rapids, Michigan / Cambridge, U.K.

Wm. B. Eerdmans Publishing Co.

255 Jefferson Ave. S.E., Grand Rapids, Michigan 49503 /
P.O. Box 163, Cambridge CB3 9PU U.K.

Printed in the United States of America

06 05 04 03 02   7 6 5 4 3 2

Library of Congress Cataloging-in-Publication Data

Gullan, Harold I., 1931-
    Faith of our mothers: the stories of presidential mothers from
Mary Washington to Barbara Bush / Harold I. Gullan
        p.   cm.
    Includes bibliographical references and index.
    ISBN 0-8028-4926-1 (pbk.: alk. paper)
    1. Mothers of presidents — United States — Biography.
    2. Mothers of presidents — Religious life — United States. I. Title.

E176.3.G85 2001
973'.09'9 — dc21
[B]
                                        2001023823

www.eerdmans.com

CONTENTS

BY WAY OF INTRODUCTION

HARRY TRUMAN once said that the only thing that is new in the world is the history we don't know. In writing *The Upset That Wasn't*, a book about Truman's dramatic victory in 1948, I was impressed by the pivotal role his mother played in instilling his ambitions. An article I later composed left me with similar impressions of Dwight Eisenhower's mother. It occurred to me that perhaps my next book should tell the stories of such presidential mothers, about whom most of us — myself included — seemed to know so little. I already had a title in mind, *First Mothers*.

It was a television interview, however, that moved me from thinking to writing. Political pundit Chris Matthews, in response to a question from Charlie Rose, suggested that Bill Clinton's legacy might have been more substantial had he a strong father figure to look up to and emulate. Wait a minute, I thought. Most of the presidents I knew anything about appeared to have been more influenced by their mothers. A year of research only confirmed that conviction, despite the limitations of the literature. It was these extraordinary women who most inspired their sons.

The American presidency, of course, has been the subject of immense and ever-expanding appraisal, scholarly and popular. Yet relatively little has been written about the parents of our presidents, and even less specifically about their mothers. When, in 1968, a talented newspaperwoman named Doris Faber completed her splendid little book, *The Mothers of American Presidents*, she could only find one prior study on the subject. That was a 1922 work by the Reverend Doctor William Judson Hampton entitled *Our Presidents and Their Mothers*. I am very much indebted to both authors. Faber and Hampton shared the view that, with the exception of Abigail Adams, who left behind a legacy of letters, the significance of presidential mothers had been shamefully neglected by historians. Faber was invaluable in locating the "missing mothers" of many nineteenth-century presidents. Hampton shaped my focus, helping this book evolve from a series of anecdotal accounts to a study with an underlying theme.

As this theme developed, I decided to reflect it in a new title, *Faith of Our Mothers*. It was just as well. As it turns out, another book named *First Mothers* was already on its way to completion. Surprises are not limited to fiction. But that draws no complaint from this quarter. Although I am not given to quoting Chairman Mao, many flowers should bloom. There have been too few in this particular garden — indeed, nothing at all since Faber's book was reprinted in 1978.

Why *Faith of Our Mothers*? Because faith is the quality these women most shared — above all, faith in the limitless potential of their sons. Often from their sons' infancy, presidential mothers sacrificed and dreamed for them, evincing a constancy and confidence that transcended love alone. Not every mother's influence turned out to be entirely beneficent, but virtually all of these women spurred their sons to achievement. It is this dedication that most unites so many disparate personalities. The mother of Bill Clinton, for example, cherished hope for her son at the center of her life no less than, say, the mothers of Rutherford B. Hayes or Grover Cleveland.

There is, however, another sort of faith manifested by many of these women. Virtually every presidential mother had faith in her son, but a remarkable number possessed a devout religious faith as well. Many hoped their favored sons would become ministers of the gospel; Nancy McKinley even prayed that her boy William might someday be a Methodist bishop. The Reverend Doctor Hampton noted how many presidential mothers were devoted Christians, a number immensely increased since his book was published. These women have followed a variety of creeds, and some have more successfully passed down their beliefs to their offspring than others. But through the years, their striving has been recognized by those it served, and their virtues reflected in their sons' best moments as president. American morality has often been grounded in Judeo-Christian faith.

Of our first twenty-five presidents, so little is known about ten of their mothers that, sadly, it is difficult to bring them back to life. (And for many presidential mothers, no image of how they looked even exists.) Were they equally supportive? Were they equally religious? I've tried to at least touch on them all, but much is conjecture. Even Thomas Jefferson, so copious in his commentary on everything else, had next to nothing to say about his mother.

Most of the mothers we do know about, for a variety of reasons, seem to have exerted more influence than their husbands on the sons who became president. Perhaps, as Doris Faber notes, one reason for such significance may be the mother's primary responsibility for childrearing. Faber also observes, as Margaret Truman Daniel did in her affectionate biography of her own father, how many of our presidents have been first or only sons — traditionally the focus of parental ambitions. (Today, thankfully, first daughters are equally valued.) Yet even in large families, presidential mothers seemed to have had an almost instinctive sense of which child held the most promise.

Did mothers have more influence because they tended to live longer than their husbands? Not necessarily. A number of potentially exceptional mothers of presidents also died young. The gifted Hulda Hoover died when Herbert was only eight. Calvin Coolidge never quite got over the death of his gentle mother, Victoria, when he was twelve. Moreover, not all presidential mothers who long outlived their husbands exerted a particularly positive influence on their sons. George Washington's disaffection with his mother is well documented. Polio-stricken Franklin Roosevelt had to overcome his mother's projection for him of a safe life limited to Hudson Valley squiredom.

Most of these mothers, however, encouraged the attainment of eminence, and the means of ascent was invariably education. Although many of them favored the ministry for their sons, they were primarily concerned with inspiring lofty aspirations. Rebekah Baines Johnson stands alone in viewing a specific public office as the career goal for her son. There is no prototype for these strong-willed women. As many were derived from destitution as from wealth. Some, like Elizabeth Jackson, literally saved their sons' lives. Some, like Maria Van Buren, created an environment in which ambition became viable. Some, like Eliza Garfield, overcame daunting odds simply to survive. Some, like Elizabeth Buchanan, used the gift of poetry to impart high ideals. Some, like Jessie Wilson, overwhelmed with supportive affection. Some, like Hannah Nixon, were called "saints" by their sons, and many more deserved to be. What they have had in common is faith, hope, and will. Although many of their sons were bound to fall short of their expectations, what a biographer once said of James Buchanan can still be applied to others: everything attractive about him derived from his mother, the better angel of his nature.

These are intended less to be capsule biographies than brief essays. With such differing amounts of material available, there has been no attempt to make them equal in length. The approach also varies. Some consideration of a president's politics (indeed, two presidents) seems relevant for the Adamses, for example. In most other instances it is not. With presidents such as William Henry Harrison and John Tyler, so little is known of their mothers that I felt obliged to dwell a little on their own careers. Fortunately, this problem recedes in the twentieth century. In the twenty-first, we will likely know too much about everyone.

In the past, I've spent many rewarding hours in presidential libraries, but this is not a book derived largely from original sources. Rather, I've relied on past and present historians and biographers, many of whom are gratefully quoted in the text, and on the recollections of the presidents themselves. The renowned historian John Lukacs made a nice distinction when he pointed out that a letter drawn from the files of a library is considered primary research, while the same letter reprinted in a book is deemed secondary. I hope that *Faith of Our Mothers* will not prove to be a secondary book, but a popular (if not a "pop") history. The ongoing saga of the American experience is a voyage of discovery for writers as well as readers. Although I've done some prior writing and speaking on the presidency, much of what I learned in assembling this book was entirely new to me — part of the history I didn't know. My earnest wish is that reading the stories of these remarkable women, so different in their talents and temperaments, will prove as rewarding an experience as writing it was.

Throughout, I have been profoundly indebted to the tireless staff of the St. Joseph's University library, especially Evelyn Minick and her associate Susan Tsiouris, the Lewis and Clark of my own corps of discovery. In coordinating the holdings of so many other libraries, they utilized a dazzling technology beyond my Luddite-like comprehension. For her equally unremitting efforts to translate my thoughts into some semblance of coherent English, I am beholden, as always, to my editor and friend, Elsa Efran. I also want to express my thanks to Ramona Flood, Joe Zuggi, Randall Miller, Ray Razzi, John Kuykendall, Jack Loughridge, Peter Munger, William McNitt, Ken Hafeli, and the generous people who provided the pictures that enhance this book. Most essential of all have been the contributions of so many people at my estimable publisher — particularly editor Hannah Timmermans, Andrew Hoogheem, Charles Van Hof, Kathryn VanderMolen, Willem Mineur, Anita Eerdmans, and Sam Eerdmans — who cemented our venture. It is my hope, to borrow a phrase, that a work so conceived and so dedicated will long endure.

In one way or another, escape was the initial goal of many of these young men who ultimately became president of our nation, their aim to rise above the circumstances of their childhoods. Often, this even involved overcoming the failures of their well-intentioned fathers. Rarely did it result in renouncing the inspiration of their mothers. Much the contrary. In this spirit I dedicate *Faith of Our Mothers* to the two people who most inspire me — my son, Bill, who knows what it is to be a president, and his mother, Betsy, whose integrity he had the good fortune to inherit.

CHAPTER ONE

The Perplexing Mary Ball Washington

WHAT TO MAKE of the mother of the father of our nation has long challenged historians. As Miriam Anne Bourne puts it, "Nineteenth-century sentimentality created a virtuous myth; twentieth-century revisionism has created a nagging monster." Of one quality there is no doubt. In an age of male domination, Mary Ball Washington was a woman of immense will — which she consistently sought to exert on her oldest son, George, and which he consistently tried to escape. The contest was protracted. Washington's mother lived into her eighty-second year, finally succumbing only a decade before her son.

That he could not have children of his own was a profound disappointment to Washington. In a circumspect letter to a nephew he implied that the fault was not his: "If Mrs. Washington should survive me there is a moral certainty of my dying without issue." The widowed Martha Dandridge Custis, however, had brought her own two surviving children, a son and a daughter, into her marriage with George Washington. On these stepchildren, his stepson's children, and a host of nieces and nephews Washington lavished attention bordering on intrusiveness. Even during the war for American independence he carried on an extensive correspondence with them, as with his brothers, sister, and cousins. Letters to his mother were few and formal. If the mature Washington's full family life substituted in some measure for the son he never had, it was also recompense for the sort of childhood he felt he had been denied. His career contradicts Lord Acton's dictum that power necessarily corrupts. Washington never lacked for ambition, but his ultimate aim was always to return, like Cincinnatus, to the home he had made. Even during the excitement of 1775 he wrote to Martha, "I should enjoy more real happiness in one month with you at home, than I have the most distant prospect of finding abroad, if my stay were to be seven times seven years."

Much is made of the patrician antecedents of our first six presidents, four of whom were the sons of Virginia planters and the other two from a well-established Massachusetts family. In the saga of the Washingtons, however, there are also humbler themes, the stuff of romantic novels, and a mobility akin to that of later generations of American immigrants. In the seventy-five years between the landing of the first of his family in Virginia and the birth of George Washington, a remarkable transition was effected.

For generations the Washingtons had lived in the Essex region of England, prosperous enough through their estates to enable young Lawrence Washington to answer a call to the Anglican priesthood. Unfortunately, his ministry became embroiled in the English Civil War of the 1640s. While the embattled son of deposed King Charles I was still able to bestow on seven of his companions in exile a million acres of "proprietary" land in the Virginia colony across the Atlantic, the Washingtons did not fare so well. Roundhead Puritans of the ascendant Oliver Cromwell found the Reverend Mr. Washington too cavalier for their tastes and expelled him from his pulpit for "immorality." Perhaps his reputation for drinking overshadowed political or doctrinal disputes, but in either event Washington was ruined.

The minister's high-spirited son John chose to go to sea, not as the naval midshipman he might once have been, but as mate on a humble merchant vessel, with hopes of trading in the New World. In 1657, the twenty-five-year-old landed in Virginia. His was no proprietary "first family," but the ambitious newcomer lost little time in finding himself a prosperous bride, the most direct form of upward mobility. His example would be followed through succeeding generations of Washingtons. Soon the couple had a son, another Lawrence, who would be George Washington's grandfather.

As Washington biographer James Thomas Flexner points out, "The Wild West was then on the Atlantic seaboard, and John Washington was a turbulent spirit well suited to so violent a world." Sued by his captain for desertion, he responded by accusing the captain of having engaged in murder during the voyage. Neither charge was resolved. After his first wife died, John married in succession two sisters who had been accused of prostitution. Neither union impeded his success. A self-taught lawyer, he rose rapidly as both judge and advocate. John Washington's extraordinary career exemplified the ambivalence of a colonial society founded on raw acquisitiveness yet already overlaid with a veneer of English sensibilities. On the one hand, he came to sit on the county court and his church vestry. On the other, as a militia officer, his greed for land led to an indictment (but not conviction) for the murder of Indian emissaries.

"As generous as he was rough and unscrupulous," Flexner writes, "John re-established the Washingtons in the fierce New World at about the rank they had occupied, before Cromwell, in the Old. He made them the equivalent of an English country family. Although no Washington ever sat in the equivalent of the House of Lords, the King's Council, they often married above themselves." They also evidenced "a passion for acreage." George Washington would fit both descriptions.

Not surprisingly, the second generation of Washingtons in North America tended to overlook the foundations of their relative prosperity. John's son Lawrence, although similarly acquisitive, was a respectable, introspective lawyer. He married well, but died young. Lawrence's second son, Augustine, enjoyed the benefits of an education in England, no longer at war with itself, and also married the daughter of a well-to-do Virginia planter. By the time he came of age in 1715 he was the master of some 1,750 fertile acres.

Relatively little is known of Augustine, though it was he who would become the father of George Washington. George recalled his father as a rather remote but gentle giant who was "fond of children." Washington biographer Douglas Southall Freeman supports this beneficent image: "Gus, as he was called by his friends, was blond, of fine proportions and great physical strength and stood six feet in his stockings. His kindly nature matched his towering strength." Flexner, however, describes another side of Augustine Washington, a businessman preoccupied with problems and anxieties, "much concerned with land speculation, prone to lawsuits; given . . . to hesitation and procrastination." Bourne suggests, "It is inconceivable that such an energetic man would not have had some influence on his best-known son." It seems likely, however, that when George, the first son of Augustine's second marriage, was growing up, his busy father simply wasn't around very much. Indeed, it was while he was on a business trip to England that Augustine Washington's first wife died. They had been married less than eight years, but had three young children. Despite his grief, Augustine understood that he could not raise them alone.

It took him two years to find a new wife. Amiable widows were rarely in short supply even in sparsely populated Virginia, but Augustine settled instead on an "old maid" of twenty-three named Mary Ball. The source of his attraction is uncertain. Flexner describes Mary as "a healthy orphan of moderate height, rounded figure, and pleasant voice," but not everyone was to find her voice so pleasant. In any case, she came to the marriage with a substantial inheritance of her own, and few emotional ties. Her father had already sired a large family when, a widower, he married a lady viewed by his progeny as far beneath their status. Out of this union Mary Ball was born. After both parents died, she went to live with family friends. Mary had inherited from her father, in the words of Flexner, "400 acres, fifteen cattle, three Negroes, and enough feathers to be made into a bed." The subsequent deaths of others in her family added substantially to her estate. Although her education was limited, Mary grew into an independent, strong-willed young woman — more than a match for her obliging husband.

Eleven months after they married, Mary gave birth to a boy large enough to seem a proper son of Augustine Washington. He was christened George — not a traditional Washington name — after her guardian George Eskridge. Within two years, George had a brother and sister, then two more brothers. After the death of his half-sister Jane in 1735 and the departure of his two half-brothers for the Appleby School in England, George was the oldest child at home. His own education was in the hands of tutors. Although George preferred riding, hunting, and exploring to indoor pursuits, he did enjoy reading, writing, and draw-

Mary Washington
Courtesy of The Library of Congress

ing, and showed a definite aptitude for mathematics, a precursor of his interest in surveying. In his preteen years, young George reflected the dual nature of his surroundings; he thirsted for adventure in the trackless wilderness only two days' hike to the west, yet laboriously wrote down all 110 maxims of the "Rules of Civility and Decent Behavior in Company and Conversation" — devised by the Jesuits for Spanish or

French nobility yet equally applicable to the emerging gentility of tide-water Virginia.

In the years following George's birth, Augustine Washington's days became busier than ever with his growing concerns, which derived not only from inheritance and his marriages but from promising specula-tive ventures as well. Iron had been found on his land near the town of Fredericksburg, and was to be mined by an English partnership. The family owned plantations and mills in Maryland as well as in Virginia. Moreover, even more than his circumspect father or his swashbuckling grandfather, Augustine embraced the obligations of a country gentle-man and community leader: vestryman, high sheriff of Westmoreland County, trustee of Fredericksburg. Augustine was the parent on the move, Mary the parent in place.

That place itself was not stationary. When George was three, the family moved from Popes Creek on the Potomac to Fairfax County and the home that would become Mount Vernon. When he was seven they moved again to Ferry Farm, on the Rappahannock, across from Fredericksburg. His most idyllic years were there. If George Washing-ton actually cut down cherry trees, it must have been at Ferry Farm. Playmates were abundant, as were nearby cousins. It was while visiting them in the spring of 1743 that a messenger arrived with the urgent summons to ride home. His father was dying. George was only eleven.

The will of Augustine Washington was predictably detailed. In-stead of the primogeniture of old England, everyone would receive something. The largest share, however, did go to Lawrence Washing-ton, the elder son of Augustine's first marriage. It included the great house Lawrence would rebuild and name Mount Vernon, after the En-glish admiral under whom he had served. To George, the oldest son of his second marriage, to be held in trust until he became twenty-one, went Ferry Farm, a great deal of land, and ten slaves. Augustine made provision for his surviving wife, Mary, but in the prevailing custom, her control of property was to be temporary — the full benefit of some land for five years and possession of Ferry Farm until George came of age. In fact, it would be twenty-eight years before she left, finally moving to a small house in Fredericksburg to be near her married daughter, Betty. From this destination she would rarely stray. For the rest of her life,

Mary Washington was obliged to rely on the generosity of her children, particularly George. In her view, he never contributed quite enough.

Widowed at thirty-six, Mary faced daunting challenges — the maintenance of substantial property, and raising the five young children who were still at home. She had made up her mind. She would not remarry. In the Virginia of the eighteenth century, however, even so self-reliant a woman needed help. Since George was the oldest, she decided that he must stay at home and watch over his siblings, but under her careful supervision. Freeman notes that Mary's weaknesses as the manager of Ferry Farm included difficulty with priorities. "A thousand trifles were her daily care to the neglect of larger interests." Similarly, Mary monitored every detail of her children's lives. A contemporary of George relates, "Of the mother I was ten times more afraid than I ever was of my own parents. She awed me in the midst of her kindness." Indeed, she *could* be kind, but at eleven George Washington had no intention of settling down, even as the man of this bustling, stifling household.

His father's death had already robbed him of the opportunity to travel, as his half-brothers had, to school in England. Much later, despite his affection for his own family hearth, Washington would refer to his regret at never having seen so great a city as London. His foreign education would likely have been supplemented by at least two years at William and Mary College, the school of Jefferson and Monroe. Despite all the triumphs that came to him, Washington always felt keenly his lack of a formal education. So would others. John Adams had a low opinion of Washington's intellect. Ambitious Alexander Hamilton felt he should guide policy, with President Washington the ideal national figurehead. To Thomas Jefferson, Washington's "mind was great and powerful without being of the very first order." It puts one in mind of a later president who also had a domineering mother; Oliver Wendell Holmes viewed Franklin D. Roosevelt (whose education had not been truncated) as having a second-rate intellect but a first-rate temperament.

If young Washington's instinct was to escape, there were soon inviting places to go. At twenty, his half-brother Lawrence had returned home from military service, just before the death of their father. More than anyone, Lawrence, although too frequently away, had been George's role model. He represented everything the young boy most admired and aspired to. As a dashing young captain in a Virginia regiment, Lawrence — to the dread of their mother — had taken part in the bloody British expedition against Spain at Cartagena in the Caribbean. He had come home unharmed, however, in resplendent uniform, a hero to all.

George not only shared his half-brother's sense of adventure, he hoped someday to also attain a semblance of the erudition and polish that put Lawrence at ease in any company. When Lawrence won the hand of Anne Fairfax, whose family stood at the very pinnacle of tidewater society, it also gained young George entry into that realm, one significant level above his own. Soon Colonel William Fairfax would come to see in this awkward younger Washington potential conspicuously lacking in his own weak-kneed sons. From the time Lawrence occupied the estate he renamed Mount Vernon, it became Washington's true home. At Belvoir, the adjoining Fairfax mansion, both Washingtons mingled with the political and social leadership of Virginia.

Lawrence's extensive landholdings encouraged George's interest in surveying and exploring; Lawrence's military prowess, George's dreams of his own future success. "My inclinations," he declared, "are strongly bent to arms." To all of this his mother was unalterably opposed. When at fourteen George was offered, under the auspices of Fairfax, an opportunity to be a midshipman in the Royal Navy, Mary Washington for a time was uncharacteristically uncertain what to do. Her difficulties in managing Ferry Farm had led to financial crisis, and the income the position brought would have been helpful, but she nevertheless decided to oppose the offer. With the aid of her brother, Joseph Ball, she dissuaded her son from accepting it. George, in any case, was more interested in a military than a naval future.

At sixteen, however, George was permitted to accept the offer of Fairfax to join an expedition surveying western lands. At seventeen, he gained his first paying job, as surveyor for the county of Culpepper, which afforded him ample opportunity for (in the family tradition) acquiring land for himself in the fertile Shenandoah Valley. On the one hand, Mary Washington wanted to keep her son safe from the dangers of the frontier, as she had from the perils of the sea. On the other, she wanted the financial help the new job provided. George was not yet of age, but he was almost a man and already an impressive figure — increasingly independent, growing to a height taller than his father's, and constructing what would become his public persona, an almost austere sense of command. One imagines that Mary Washington wasn't quite certain what to make of him, even though she might see there something of herself.

One Fairfax influence nearly led to George's ruin. At sixteen he fell quite suddenly in love, but, unfortunately, the lady was already married. Fairfax's son George William, after attending a session of the House of Burgesses in Williamsburg with his friend, Lawrence Washington, had returned to Belvoir with his future bride, the dazzling Sally Cary. Since her union with her husband was as much dynastic as romantic, Sally may well have felt an attraction to young George and wished she could reciprocate his attentions. A sensible young woman of eighteen, however, she apparently contained the relationship to one of harmless flirtation, saving herself from scandal and preserving for George the continued patronage of the powerful. When he finally did marry, it was to the sensible, amiable, wealthy, and widowed Martha Dandridge Custis.

Lawrence Washington, however, had returned from Williamsburg with a serious problem of his own. His chronic cough had escalated to "consumption," likely a form of tuberculosis. Seeking a cure in the warm springs of the south, Lawrence eventually decided to sail for the beneficent climate of Barbados. George accompanied him, embarking at nineteen on the only ocean voyage of his life. His mother could do little to dissuade him. The tropical locale enthralled George, but unfortunately he contracted smallpox and had to return home. Lawrence went on to Bermuda. George recovered, but Lawrence did not. He died at the age of only thirty-four. George's father, Augustine, had died at forty-nine. By the time he was twenty, George Washington had lost both of the male role models from his own family.

Lawrence's will gave George in "love and affection" several lots in Fredericksburg, and in the event of contingencies, the ultimate possession of Mount Vernon. George's education by tutors had ended by the time he was in his early teens. His wider exposure to the world had been through Lawrence and the Fairfax family. On the verge of his majority, beyond the restraint of his mother's hand, Washington embarked on his true vocation, military adventure. Assuming Lawrence's position as adjutant of the Virginia militia, he undertook a dangerous mission from the provincial governor to convince the French to abandon their plans for expansion in the Ohio Valley. The ultimatum failed, the French and Indian War followed, and Washington was engaged in periodic combat for the better part of the next eight years.

Returning home in 1759 as a full colonel who had commanded all of Virginia's forces, Washington had important decisions to make. He had suffered many military setbacks, but he had vast experience; despite this he had been denied a commission in the regular British Army. It was to be a source of enduring resentment, likely influencing his later views. Washington resigned his commission, married Martha, and set about becoming the country gentleman his mother had envisioned. By now George had inherited both Mount Vernon and a new family to inhabit it.

Throughout his campaigns he had found time to write his remaining half-brother Austin and his own brothers and sister with surprising frequency, letters of warmth and candor, often with assurances that all was well. "As I have heard since my arriv'l at this place a circumstantial acct. of my death and dying speech," George wrote his brother John Augustine, "I take this early opportunity of contradicting both and of assuring you that I now exist." To his terrified mother Washington wrote little, although he once asked Austin not to tell her of a "shameful defeat." Apparently he still valued her grudging favor. Despite its perils and hardships, Washington savored the military life. Comparing the valor of his Virginia militia to the "cowardice" of the British regulars, he made it plain, as relations became strained with the mother country, that he was experienced in war as well as agricultural management.

After Mary Washington finally moved from Ferry Farm to her modest home in Fredericksburg, she saw little of her son. She avoided sharing in his subsequent success, sometimes seeming almost to resent it. In Flexner's view "She was clearly a powerful woman, but all her power was centered on herself." Most of her letters, even during the war for American independence, complain of her own want and of her son's neglect. A notably affectionate exception in 1782 to "My dear George" thanks him for the "2 five ginnes" he sent, expresses grief at family deaths, and regrets her absence when George happened to come through Fredericksburg on short notice. "I am afraid I never shall have that pleasure agin." Only the year before, however, her discontent had become so public that the Virginia House of Delegates proposed to raise a pension for the destitute mother of the commanding general of the Continental Army. An embarrassed and infuriated Washington protested, "Before I left Virginia, I answered all her calls for money; and since that period, have directed my steward to do the same. Whence her distresses can arise therefore I know not."

Washington's sister Betty and her family resided near enough their mother to attend to many of her immediate needs. In addition, Washington ultimately tried to make his patient brother John a sort of intermediary, while doing a bit of complaining on his own. Waiting anxiously for the peace treaty in 1783, George wrote John of yet another plea for funds from their mother: "It is too much while I am suffering in every other way . . . to be saddled with all the expense of hers." John was implored to please "represent to her in delicate terms the impropriety of her complaints." After he did so, their mother simply switched these complaints to her younger son, writing John, "I am going fast, and . . . the time is hard. . . . I never lived so poore in my life." Contemporary accounts from Mary Washington's neighbors portray less want, but a dignified simplicity of life, putting to question both Washington's view of his mother as profligate and his mother's insistence that she was "almost starved."

After reliable John Washington died in 1787, George turned his attention back to the parent he now admitted to be "aged and infirm." In a letter to his mother of unaccustomed length, he advised her to wind up her own affairs and come to "live with one of your children." Washington cautioned, however, that life at Mount Vernon, so frenetic it might be "compared to a well resorted tavern," would "never answer your purposes." There is no record of a response. On his way to the Constitutional Convention, however, Washington did finally manage to visit his mother in Fredericksburg. She seemed to him as mentally alert as ever, but now "reduced . . . to a skeleton." He feared, as well, for his sister Betty, whose constant solicitousness appeared to have impaired her own health. Both recovered, but two years later, on September 1, 1789, Mary Ball Washington finally passed away, probably of a form of cancer. Perhaps George viewed his final letter and visits as a form of reconciliation, but even in paying his mother tribute, he could not resist referring to her constant and excessive demands: "She has had a great deal of money from me."

Many years later Washington's step-grandson, George Washington Parke Custis, reflected, as Bourne characterizes it, on "the tempestuous relationship between Mary Ball Washington and her oldest son." To Custis the embattled widow's rigidity was not without merit in instilling the discipline that underlay her son's career. She must have viewed herself, Curtis wrote, as "the guide who directed your steps when they needed the guidance of age and wisdom, the parental affection which claimed your love, the parental authority which commanded your obedience."

The operative word is "command." That childhood friend of George Washington who had been so impressed by Mary Washington looked back from the perspective of time and continued, "Whoever has seen that awe-inspiring air and manner so characteristic in the father of his country, will remember the matron as she appeared when the presiding genius of her well-ordered household, commanding and being obeyed." There is certainly much of his mother in Washington's own complaints, however justified, of the criminal penury of Congress through the Revolutionary War, and of the apparent hopelessness of his own position. In the first year of that war he wrote his stepson "Jacky" Custis, "I do not think that any officer since the creation had susch [sic] a variety of difficulties and perplexities to encounter as I have. How we shall be able to rub along until the new army is raised, I know not." In peace as well as war, anger and resentment so often boiled beneath his seemingly serene countenance.

There is also much of his mother's strength in Washington's stubborn reliance on his own judgment, even in the face of the military and political advice of others, and in his passion for order and organization.

Washington took no salary for his service in the war but kept an account of his every expense, to be presented to Congress, so detailed it would have elicited the admiration of his mother, immersed as she had been in her own "thousand trivialities." Even Washington's willful avoidance of the constricted life his mother envisioned for him — an instinct to escape that would be repeated so frequently by American presidents in the twentieth century — was reminiscent of his mother's refusal to fulfill society's expectations for a young woman or an older widow. Washington's ultimate desire for settled domesticity may have been a reaction to its denial in his own youth, but it also mirrored his mother's will to raise her own family as she saw fit.

But, one may ask, did Mary Washington leave a spiritual legacy to her son as well? Though her life is better documented than the lives of many of the other early mothers, the nature of her faith remains somewhat hazy. The evidence does show that Mary Washington's religious and moral convictions were, as Doris Faber puts it, "strictly orthodox." That much at least is beyond doubt. From Faber also we get the anecdotal testimony of one of Mary's grandsons, who described the long walks on which she would take him for the purpose of viewing the grandeur of nature; she would "point out the different forest trees visible on the hills across the river and impress on him the majesty of the Creator of all things." In addition, Washington Irving claimed that Mary Washington's favorite book was Sir Matthew Hale's *Contemplations, moral and divine,* a collection of moral and religious maxims. According to tradition, at least, she would read from some work of religion and morality daily to her children, frequently from this volume, and these readings so impressed George that the small volume of contemplations, inscribed with his mother's autograph, became among his most treasured possessions. How accurate that rosy picture is can be questioned, but Mary's ownership of the volume itself cannot; her autographed copy is preserved at Mount Vernon.

That there was a spiritual quality to her ministrations, therefore, is clear, even if it cannot be fully described. Perhaps it was this background that helped her son, through all his difficulties, to never lose sight of the ultimate goal of his mature efforts — an entirely new kind of nation, as he said, "designed by Providence for the display of human greatness and felicity." Religion would be an essential element, but without the established authority of any single denomination. Bigotry, Washington vowed, would be given "no sanction."

CHAPTER TWO

The Missing Mothers of Virginia

⋙ Jane Jefferson
⋙ Nelly Madison
⋙ Elizabeth Monroe

IF THE INFLUENCE of George Washington's mother is difficult to discern, at least she had a college named after her (Mary Washington College in Virginia). No similar honor was bestowed on the parents of Washington's notable Virginia successors — Jefferson, Madison, and Monroe — although their sons, unlike Washington, enjoyed the advantages of higher education. It was in fact to their teachers more than to their parents — about whom relatively little is known — that each credited his subsequent success.

In Jefferson's case, his notable mentor was an enlightened Scottish émigré named William Small, whom he encountered at the College of William and Mary. Small was the only faculty member not of the Anglican clergy. His province of "natural philosophy" encompassed mathematics and science, but his interests extended to every field of learning. In his autobiography, Jefferson evaluated his friendship with Small as "my great good fortune, and what probably fixed the destinies of my life." Small's "enlarged and liberal mind" widened Jefferson's intellectual horizons far beyond the confining regimen of the classroom. Through Small, Jefferson gained the acquaintance of the most stimulating circle in the colonial capital of Williamsburg. Particularly influential was a young member of the House of Burgesses, destined to become a distinguished jurist and patriot, who was Jefferson's "most affectionate" friend and inspiration, George Wythe.

Similarly, James Madison considered his first schoolmaster, James Robertson, another Scot, as the strongest influence on his own career. From the ages of eleven through fifteen, Madison boarded at Mr. Robertson's school, receiving a classical foundation of remarkable scope for the American colonies. The adult Madison wrote of Robertson, "All I have in life I owe largely to that man." At the College of New Jersey at Princeton, Madison encountered yet another formidable Scot, Dr. John Witherspoon. A college president personally acquainted with every student (what a refreshing anomaly today), Witherspoon encouraged Madison's interests in literature, philosophy, and — most significantly — the foundations of equitable government.

To young James Monroe, the very buildings of William and Mary, which had been described by the more aesthetic Jefferson as "rude misshapen piles," made an impression he never forgot. On the eve of the American Revolution, the college seemed to Monroe a font of enlightened energy, headed by a "liberal and patriotic regime." This followed Monroe's grounding at the academy of Parson Archibald Campbell, a school also attended by John Marshall. Here Monroe garnered, as biographer William Penn Cresson describes it, "a solid foundation in the classics, a respect for the factual exactness of mathematics, and an understanding of such words as loyalty, honesty, honor, and devotion."

But what of the parents who made such educational opportunities possible? Jefferson credits only his father, and in remarkably few words for one so given to written expression. No American president has been subjected to more speculative psychohistory than Thomas Jefferson. Consider such typical titles in recent years as *Jefferson: A Revealing Biography, Thomas Jefferson: An Intimate History,* and *The Jefferson Scandals: A Rebuttal.* Such books aren't simply concerned with affirming or explaining Jefferson's relationship with Sally Hemings or uncovering other details of his private life. DNA evidence is of little help in unlocking the authentic sentiments of so complex a president. As noted Jefferson biographer Merrill Peterson puts it, although Jefferson left to posterity a vast corpus of papers, public and private, his personality remains "elusive." The little Jefferson wrote about his father is reminiscent of Washington's spare recollection of his own father. Physically and temperamentally, the two seem almost carbon copies of one another: immensely strong, acquisitive men, full of ambition and energy.

If Washington was born near the American frontier, the Jefferson family had settled directly on it. Deriving from Wales and originally landing in tidewater Virginia, by the 1680s Jefferson's grandfather had acquired abundant farmlands to the west. His wife brought additional property and the slaves to work it. The transition from yeoman to gentleman took little more than a generation. By the time of Thomas Jefferson's birth, his father Peter had risen to serve on the Chancery Court and in the Virginia House of Burgesses, on the same hierarchical level as Augustine Washington. Like the Washingtons, the Jeffersons married above themselves. Peter Jefferson won the hand of Jane Randolph, a member of one of the most prominent Virginia families. Together they established a plantation, named Shadwell after her ancestral home, on the Rivanna River in the foothills of the Blue Ridge Mountains. They were among the earliest settlers in the region. Here Thomas Jefferson was born in 1743, their third child and first son.

Perhaps some of Jefferson's ambivalence about his parents derives from the ambulatory, if comfortable, nature of his childhood. Shortly after Thomas's birth, his father agreed to care for the four children of William Randolph, his wife's cousin and a close friend, who had died at the age of only thirty-three. Unfortunately, the Randolph estate at Tuckahoe was some fifty miles to the east. For years the dutiful Peter and Jane Jefferson would have two sets of children and two plantations to manage. Indeed, Thomas Jefferson's earliest recollection was of being carried, at the age of two or three, on a pillow by horseback between his two domiciles.

For five years, from the age of nine, Jefferson was under the tutelage of an Anglican minister named William Douglas. Douglas, too, was of Scotch extraction. The colony of Virginia may have been Anglican, ultimately Episcopalian, but most of the significant teachers seem to have been Scotch Presbyterians. For Douglas, Jefferson developed little regard or respect. Despite frequent visits to his family, now back at Shadwell, the lonely young scholar may well have felt abandoned by both parents.

As biographer Page Smith puts it, "Even though his later references to his father are respectful and admiring, there is about them an unmistakable reserve. Perhaps even more striking is that he never during a long lifetime spoke with any warmth or feeling about his mother. Indeed he hardly spoke about her at all." In one vital regard, however, Peter Jefferson was anything but neglectful. He determined that his son would have the education he lacked, even if it started with the small school of Mr. Douglas. In his autobiography, written when he was seventy-seven, Jefferson wrote, "My father's education had been quite neglected, but being of a strong mind, sound judgment and eager after information, he read much and improved himself." Certainly young Jefferson must have longed for a more constant acquaintance with such a man as his father, one as admired in his own community as Augustine Washington was in his. Unfortunately, both Peter Jefferson and Augustine Washington died too soon. George Washington became the reluctant head of his household at eleven; the sensitive Thomas Jefferson at fourteen. A lifetime later he recalled his sense of isolation: "At fourteen years of age the whole care and direction of myself was thrown on myself entirely, without a relation or friend to advise or guide me." What of his mother? What of the five guardians chosen by his father — men of probity and experience? As the oldest in a house with six sisters and an infant brother, Jefferson certainly assumed responsibilities, but he was hardly bereft of assistance or advice.

By the terms of his father's will, Jefferson would inherit Shadwell at twenty-one, and in the interim he was to receive as thorough a classical education as possible. After three years of study with the Reverend James Maury, whose scholarship was of a higher order than Douglas's, Jefferson felt ready to enter William and Mary. In a letter to one of his guardians, Jefferson complains not of the isolation or provincialism of his home but of its distractions: "As long as I stay . . . the Loss of one-fourth of my Time is inevitable, by Company's coming here and detaining me from School." Peter Jefferson had preached self-reliance, to be both strong in body and "strong and free" in mind. He had lived just long enough to at least teach Thomas the rudiments of riding, hunting, swimming, and surveying, but most of all to instill in him the desire to be "eager after information." Tall and slender, Jefferson would never match his father's legendary strength, but he would exceed the elder's immense curiosity. The most treasured legacy of father to son was Peter Jefferson's modest library of English classics.

With his father gone, and his brother too young to be a true companion, Jefferson clearly felt little attraction for the company of the females in his family. From the first, Jefferson's biographers have tried to fathom this. Henry Randall, noting that Jefferson was "singularly shy" when writing about women, even his own mother, nonetheless conjectured that Jane Randolph Jefferson "was in every respect worthy of his highest respect and deepest love, and she received them." How does he know? Dumas Malone refers to Jefferson's "characteristic reticence about the women of his family . . . at no time in his life did he turn to women for serious advice, anyway." Such later biographers as Fawn Brodie refer to the high esteem in which Jane Jefferson was held by her contemporaries, who described her as a lady of "amiable and affectionate disposition . . . lively cheerful temper . . . a great fund of humor," in addition to an air of refinement and elegance. She must have been devoted to her precocious son. Other than resenting their years of separation, what fault could Jefferson find with such a mother? She was surely no nagging Mary Washington.

Perhaps her very gentility offended Jefferson. As he grew older, he cherished the premise of a peculiarly American aristocracy of achievement, buttressed by self-made men like his father. Jefferson may have profited by it, but his maternal lineage was not in itself a source of pride or even of very much interest to him. Jefferson's entire family history on both sides is compressed into one brief paragraph in his 1821 autobiography: "The tradition in my father's family is that their ancestor came to this country from Wales and from near the mountain of Snowden," he writes. In 1739, he continues, Peter Jefferson married nineteen-year-old Jane Randolph, of a family tracing "their pedigree far back in England & Scotland, to which let everyone ascribe the faith & merit he chuses [sic]." Such a summary is not only brief, but peculiar.

Jefferson may have believed in a more egalitarian society, one in which status was based on achievement rather than ancestry, but how did women fit into this society? Here his views seem very traditional, valuing wives as supportive helpmates and praising feminine "modesty and diffidence." Jefferson's own wife, Martha, who died young, was re-

called by her granddaughter as being renowned for her "domestic virtues," her wit and vivacity, and her "most agreeable person and manners." She sounds very much like Jefferson's mother. That after his
wife's death Jefferson apparently came to love at least two highly independent women seems as ironic as so much else in his life, but he could
marry neither; one was already married, the other at least technically
black.

Peterson, in an opinion shared by other Jefferson biographers,
writes that by Jefferson's "own reckoning" his mother "was a zero quan-
tity in his life," but Brodie suggests a scenario more like that of Washington's youth: "The astonishing fact," she writes, is that after his
schooling Jefferson lived with his mother until he was twenty-seven.
His avoidance of even mentioning her "seems evidence rather of very
great influence which he deeply resented, and which he struggled to escape." We will never know the true nature of the relationship. In that
"vast corpus" of Jefferson's documents that have come down to us,
there is not a single letter between mother and son. He burned them all,
as he did later letters between him and his wife. He refers to his mother
only four times — in one of his account books, in that equivocal sentence in his autobiography, and in two letters that are equally curious.
To his friend John Page in 1770 Jefferson bemoans "the loss of my
mother's house by fire, and in it of every paper I had in the world, and
almost every book." What of his mother's loss? By then Jefferson had
begun work on his own mountaintop home at Monticello. Six years
later, on March 31, 1776, Jefferson wrote in his account book only that
"my mother died about eight o'clock this morning in the 57th year of
her life." It took Jefferson two months to write to an uncle living in
England: "The death of my mother you have probably not heard of.
This happened on the last day of March after an illness of not more
than an hour. We supposed it to have been apoplectic." Nothing more
on the subject.

Of course, 1776 was a tumultuous year in the life of England's
American colonies. Jefferson's illness, six weeks of agonizing headaches
beginning directly after his mother's death, took him away from the
Continental Congress at a most pivotal juncture. He would have such
debilitating headaches again in future years, most severely after the

death of his wife. Of Jefferson's deep love for his wife there is no doubt. Yet he found it difficult to speak or write of her after her death. Might he not have harbored some reservoir of unspoken affection for his mother, as well? As Smith suggests, "We are by now familiar with Jefferson's impulse to hide or dissemble his deepest feelings.... [H]is silence about his mother, like his silence about his dead wife, *may* have been the consequences of a dependence too profound for him to speak of."

Of his father, Jefferson did manage to write a bit, implying a good deal more. In the opinion of Malone, the loss of Peter Jefferson "created a chasm" in his son's life "which remained unfilled until his years in Williamsburg." In William Small and George Wythe, Thomas Jefferson found his mature role models, but he was positioned to meet them only because of self-taught Peter Jefferson's love of learning. Jane Randolph Jefferson was at her son's side many more years, and was obviously a woman of cultivated tastes and pleasant demeanor. Whatever the degree of her influence, it merits recognition, and it is unfortunate that we are not able to appreciate it better.

It is also unfortunate that we know so little about her faith or the faiths of the mothers of Madison and Monroe. In religion Jefferson was a rational deist, but as president he rejoiced in the healthy diversity of America's "benign religion . . . practiced in various forms, yet all of them inculcating honesty, truth, temperance, gratitude, and the love of man." When he attended services held in the House chamber, it may have been merely good politics — or it may have been the residue of his parents' deeper belief in more than only creation. Like all the Founders, Jefferson favored the diverse over the doctrinaire, but freedom of religion did not require freedom from religion.

FIVE GENERATIONS before the birth of James Madison, the first of his family arrived in the Virginia Colony. John Maddison (the extra "d" would be dropped later) possessed the same sort of innovative energy that launched the earliest Washingtons and Jeffersons who reached the New World. A ship's carpenter by trade, Maddison was also quite a salesman. His great success lay in recruiting others to make the perilous journey across the Atlantic. Under the headright system a man could "patent" fifty acres of land for every immigrant he brought over. Soon

Maddison had amassed over thirteen hundred fertile acres. His sons and grandsons fared even better, and married well, in the familiar pattern. By 1751, when James Madison was born, his family possessed immense acreage in the piedmont of the Shenandoah Valley, beyond the Blue Ridge, where land was still abundant.

The Madisons, however, were not quite landed gentry. Theirs was a working plantation, and the family was acquainted with strenuous physical labor. As described by biographer Virginia Moore, James's father, the original James Madison, "was a man before he was a boy." One of his responsibilities was delivering great hogsheads of tobacco to the warehouse of the affluent Conway family. At the Conway's nearby home at Belle Grove, twenty-one-year-old James Madison Sr. fell in love with seventeen-year-old Nelly Conway. The attraction was mutual, and they were married in 1749. Their first child, James Madison Jr., was born two years later. To avoid confusion they called him "Jemmy." Growing to a height of only about five foot three or five foot six (depending on which account one believes), he would also be known as "Little Jemmy." Although his mother claimed descent from Scottish king Robert the Bruce, young James Madison was no more impressed with genealogy than Jefferson had been. As an adult he wrote of his forebears, "In both the paternal and maternal line . . . they were planters and among the respectable, though not the most opulent, class."

Madison's was a public life. To him there was, even in later years, little impetus to elaborate beyond his public career. In finally agreeing to dictate an autobiography of sorts, Madison provided but the "merest skeleton" of his life prior to going off to college, only some two hundred words to describe his first eighteen years. It is sufficient, however, to convey something not only of what his childhood was like, but of the debt he owed to both his parents. Only seven of their twelve children survived infancy. Epidemics were frequent, although the climate of the Virginia uplands was more salubrious than that of the more settled tidewater. Jemmy was not a robust child, his apparent fragility a constant concern. That he survived to be eighty-five would have astonished his parents, as it did Madison himself. Not only had he outlived most of his contemporaries, he noted, "I may be thought to have outlived myself."

To his father, Madison owed his appreciation of the natural world and the focused nature of his education; to his mother, the unconditional love that made his childhood more ordered than that of Washington or Jefferson. As the hills of what is now Orange County, Virginia, became more populated, Madison lacked little for playmates, black or white. His lifelong hatred of slavery must have derived from these experiences. While taking naturally to neither riding nor other outdoor pursuits, young Jemmy daily followed his father around their seemingly vast domain, exploring its wonders. The elder Madison, now called "Squire" or "Colonel" because he headed the King's Militia, was a more scientific farmer than his neighbors. He grew wheat and other crops, as well as tobacco, becoming less dependent on the vagaries of nature. When the Squire had a larger home constructed, named Montpelier, his eight-year-old son helped bring in the furniture.

It appears that both his grandmothers early appreciated bright young Jemmy's possibilities. He was taught to read, write, and compute at home. His father, now burdened with such additional responsibilities as presiding magistrate, sought out the best school in the region for his eleven-year-old son, and settled on that of Donald Robertson. Unlike Jefferson, Madison relished his time at boarding school, came to revere Robertson, and was none too anxious to leave five years later, despite his fondness for the comforts of home. The youthful rector of the nearby Brick Church, the Reverend Thomas Martin, had been engaged to tutor young Madison to prepare him for college, a destination desired by both his parents. Although a devout Anglican, Squire Madison was none too pleased with the reputed licentiousness then prevailing at William and Mary, the college of choice for the sons of Virginia's planters. Reverend Martin had graduated from the College of New Jersey at Princeton and thought highly of its celebrated new president, the Reverend Dr. John Witherspoon. That both school and president were Presbyterian mattered not at all to the Madisons. Moreover, the northern climate was considered more healthful than even the Virginia uplands, and the family had come to trust Martin's judgment.

In 1769, James Madison Jr. became one of the first southerners to matriculate at Princeton. The college and Witherspoon would have as profound an impact on Madison's future course in public life as Rob-

ertson's school had on his intellectual foundations. Rather than separating church and state, Witherspoon merged the civil with the clerical,
teaching a renowned course in moral philosophy. As historians Oscar
and Lilian Handlin point out, the college of New Jersey, although
founded to preserve "doctrinal purity," had by 1770 become "the center
of the new learning, linking rationalism and evangelical forces. All people possessed the capacity for reason, just as all possessed souls to
save." Under Witherspoon's leadership the college also became a hot-
bed of patriotism and of emerging American nationalism. As Merrill
Peterson writes, sober-sided Squire Madison knew what he was doing
in directing his equally serious son to New Jersey: "It was a venturesome
step, and it paid off not simply in the standard currency of education
but in the education of a man whose personal identifications were neither Virginian nor Anglican, but American."

The elder Madison lived to see his son achieve a prominent place in
the formation of the new republic. The Squire died just as Jemmy was
planning his family's departure from Montpelier to become Secretary
of State in the Jefferson administration. "Yesterday morning," the
grieving Madison wrote on February 28, 1801, "rather suddenly,
though very gently, the flame of life went out." Just as with Augustine
Washington and Peter Jefferson, James Madison Sr., though far from
being the largest landowner, had earned his place as the first citizen of
his community. Madison's mother lived to witness her son's presidency
and, unlike Mary Ball Washington, was immensely gratified by it. As
Doris Faber writes, the picture of Nelly Conway Madison that emerges
from the few letters written about her is one of caring, "of an unpretentious lady who sew[ed] shirts for young James while he studie[d] at
Princeton, who sen[t] tubs of fresh butter to him when he [went] on the
public's business in Richmond."

During Madison's presidential tenure, St. John's Episcopal Church
was founded across the street from the White House. It became an ecumenical "Church of the President." Historian Carl Anthony points out
that starting with Madison "Every President has attended at least one
service there." The Madisons became parishioners, their regular attendance a source of satisfaction to Madison's mother. As she aged, Nelly
lived in a separate apartment at Montpelier, in kindly concord with the

new mistress of the mansion, her admiring and celebrated daughter-in-law, Dolley Madison. Favored guests looked forward to visiting the venerable lady in her quarters. Nelly Conway Madison said to one of them a year before she died, at the age of ninety-seven, that "I have been a blest woman, blest all my life, and blest in this my old age." Her son, at seventy-seven, had a face more lined with care than his mother's. Both of them "may be thought to have outlived" themselves.

IF MADISON was "the last of the founders," Monroe came close behind, completing a talented trilogy of Virginians. We know less about his childhood than about Madison's, and even less about his parents. That is all the more regrettable because what little can be gleaned implies that Spence and Elizabeth Jones Monroe were remarkable people. Monroe's father, generally referred to by such puzzling appellations as "a well-established Virginia planter of modest means," doesn't quite fit into any neat category. He was as much a carpenter or "joiner" as a planter. In the interior of Virginia, however stratified tidewater society was evolving, one could still be both a carpenter and a gentleman. Practical ability was of immense value. As for "well-established," there had been Monroes in what became Westmoreland County since the mid-1600s, and some had attained positions of prominence. As for "modest means," after Spence's death, his son's college bills were settled by his wife's affluent brother. Monroe, however, recalled his father as "a worthy and respectable citizen possessed of good land and other property."

There was obviously some financial volatility in the life of Spence Monroe. His sandy-soiled plantation, such as it was, near a virgin forest on Monroe Creek, included an unpretentious home likely remodeled by his own hand. At its height, the property was light years removed from the sixty-thousand-acre estates of the aristocats who lived in the "Northern Neck" of Virginia, many already inclined to English-aping indolence and frivolity. Three things we do know about the father of James Monroe: Like so many other presidential fathers, he, too, married well; he, too, believed in education; and he was a patriot.

His wife, Elizabeth Jones, often called "Eliza," is sketchily described as "amiable," lively, and a very well-educated young woman for that time and place. Monroe described her as "respectable" as well, "possessing the best domestic qualities of a good wife and a good parent." She was the daughter of an "undertaker in architecture" (presumably a higher calling than carpenter). Her father, however, was both rich and married to the daughter of a prominent lawyer. Her distinguished brother, Judge Joseph Jones of Fredericksburg, presided over the Virginia General Court, would later serve in congress, and was a confidant of Washington, Jefferson, and Madison.

Spence Monroe's patriotism was confirmed in 1776 when, in answer to Richard Henry Lee's summons to import no more English goods until the Stamp Act was repealed, he courageously signed a pledge to that effect. At that time, James Monroe was already eight, the eldest of his parents' five children, and surely had a sense of the growing turmoil in the colonies. Monroe's early education was not at the hands of imported English tutors but took place in the schoolhouse of stern Parson Archibald Campbell, to which he trudged each day. He was joined in that laborious two-way trek by his classmate, future chief justice John Marshall. Each carried a rifle over one shoulder and books under the other. Marshall was as light-hearted as his companion was solemn. By his teens, tall, sturdy James Monroe, so physically unlike Madison, shared with him a profoundly serious demeanor that transcended the environment of either's home life.

Perhaps in Monroe's case, the influence of Parson Campbell played a part. He stressed discipline and constancy. As a Monroe descendant put it, beyond being "especially well-grounded in mathematics and Latin," the parson's pupils "in their various subsequent careers . . . were noted for solidity of character." We know that Marshall's father read him classic literature by candlelight in their frontier cabin, and it is certainly possible to imagine Elizabeth Jones Monroe doing the same for James. A crack shot, he often added fresh game to the family table, making practical use of the lengthy walk home from school. Such a youth might have been of immense assistance on the farm of his apparently hard-pressed parents.

Still, at sixteen, he went off to the College of William and Mary, at least initially financed by his father, and carrying the expectations of both Spence and Eliza with him. Under a new president the college was regaining some of the qualities Madison's father had found so lacking, but greater issues were at hand. After only two years, Monroe left to serve in the Continental Army, and his notable bravery in a number of Revolutionary War engagements won Washington's personal commendation. At scarcely twenty years of age, Monroe became a lieutenant colonel. His father had died in 1774; his mother's precise date of death is uncertain. Perhaps her most significant contribution was posthumous. At his death, her brother Joseph directed that his sizeable estate be divided among the children of his late sisters, "allowing my nephew Colonel James Monroe the first choice." This bequest helped immeasurably in launching the young man's career, validating his parents' judgment. If their means were modest, so much greater was their achievement.

Meanwhile, six hundred miles to the north, the first American political dynasty was already taking shape. Of Virginia's missing mothers we know far too little. Fortunately, of the Adams women we know a great deal more. Abigail Adams made certain of that. She put the story in her own words.

CHAPTER THREE

Players in the "Great Theatre of Life"

ᴥ Susanna and Abigail Adams

HAD SUSANNA ADAMS written as much as her daughter-in-law Abigail, she might be equally renowned. Both women were strong as well as supportive. Though the man who connected them, Susanna's son John, would become the second president of the United States, his ambitions did not encompass the establishment of a political dynasty. Political leadership in the colonies and even in the early years of the American republic was not a profession in itself, but the obligation of men who had the leisure and learning, or who felt the practical necessity to engage in it as a part-time pursuit. After all, there had to be some form of government, especially on the local level. It was not until eight years after the son of John Adams relinquished the office of the presidency that the first American president immersed in politics as a livelihood — Martin Van Buren — assumed the office.

To Adams, who in the manner of Washington, Jefferson, and Monroe liked to view himself fundamentally as a farmer, the realities of his life represented the first stage of a progression. "I must study politics and war," he wrote, "that my sons may have liberty to study mathematics and philosophy. My sons ought to study mathematics and philosophy, geography, naval history, naval architecture, navigation, commerce, and agriculture, in order to give their sons the right to study painting, poetry, music, architecture, statuary, tapestry, and porcelain."

That anyone might deem the study of porcelain more elevated than the study of philosophy would have bemused bright young Abigail Smith, growing up a few miles from Adams. As a girl, she had been afforded the opportunity to study neither. Yet after she married John Adams, ultimately becoming both the wife and mother of American presidents, her advice to both was limited by no inhibitions of intellectual inferiority. "Nabby," as she was called as a child, insisted that since women played no less a role in the "Great Theatre" of life than men, they should be equally educated. This was no premature feminism, but simple sense. As biographer Phyllis Lee Levin puts it, since women "were responsible for the care and early instruction of their children, she mourned their lack of training for this trust." To Abigail, matrimony and motherhood would always be a woman's most important priorities, but to both Abigail Smith and John Adams, growing up in the neighboring Massachusetts towns of Braintree and Weymouth, the interests of their tight-knit communities were also of great importance.

It was a world removed from the expansive plantations of even the western reaches of Virginia, and represented a harsher if healthier environment. Modest, hard-worked farmland extended out from towns like Braintree, but families lived closely together at the core. Their sense of community could be comforting but also inhibiting, based on a Puritan rigor utterly foreign to the more permissive Anglicanism of the decentralized South. A pious, structured Christian life was both the foundation and aim of every family. As biographer Page Smith writes, "A good Puritan . . . kept a kind of daily audit of his soul's state of grace. . . . The result was life led, within the confines of the rural village, on the highest plateau of self-consciousness . . . with an intensity that modern man cannot imagine." When the first American Adams, John's great-great-grandfather, both a farmer and a "malter," settled in Braintree around 1640, Anne Hutchinson had only recently been expelled from the Massachusetts Bay Colony for theological subversion, and the Salem witch trials were still decades in the future.

By the time John Adams was born in 1735, only the residue of such rigidity remained, but the meetinghouse still merged with the family hearth at the center of both religious and civic life. Around them, much else was changing. In fifty years, Britain's American colonies had grown fourfold in population and had tripled in size. John Adams's father, also named John, had achieved public esteem second only to that of Braintree's leading citizen, Colonel John Quincy. A shoemaker as well as a farmer, Adams was known as "Deacon" for his devotion to the church, but also served as "tithingman," town selectman, constable, and lieutenant of the militia. Calm and self-sufficient, he was a man people instinctively looked to for leadership. An aristocratic descendant referred to this original John Adams as only a "typical New England yeoman," but that is hardly adequate. When he died, his son John recalled the Deacon as "the honestest man I ever knew," who had managed "nearly all the business of the town. . . . In wisdom, piety, benevolence and charity in proportion to his education and sphere of life I have never seen his equal."

That young John Adams's own "sphere of life" would so exceed his father's was due at least as much to his mother, the elegant, volatile Susanna Boylston of Brookline and Boston. The wonder is what Susanna, born to a family of wealth and distinction, saw in this stolid shoemaker of Braintree. Moreover, Deacon John Adams was eighteen years her senior. Perhaps, at twenty-five, strong-willed Sarah, as she was called, had discouraged too many other suitors. It may be she sensed something of the strength and reliability others recognized in the Deacon. In any case, their union elevated the Adams family even in relatively egalitarian Massachusetts, as had Sarah's sister's marriage to the Deacon's clergyman brother. Their means of ascent, at least, was not so different from those of colonial Virginia.

The first of Sarah and John Adams's three sons was born a year later, and named for his father. On this first male offspring — as, fairly or not, was so often the case — the expectations of both parents were centered. Somehow, it was decided early on that he should be afforded the opportunity to attend Harvard. His father's earnest hope was that young John might become a learned Congregational minister, or, failing that, perhaps a physician in the Boylston family tradition. Adams recalled, "My father had destined his first-born, long before his birth, to a public education." He meant "public" in the English sense. John Adams would be the first of his family to go to college.

Although Adams matured to a demeanor so serious it might rival Monroe's, this cannot be attributed to the severity of his childhood.

Adams loved the outdoors, excelled at sports, each in its season, and was drawn particularly to the company of young women. By his teens, he was warned by both parents with some clarity of such conduct's potential dangers. But it was more his own self-discipline than Calvinist theology that kept John Adams from fathering illegitimate children, a common occurrence even in such towns as Braintree.

The Adamses, like other respectable families in the region, believed in at least rudimentary reading and writing for girls as well as boys. Reading the Bible reinforced the primacy of their religion. For Abigail Smith, however, over in Weymouth, learning to read provided the means to consume on her own every other book she could lay her hands on. John's parents taught him to read at home, even before dispatching him to the town's one-room schoolhouse. Soon he was advanced, with the town's other more promising scholars, to Braintree's Latin School. That the school was presided over by a Harvard graduate named Joseph Cleverly must have pleased the Adamses, despite Cleverly's Anglican affiliation. But the learned schoolmaster unfortunately was an indifferent and uninspired teacher and did little to hasten their son's intellectual development.

When asked by the Deacon what he proposed to do with his life, young John volunteered that he longed for nothing more than to be a good farmer like his father. Accordingly, John Sr. had his son join him in a particularly rigorous day of farm work and then asked if such hard physical labor still represented the sort of future the boy envisioned for himself. "Yes, sir," young John replied, "I like it very well." "Aye," his exasperated father answered, "but I don't like it so well, so you shall go to school." Fortuitously, a more invigorating year of instruction followed under a new schoolmaster named Joseph Marsh. It finally awakened in John the potential his parents had hoped for. Solving mathematical problems and reading books, even in Latin, could actually be stimulating. But was John ready for the challenge of Harvard?

The sixteen-year-old was to have ridden to his entrance examinations in Cambridge in the supportive company of Marsh, but the schoolmaster fell ill. John would have to face the formidable Harvard elders alone. It turned out, however, that though formidable they were also benign, allowing the apprehensive young scholar to use a dictionary in translating a difficult Latin passage into English. Assigning a theme for John to compose over the summer, they accepted him on the spot, an admissions process that certainly compares favorably with today's. As was the case with the three Virginians who succeeded him in the presidency, the great contribution of John Adams's parents was to insist on the sort of education that made his future career possible. Smith writes, "The father's influence on the son was strong and enduring . . . [Adams's] attachment to his mother was equally close . . . she had, moreover, an inexhaustible stock of improving precepts which her son took to heart." There was, as well, an even earlier influence. Biographer Paul Nagel notes Adams's tribute in his autobiography to his grandmother, Hanna Bass Adams. She composed "a wonderfully fine" document for her descendants, a plea for the value of learning. Had it not been for the strength of this exhortation, Adams was uncertain whether his father, the Deacon, would have had so unshakable a "determination to give his first son a liberal education."

In the opinion of historian Daniel Boorstin, John Adams seems almost to have "leaped" into eminence, launched by his experiences at Harvard to become something of a "self-made aristocrat." Choosing a career in the law rather than the ministry, Adams was influenced by such giants as Edward Holyoke and John Winthrop. The Harvard of 1750, however, was not quite a bastion of pure merit. Although, as biographer Jack Shepherd writes, Adams's admission was less a tribute to his family's distinction than to the college's insistence on opening "its doors to young men of promise," his ranking of fifteenth in his incoming class of twenty-four was based on an evaluation of the social status of his family. Without his mother's Boylston heritage, he would have been ranked even lower, or might not have gained entrance at all. In her family, learning was already a tradition. Had she been born in a later era, Susanna would likely have shared in that tradition herself.

While John was discovering the wonders of Harvard and Cambridge, seven-year-old Abigail Smith of Weymouth was already displaying what her biographer Lynne Withey cites as a "certain stubbornness of spirit." Small, sickly, and initially very shy, Nabby Smith was nonetheless the highly spirited daughter of a minister less doctrinaire than those the Adamses were acquainted with. Congregational Parson William Smith, who did study for the ministry at Harvard, was the son of a prosperous Boston merchant. Called to Weymouth and the North Parish Church, where his equanimity enabled him to enjoy a notably extended tenure, he had the means to buy not only its parsonage but also acres of surrounding farmland. His wife, Elizabeth Quincy Smith, daughter of the distinguished John Quincy of Braintree, added more than wealth and cachet to their union. Of a more practical bent than her affable, intellectual husband, she helped assure the success of their forty-five-year ministry, despite the religious turmoil of the times, in the oldest town of the original Massachusetts Bay Colony. The Smiths had four children. All three girls, of whom Nabby was the middle, grew to be lively and bright. Only the son, William, seems to have lacked their spark.

Girls growing up in the 1750s, however, even to families of prominence, were expected to lead narrowly circumscribed lives. The Smith daughters, particularly Abigail, were determined to be different, which, as Withey recounts, "dismayed [Abigail's] mother and delighted her father." Taught to read the Bible, Nabby spent every available hour devouring not only Scripture but her father's Shakespeare, Milton, Pope, Swift, even John Locke — and then discussing it all with him and his astonished friends. She hadn't stayed shy for long. Unlike John Adams, Abigail provided her own motivation. It was not, however, a form of rebellion. To Abigail, exploring the realm of the mind need not be at the sacrifice of her expected domestic diligence. She was never overtly disobedient to her parents or resentful of the role accorded her gender. She simply wanted more and was adroit at getting her own way, especially from her adoring father. Her grandmother Quincy also doted on the precocious young woman, while Abigail's mother, loving but perplexed, became inclined to focus her attention on her less challenging children. Still, the slights of Nabby's neglected education were never quite forgotten. Nearly a lifetime later she lamented, "I never was sent to any school."

Although something less than a classic beauty, Abigail at fifteen had grown into a striking, slender, dark-eyed, and quite popular young woman. Her proclivity for argumentation and her wit were generally taken as tokens of a distinctive personality. The young people of

Weymouth and Braintree intermingled frequently, and the three viva-cious Smith sisters enjoyed a wide acquaintance. Into the midst of their bustling household around 1758 was introduced an already rather chubby and unusually solemn young lawyer named John Adams. He was very free with his opinions, yet ill at ease in company. Abigail was less attracted than intrigued by this odd combination of uncertainty and outspokenness. It was her lovely cousin Hannah Quincy, however, who was the object of Adams's tentative affections. To no one's sur-prise, they were not reciprocated. As for the Smiths, Adams was not im-pressed. He viewed the father as rather worldly and crafty for a parson, concealing his wealth under a veneer of piety, and the daughters as "not fond, not frank, not candid."

Two years later, however, when Abigail and John were reintroduced by a mutual friend, they fell in love almost despite themselves. Oppo-sites may attract, but so can similarities. If John Adams was outspoken, could he find a better match in all of Massachusetts than acerbic Abi-gail Smith? Although nine years younger, she stood up to him, and he discovered he liked it. Frugality was also in Adams's nature, and he would not take upon himself a wife without carefully calculating his professional prospects. That it took another three years for them to marry was not, however, his doing. Abigail's parents felt she might do better socially and urged delay, but John had at least made progress ma-terially. A struggling young lawyer when he first met the Smiths, Ad-ams's practice had grown and, at the death of his father, he had also in-herited the family farm.

Perhaps it was John's keen mind that first appealed to Abigail, but his passionate nature, so early noted by his parents and so apparently at odds with his sober mien, was sorely tested during the lengthy court-ship. Abigail's earliest letters to John reciprocated his ardor, and his im-patience. Their bonds grew strong, maturing into lifelong affection and a genuine partnership. Ironically, it is to their lengthy separations that we owe the documentation of that relationship, their remarkable and revealing correspondence. What if these letters had been destroyed, as were Jefferson's to his wife, and so many of Lincoln's private papers? If Abigail Adams's letters are her enduring legacy, they also tell us a great deal about two presidents of the United States.

During the first decade of their marriage, letters were few and perfunctory, with John away largely on legal business. Abigail was busily engaged in the essential task she embraced, raising their four children. (A fifth had died in infancy.) Unlike the Virginians who preceded and succeeded him in the presidency, John Adams was blessed with a male heir. John and Sarah's oldest son and second child they named John Quincy, after his esteemed great-grandfather, who died on the day of the christening in 1767. The name was favored by John Adams, who fondly remembered Colonel Quincy, and by his mother-in-law, now reconciled to the marriage. John Quincy Adams, whose parents called him "Johnny," would be a child of the American Revolution, thrust into a world of turmoil and danger and yet also of exhilaration. When he was six, British tea was dumped into the sea in nearby Boston. At the age of eight, he witnessed with his mother the flames of the Battle of Bunker Hill from a summit near their home in Braintree.

Abigail's activities belied her supposedly frail health. Her husband was now away for longer periods, not only practicing his profession but, increasingly, becoming involved in seditious activities. Young Johnny was also imbued with patriotic fervor. These sentiments, like his lifelong sense of duty, derived from both parents, but at firsthand from the mother who raised him. At first, John Quincy was tutored by his father's law clerks, but they were soon obliged to depart, and he became his mother's prize pupil as well as her household assistant. Of necessity Abigail became supervisor and schoolmaster, running a substantial property on her own with remarkable efficiency, while imparting to all four children a smattering of everything from geography and drawing to poetry and French. She even taught them Latin, after first teaching herself. What could have better confirmed her conviction that she should have been better prepared to play her own role in the "Great Theatre" of life? Even her haphazard spelling and punctuation would always be a source of consternation, and she urged greater precision on her children and grandchildren of both sexes.

With home schooling added to all her other responsibilities, Abigail's exhausting hours were little brightened by the insensitive nature of her missing husband's missives. Combining advice with alarm, he insisted their progeny be taught, even in wartime, "not only to do virtuously but to excell," while urging that she "fly to the woods with our children" should the British land on the coast near their home. As the war intensified, Abigail not only feared for her husband's safety but bore family tragedy alone. Her mother died during an epidemic of dysentery. A daughter was delivered stillborn. The family witnessed dramatic events as well. When he was nine, Johnny heard the Declaration of Independence proclaimed, and he was urged by his mother to write his own reactions to his father. Despite the sporadic nature of his education, Johnny came to enjoy reading of every kind, especially fanciful fiction. He struggled to get through *Paradise Lost* because he knew it would please his parents, and his letters to his father testify that he was hardly self-taught.

In fairness, John Adams suffered immense guilt at his long absences from Abigail, guilt exacerbated by his inability to participate in rearing his children during their formative years. For her part, Abigail bore suffering with fortitude. As biographer Marie Hecht writes, Abigail "took the view that the separation was her sacrifice for her country, but she did regret that it happened to the children 'at the time in life when the joint instruction and admonitions of parents sink deeper than in mature years.'" Greater challenges were to come. At the end of 1777, Congress selected John Adams to replace Silas Deane as commissioner to France, where he was to join Benjamin Franklin and Arthur Lee in the critical task of gaining foreign support. Despite the perils and discomfort of an ocean crossing and the danger of capture by the British, Abigail longed to accompany her husband. She hoped to take with them the two oldest children, leaving the younger two with trusted friends. John would not hear of it, but somehow by "earnest entreaty" ten-year-old Johnny persuaded his father to take him to Paris. Abigail would lose both husband and son for the better part of the next six years to the demands of diplomatic duty.

During this even more desolate time, as Boorstin writes, Abigail continued her "heavy and diverse responsibilities, directing and financing the farm, keeping it afloat, reporting political facts, being both mother and father to the children at home, and instructing her absent eldest son in his morals and his duties." She must have appreciated the irony of her husband's earnest admonitions that his "dear partner in all the joys and sorrows of life" devote her "whole attention to the family, the stock, the farm, the dairy." She had already proven a better manager than he. Her interest in politics was also growing steadily during this time, and it did not simply mirror her husband's. That, by and large, their views coincided is the product of two independent minds reaching similar conclusions. Even during a revolution, both valued public order. The goal was not anarchy but a more equitable government.

In 1778, however, Abigail's more immediate concerns were the welfare of her children and the safety of her spouse. In the uncertain circumstances, letters could take months to arrive — or might never arrive at all. Frustrations finally surfaced in her communications to John. As the war intensified, money became tighter, food became scarcer, and a smallpox epidemic threatened throughout the harsh Massachusetts winter. "How lonely are my days?" she wrote. "How solitary are my nights? Secluded from all Society but my two little Boys, and my domesticks, by the Mountains of snow which surround me I could almost fancy myself in Greenland. . . . In the very few lines I have received from you not the least mention is made that you have ever received a line from me." More often than not it was now eleven-year-old Johnny, fiercely protective of his father, who would remind her that "Poppa" had "[so] many other things to think about" that it was admirable he could find time to write home at all. "It really hurts him to receive such letters," the boy reproved his mother.

One imagines that Abigail, even if chagrined, was also proud of her first son's loyalty and assertiveness. In the cause of self-improvement, she never ceased to admonish all her children, but most of all, at whatever distance, aimed her advice at John Quincy: "Improve your understanding for acquiring useful knowledge and virtue, such as will render you an ornament to society, an Honour to your Country, and a Blessing to your Parents." "[Follow] the precepts of your father as you value the happiness of your mother and your own welfare. . . . I had much rather you should have found your Grave in the ocean . . . rather than see you an immoral profligate or a Graceless child." If she seemed to lay it on a bit thick, Abigail later confided to Johnny that "I have sometimes found great address necessary to carry a point." Ever the parson's daughter, she valued repetition.

To her great joy, husband and son returned home for a brief interlude in 1779. John was elected to the Massachusetts Constitutional Convention and helped frame the document, but soon returned to his multiple tasks as "minister plenipotentiary" to France, where he had been placed in the hope that he could negotiate ultimate treaties of peace and commerce with Great Britain. This time he took not only John Quincy but his younger son Charles back to Europe with him, and the trip over was even more arduous and protracted than normal. One can only imagine Abigail's dismay. At least Johnny's education was not neglected in Europe. Attending schools in France and the Netherlands, he became so fluent in foreign languages that at the age of only fourteen he was selected to accompany Francis Dana, the American minister to Russia, as both secretary and translator — an extraordinary appointment.

Finally, in 1784, after American independence had been secured, Abigail Adams sailed to London to rejoin her husband. As the first ambassador (although the term in use was still "minister") of a free United States to Great Britain, his would be a delicate assignment. But Adams had already demonstrated considerable dexterity in working out a peace treaty balanced between the interests of his own country, Britain, France, and Spain — and reconciling the "subtle spirits" of his contrasting colleagues, Benjamin Franklin and John Jay. Finally reunited with his steadfast wife, Adams extolled her as a "heroine" of unexampled courage, sacrifice, and patriotism. For her part, Abigail was understandably delighted at the reunion and the acquaintance of such new friends as Thomas Jefferson, but she chafed at the artifice and snobbery of official society in London and Paris. She was even happier than her husband to return home in 1788. Their son Johnny had preceded them. Matured perhaps too quickly by his own responsibilities, he had already developed a preoccupation with self-improvement and at least a public demeanor as somber as his father's. Well prepared by his European education, he graduated from Harvard in only two years. Eventually he passed the bar and set about establishing his own law practice in Boston. Yet the attraction of diplomacy remained strong, bolstered by the example of his father's notable service and the awareness of his mother's expectations.

The new nation would need more than diplomats. Like his humbler forebears, John Adams had been obliged to "study" politics, participating in local government as a duty. Now he would be called upon to engage in it on a far broader scale, indeed to make it his preoccupation. An active supporter of the Constitution even while in Europe, and already named to the new Congress in 1789, Adams came in a distant second to George Washington in the initial vote of electors, making him the first vice president of the United States. Although describing the office to Abigail as "the most insignificant . . . that ever the invention of man contrived," Adams could not responsibly decline it. His main task was simply to preside over a Senate consisting of only twenty-two members, but his tie-breaking vote was often necessary to allow legislation to move forward. Despite Washington's abhorrence of factionalism, the young nation was already evolving into two distinct political parties, Federalists and Democratic-Republicans. Believing with Hamilton in a centralized financial structure, government by elites, and closer ties with the British, Adams was clearly a Federalist. Abigail shared his sentiments. Although she detested the increasingly vituperative nature of American politics, particularly as it came to be directed against her husband, she was also fascinated by it and was proud of the Adams family's growing prominence.

Unfortunately for John and Abigail, their times of separation were not at an end. Living in the temporary capital of Philadelphia, already a relative metropolis, was terribly costly, the wages of public office were woefully meager, and Abigail was often ill. She returned for lengthy periods to Quincy, as their home area of Braintree had been respectfully renamed. Even after her husband was narrowly elected as Washington's successor in 1796, Abigail was not always able to be at his side. Both understood fully the "honorable trials," as John put it, awaiting whoever followed Washington. Although Washington's second term was more troubled than his first, the squire of Mount Vernon, had he desired it, could have been elected president in perpetuity.

Meanwhile, John Quincy was finding his own way in Boston, heartened, if sometimes burdened, by the customary stream of correspondence from both parents, whose standards he strove to satisfy. His father's advice was general, reminding Johnny to care for his health, keep up his spirits, and trust that sustained effort would ultimately bring its rewards. His mother's counsel was equally supportive but far more specific. She delved into everything, as she would with her children and grandchildren to the end of her life, but particularly with her oldest son. It was turning out to be more costly than he had anticipated to establish a legal practice in Boston, but he was hesitant to ask for financial aid, considering the "innumerable favors" he had already received from his "best of parents." Abigail assured him that any devoted parent would do no less and urged him to "make yourself easy," all the while reminding him how superior his situation was to most others. This touch of vinegar frequently flavored her advice. When Johnny fell in love with a local belle named Mary Frazier, it must have reminded his mother of her husband's infatuation with the lovely Hannah Quincy prior to their own marriage. Without criticizing the young woman specifically, she warned John Quincy that "Too early a marriage will involve you in troubles that may render you . . . unhappy the remainder of your life." Perhaps Abigail's unspoken concern was that she might have to share her son too soon, or that there wasn't anyone truly worthy of him. Johnny assured his mother that he would never ask her consent to any "connection" until he was fully able to support it "with honor and independence." When he finally did marry another, however, he made the decision on his own — and announced it afterward.

Johnny's legal career was interrupted by President Washington, who in 1794 named the twenty-seven-year-old as Minister to the Netherlands, where he served with distinction. Upon leaving office, Washington conveyed to his successor his "strong hope" that "merited promotion" should not be withheld from John Quincy Adams, "the most valued public character we have abroad," simply because accusations of nepotism might result. The senior Adams was in a delicate position, already assailed on many fronts by an opposition party and press that had not spared even Washington. As Adams took office, his son was to be transferred from The Hague to Portugal. His father reassigned him, with his concurrence, to the ostensibly more prominent position of Minister to Prussia, despite the inevitable criticism such a move would bring. To Abigail's suggestion that this smacked of opportunism, John Quincy replied, "I had hoped that my mother knew me better . . . I have not been so totally regardless of the principles which education had instilled, nor so totally destitute of a sense of delicacy." Hecht writes that "The bond between John Quincy Adams and his mother was deep, subtle, and complex. As a lad, because of his father's constant absences . . . Abigail depended on her eldest son. As he grew older, she saw that her hopes and her ambitions must center upon him, the most stable and gifted of her children." Despite his growing resentment at her intrusiveness as he matured, "what John Quincy never lost was a need for his mother's approval." His father was equally revered but not so difficult to please.

Together or apart, John and Abigail Adams had a sort of telepathy. Although they shared similar views on many issues, Abigail did not merely echo her husband's opinions during his troubled term as president. She had been his closest collaborator in maneuvering for the election of 1796, all the while proclaiming that she wanted only to "reign in the heart of my husband." When he so narrowly won, he needed her counsel all the more. Opposed by Vice President Jefferson, and with his Federalist cabinet filled with men more loyal to Alexander Hamilton, Adams felt that Abigail was, as historian Joseph Ellis points out, the only confidant he "could truly trust." When she absented herself from the capital city, Adams's letters were plaintive. "I never wanted your advice and assistance more in my life. . . . The times are critical and dangerous and I must have you here to assist me. . . . I can do nothing without you."

Abigail detested the subjugation of anyone, whether slaves kidnapped from Africa, women denied opportunity, or the American colonies deprived of their rights by the Mother Country. As early as 1775 she had urged John to support the demand for outright independence, a stand he had been more gradually moving toward since his opposition to the Stamp Act a decade earlier. They both feared the growing recklessness of revolutionary France, which was reflected in the sentiments of many Americans. It led to a lengthy break in their friendship with Thomas Jefferson. They both favored a strong national defense but a prudent foreign policy. They both accepted the necessity for internal order, although Abigail was more in favor of such extreme measures as the Alien and Sedition Acts. She was particularly resentful of the

Abigail Adams
Courtesy of The Library of Congress

"vile misrepresentations" of a press she viewed as dangerously partisan. When she urged her husband to "remember the ladies," it was not so much an Eleanor Roosevelt-like plea that he do more than he deemed possible as it was a reminder of views they shared. Critics who complained that Abigail was John's most trusted advisor were right, but he was not under her spell. Their partnership predated his presidency, and it was not purely political. Abigail may have felt herself inferior to Martha Washington as an ideal first lady, but she could not resist her life-long proclivity to speak her mind. To Abigail, expressing thoughtful opinions on any subject was simply part of a full, "busy," useful life, completing rather than competing with a woman's essential tasks of wife and mother. To influence those who exercise power is not to usurp it.

It was not the advanced views of either Abigail or John, however, that led to the defeat of his bid for a second term in 1800, but the unpopularity of his policies. By adroitly avoiding war with France, he angered the more truculent of his Federalist constituency, while his domestic agenda was opposed by the increasingly powerful Democratic-Republicans. Of course, the daunting task of succeeding George Washington, who himself had come under partisan attack in his second term, would have been a challenge for anyone. Adams's autocratic governing style didn't help either. Earlier that year, the Adams family had finally moved to the unfinished executive mansion in the new capital city, marshy, muddy Washington. Abigail hung laundry in some of its rooms while spending a few miserable months preparing the premises for incoming President Jefferson. The Adamses did not remain for his inauguration, but returned to Quincy, from which they were rarely to stray. Both may well have longed for the serenity of such familiar surroundings, to be immersed again in farming and family life, but it was not the limelight that had lost its allure. It was the bitterness and turmoil of fractured government that they were happy to leave behind, especially the "basest libels and vilest slander" Abigail felt had been unfairly inflicted on her husband.

Back at home, John wrote his autobiography and attended to a wide range of correspondence, almost all of which he saved for future generations. He also continued the diary he had written virtually all of his life, providing an extraordinary picture of the times far more vivid than the aged recollections of some of the other Founding Fathers. (Nevertheless, he was uneasy, feeling that his role in the struggle for independence would be overshadowed by others'.) Jefferson believed each generation should be a separate entity, but to Adams there was a continuity from one generation to the next. His own family had already made the transition from governing a town to guiding a nation. Characteristically, during the remaining seventeen years of her life Abigail's focus was on the future. She never ceased to pour out advice, solicited or not, particularly to the cynosure of her hopes, the son she may already have foreseen as a potential president of the United States.

When John Quincy Adams, tired of "foreign climes" and recalled from Prussia at the end of his father's term, finally returned to the United States in 1801, he brought home a wife. Lively, cosmopolitan Louisa Catherine Johnson had never set foot on the American continent. Born to an American father and a British mother and raised in France, she had met her future husband in London. Her father, a tobacco merchant as well as American consul-general, had fallen on hard financial times. Louisa was loath to inflict her problems on others. Her warmth, however, melted John Quincy's icy New England reserve. He chafed at delays, revealing the same unsuspected passionate nature his father had thirty-three years before. Once John Quincy had argued at Harvard that money made a better foundation for matrimony than love, but just before being dispatched to Prussia, he wed destitute Louisa in a quiet London ceremony. In a joint letter to both his "dear and honored" parents, their buoyant son urged that they banish any possible anxiety. "You will find her [to] prove such a daughter as you would wish for your son." Abigail, however, was apprehensive, perhaps regretting her earlier interference in John Quincy's romance with Mary Frazier. It wasn't so much money that was on her mind. Might not Louisa be too fine a lady, too delicate and aristocratic to provide the kind of supportive partnership Abigail had given John to advance his career? Abigail's reaction reminds one of the early appraisal of Jacqueline Bouvier by some of the Kennedys. Still, it was heartening to the patriotic Abigail "by the love I bear my Country that the Syren is at least half blood."

As it turned out, it was Louisa who was intimidated by her tiny but overwhelming mother-in-law. After a fifty-eight-day passage from Hamburg, John Quincy, Louisa, and their five-month-old child, appropriately named George Washington Adams, arrived in Philadelphia and hastened to Massachusetts where their excited, impatient parents waited. Her joy at seeing her son again did not prevent Abigail from inquiring rather too quickly about just what he proposed to do in the future. Would he again take up the law in Boston? Circumstances intervened. John Adams was still highly esteemed in New England, and in

1802 his son was elected to the Massachusetts Senate as a Federalist; the following year he was elected to the Senate of the United States. Apparently the next generation of Adamses would not be studying "mathematics and philosophy" after all. Unfortunately, John Quincy Adams was as stubborn as his father — and as independent-minded as his mother. He insisted on considering every issue on its merits, not always following the party line, and broke most significantly with the Federalists in 1807 by supporting President Jefferson's Embargo Act. During his years in the Senate, he often returned to Quincy for relief from the Washington heat, political as well as climatic.

Happily back in the arena, his mother cautioned, "No man in Congress is so delicately situated." You should expect jealousy and opposition on all sides, she cautioned her son, yet you must continue to speak your mind. "I wish not to see you a cypher, nor is it possible you can be one. . . . I know your vote will always proceed from a sense of what you consider right and proper divested of party spirit. . . . [It is my] sincere wish and fervent prayer [that] so long as you live, may you hold fast your integrity." Still, the old maternal maxims always returned. She worried about his weight, his health, his sociability, his appearance. If he demanded much of himself, his mother expected perfection. While prescribing homemade remedies for every ailment, she cautioned, "You must not let the mind wear so much with the body . . . unbend in company . . . you eat too little and study too much . . . [beware] stiffness, reserve, and a coldness of address in company." Perhaps excessive formality had developed in Europe. One could be very careful, yet congenial. He looked too "pale, thin, and slender," Abigail observed, and was much too careless in dress. "A good coat is tantamount to a good character." A clean-shaven, healthy appearance is as important as a proper wig and neck-cloth. Were such brisk admonitions addressed to a fourteen-year-old schoolboy or to a forty-year-old member of Congress?

In everything, Abigail sought that Louisa should "unite" with her. The young woman hardly knew what to make of such a combination of parental protectiveness and intrusiveness. Certainly Abigail understood American realities better than did her daughter-in-law. Abigail understood John Quincy as well, and was utterly devoted to his success — but perhaps almost too devoted? Father Adams's perceptive advice came when it was solicited; the mother seemed obsessed with her son's success. Yet, over time, a close bond developed between these two very dissimilar women. They had ample opportunity to get to know one another; while John Quincy labored in Washington, Louisa and their children stayed behind in Massachusetts, just as frugal Abigail had when John was serving as vice president.

The young family itself was growing. Another John was born before John Quincy went to the Senate, a third son and a daughter later. Meanwhile, despite his political pedigree, the Federalist Party had seen quite enough of the intransigence of John Quincy Adams. The Massachusetts legislature named his successor six months before his term expired. Angered at this affront, Adams resigned and returned to Massachusetts to practice law and teach at Harvard. In 1808 he broke with his father's party, supporting Democratic-Republican James Madison, another former Federalist, for president. Again, his mother, with a mixture of political prescience and confidence, supported his decision. She could see that the Federalists, with their narrowing political base and craven acquiescence to British interests, were on their way out as a national party. And, in fact, she had never believed much in rigid adherence to political parties.

When Madison appointed John Quincy to become Minister to Russia, Abigail was concerned. Why go even farther abroad when the developing American political and legal scene offered such possibilities? In addition, John Quincy's financial success, and his father's, had been little advanced by such official missions. Indeed, the whole family's security was uncertain. Perhaps most of all, she would miss him. She had spent too many years separated from both her husband and her first son. Hers was "a life of farewells." To a friend, Abigail confided that a man of John Quincy's merit "ought not to be permitted to leave the Country — a Country which wants such supports." Louisa, too, was deeply distressed at the impending departure. Despite their early passion, life with her intensely serious husband was never easy. The financial ruin of her own family and the impoverished state of the foreign service would allow for little entertainment or diversion in so distant a posting. She dreaded the Russian winters, the primitive conditions even in St. Petersburg, the likelihood of European conflict, and the distance from a new family she was just coming to know. Worst of all, to save money, her husband insisted she leave her two oldest sons, then eight and six, home in the care of their grandparents.

It was during the lonely years to come that Louisa's bond with Abigail strengthened, that the letters that took so many months to arrive were addressed to a "dear mother" from an "affectionate daughter." The shared experience of so many separations made them closer. Louisa's health deteriorated in the harsh climate, and her only daughter died after but a year of life. Her mourning could be appreciated by Abigail, whose own daughter, Susanna, had lived for only two years. Louisa was "solicitous" to return home, where in "Mrs. Adams I should have found a comforter, a friend who would pity my sufferings which she would have understood." Both mother and daughter-in-law were cheered when John Quincy was sent to Ghent in 1814 to help negotiate an end to the War of 1812, but he traveled alone. It was only in 1815 that, his mission to Russia finally completed, John Quincy sent for his wife and youngest son to join him in Paris. Delicate Louisa, negotiating the perils of that 2000-mile journey, proved herself as resourceful as any Adams.

It cheered Abigail, now in her seventies, that at least her son and his family were closer to the warmth of home. In 1815, Boston's church bells rang in the advent of peace, portending — despite the depredations the British had committed in the War of 1812 — an era of enhanced American influence. Abigail, ever-alert to events even if diminished physically, delighted in the "late glorious victory" at New Orleans and was so impressed with her son's lengthy letter thoroughly explaining the peace treaty that she laboriously copied every word. To make certain her John Quincy's role was appreciated, she had his letter published and distributed as an anonymous communication "from one of the ministers to his friend."

John wrote to John Quincy that he would be "overjoyed" to see how his mother had recovered "her former alacrity, spirit, wit" and that he took "great delight in riding out with her every fair day." Their adored daughter, also nicknamed Nabby by her mother, had died in 1813. Now only two sons remained of their original five children. Yet Abigail's letters to John Quincy were, as always, most focused on his own future.

After the peace treaty was signed, he had been dispatched to London, as had his father following the previous Anglo-American conflict, as Minister to Great Britain. Throughout the spring of 1817, Abigail implored John Quincy to return: "The voice of the nation calls you home. The government calls you home — and your parents unite in the call." She was already very critical of what she viewed as the excessive pomp of the incoming Monroe administration. Jefferson was looking better. Although she never wrote in so many words that she anticipated John Quincy would be called upon to serve as a future president, now the hope was implicit. Urged by their mutual friend Benjamin Rush, John Adams joined his wife in resuming their correspondence with Thomas Jefferson, who wrote empathetically on the death of their daughter but prescribed "time and silence" as "the only medicine for grief."

Abigail knew she had little time left, but serenity was never her style. Limited physically to the reduced world of family and friends, Abigail's mind remained boundless. From her theocratic childhood, Abigail had always thought deeply about religion. She had made the transition from the Congregational beliefs of her parents to the Episcopalian Church of her daughter-in-law. Now she sought simplicity, to take the Christian faith to its foundations. Early in 1818 she wrote to Louisa, "True religion is from the Heart, between Man and his Creator." She declared herself to be a Unitarian, believing that "the Father alone is the supreme God. . . . Jesus Christ derived his Being, and all his powers and honours from the Father." John Quincy, always more religious than his father and, in fact, something of a biblical scholar, also became a Unitarian. With the city of Washington's proliferation of new churches, he sometimes attended services in various venues three times a day — his own quest another reflection of his mother's ceaseless inquiry into truth.

To her grandchildren Abigail remained a font of advice, instructing them on everything from the profitable use of the precious commodity of time to the importance of polished penmanship, spelling, and punctuation. Abigail remained concerned about feminine decorum. To her granddaughter Caroline, Nabby's child, who had come to live with them prior to her own marriage, Abigail stressed that American women should be content "with the show which nature bestows," rather than falling prey to the low bodices, suggestive glances, and general libertinism of radical French influences. "Chastity, modesty, decency, and conjugal faith are the pillars of society [without which] the whole fabrick falls sooner or later." Abigail remained ever the political innovator, the domestic conservative.

John Quincy and his family finally returned home in 1817. He had been named Secretary of State by President Monroe, a post previously held by Jefferson, Madison, and Monroe himself. John Adams would live to see his son elected president only seven years later. Abigail would not. Despite meddling in everyone's lives, she remained always "a mortal enemy of anything but a cheerful countenance and a merry heart." All in all, she reasoned, "This is a very good world," only capable of improvement. She and her husband had enjoyed much stimulating company in their retirement, and finally the return of John Quincy. He seemed to sense that his mother was weakening and spent as much time as he could manage in Quincy, whatever the rush of events in Washington. Abigail's mind was as alert as ever, full of such ideas as the formation of a "council of the ladies" made up of the wives of government officials. But by the fall of 1817 she suffered severe chills and a variety of other ailments. On October 28, 1818, she finally succumbed to typhoid fever. Her last letter to Thomas Jefferson was signed "your old and steady friend." To a grief-stricken John Adams, Jefferson wrote with unaccustomed emotion of "mingling my tears with yours."

When he heard the news, John Quincy suffered something akin to an emotional collapse. Louisa observed that he was "totally incapacitated." Later he wrote, "In the agitation of my own heart I knew not how to order my speech." Despite his frequent absences from his mother's side, to John Quincy, denied the comforting knowledge of her unwavering solicitude, "The world feels to me like a solitude." He also paid tribute to her spiritual qualities: "There is not a virtue that can abide in the human heart, but it was the ornament of hers. . . . The God of my Father and Mother shall be my God." To Louisa, Abigail was "the guiding planet around which all revolved." Toward the end, however, Abigail seems finally to have surmised how burdensome were her ambitions for her fifty-year-old son. She wrote to Louisa, "My love to my Son, I have not the heart to ask him to write tho it would give me so much pleasure." Although John Quincy remarked that while his mother lived, "Whenever I returned . . . I felt as if the joys of childhood had returned to make me happy. All was kindness and affection," he also said, "I cannot escape my destiny." Intended or not, that legacy could be a burden. Of his own three sons, only the youngest, Charles Francis, achieved a career of great distinction. One died of alcoholism, the other committed suicide.

John Adams and John Quincy Adams were both first sons, to whom much was given and from whom much was expected. John Quincy's eventual focus on a political career seems to have been more encouraged by his mother than by his father. Based on his own unhappy tenure as Washington's successor, John Adams harbored no presidential ambitions for his son. There is little doubt Abigail contributed to her husband's administration, but did her thinking also influence her son's term in the presidency? Certainly she would have approved of his extraordinarily ambitious plans for public works and stimulation of the economy and his courageous espousal of Indian rights. She would have been overjoyed by his subsequent opposition to slavery as "old man eloquent" in the House of Representatives. That John Quincy Adams's four years in the White House were the unhappiest of his life was due more to the controversial nature of his election and a personality even more inflexible than his father's than to the content of his proposals. He inherited the drive, domineering personality, and self-discipline of his mother, but without the grace of her wit and generosity.

It has been suggested that Abigail Adams was contradictory, that she became more conservative, even reactionary, as she grew older. It is not true. Her children and grandchildren may have resented her interference in their lives, yet it never diminished their appreciation of her loving concern for them. She insisted on thinking and speaking for herself even when very young, and hoped to instill in others not a blind acceptance of her views but a similar independence of thought. Abigail's support of the American Revolution and opposition to the French is testament to the differences between the two — the first opposed tyranny, the other replaced one form with another. Her fear of "foreign" influences, even to the point of advocating suppression of the Ameri can press, can be questioned as prudent policy, but it is consistent with her belief in the vital importance of public order. Her life-long advocacy of women's rights but also of feminine modesty was no contradiction but was based on the conviction that all lives have limitless potential. Such potential should not make women more like men, she felt, but more fulfilled as women. In her own life, Abigail was obliged to fill many roles — wife, mother, grandmother, homemaker, writer, educator, farm manager, financial planner, patriot, and counselor to statesmen.

Books chronicling the saga of the Adamses often focus primarily on the Adams men and the offices they occupied. Yet much of what we know about these men comes from the letters and journal of Abigail Adams, and it was a woman, Abigail's granddaughter Caroline Smith Dewindt, who kept Abigail's thoughts alive by publishing selections from her journal and letters in 1841. That most fitting memorial was more than Abigail would have wished. Despite her self-confidence, she always considered her husband's and son's lives and careers more significant than her own. In this singular sense she may finally be viewed as a victim of her times. That her husband and son were less successful than they should have been as presidents, despite representing views she espoused, leads to the inescapable conclusion that with her more practical, outgoing, positive outlook, Abigail Smith Adams would have made an outstanding president of the United States.

CHAPTER FOUR

Immigrants and Pioneers

- ॐ Elizabeth Jackson
- ॐ Maria Van Buren
- ॐ Elizabeth Harrison
- ॐ Mary Tyler
- ॐ Jane Polk
- ॐ Sarah Taylor

ANDREW JACKSON marks a point of departure from the previous six presidents. Even the most egalitarian of the Founders, Thomas Jefferson, hardly anticipated that an enlarged electorate would bring forth from its humblest recesses an Andrew Jackson. Unlike many previous presidential mothers, those of Jackson and a number of his immediate successors did not so much confer status on their offspring as inspire aspirations others could scarcely comprehend. In Jackson's case, his mother quite literally saved his life.

Certainly Elizabeth (Betty) Hutchinson came to her marriage with no more in the way of worldly goods than her husband, who was also named Andrew Jackson. Described by biographer Burke Davis as "a small, spirited woman," she had her hands full tending to two young sons by day and weaving throughout the night. Their third son, Andrew, had not yet been conceived when both husband and wife were earning a meager living as "linen drapers" in the Irish town of Carrickfergus. Their life afforded little leisure to enjoy the natural beauty of their surroundings. The Jacksons were more Scotch than Irish, residing near Belfast in Ulster, where ancient antipathies still fester. Perhaps violence was part of the ethnic inheritance of the seventh president of the United States, but from his parents came fortitude and tenacity. The Jacksons had some relatives in the region who had achieved a degree of prosperity, but the senior Andrew and his wife were, in the words of biographer Gerald Johnson, "worse than poor. They were luckless." The conclusion of the French and Indian War had opened up vast territories in North America, promising abundant opportunity for anyone willing to work. It took little encouragement to induce Jackson in 1765 to add his family to twenty others planning to emigrate.

They had been preceded by such optimistic pioneers as Jackson's brother, Hugh, and his uncle by marriage, James Crawford. Already a semblance of their old community had been established in a fertile valley known as "the Waxhaws" by the Catawba Creek, near the border of what is now North and South Carolina. Betty Jackson's four married sisters also lived nearby. With so extensive a colony of connections the Jacksons were warmly welcomed, and set about to build a better life. But it took more than encouragement to succeed, and Jackson's luck proved no better in the new world than it had in the old.

Despite his inexperience, the linen draper was determined to be a successful farmer. Obtaining land at the edge of the forest surrounding the Waxhaws, near Twelve Mile Creek, Jackson started laboriously to clear it. Those with money had purchased land within the settlement. Jackson lacked the means to do so. Unfortunately, his tract had not yet been surveyed, and his possession of it was contested by the claims of others. It is uncertain whether Jackson ever had clear title to the land he worked — or was only an unwilling tenant. In any event, as Johnson writes, "He attacked the forest resolutely and not without success, for the record testifies that he cleared his land, raised at least one crop and built his log house by the beginning of the year 1767." The family entered into the life of their community, traveling the twelve miles every Sunday to worship with Mrs. Jackson's relatives at the Waxhaw Church. Before long, however, the wilderness won out. Among the charred stumps of the trees he'd felled, Jackson severely injured himself straining to lift a giant log. Within hours, he was dead. Betty Jackson was pregnant with their third child.

In a crude farm wagon, Jackson's body was brought down to the Waxhaw churchyard and buried without even a stone to mark its place. The family would never return to the farm he had labored so earnestly to wrest from the forest. A few days later, at a kindly relative's house near the church, Betty gave birth. It was another son. At least she could honor her late husband by naming the boy Andrew. Penniless but determined to keep her family together, she ventured a few miles south to the home of a sister who had become an invalid. In return for her brother-in-law's hospitality, Betty Jackson undertook to manage the entire household. It was not so much a dependency as a contract between equals. A strong, energetic woman who could cook, clean, and sew was a valuable commodity on the American frontier. Able to read and write a little, Betty especially wanted all three of her sons to be educated, not only the oldest — a great boon for young Andrew.

The best local school was affiliated with the Presbyterian Church, not surprising in an area where ministers were generally the most learned and esteemed men in the community. Although the loosely governed Carolinas were hardly a New England theocracy, a clergyman's views were often followed in temporal matters as well. When it became clear that her youngest son was the most promising scholar of her three boys, indomitable Betty Jackson determined that ultimately he should become a man of the cloth. It may be hard to imagine the Andrew Jackson of our history books as a Presbyterian minister, but he surely developed the capacity to command respect.

Unfortunately, young Andrew was far more interested in riding, running, and fighting than in reading, writing, and keeping accounts. Still, by the age of five he could read well, by the age of eight he wrote in "a neat, legible hand," and by nine he was even employed as a "public reader." Since most of the men and women of the Waxhaw settlement were illiterate, they gathered daily to have the news and important documents read to them by the equivalent of town criers. Andrew was proud of his ability to perform this task, generally accorded to adults. In July, 1776, he was chosen to read to the assembled community the entire Declaration of Independence from a newspaper. His mother might well imagine him in a pulpit, but Andrew was likely more focused on the import of the words he uttered. Only a month earlier, his relative, Captain Robert Crawford, had led a local company of militia to help repel a British assault on Charleston. A war of independence was already under way. Indeed, skirmishes had taken place sporadically for over four years.

At thirteen, Andrew Jackson was a volatile combination of confidence, energy, and emotion. Burke Davis writes, "Lean and graceful, with a thick shock of dark reddish hair and bright blue eyes deeply set in a freckled face, he was already notorious for his temper." Protective of younger children, he was nonetheless feared by all. Any sign of ridicule could set him off. When a childhood affliction caused him to slobber uncontrollably, Jackson warned, "By God, if one of you laughs, I'll kill him." His "Spartan Mother" insisted that her son never cry and always defend himself, whatever the odds; she was religious, but felt that a Christian need not be a pacifist. The temper of the times did little to soften Andrew's belligerence. Neighbors and even families were divided by what would become as much a civil as a revolutionary war. The Scotch derived from the highlands would stay largely loyal to the crown; Scotch-Irish like the Jacksons were more inclined to independence. As the regular armies came and went, the war in the Carolinas degenerated into ferocious blood feuds between bands of Loyalist and insurgent bushwhackers not unlike those in Missouri and Kansas in the later Civil War. No one was spared, civilian or soldier.

Betty Jackson feared for her sons, but where was she to go? She was powerless to prevent her oldest, eighteen-year-old Hugh, from fighting for independence with the local militia. In 1779 he was killed at the Battle of Stono Bridge. With her two remaining sons she helped tend the wounded, their old church turned into a makeshift hospital. Afterward, she wandered about the countryside, hoping to keep her family safe until hostilities receded. Instead, they heightened, as feared British Colonel Banastre Tarleton's troops tore through the Waxhaws. Pugnacious Andrew could no longer be restrained. Only thirteen years and four months old, he joined his sixteen-year-old brother, Robert, in the backwoods cavalry of Colonel William R. Davie. These hard-pressed volunteers weren't very particular about age. At first Davie tried to protect Andrew by limiting him to duty as a mounted messenger, but the youth was so skilled a rider and so knowledgeable about local terrain that he became a favorite of his commander, who gave him a handsome pistol with which to protect himself. Andrew had no intention of being a noncombatant, already possessing a valuable Irish rifle.

Unfortunately, he would see no action. A patrol of British dragoons surprised Jackson's band. It scattered, and Robert and Andrew took refuge in a relative's home. Betrayed by a Tory neighbor, the two boys were ignominiously captured without firing a shot. When an imperious British officer ordered them to clean his muddy boots, Andrew insisted that they be treated as prisoners of war. His reply was a saber slash. Andrew thrust his hand up to ward it off. Blood gushed from wounds in both his scalp and his hand. Robert was even less fortunate, knocked to the floor by the saber, opening a deeper wound, which soon became infected. After the house was plundered and burned, both were marched away to a foul prison camp in Camden, forty miles distant. A smallpox epidemic, the periodic and lethal affliction of the American colonies, made the condition of the captives even more perilous.

When word reached the boys' mother, she somehow kept her head. From a militia captain she secured the promise that thirteen British prisoners would be released in exchange for her two sons and several of their companions. Then she hastened by horseback the forty miles to the prison camp, insisting that she see the local British commander, Lord Rawdon, personally. As biographer Marquis James writes, perhaps he admired the "pluck" of this "brisk, blue-eyed little Irishwoman whose country attire showed the stains of travel." The exchange was made, her sons were liberated, but they were more dead than alive. The ragged little group set off, all the way back to the Waxhaws. Betty could obtain only two horses. On one, Robert was held so that he would not fall off. His mother rode on the other horse. Andrew, barefoot, bareheaded, coatless, and burning with fever but still ambulatory, managed to walk, with the other freed men. Almost home, a drenching rainstorm added to their miseries.

Within forty-eight hours of his arrival, Robert was dead, his wound and the effects of smallpox too severe to overcome. It was touch-and-go with Andrew. Having lost her husband and two of her three sons to the claims of wilderness and war, Elizabeth Jackson all but willed her last child to survive. After months of her ministrations, he was finally out of danger. All his life, Andrew Jackson would carry the scars that symbolized his hatred of the British. But they would also remind him of his mother's nobility. She, as well as he, had seen firsthand the horrors of British prison camps. Through tragic years, the Waxhaws had been their home, their kinfolk a source of comfort and support. Now two of the Crawfords' sons lay ill with "ship fever" in British prison ships in the harbor of Charleston, along with others of her neighbors' children. Elizabeth had to try to save them, just has she had saved Andrew and nearly saved Robert.

In the summer of 1781, convinced that Andrew would be safe, she set out with two other Waxhaw women to find the prisoners and help nurse them back to health. She may have gone the whole 160 miles by foot, but it is more likely she traveled the distance on horseback, leading pack animals loaded with medicines and supplies. With the likelihood of contagion, she must have known her farewell from Andrew would be final, but she also must have harbored a mother's confidence in his ability to provide for himself. In light of his subsequent career, her tearful last words to him, as he recalled them, were both characteristic and prophetic: "Andy . . . never tell a lie, nor take what is not your own, nor sue for slander . . . settle them cases yourself."

Inevitably, although she did save at least one of the Crawfords, she soon contracted the fever herself and died at the home of a friend. She was hastily buried on a plain outside of Charleston, her grave as unmarked as that of her husband. All Andrew received by way of remembrance was a bundle of her spare clothes. At only fifteen, he had learned a great deal about poverty, war, and loss — a hard preparation for almost anything life might offer. Yet he said, as Jefferson had with less justification at the death of his father, "I felt utterly alone." In old age, Jackson would still remember his mother as having been "gentle as a dove and brave as a lioness."

It did not take long to justify her confidence that he could make his way in the world. He lived with friends and relatives for three years. When the British finally departed from Charleston, he served as a saddler's apprentice, and might well have made working with horses his career. An unexpected bequest of several hundred pounds from his paternal grandfather, an Irish weaver and merchant who had prospered, raised his sights. He gambled the money away, but his new taste for high living also hastened his acquaintance with Charleston aristocrats, enhancing his ease in any company. Somehow he found the means to spend a short time at a "classical" school, and even briefly became a schoolmaster. Ultimately, with all the Tory barristers gone, Jackson saw his opportunity and took up the study of law in the office of a North Carolina attorney. In 1788, he moved to the new settlement of Nashville in what was then the western district of the state. In his twenties, he was already an established success; by thirty, he represented the new state of Tennessee in the United States House of Representatives. Throughout his life, for good or ill, Andrew Jackson followed his mother's admonition to "settle them cases yourself." As president, Jackson would personally subdue an assailant whose two pistols had miraculously misfired at point blank range. (The man's grievance: that Jackson had prevented his ascension as King of England.) Elizabeth Jackson had not saved her son to be a weakling.

Nor to be an unbeliever. Jackson's wife, Rachel, devout as his mother had been, urged him to join the Presbyterian church, but while he held office Jackson insisted that a public confession of faith would be misconstrued as politically motivated. No friend of religious bigotry, however, he hosted the Roman Catholic wedding of an aide's daughter in the White House. Out of office, both his wife and mother long deceased, seventy-year-old Andrew Jackson finally joined the little brick church he had built on the grounds of his home, the Hermitage. He died eight years later, a committed Christian, convinced that "Heaven [would] not be Heaven" were he not to be reunited with his beloved wife and saintly mother.

UNLIKE Elizabeth Jackson, Maria Van Buren did not save the life of her most promising son, but what she gave him was of almost equal value. Maria provided Martin with an example of diligence to inspire his future success, overcoming the influence of his good-natured but unambitious father. Martin Van Buren was the first American president whose family was not descended from the British Isles. The Van Burens were Dutch on both sides and had been for generations. They resided in the little town of Kinderhook ("Old Kinderhook" would be transposed to "OK" in Van Buren's campaign for the presidency) in an area of the Hudson Valley of New York later celebrated by Washington Irving. The residents spoke Dutch among themselves and attended their own Dutch Reformed Church. Intermarriage reinforced their shared heritage, but a hierarchy necessarily developed to preserve their traditions. At the top, just as in Massachusetts or Virginia, were established families of education and property. The Van Burens, despite their kinship of blood with many of them, occupied a humbler place in the community.

This did not particularly upset Martin's easygoing father, Abraham, who took things as they came. He was a thirty-nine-year-old bachelor when he married the widow Maria Hoes Van Alen in 1776. As biographer John Niven writes, "Maria was a capable woman, and her condition, struggling to provide a home for her three children, appealed to the sentimental side of his nature." Perhaps Abraham also recognized in Maria a potentially stabilizing influence. She had known better times as the daughter of a respected family who had been among the original emigrants from Holland. The couple had two children before Abraham went off to fight in the Revolutionary War. A third child, Martin, their first son, was born on December 5, 1782, just before the war ended. Eventually there would be nine children in all, including those from Maria's first marriage, living in exceedingly cramped quarters above Abraham Van Buren's tavern.

His thrifty forebears had bequeathed him both this tavern, ideally situated on the Post Road between Albany and New York, and substantial acreage of fertile farmland. An enterprising entrepreneur, particularly one with Abraham's congenial nature, might have made much of such property. As Martin recalled, his father "was never known to have an enemy." Moreover, Abraham Van Buren served as town clerk and earned extra money by renting out the tavern for political meetings and as a polling place. Martin's early taste for politics developed at home. If he wanted to hear Federalists debate Jeffersonians, he needed only go downstairs. Unfortunately, his father was that notable exception to ethnic generalities, an improvident Dutchman. Satisfaction came too easily to him. He enjoyed the company his tavern afforded, but had neither the ability to run it efficiently nor the energy to make the most profitable use of his farm. As Martin was later to put it, succinctly, his father was "utterly devoid of the spirit of accumulation." Abraham was also a soft touch, and he rarely pressed anyone for repayment. As his children and stepchildren grew, the family's already modest circumstances were reduced to a state of penury.

Dutiful but determined, Maria came to understand that she must provide both stability and respectability if the family were to survive. Under her unobtrusive but well-ordered auspices, each of the children worked out their assigned tasks in both family enterprises, under a stringent budget. Beyond providing for immediate necessities, Maria had larger ambitions for her children and early recognized particular promise in Martin. If she could help it, he would not wind up like the father of whom he was so fond. As Niven writes, "Even as a very young child there was something, some indefinable quality that set Martin Van Buren apart. . . . A handsome child, small, rather delicate in appearance . . . [he had] a merry disposition and an infectious smile [that] made him popular among his friends. But it was his quickness of mind, his poise that appealed to his elders." Some of these elders were the leading citizens of the community. They could overlook the youth's humble origins when they heard him discuss adult subjects with such clarity and ease. One thinks of Harry Truman's observation that his own success was based on finding out what would please others, and then doing it. Clearly, Martin Van Buren was meant for bigger things, but only the patronage of the powerful, not his father's cronies, could launch his career. His mother fully realized this. Even after a day in the fields, she made certain that Martin's simple homespun was cleaner than anyone else's. He was always mannerly, deferential without being obsequious to those in authority, considerate of those younger than himself.

Most important, of course, was that he be educated. Maria was realistic enough to understand that college would be a financial impossibility, even for her most talented son. She had, however, already squeezed enough out of the family's meager resources to somehow grant the sons of her earlier marriage sufficient education that they could be accepted as law clerks. Ultimately one would serve as a member of Congress. She managed to keep Martin in school until the age of fifteen, a considerable loss of free labor to her hard-pressed husband. Yet agreeable Abraham consented, as he invariably did, not so much because he could see the point of it as to please his overworked wife.

The school, which became the distinguished Kinderhook Academy, was in those times only a single room. It was administered, however, by a dedicated schoolmaster, David Warden, who was perceptive enough to grasp Martin's potential and work with him almost as a tutor. Although in later years Van Buren, like Washington before him, would regret his educational limitations, he amassed the essential tools for a public career under Warden's tutelage. Beyond Latin and arithmetic, the grammar, rhetoric, and logic Martin absorbed provided the foundation for him to learn to speak and write more forcefully. The mature Van Buren's temperament and tenacity, however, derived most of all from his mother.

Unlike some subsequent presidents who sought to escape their childhood circumstances, Van Buren genuinely loved both his parents. When his father died at the age of eighty-one, Martin accurately appraised him as an "amiable and loving" parent, a generous friend to all. Yet even as a youth, Martin understood that success lay in overcoming his father's weaknesses and embracing his mother's strengths. He saw in himself, rightly or not, too much of the aimless conviviality of his father, and a tendency to act much too hastily. If he were to succeed, he must use his time efficiently, plan thoroughly, and work harder than others. In everything he must emulate his mother's carefulness, if not her quietness. After his schooling he returned neither to the taproom nor to farm chores. His family succeeded in finding him a place in the office of the town's leading lawyer, Francis Silvester. In return for sweeping out his offices and clerking part-time at the store of the attorney's brother, Van Buren was given a bedroom at the store, and the opportunity to learn the law. He made the most of it.

By the age of seventeen, Van Buren had not only mastered the complex New York legal code, he was well on his way to becoming a professional politician. He would ultimately practice law and be elected to his first public office by the age of thirty, but even while clerking for Silvester, Van Buren was already evidencing political skill. His patron and most of the prominent folk in Kinderhook were Federalists, but like Abigail Adams, Van Buren could see that so diminished a political party was headed for oblivion. Adroitly, he helped obtain the Democratic-Republican nomination to Congress for his townsman and relative, John P. Van Ness, at their regional convention in Troy. Despite this defection, Van Buren had inherited enough of his father's charm to be forgiven by Silvester. Still, the ambitious youth did not become active himself as a Democratic-Republican until the grateful Van Ness paid his way to New York City, enabling Van Buren to continue his studies in the metropolis and pass the bar. That quality of calculation did not derive from his father.

Maria Hoes Van Alen Van Buren died less than a year after her second husband, Abraham Van Buren. By then, their son Martin was simultaneously a state senator and attorney general of New York — a power broker well on his way to a national political career. Doris Faber notes that Maria's epitaph was limited to such observations as, "her long life was adorned by domestic virtues of the most useful kind." Useful indeed. Her true memorial would be the career of the eighth president of the United States.

THE "Age of Jackson" extended far beyond Andrew Jackson's actual tenure in the White House and wrought many changes, not the least in the structure of American political parties. Martin Van Buren, Jackson's devoted but luckless successor, was writing a study on that subject when he died in 1862. By the time his sons completed it, our present two-party system was essentially in place. The Federalists had hastened to oblivion after the War of 1812. Jefferson's Democratic-Republicans (with the emphasis on Republican) became simply the Democratic Party as we know it today. Disparate elements of the old party, united initially by their opposition to Jackson, formed the Whig Party. They fielded candidates in 1836, and by 1840 had just enough strength to elect their first president, William Henry Harrison. A new Republican party would enter the lists in 1856, as the Whigs declined.

The election of Harrison and his running mate, John Tyler, marked a short-lived return to the primacy of Southern gentlemen, although it was hardly characterized in that way at the time. It also, unfortunately, reprises the lack of information that characterizes the missing mothers of Virginia. All we know of Elizabeth Bassett Harrison is that she was born to a prominent family remotely related to Martha Washington; was reputed to be both beautiful and beneficent; married the fifth Benjamin Harrison (there would be more); gave birth to seven children, of whom William Henry was the youngest; and died in her sixties at the

Harrisons' Berkeley estate. All we know of Mary Armistead Tyler is that she, too, was born to a prominent family; was reputed to be both beautiful and beneficent; at sixteen married the third John Tyler, a widower far older than she; had eight children, of whom young John was the sixth; and died when the boy was only seven. In the most noted biography of President John Tyler, his mother rates only a single mention and isn't even included in the index.

The fathers of Harrison and Tyler fare better. Both were prominent planters who enjoyed similarly successful and thoroughly documented public careers, each serving as governor of Virginia. Their most successful sons, born within the same county sixteen years apart, shared little beyond their origins and the extent of their ambitions. Harrison left Hampden-Sydney College to study medicine in Philadelphia, but joined the army after his father died, rising to the rank of brigadier-general. After well-publicized campaigns of Indian fighting, he settled in Ohio and was eventually elected to the United States Senate. He returned to manage his new farm and take on a government post in order to settle substantial debts he had accumulated. It also occurred to him that his military renown might translate to consideration for the presidency, under the auspices of the emerging Whig Party. The courtly Tyler was no less ambitious but far less traveled. After attending William and Mary, he had studied law with his father, served in the War of 1812, and climbed the political ladder, eventually being elected governor of Virginia and United States senator. He became a Whig not because he concurred with the big-government emphasis of many of its leaders but because of his disaffection with Jackson, whom he had previously supported. It was an era of shifting loyalties.

Despite their differences, Harrison and Tyler are tied together in perpetuity not only by their peculiarly shared administration but also because of the extraordinary political campaign that brought it about. Each had shown sufficient promise in regional opposition to Van Buren in 1836 to make them together a seemingly logical Whig ticket to block "Old Kinderhook's" reelection bid in 1840. Harrison was pliable and was increasingly viewed as a man of the West. Tyler, still firmly a son of the old South, nicely balanced the ticket. His support of slavery and states' rights was anathema to many Whigs, but, after all, he would only be vice president — less significant than members of the cabinet. Besides, the way to win was to market personalities, not debate issues. To our eyes, 1840 seems almost a contemporary campaign.

The main thrust of the Whigs' effort was to build up Harrison as their own equivalent of Jackson. Unfortunately, Harrison's military opponents had not been foreign foes but the Native American confederation headed by Chief Tecumseh, who had received only tepid British support. Harrison's notable victory came in Ontario, but it was his earlier, inconclusive confrontation at Tippecanoe Creek in the Indiana Territory that resonated with the image-makers. Politics as an entertainment form reached its manipulative zenith in 1840, with a proliferation of picnics, parades, and paraphernalia of all kinds. Under the catchy slogan "Tippecanoe and Tyler too," the patrician Harrison was promoted not only as a champion of the common man but also as one derived from the humblest origins, reared in a log cabin, and a devotee of hard cider. The Democrats had only themselves to blame. The whole Whig campaign took its cue from a satiric attempt by a newspaper sympathetic to Van Buren to picture the nearly sixty-eight-year-old Harrison as fit only for bucolic retirement, contentedly sipping cider in his rustic cabin. As for Van Buren, the only candidate personally acquainted with poverty, the Whigs portrayed him as the prissy embodiment of luxurious living, a "used up" tool of Eastern money interests. Already saddled with an economic depression inherited from Jackson, Van Buren was swamped in the election.

Equivocation over slavery would bring down the Whig Party in less than two decades, but its leaders' emphasis on nationalism, a central banking system, protectionism, and internal improvements was embraced by Harrison after the election of 1840. He returned home — not to a log cabin but to the very room in which his mother had died at his family's Berkeley estate — to weave these themes together. His comprehensive inaugural address, the longest ever written, was delivered in its entirety in a driving rainstorm. Harrison also insisted on the dramatic gesture of riding his white steed through the downpour to the Capitol. Among his recommendations was a constitutional amendment limiting presidents to one term. His own lasted precisely one month. He caught pneumonia and died, making John Tyler the nation's first accidental president. The Constitution had failed to clearly specify whether he was to be more than merely an acting chief executive until the next election. Tyler settled the matter, assuming the reins of office in their entirety, thereby establishing the precedent that endures to this day.

Unfailingly courteous but obstinate, Tyler could neither control the strong cabinet he had inherited nor work effectively with Congress. His own priorities, so different than Harrison's would have been, alienated Whigs and divided Democrats. Unable to assemble a new party to champion states' rights and support the preservation — if not the expansion — of slavery, Tyler despaired of being elected president in his own right, and at the conclusion of what was to have been Harrison's term, he retired to his estate. Perhaps because he transcended identification with any faction, Tyler was called upon early in 1861 by the Virginia legislature to return to Washington, under the auspices of outgoing President Buchanan, to preside over a last-ditch peace conference to avoid civil war. When it failed, he pledged his loyalty to the Southern cause, and was elected to the new Confederate Congress. Before he could take his seat, however, he died in Richmond, at the same age as had Harrison, reviled in the North and misunderstood in the South.

So far as one can tell, unlike Harrison and Tyler themselves, their mothers were very similar. Tyler must have taken from his own experiences his memorable tribute to motherhood: "She who nurtured us in our infancy . . . taught us to raise our little hands in prayer . . . and reared us to manhood in the love and practice of virtue — such a mother is of priceless value." It is unfortunate that he and his predecessor did not say more to better illuminate for us the lives of Elizabeth Bassett Harrison and Mary Armistead Tyler.

EZEKIAL POLK was that contradiction in terms, a restless farmer. As biographer Martha Morrel writes, "The same venturesome spirit that had brought his great-grandfather to America more than a century earlier flowed through his veins with undiluted vigor." His great chance came when he received a land grant because of his service in the Revolutionary War. He bought up additional grants from other veterans and set out for the western territory of North Carolina. Ezekial's energetic wanderlust would be shared by his son, Samuel.

Meanwhile, not very far away, James Knox was returning to the farm he had already established near Mechlenburg, not far from Charlotte, the growing town that, ironically, had been named for the wife of King George III. Knox had distinguished himself in the Revolutionary War, rising to the rank of colonel. Among those especially happy to welcome him home was his young daughter, Jane, who had been born in 1776 just before her father went off to fight. That the Knox family was renowned for piety as well as industriousness is not surprising. Jane Knox was the great-great-grandniece of John Knox, the father of Scotch Presbyterianism. It was a legacy she did not take lightly.

As both Jane Knox and Samuel Polk grew to adulthood, the boundaries of their region moved inexorably westward. A projected road thirty feet wide was being constructed all the way to Nashville. Soon it would be safe for families to settle west of the Appalachians, and the population in the western territory of North Carolina would reach the sixty thousand necessary to make it eligible for separate statehood. Even in this relative wilderness, opportunities for young people to meet socially were not lacking. Whatever attracted these two to each other, it was not Jane's frivolity, although she didn't mind being called "Jenny." Nor could it have had anything to do with Sam's religious fervor. He was no more a churchgoer than was his freethinking father. What both Jane and Sam possessed, however, was something of their parents' energy and enterprise. Shared ambition can transcend many differences. However they came together, Sam Polk and Jane Knox were married on Christmas Day, 1795, and the first of their children was born less than a year later. Although Sam agreed to name the boy James Knox Polk after his father-in-law, he refused to have his son baptized as a Presbyterian, since it would require his own profession of faith. This discord would be one of few between husband and wife, but it remained a concern of Jane's to the very end of her son's life.

James Polk was born in the same year as the new state of Tennessee. From the start, he seemed ill suited for the rigorous rural routine that awaited him. Morrel describes the child as "frail" but "well-formed," small but handsome. He was never to develop the physical strength to be much help to his father, although he willingly undertook the farm chores he hated. Horses, the outdoors, hunting, and fishing, however,

Jane Polk

Courtesy of James K. Polk Memorial Association, Columbia, Tennessee

James came to love. As the family grew, his primary task was to be his mother's helper, assuming responsibility for the care and direction of his nine younger brothers and sisters. The Polk household was no military academy, but discipline and duty were lessons absorbed early by each child.

Both parents had received enough rudimentary learning to want to teach at least their oldest son how to read, write, and compute. Their keen interest in events outside their community, particularly politics, was also imparted to James. Jane and Sam Polk may not have agreed about theology, but they were of one mind about government. Both were devoted Jeffersonians. In the temporal realm, Jane was no dogmatist. James Polk was encouraged to think independently. As a child he thrilled to stories of his grandfather's involvement in the Revolutionary War, memories that were still fresh. He also grew up listening to lively frontier debates between his parents and their neighbors about the future course of the Republic.

No one doubted that the frontier would ultimately reach the Pacific, an eventuality that was to be hastened by Polk himself, although his ever-restless father only moved as far as the western edge of Tennessee. It was when James was ten that his family pulled up stakes for what Sam characteristically viewed as a bountiful "land of promise" over the western horizon. For the absence of either a church or a school, Jane Polk could compensate by imparting knowledge and religion on her own. The absence of a doctor, however, was of immediate concern. James was not only still delicate, but his increasingly frequent illnesses alarmed both parents. They determined to do whatever they could to find the cause, even though it meant traveling 250 miles to the nearest doctor, in Kentucky. His diagnosis was gallstones. James faced an immediate operation to remove them, without benefit of anesthesia, and demonstrated the fearlessness one might expect from one who was born of such sturdy parents. After the operation, his health markedly improved.

In Tennessee, Sam Polk expanded from agriculture to surveying and storekeeping, turning a profit at everything. For a time, he apprenticed his oldest son to another merchant, but James disliked retailing as much as farming. His mother understood that her boy was not averse to hard work, but that it was his mind he longed to exercise. Even more than had Betty Jackson, Jane Polk longed to see her brightest boy become a learned Presbyterian minister. Despite not being baptized, he had followed her faith since childhood. James's own hopes were to teach or practice law or medicine. Whatever the future might hold, mother and son together convinced stubborn Sam Polk, who now had the means, to invest in the best education available in their environs. "Do well in your studies," the father promised, "and I'll send you to college. But mind — I'll not waste my money if you waste your time."

Wasting time was hardly James Polk's inheritance from either parent. Starting with a tutor in the nearby town of Columbia, James advanced to a well-regarded academy in Murfreesboro, fifty miles away.

He proved a conscientious if not brilliant student, a restless perfectionist. Certainly the nature of Polk's presidency was foreshadowed by his approach to this belated exposure to formal education. It opened vistas beyond his imagining, and his academic success was largely based on outworking everyone else. In Murfreesboro he made friends outside his family circle for the first time. He even managed to meet young girls, who came for lessons after hours. Eventually he would marry the brightest of them, Sarah Childress, at least in part because she reminded him so much of his mother. He made time in his intensive schedule for the sort of long walks he had enjoyed as a child, sustaining his improved health. His father, as good as his word, sent James to the University of North Carolina. Entering as a sophomore, he graduated with honors. Polk disappointed his mother only in his choice of profession. He moved to Nashville, studied law for two years, passed the bar, and with a Carolina classmate set up a legal partnership. "It's a fine looking sign," Jane Polk admitted, looking up at their freshly painted shingle. "Never do anything to dishonor it."

His parents had worked their way up to affluence. Most of his siblings would also prosper, but none matched the drive of James Knox Polk. By the age of twenty-seven he was elected to the state legislature, two years later to the same congressional seat that had been occupied by Andrew Jackson, an old acquaintance of his family. Jackson was such a hero to Polk that he enjoyed his new appellation of "Young Hickory." Eventually he was elected governor of Tennessee, and in 1844 he emerged as a compromise candidate — the first "dark horse" — of the Democratic Party for the presidency itself. Running on an expansionist platform and supported by Jackson, Polk won a narrow victory over the more renowned Whig candidate, Henry Clay. In the White House, Polk would be no imitation of Jackson but, just as his parents had encouraged, very much his own man. Perhaps too much so.

Academics are prone to cite Polk as an example of the difference between success and esteem. By any measure, he was one of the most successful presidents in American history, and far the strongest national leader between Jackson and Lincoln. Polk did not require the Constitutional amendment proposed by Harrison, but stated at the outset that he would serve only a single term. He then proceeded to work himself to death. He achieved all four of the major goals he had outlined. He reduced tariffs and reestablished the subtreasury system, but his fundamental objective was to double the size of the nation. Polk achieved this by outmaneuvering the British to gain all of Oregon and precipitating a war with the weaker Mexicans to obtain California, Texas, and the Southwest. This aggressively expansionist conflict bitterly divided the nation. Among Polk's detractors were a young legislator from Illinois named Abraham Lincoln and even many of those obliged to fight in the Mexican War, including a lieutenant named Ulysses S. Grant.

Despite his vow to be a one-term president, Polk was suspicious of everyone, gathering as much power in his own hands as possible. He tried to limit the popularity of his two commanding generals in Mexico, Winfield Scott and Zachary Taylor, by playing them off against each other, fearing either or both, with no visible qualifications, might run for president. As it turned out, both did, and one won. Manifesting self-righteousness bordering on paranoia, Polk gained many admirers but few friends. It is not difficult to discern the source of his immense energy and will, but there is no indication that either of Polk's parents had so distrustful a disposition. Despite his successes, Polk never assembled the support that would have made a second term possible, even had he been willing to reconsider his earlier vow. Instead, in 1849 he returned to his newly purchased mansion in Nashville, accompanied by his devoted wife. They had no children. Polk was so utterly worn out his mother noted that he looked older than she. He would die sooner, at the age of fifty-three, only three and a half months into his retirement. His father had passed away long before, but his mother would outlive him by two years. As her son declined, Jane Polk urged her daughter-in-law, Sarah, also a devout Presbyterian, to help convince him to finally be baptized into her church. Instead, because he felt committed to a minister he particularly respected, James Knox Polk died a Methodist. Near the end he is reported to have told his mother that he had never disobeyed her. He finally did, on his deathbed, but she must have understood. Whatever her son's failings, fidelity was a trait that they shared.

POLK'S FEARS were realized in the very next election, in the person of Zachary Taylor. An unpretentious Mexican War general known as "Old Rough and Ready," Taylor was narrowly elected president. He ran under Whig auspices but cared little about political parties, viewing himself as a candidate of national unity. Although a slave-owning Southerner, he fervently believed in the preservation of the Union, and had he served longer, might well have had a significant role in American history. To Polk, Taylor was simply a potential figurehead, propped up by an ambitious political party and "exceedingly ignorant of public affairs." That Taylor was not ignorant of virtually everything else was almost entirely due to his mother.

His childhood reversed the upward striving of the families of most of our early presidents. Both of his parents were better educated than Zachary Taylor would be. The problem was land. His father, Richard Taylor, did not feel his Virginia estate was of sufficient size to support a growing family, at least in the style to which he and his wife were accustomed. Both were from prominent families, with deep Virginia roots. The Taylors, related to both the Madisons and the Lees, had been in the "Old Dominion" of Virginia for over a hundred and fifty years. Sarah Dabney Strother, called "Sally," who married Richard when she was eighteen, had been educated by European tutors at her family's estate near Fredericksburg. Her husband, yet another graduate of William and Mary, had risen to the rank of lieutenant colonel in the Revolutionary War, then returned to acquire his relatively modest Hare Forest plantation in Orange County and serve in the Virginia Assembly. By 1784 Sarah had produced two sons, with a third on the way. Eventually there would be nine children.

As biographer K. Jack Bauer points out, the first decade after American independence was a time of political uncertainty, social upheaval, and economic instability, to which even well-positioned families like the Taylors were not impervious. The lure of a fresh start appealed to young men whose wartime exploits had given them "a sense of their own strength and competence." Unable to pay returning veterans in cash for their services, hard-pressed states like Virginia offered them vast tracts of land in their western preserves. This was especially appealing to former officers like Richard Taylor, who were not their families' first sons. The grant made to him of over eight thousand acres in sparsely settled Kentucky was too substantial to be refused. He sold his Virginia property and set out to the frontier post of Louisville to claim his first one thousand acres.

Taylor's return to Kentucky was delayed by the advanced state of his wife's pregnancy. She completed her confinement at the home of her husband's cousin, only twelve miles into their journey west, and on March 4, 1784, a third son was born to Richard and Sarah Taylor. They named him Zachary after his paternal grandfather. Then they ventured on to Kentucky to begin their new life, endowing what would become the "Bluegrass State" with its claim to our twelfth president.

Eventually, the Taylors' new domain would transcend the scale of anything they had enjoyed in Virginia, but it took years of toil. Accordingly, Zachary Taylor may well have started life in a log cabin, a claim so often accorded to others with less justification. The move denied him the sort of education he would have enjoyed in Virginia. He was eight before Kentucky became a state, its schools still primitive at best. About a good deal of his childhood, and that of his siblings, we can only conjecture. Apparently tutors did come by from time to time, but with Zachary's father busy hacking their new home out of the wilderness, it fell to Sally Taylor to instruct her children. As Doris Faber writes, "Whatever learning [Zachary] had came from her, and one must doubt whether he would have been able to write even one page if she had not taught him his letters." Despite such a debt, Faber points out that Taylor never so much as mentions his mother in the fifteen-page autobiography he wrote later in life.

It is not surprising that, living on the frontier with a father who relished his own role in the Revolution, young Zachary early envisioned a military career for himself. By his twenties, he was a first lieutenant in the United States Infantry. Despite his lack of any formal schooling and his reputation for common sense rather than for knowledge, Taylor developed a heightened appreciation of the importance of education. As Bauer relates, Taylor paid great attention to the schools maintained for the children of those stationed at every post he commanded. At least three of his four surviving children (two daughters died in an 1820 malaria outbreak in Louisiana) would attend prominent schools in the east; his only son, Richard, studied in Edinburgh and Paris before graduating from Yale. Sarah Taylor did not live to see her son elected president, dying in 1822, just before her sixty-second birthday. Zachary was only a lieutenant colonel then, the same rank previously attained by his father. Taylor's semi-invalid wife, Margaret, utterly opposed to her husband's nomination and election, was devastated by his death from typhoid fever in 1850, only fifteen months into his presidency. Ironically, this firm Unionist's son would serve as a Confederate general, and his daughter, Sarah Knox, was the first wife of Jefferson Davis. She died only three months after the wedding, of malaria, the same malady that had struck down her sisters.

It was probably Zachary Taylor's lifelong preoccupation with soldiering that precluded a suitable expression of his debt to his mother. Having enjoyed in her childhood the instruction of well-educated tutors, she would be her son's only consistent teacher, keeping at least a flickering light of learning alive in the wilderness. Without the influence of Sarah Strother Taylor, this gently bred but resourceful pioneer woman, Zachary could not even have qualified for a command.

CHAPTER FIVE

Mothers of the Ante-bellum Presidents

- Phoebe Fillmore
- Anna Pierce
- Elizabeth Buchanan

ZACHARY TAYLOR, unlike William Henry Harrison, was succeeded by a vice president who largely agreed with him. The problem was that Millard Fillmore, nominated by the Whigs to balance their ticket in 1848, was weak where Taylor was strong. Handsome and well liked, the early equivalent of a Warren Harding, Fillmore had served in the House of Representatives and was New York state controller when he was chosen to run with Taylor. As vice president, he was largely excluded from policy-making, but as president he approved Henry Clay's Compromise of 1850, which Taylor would have strenuously opposed. Its concessions assured a few more years of tenuous peace but satisfied virtually no one. Fillmore hated slavery but invariably counseled moderation. His peculiar political career, however, had originated with the Anti-Masonic Party and ended embarrassingly with the bigoted American Party of "Know-Nothings." Yet his presidency was well intentioned, and not without its achievements. Whatever Fillmore's personal limitations, his whole career is a testament to making the most of every opportunity. His most significant achievements could not have occurred without his mother's early guidance.

Fillmore's childhood was one of almost Dickensian privation. His mother, Phoebe Millard, the daughter of a prosperous Massachusetts physician, fell in love with a young farmer as ambitious as young Samuel Polk. Nathaniel Fillmore, however, was no Polk. Hasty and improvident, he bought land, sight unseen, in upstate New York, and because of conflicting claims wound up as only a struggling tenant farmer. Phoebe, who loyally stood by her husband through years of grinding poverty, also gave him eight children. Her health, always tenuous, was little enhanced by the squalor of their surroundings. It is a wonder she lived to be fifty-one. As would so many other mothers of American presidents, Phoebe Fillmore endowed her first-born son, born on January 7, 1800, with all her surviving expectations. She also gave him her family's name. As Millard Fillmore grew, his mother used the few books she had brought into her marriage to teach him to read, and, she hoped, to fire his ambition. It worked. By the age of fourteen, apprenticed to a cloth-maker in the next county, Millard was reading on his own, seeking out new books from a circulating library, and attending a local academy on his hours off. Ultimately, he saved enough from his meager earnings to pay off his employer and get a job teaching school.

When he came home for a visit, his mother gave him a final gift. She had persuaded her husband to ask their landlord, a local county judge, to try their son out as a clerk. When he heard the news, Millard was so touched that he burst into tears. He knew he was on his way. In only a few years, Fillmore was admitted to the New York bar. At twenty-eight, he was elected to the New York State Assembly. His mother did not live to see him establish his lucrative law practice in Buffalo or go to the House of Representatives in Washington. His proud departure for Albany, a precursor of things to come, was satisfaction enough.

FRANKLIN PIERCE, the Democrat who succeeded Fillmore and shares his subsequent obscurity, enjoyed a childhood as privileged as Fillmore's was deprived. After the death of his mother, Anna Kendrick Pierce, Franklin wrote a rather equivocal tribute: "She was a most affectionate and tender mother, strong in many points and weak in some but always weak on the side of kindness and deep affection." What were these "weak" points that required justification? The most obvious is that Anna Pierce could not hold her liquor, a failing her son inherited. They both drank excessively, but only Franklin overcame the addiction, and not without inner turmoil. His mother's failing for spirits, however, did not prevent her from successfully raising eight children, as well as the stepdaughter she acquired when she married widower Benjamin Pierce.

Temperamentally, they were an unlikely couple, the disciplined but ambitious military man and his fun-loving, unpredictable wife, twelve years his junior. Yet they lived together with apparent concord for nearly half a century, dying within a year of each other. Franklin Pierce's father, the seventh of ten children of a prior Benjamin Pierce of Chelmsford, Massachusetts, grew up poor but proud in the care of an uncle, after both his parents died. When Benjamin was only eighteen, fighting broke out at Lexington and Concord. Emulating the Minutemen, the young man dropped his plow, took his uncle's fowling piece, pouch, and powder horn, and by the next morning had volunteered in the local militia. He wrote succinctly of his experiences, "I remained in the Army during the war. I enjoyed it much." Pierce ended the war as a captain. The title of "General" he later bestowed on himself, as head of his own militia.

After the conflict, suspecting there might be greater opportunity in the less-settled north, Pierce headed for New Hampshire. His first wife died giving birth to their daughter. When he met lively Anna Kendrick, it did not take him long to propose. Nor did it take her long to accept. The dashing newcomer and his twenty-one-year-old bride set up housekeeping in Hillsborough County, among the first settlers in this pristine region of New Hampshire. The sixth of eight children, Franklin was born in 1804. Although his parents still lived in the log cottage his father had constructed, by a stream leading to Contoocook Pond, they had far grander plans. Benjamin Pierce was already the most prominent figure of his community. Biographer Roy Franklin Nichols writes, "He was a typical back country leader who, though rough in manners and lacking in education and culture, had a vivid personality with much native force and strength which made him a domineering yet generous 'squire.'" General Pierce not only headed the local militia, he was very active in politics, helping to supplant the prevailing Federalists with his more egalitarian Jeffersonians. He would go on to become governor of New Hampshire.

Not long after Franklin's birth, his family moved into a much larger home, almost a mansion. It was also closer to the turnpike that brought visitors and news to their remote region by regular stagecoach service. General Pierce was so renowned for his hospitality that he took out a liquor license and converted part of his property to a tavern. Could he have been less conscious of his wife's drinking problem than his neighbors were? Vivacious, mercurial Anna Pierce didn't seem to mind, taking delight in shocking the prim paragons who disdained her imbibing, her outspokenness, and her colorfully provocative dress. Gossip about her appears to have been the major diversion of Hillsborough.

Young Frank, as his parents called him, was genuinely fond of both of them. He loved to listen to his father's war stories. Frank's mother did little to inhibit his outdoor diversions — swimming, skating, hunting, and fishing, each in its season. Her free spirit also blunted the mix of Calvinist and Puritan theology that still pervaded the area. For so lively a lad, as Nichols writes, "Between his father's strictness and his mother's easygoing ways there was sure to be a chance for the quick-witted to escape many of the consequences of boyish disobedience." When Frank was eight, this idyll was rudely interrupted by the War of 1812. His older brothers and his sister's husband enlisted, and his father was frequently called to councils at the state capital in Concord. Although thrilled with accounts of their activities, the family felt immense relief when each of them returned home safely.

Still, life had to go on, and for Frank that meant the start of his education at the local school. In the opinion of his parents, however, it was not quite sufficient, and eventually Frank was dispatched to the prestigious Hancock Academy in a nearby town. As Nichols relates, Pierce considered an early incident there to be "a turning point in his career." It also reveals much about his father. On a Sunday morning at Hancock Academy, twelve-year-old Frank was homesick. Without permission, he walked all the way home. After the church service, his father calmly asked him to stay for dinner. Benjamin Pierce made no comment, uttered no reproach, and after dinner drove his son back toward Hancock. Midway, he dropped the boy off in the road and returned home alone. A drenching rain added to Frank's discomfort as he approached the academy. He never left school again without approval. His father's expectations did not need to be voiced to be understood.

Frank proved so adept a student, they chose only him and his older brother, another Benjamin, to go off to college. Ben went to Dartmouth, but his father liked what he had heard about Bowdoin College in the new state of Maine and selected it for Frank, who rode all the way there in the family chaise, in excited anticipation, wedged symbolically between both his parents. The personal charm that, more than anything else, carried Franklin Pierce so unexpectedly far bloomed at Bowdoin. He graduated third in his class and went on to the study of law. He also became more religious, impressed by Congregationalists' preaching. This new ardor instilled in Pierce a degree of introspection, but perhaps also a recognition of his own shortcomings.

Anna Kendrick Pierce lived to the age of seventy, long enough to witness her son serving in the state legislature at the same time his father was governor. Franklin emulated his straightforward father's devotion to Jefferson and particularly to Jackson. But as president he could find no simple solutions to the long-simmering conflicts of the 1850s. His politics may have derived from his father, but Pierce's personality came straight from his vivacious mother. She was charming even when sober.

BECAUSE James Buchanan, our only bachelor president, had at least one male friend of whom he was inordinately fond, there has been recurrent speculation that he may have been a homosexual. This would have come as quite a shock to Ann Coleman, the belle of Lancaster, Pennsylvania. She had fallen deeply in love with Buchanan, a handsome, twenty-eight-year-old lawyer, and was engaged to him in the summer of 1819. That she died so suddenly and mysteriously, perhaps a suicide, only a few months later during a visit to Philadelphia has been ascribed to many possible causes. Perhaps it was an agitated reaction to her wealthy parents' insistence that Buchanan was little more than a fortune-hunter, perhaps a result of his attentions to other women, or maybe simply the result of her own emotional fragility. Nowhere was it suggested that his fiancée's belated discovery of Buchanan's sexual preference caused her to take her own life.

Whatever the cause, the despair that gripped Buchanan after Ann Coleman's death was undeniable. So was the unrelenting hatred for him by her family, and the suspicion of much of Lancaster that somehow Buchanan was to blame for the tragedy. He wrote in a letter to Ann's father, which was refused and returned, that "she, as well as I, have been much abused. God forgive the authors of it. . . . I feel that happiness has fled from me forever." Perhaps this devastating experience triggered in Buchanan a determination that nothing like it must ever happen again, and set him on a course that precluded matrimony. We do know that, despite not marrying, it was only in the company of other women — his mother and sisters — that he found solace. They surrounded him that lonely Christmas, by the warm hearth of their Mercersburg home, offering a sympathy available nowhere else, and instilled in him a renewed confidence to continue a career that had previously seemed so promising. The solace came most of all from his devoutly Presbyterian mother. As biographer Philip Shriver Klein writes, "She had the kind of faith which assumed that whatever happened was an act of the deity intended especially for her instruction and benefit." And, one might add, for the benefit of others.

It was not only the faith of Elizabeth Speer Buchanan that sustained her oldest son. From her he also derived whatever qualities made him a more attractive personality. The ambition came from his father, the poetry from his mother. Buchanan described his feelings about his mother in more detail than had any previous president. Late in his life he wrote, "Under providence I attribute any little distinction which I may have acquired in this world to the blessing which he conferred to me in granting me such a mother."

Buchanan's father, also named James, was restless, energetic, and ambitious. The family had lived in Scotland and the north of Ireland for seven generations, but this James Buchanan, in the wake of the American Revolution, glimpsed greater opportunities across the ocean. His uncle's brother, Joshua Russell, had already settled near Gettysburg, Pennsylvania, and was the proprietor of a thriving tavern. James liked the look of the new land of opportunity almost as soon as he set foot in Philadelphia and was greeted by Russell. He liked it even more when he reached central Pennsylvania and encountered comely sixteen-year-old Elizabeth Speer. She kept house for her widower father and her four older brothers on the farm adjacent to Russell's tavern.

It didn't take long for James Buchanan to discover economic opportunity, although it would be a few years before he could capitalize on it. He found work some forty miles to the west at a trading post and warehouse unappealingly called "The Stony Batter" and operated by one John Tom. Situated at a busy junction called Cove Gap, the establishment sold provisions to wagons and packhorses heading off to many different destinations. Eventually, after some convoluted negotiations, Buchanan was able to purchase the whole operation from Tom. Returning to Gettysburg, James rekindled his acquaintance with Elizabeth Speer. They were married in 1788, when she was twenty-one and he twenty-seven, and they moved into his log cabin (although there were a number of other buildings on his new property as well).

The following year the couple was blessed with their first child, a daughter they named Mary. On April 23, 1791, they had their first son, and named him James after his father. When little Mary died later that year, a tragedy not uncommon in eighteenth-century America, it sorely tested Elizabeth's faith. She followed the firm belief in predestination of her Scotch Presbyterian father, who had moved from his former home in Lancaster County because of a theological dispute with his less doctrinaire pastor there. Only her trust in the certainty of God's will made Elizabeth's grief bearable, just as it would later help her comfort her son after the death of Ann Coleman. Still, as Klein writes, "It would have been an unnatural mother that after this experience did not lavish more than the usual care upon her surviving child. James Buchanan, from the very first year of his life, occupied a position of special importance in the household." The Buchanans would have eleven children in all, two of whom died in infancy and three others who died much too young, but there were no surviving boys for another fourteen years. Throughout his childhood, young James was at the center of a circle of adoring females. He was also the object of his ever-striving father's hopes for the future.

Like Franklin Pierce, James Buchanan was influenced by both parents, but in Buchanan's case his dual inheritance represented a more complementary contrast. In the "Autobiographical Sketch" that opened his self-justifying 1866 memoirs, Buchanan accurately described his father as "a man of practical judgment and of great industry and perseverance." Then, enhancing it a bit, James added that the senior Buchanan had been "respected . . . by everyone who approached him," and "was a kind father, a sincere friend, and an honest and reliable man." Of his mother, Buchanan wrote that "considering her limited opportunities in early life, she was a very remarkable woman." Despite her household labors, "she yet found time to read much and reflect deeply on what she read. . . . For her sons, as they successively grew up, she was a delightful and instructive companion. . . . It was chiefly to her influence that all her sons were indebted for a liberal education."

Apparently, for all her enlightened reading and reflection, Elizabeth Buchanan was not convinced of the necessity of providing her daughters with a similarly complete "liberal education." Still, at the outset, she was the sole teacher of all her children. In her informal lyceum, she revealed the delights of Milton and Pope as well as the lessons of Scripture and the basics of reading, writing, and calculation. Decades later, Buchanan still marveled at the breadth of her intellectual curiosity. Even after her successful husband insisted it was no longer necessary, Elizabeth Buchanan continued to personally perform all the household chores, perhaps out of habit, perhaps out of a sense of propriety. Her son wrote, "I have often myself, during the vacations at school or college, sat down at the kitchen and whilst she was at the wash tub, entirely by choice, have spent hours pleasantly and instructively conversing with her. . . . She had a great fondness for poetry and could repeat with ease all the passages of her favorite authors. . . . [She] had read much on the subject of theology, and what she read once, she remembered forever." She delighted in encouraging all her children's interests and entering "into all their joys and sorrows."

As Klein writes, Stony Batter was not the ideal place to raise a family. "The clearing resounded with the turmoil of stamping horses, drunken drovers, and cursing wagoners. Elizabeth Buchanan disliked this raw and uncouth society and lived in constant fear for the safety of her small children." Fortunately, her ambitious husband had no intention of settling there permanently. The trading post was only a way station on the family's road to respectability. By 1794, Buchanan had prospered sufficiently to buy "Dunwoodie Farm," a spacious three-hundred-acre estate, and two years later he built and moved his family into a handsome home in the settled town of Mercersburg. It would also serve as the headquarters of his expanding interests. His brother-in-law was put in charge of the store that had started it all. The move to town was salubrious for both of young James's parents. His mother enjoyed the company of earnest, literate Presbyterians like herself. His father was able to earn the regard of well-established families, becoming for a time, among other distinctions, their justice of the peace.

For six-year-old James, the move seemed a mixed blessing. It meant accepting the structure of a real school. He had enjoyed being the center of attention, learning at home from his devoted mother. The move also resulted in more sustained contact with his father, whose expectations would never diminish. There is little doubt that the senior James Buchanan admired his wife's qualities, but beyond their mutual affection they shared little except a boundless energy. In her spirituality, despite many trials, she found a contentment he was denied. She was self-educated and satisfied; he was self-made, a process that could never be quite completed. A firm Federalist in politics, as were many others who had risen by their own efforts, the senior Buchanan was hard-driving and scrupulously honest, but hardly known for Christian compassion or idealism. He had little use for small talk or time for leisure, even if shared with his first son. When the two worked together, the father was particularly demanding, expecting more than he would of another's child. From his father, James inherited not only ambition but also an excessive passion for precision. Everything must be accounted for. He respected, even loved, his father, but there was nothing of the intimacy he enjoyed with his mother.

James's first school was the old Stone Academy, which would evolve into the renowned Mercersburg Academy. The Latin and Greek he learned formed the basis of a classical education, but it was rarely imparted with his mother's affectionate enthusiasm. Still, James did well enough to gain the notice of the family's learned pastor, Dr. John King. He had been named a trustee of Dickinson College in Carlisle, a struggling but well-regarded institution of higher learning. When James turned sixteen, his father was encouraged to enroll him. Like many another presidential mother, Elizabeth Buchanan harbored hopes that her son would be a minister, but here the father prevailed. He wanted young James to be a practical-minded lawyer, but James first had to get through college. It began promisingly enough, with James allowed to start as a junior, and doing very well in his studies. Soon, however, he became critical of a great many things about the school.

Conditioned to being the focus of his family, it is not surprising that, thrust among the other forty-one students, James Buchanan was even more obliged than he had been at Old Stone Academy to court popularity. "Without much natural tendency to become dissipated," he recalled, "and chiefly from the examples of others . . . I engaged in every sort of extravagance and mischief." He drank excessively, smoked cigars, and took part in pranks, but, most offensively, he showed off his intellectual prowess at the expense of some of his professors. Yet, with outstanding grades and the esteem of his peers, Buchanan returned home after his first year at Dickinson secure in his place on the campus and looking forward to his senior year. Instead, he received a letter stating that he had been expelled for "disorderly conduct." One can imagine the reaction of his father.

Only the intervention of their kindly Presbyterian pastor, Dr. King, who by then had been named president of the board of trustees, permitted the ostensibly chastened young man to return. He was denied the coveted first honor at graduation, however, which he probably merited, largely because of his own machinations and the residual disdain of much of the faculty. His chagrined father suggested that he take the disappointment "like a man," but even in his memoirs Buchanan regretted that he had not attended a different college. His mother was simply heartened by his academic accomplishments. To her, knowledge was its own reward.

Discouraged but little deterred, Buchanan plowed straight ahead, studying law in Lancaster. Admitted to the bar in 1812, he opposed the war but felt it was his duty to help defend his country. He volunteered in 1814, after making his first public address. Following brief military service, he was elected to the Pennsylvania legislature. In 1820, only a year after the tragedy of Ann Coleman's death, Buchanan was elected to the United States House of Representatives. All this his father proudly witnessed, although his son did run as a Democrat. James Buchanan Sr.

died in 1821 at the age of sixty. His son marveled at how his mother accepted the loss of her beloved husband, as well as the subsequent deaths of her favorite daughter and two cherished sons, one of whom had been named for George Washington. "She was a woman of great firmness of character," James wrote, "and bore the afflictions of her life with Christian philosophy." He couldn't remotely approximate her saintly demeanor, but he never ceased admiring and being inspired by it. His mother continued her acute interest in his career. In 1831 she urged, without success, that he decline appointment to be minister to Russia. She was worldly enough to recognize domestic political opportunities for her son. Elizabeth added a poignant postscript in a letter to him, asking, "At what time do you intend paying us that visit, previous to your departure from the country which gave you birth, and I expect, to me, the last visit? Do not disappoint me, but certainly come." James did come, but it was indeed the last time he would see his mother.

On May 14, 1833, at the age of sixty-six, Elizabeth Speer Buchanan died at the home of her son-in-law, appropriately a member of the clergy. Her son James, about to return from St. Petersburg, had written her, "You may rest assured that I shall . . . lose no time in paying you a visit; when I trust in Heaven you will still be in the enjoyment of your usual health." She had already peacefully expired before the letter arrived, as Buchanan later observed, "in the calm but firm assurance that she was going home to her Father and her God."

Over twenty years later, President James Buchanan would be no more successful than had been his predecessors, Fillmore and Pierce, in settling the divisive issues that led to the Civil War. Buchanan had been a compromise candidate, and as president he never ceased urging compromise, until almost the moment of Lincoln's inauguration. Had he been alive to do so, Buchanan's father might have severely judged his son's failure to forestall the conflict, but Buchanan's mother would have applauded his efforts — and then prayed for their success.

CHAPTER SIX

"All That I Am . . . I Get from My Angel Mother"

❧ Nancy and Sarah Lincoln

ABOUT EIGHTY years ago, H. L. Mencken wrote that there are four kinds of books that seem always to sell well in the United States: murder mysteries, books on spiritualism, books featuring damsels in distress, and biographies of Abraham Lincoln. If writing about the Great Emancipator was already a cottage industry then, it has since expanded to an empire of enterprise. Biographies of Lincoln are estimated to total between two and ten thousand, with no end in view.

For our purpose — evaluating the influence of Lincoln's parents — however, little of significance has been discovered in recent years. In this regard, some of the earlier biographies of Lincoln still hold up well, even that of the noted "muckraker" Ida Tarbell, who wrote about Lincoln late in the nineteenth century when many of his contemporaries were still alive. Carl Sandburg's poetic volumes of the 1920s and '30s are still compelling reading. Yet, if it weren't for revisionism, who would need historians? The first revisionist account of Lincoln's life was also one of the first serious biographies. It originated almost on the day Lincoln died in 1865 and was intended as an authentic antidote to the instant mythology of the martyred president. It was written by Lincoln's devoted law partner, William Herndon, who was intent on honestly portraying the flesh-and-blood man he knew, no less great or humane for all his imperfections. Herndon, who was known to imbibe, may have paused for an occasional snifter in assembling his work, because it was not published for another twenty-four years.

His revelation about Lincoln's mother, Nancy Hanks Lincoln, still engages our attention. According to Herndon, Lincoln was convinced she was illegitimate, which puts a different spin on the quotation that heads this chapter. Lincoln owed "all that I am" to his mother because, as he confided to Herndon alone (at least as Herndon relates it), he believed she had been born of a union between her mother and an aristocratic Virginia planter. The resulting blood he carried in his veins accounted for qualities that elevated him above his backwoods playmates. Such an emphasis on antecedents doesn't sound very Lincolnesque, but the story has persisted. Nancy Hanks Lincoln died when her son was only nine or ten (sources vary). Lincoln scholar and biographer David Herbert Donald suggests that Lincoln's references to his departed "angel mother" were intended at least in part to differentiate her from his stepmother, who was very much alive, and the person he most loved. His avowal that he owed everything to his mother was not so much a tribute to her loving care, which was even more exemplified by her successor, as "to the genes which she allegedly transmitted from an unnamed grandfather."

Donald also stresses, however, that Lincoln, although he also tried to trace back his father's ancestry, was far more concerned about where he was headed. "In his mind he was a self-made man, who had little need to care about his family tree." To inquiries about his family in 1859, as he was gearing up for his presidential run, Lincoln replied with this succinct summation: "I was born February 12, 1809, in Hardin County, Kentucky. My parents were both born in Virginia, of undistinguished families — second families, perhaps I should say. My mother, who died in my tenth year, was of a family of the name of Hanks." The following year, replying to a writer who wanted to assemble a campaign biography, Lincoln insisted, "It is a great piece of folly to attempt to make anything out of my early life. It can all be condensed into a single sentence and that sentence you will find in Gray's Elegy, 'the short and simple annals of the poor.' That's my life and that's about all you or anyone else can make of it."

Yet, by many accounts, Lincoln did not see himself as entirely "self-made," and he definitely did not view each of his parents in the same light. He never openly maligned his father, only by inference, but no one could ever recall him uttering a single favorable word about Thomas Lincoln. However brief their life together, there is little doubt that Abraham genuinely loved his mother. There is no doubt whatsoever that he adored his stepmother. She would outlive him, and near the end of her life still recalled young Abe as "the best boy I ever saw." Mostly because of her, the "simple annals" of his childhood were not entirely bleak.

Much is made of the fact that Lincoln did not even attend the funeral of his father, but that was not because he hated him. The opposite of love is not so much hatred as indifference. By the time Thomas Lincoln died in 1851, Abraham was pursuing a busy and successful career, for which his father had provided little inspiration. He had visited the ailing Tom Lincoln previously and could not break away a second time. His letter of condolence was perfunctory. Had Lincoln succeeded in tracing his paternal ancestry beyond his grandfather, also named Abraham, he might have been surprised to find a degree of authentic achievement. The first Lincoln to emigrate from England, where the family name is encountered in the names of localities and cathedrals, was a weaver's apprentice who arrived in Massachusetts in 1637 and ultimately became a prosperous trader and businessman. Other Lincolns also improved their circumstances, maintaining prosperous farms in Virginia and Pennsylvania and engaging in public service. Biographer Benjamin Thomas writes, "Without exception Lincoln's forebears proved to be self-reliant, upright men of even comfortable means, who earned the respect of their neighbors. Some Lincolns in collateral lines even earned distinction. . . . In the father, Thomas, there seemed to be a falling off in the general level of Abraham's ancestry."

Perhaps Thomas Lincoln was simply worn out by the wilderness. His father, Abraham, had moved the family from Virginia to Kentucky in 1782 after his distant relative Daniel Boone had returned with visions of "a second paradise" of bountiful acreage just over the mountains. This elder Abraham Lincoln, who, like his father before him, had worked the rich soil of Rockingham County without benefit of slaves, had been a captain in the Virginia militia but did not serve in the Revolutionary War. Heightened wartime taxes and fluctuating currency made farming in Virginia less attractive, but it was more ambition that led him to Kentucky. He managed to accumulate some 5,500 acres near the town of Louisville. Of course, there were perils on the frontier. Indians in the vicinity questioned the legitimacy of any of these land claims, using the only means at their disposal. In 1786, when Abraham was planting corn with his three sons, they were ambushed and Abraham was killed. Mordecai, the oldest son, managed to find a rifle and shot an Indian taking off for the woods with young Thomas. The third son also escaped. Mordecai, young Abraham would say, in an implicit criticism of his father, "ran off with all the talents in the family." He also inherited all the property.

Thomas moved with his widowed mother to a number of locations before settling on 238 acres in Harlan County, Kentucky, the first of many farms he would own. These years were fraught with difficulty. He did manual labor for a time and learned carpentry and cabinetmaking, reportedly from one Joseph Hanks, who had a niece named Nancy. This was a period of sustained activity for Tom Lincoln. Uneducated but energetic, he earned the money to buy his first farm, served in the militia and on jury duty, and was well regarded in the community. By 1806 he felt settled enough to seek a bride. When his attentions were not reciprocated by Sarah Bush, the young lady of whom he was enamored, he redirected them toward twenty-two year-old Nancy Hanks. She accepted his proposal. Apparently she liked his robust looks and his respectful manner — he rarely cursed or drank. Less is known of the Hanks family than of the Lincolns, partially because — even more than the Lincolns — they tended to use the same names over and over, generation after generation.

Nancy was then living with one of her sisters, who was married to a man named Sparrow. Trained as a seamstress, Nancy possessed skills a potential husband might find attractive. Most of her people were illiterate, but Nancy could read, although she never learned to write. Carl Sandburg speculates, "Tom Lincoln had seen this particular Nancy Hanks . . . and noticed that she was shrewd, dry, and lonesome. He knew that she could read the Bible and . . . other books, and had read her way through newspapers." Benjamin Thomas adds, "Acquaintances agree that . . . she was intelligent, deeply religious, kindly and affection-ate." No one is quite certain what she looked like, the consensus tend-ing to be that she was small, dark, and pretty.

Nancy and Tom were married in 1806. Soon after, he bought a larger farm, called Sinking Spring, and with the carpentry skills he was already using to supplement his income constructed a sturdier home for his bride. The next year their daughter, Sarah, was born. Two years later, on February 12, 1809, the couple had a son, named Abraham for his grandfather. Even the larger log cabin was by no means spacious, only a single room with a dirt floor and a roof held up by poles. While the boy inherited Tom Lincoln's dark thatch of hair and coarse skin, he would grow to be much taller than his father (eventually 6 feet, 4 inches) and would be raw-boned rather than stocky. By the time Abra-ham was two, his family moved again, this time to a farm near Knob Creek, Kentucky. Water seems always to figure in the names of Thomas Lincoln's farms, but its availability failed to bring him fortune. Only about thirty of his two hundred and thirty acres at Knob Creek turned out to be tillable. During the five years the family lived there, Tom's spirit, if not his energy, seems to have declined, although hardly with-out cause. A second son had died in infancy. Tom may well have been better at carpentry than farming, yet the quality of his largest wood-working commission was disputed by the man who paid for it. Biogra-pher Albert Beveridge writes that "He was improvident, yet in a slow and plodding way industrious. He was good-natured, inoffensive, law abiding, notably honest . . . [but] he had no use for books." Opportu-nity to Tom Lincoln was limited to a more fertile farm somewhere over the horizon.

His wife, however, loved books, at least the few she had read, and when her son showed promise, she encouraged him to go to school "and larn all you can." In this land, she appears to have been convinced, there were no limitations. If you learned enough, you could be any-thing, and go anywhere. Contemporaries recalled her as largely silent, seemingly sad and reflective, but she read her son stories. Lincoln's only memory of the War of 1812 was of his mother's gentle care of in-jured soldiers. His earliest memory of his father reflected ominously on the latter's problems. Abraham recalled dropping pumpkin seeds behind his father, and using a hoe with the bottomland, and then seeing all their work washed away by a thunderstorm. Yet records reveal that Thomas Lincoln was an apparently successful farmer, at least at this time, ranking fifteenth out of ninety-eight property owners in the county. He was also held in high esteem by his neighbors and was celebrated for his good nature and ability to tell stories — one quality his son inherited.

It may be that Tom Lincoln simply couldn't stand success. In 1816, when Abraham was seven, his father decided to move again, this time across the Ohio River to Indiana. In part, Thomas made this decision because of slavery, which he opposed on both religious and practical grounds. His "separate" Baptist faith told him that slavery was immoral, and the labor of slaves in states like Kentucky enabled major landholders to drive out subsistence farmers like himself. In the wilderness around Pigeon Creek, they at first set up a rough shelter and survived largely on game. After shooting his first wild turkey, Abraham lost his taste for hunting. He enjoyed other outdoor activities, however, and wielded an ax, planted crops, and tended livestock — anything to help his parents, up to a point. As he later said, "My father taught me to work, but never taught me to love it." Abraham vowed that whatever else might happen in his life, he would never be a farmer or a rail splitter. Most of all, he followed his mother's admonition to "larn all you can." Any book in the vicinity was soon in his possession. He was a lively, outwardly friendly child, gangling as he outgrew his crude homespun clothing, but he also developed a less obvious sense of remoteness that he would retain all his life. He was different from his companions, and he knew it. In keeping with his character, he didn't like to be called "Abe."

The precipitous move to Indiana not only resulted in failure, it also proved fatal. Nancy's aunt and uncle, the Sparrows, and their eighteen-year-old nephew, Dennis Hanks, who became Abraham's closest companion, had come to join the Lincolns, and together they erected a more permanent dwelling. In the summer of 1818, however, a mysterious disease swept through southwestern Indiana. It was called "milk-sickness," or simply "milk-sick," since it was caused by drinking the milk of local cows. The ultimate cause turned out to be the poisonous roots these free-roaming cows had consumed. The nearest doctor was thirty miles away, but there was no known cure, in any case. First the Sparrows died. Then, in the seventh day of her own illness, Nancy Hanks Lincoln died as well, at the age of thirty-four or thirty-five, a "pioneer sacrifice," as Sandburg put it. Near the end, she had called her children to her bedside, telling them "to be good and kind to their father — and to one another and to the world." Thomas Lincoln constructed a casket, and his grief-stricken children watched him bury their mother next to the Sparrows. A few months later, a visiting Baptist preacher said a few words over their graves.

David Donald believes that the death of Abraham Lincoln's mother gave him "a sense of isolation" he never fully lost. Lincoln was so moved by his return to her gravesite in 1844 that he could only express himself in poetry. It fell to twelve-year-old Sarah to try to cook, mend, and clean for the men now in her charge, but inevitably the domicile sank into squalor. In less than a year, Tom felt impelled to go back to Kentucky, to Elizabethtown, to seek another wife. She turned out to be the lady who had rejected him originally. In the intervening years, Sarah Bush had married a man named Daniel Johnson, borne three children, and been widowed. Tom Lincoln may have felt some residual affection for her — Benjamin Thomas describes Sarah as "tall and attractive" — but the arrangement would be motivated more by practicality than romance. Tom urgently needed a competent woman to take charge of his household. Sarah needed someone to pay her debts, which — despite the reduced state of his own liquidity — Tom Lincoln was still able to do. It must be said to her credit that Sarah was reluctant to bring the subject up. Despite her circumstances, she had accumulated and managed to save possessions that in a place like Pigeon Creek would seem the luxuries of a potentate: a solid table and chairs, a magnificent walnut bureau, a spinning wheel, featherbeds, dishware, and matched sets of knives, forks, and spoons. Most astonishing, although Sarah, unlike Nancy Hanks Lincoln, could not read, she brought books: a handsome family Bible, *Pilgrim's Progress, Robinson Crusoe, Sinbad the Sailor, Aesop's Fables,* Weem's *Life of Washington,* Grimshaw's *History of the United States,* and such practical guides as the *Lessons of Elocution.*

When Sarah finally arrived, with her three young children in tow and all her possessions in a large, borrowed wagon, and Thomas Lincoln announced, "Here's your new mammy," Abraham simply fell in love with her. Reportedly he was so starved for affection that he called her "Mama" from the start, and hid himself in her ample skirts, hoping it would not be taken as disrespect for her predecessor. Sandburg reconstructs Sarah Bush Lincoln as "a strong, large-boned, rosy woman, with a kindly face and eyes, with a steady voice, steady ways." A granddaughter recalled her as "a very tall woman, straight as an Indian, fair complexion, and when I first remember her, very handsome, sprightly talking and proud. Wore her hair curled till gray . . . kind hearted and very charitable and also very industrious." If Sarah did not quite save Abraham's life, it is not too much to say that she made it possible. Thomas Lincoln was not a cruel man, although he sometimes treated Abraham roughly as their relationship deteriorated. But he was a limited man, and by this time had no fixed purpose in life. He had never developed a regard for learning. Suppose he had brought back from Kentucky a wife who shared his limitations?

Instead, Abraham's already evident determination to make something of himself, encouraged by his mother, was even more motivated by the extended tenure of his stepmother. "These two women," in the words of Tarbell, "both of unusual earnestness and sweetness of spirit were one or the other at his side throughout his youth and young manhood." Sarah's first task was simply to clean the place up. Beveridge cites her formidable abilities as a housekeeper, this woman "with a systematic passion for cleanliness" who combined prudence, "energy and sense." The change in living conditions was so pronounced that some thirty-five years later Lincoln still marveled at it. Somehow Sarah accommodated eight people in a rough-hewn cabin that had already been cramped with four, and in a reasonably amicable and equitable fashion. All the children were assigned tasks in cleaning and reconfiguring before they were permitted to go outdoors to help their father. There was inevitable grumbling, not the least from Tom Lincoln himself, but as Benjamin Thomas writes, "Despite the overcrowding, the conditions of the Lincolns became better as the kindly, hardworking stepmother brought order out of the chaos and took the motherless children to her heart."

She loved them almost better than her own children, since they were older and more fully formed. She sensed the promise in Abraham almost at once, and determined, as Nancy had vowed, that he should "larn" all he could. In his entire life, Abraham Lincoln attended school for less than a full year, and such education as he gained — first, the limited "blab" schools of Kentucky, later any rural academy Sarah could find in Indiana — was due entirely to these two women. Fortunately a school opened only a mile and a half away soon after Sarah's arrival. The winter she arrived, Sarah insisted that Abraham study there at least until the spring planting. There was as yet no public education in Indiana, only such small schools, supported by the irregular tuition of parents and administered by largely itinerant schoolmasters who rarely stayed long. Sarah also suggested that Abraham read all the books she had brought, for which he required little encouragement. "The things I want to know," he insisted, "are in books," and he would often discuss with Sarah what he had read.

Lincoln was later to recall that when he came of age he might not have known very much, but most of what he did know had come from reading books of at least "some literary or historical value," even *Aesop's Fables*. With this and a smattering of math he was able to further educate himself prior to learning the law. Until she could get paper or slate, Sarah helped him cipher on boards at home. With her help, reading became even more of a passion for Abraham. Unlike most of his neighbors, he could not only read, but write and compute as well. As the community grew, he became renowned as much for his learning as for his storytelling and athletic feats (and reluctance to work very hard). He did all the writing for his family, and both read and wrote for his neighbors, composing most of their letters. Although he did not attend the local Baptist Church regularly, as his parents did, he was thoroughly acquainted with both the Old and New Testaments. Even his father, who, now hard pressed with more mouths to feed, criticized Abraham's laziness when he was hired out to work at other farms and questioned the point of all this reading, sometimes found himself boasting to friends of how much his boy knew.

Abraham worked many odd jobs in his teens, but he would learn incomparably more of the world as a deckhand on two adventurous trips to New Orleans for a local merchant. The first trip in particular — taking a flatboat down, loaded with provisions — was a revelation, although when he returned to Indiana he was obliged to give his earnings to his father. After his second trip, Lincoln was twenty-one. He could not only keep his pay, he could prepare to make his own way in the world. In New Orleans he had seen the brutal face of slavery for the first time, a memory he carried vividly into his public life. His father and stepmother moved again, to Illinois. After accompanying them for a final time, Abraham, at twenty-two, left home for good. The death of his sister Sarah in childbirth deepened his melancholy and separation from his roots. He knew his future course must be set only by himself, far from his parents' new home and even removed from Sarah Bush Lincoln, the person he loved best in the world.

Particularly after the death of his father, Lincoln was even more solicitous of his stepmother's welfare, concerned that the money he sent her or her own modest inheritance might be diverted by avaricious relatives. Writing to slothful and unreliable John Johnson, the natural son of his stepmother, Lincoln the stepson sounds much like his own father. Johnson not only wanted money, he wanted to sell the small homestead in Coles County, Illinois, that now sheltered Sarah. Lincoln remonstrated. "Work is the only cure for your case." One way or another, Lincoln made certain his stepmother was provided for. She never experienced the want, real or imagined, of Mary Ball Washington.

Shortly before going to Washington in 1860, Lincoln paid a long and emotional visit to his seventy-three-year-old stepmother. She was deeply distressed, convinced that something terrible would happen to him. Abraham insisted, in the spirit of her own faith, that if she trusted in the Lord all would be well. Then, for a final time, he embraced the woman who had supplanted his mother as first in his affections.

After his death, and shortly before hers, Sarah Bush Lincoln reflected on her special relationship with her stepson, whom probably only she could comfortably call "Abe." She told a writer, "I induced my husband to permit Abe to read and study at home, as well as at school. At first he was not easily reconciled to it, but finally he too seemed willing to encourage him to a certain extent. . . . Abe was a dutiful son to me always, and we took particular care not to disturb him. . . . Abe was a

Sarah Bush Lincoln
Courtesy of the Illinois State Historical Library

good boy and I can say what scarcely one woman — a mother — can say in a thousand: Abe never gave me a cross word in all my life. . . . His mind and mine — what little I had — seemed to run together. He was here after he was elected president. . . . I think he loved me truly. . . . I had a son, John, who was raised with Abe. Both were good boys, but I must say, both now being dead, that Abe was the best boy I ever saw, or expect to see."

Abraham Lincoln, who bore so much, was spared enduring the death of his second mother, a death which came, unlike that of Nancy Hanks Lincoln, to one full of years. He did in fact "owe all that he was" to these two devoted woman. It is true that he once called his families "undistinguished" and characterized his early life as simply a chronicle of unremitting poverty, but he is not the only president who said different things at different times. His two mothers did more than render his childhood tolerable. They inspired his ambition. Even if he was essentially "self-made," they provided the ingredients. That he was profoundly grateful for their gifts there can be no doubt.

Among these gifts was their religious piety. Nancy Hanks Lincoln was reputed to have said, "I would rather my son would be able to read the Bible than to own a farm, if he cannot have but one," sentiments with which Sarah Bush Lincoln would have concurred. Abraham Lincoln did more than exhaustively read the Bible. It formed the foundation of his most enduring public utterances. "I know that there is a God," he declared on the eve of the coming conflict. "If He has a place for me . . . I believe I am ready. I am nothing but truth is everything." In 1858 Lincoln said, "The Saviour, I suppose, did not expect that any human creature could be as perfect as the Father in Heaven." Throughout the Civil War he found solace in the righteous "providence of God." He read his Bible daily, and and viewed organized religion as a "sanctifying" influence on the nation. His second inaugural address in particular reads like a sermon: "the judgments of the Lord are true and righteous altogether." His call for days of national consecration, fasting, and prayer were far more than expressions of pragmatism. Lincoln's wish was not only for reconciliation but for righteousness. As a political candidate said almost seven score years later, Americans should not indulge in "the supposition that morality can be maintained without religion."

But what did Lincoln believe in his heart? He belonged to no denomination. Some historians consider that his inherited Calvinism was finally consecrated at Gettysburg. Biographer Allen C. Guelzo offers as balanced an analysis as is possible at this distance. Lincoln acknowledged "a Creator of all things, who had neither beginning nor end," and viewed Jesus Christ as the redeemer of the world. And yet, he could not quite come "the whole way to belief." Acquainted with anguish, given to periods of private depression masked by public confidence, Lincoln would never escape a kind of fatalism. It precluded full acceptance of a personal relationship with a God who directed individual lives. As Guelzo writes, "Lincoln often wished that 'I was a more devout man than I am.'" If he lacked the certitude of his mother's beliefs, or his stepmother's, nonetheless, he must have been sustained by their example. They provided for him a framework of faith to endure the nation's greatest trial.

CHAPTER SEVEN

Scarcity and Silence

- ✒ Mary Johnson
- ✒ Hannah Grant

IT IS NOT difficult to determine which American presidents came from families of the greatest affluence. With so many real and reconstructed log cabins dotting the presidential landscape, however, which chief executive came from conditions of the direst deprivation? Certainly Fillmore, Jackson, and Lincoln come to mind, but my choice would be Andrew Johnson.

Johnson was, by necessity, the most thoroughly self-made man to ever occupy the office. His mother undoubtedly wanted to help him, but Mary McDonough Johnson lacked the means. Her first husband was a good man who died too soon, her second a wastrel who lived too long. When Andrew Johnson was selected to run with Abraham Lincoln on a ticket of national unity in the extraordinary wartime election of 1864, much was made of the similarity of their humble origins. They were born six weeks apart in genuine log cabins and grew up in states on the Southern border. Both overcame immense hardships in their rise to prominence. What a childhood friend said of Johnson might just as well have been said of Lincoln: "I reckon he started underground." In all, Lincoln had perhaps one year of formal schooling, but as biographer Lately Thomas notes, "Johnson did not attend school a single day in his life."

He was the son not of the customarily struggling pioneer family, a hardscrabble farmer and his resourceful wife, but of a porter and a chambermaid. Neither could read or write. Andrew's father, Jacob Johnson, however, never lacked for energy. He emigrated from England around the end of the eighteenth century with no particular goal in mind. An eminently congenial man of all work, he sought to settle down where he might achieve at least a modicum of security. Wandering aimlessly around the country, doing all sorts of odd jobs to support himself, Jacob came to Raleigh, North Carolina. He found it to his liking. The capital of a state only recently admitted to the Union, Raleigh boasted a population of over a thousand and was bustling with lawyers, legislators, and visitors. There was already an aristocracy of sorts in place, with the means to employ anyone willing to work.

That suited Jacob, who would try anything. He quickly established a reputation for availability, reliability, and honesty. He served as everything from county constable and sexton to porter of the state bank. He even tolled the town bell, announcing major events in the community. Before long he was popular enough to be elected captain of a company of militia composed of workingmen like himself. Much of his time was spent helping out at the lively new inn opposite the bank, known as Cassio's Tavern.

Here he met and fell in love with an eighteen-year-old chambermaid named Mary McDonough, known to all as "Polly." As industrious as Jacob Johnson, Polly was also a skilled seamstress. Little is known of her life prior to marrying Jacob in 1801, and not much more afterward. Apparently they both felt sufficiently optimistic about their future to enter into a union, signified by making their marks in the town registry. The couple then moved into a small log house adjacent to the inn. Polly took in washing and mending to supplement her husband's modest income. Their first child, a girl, died in infancy. Their second survived, a sturdy fair-haired boy born in 1803, whom they named William.

It would be six years before the arrival of their next child, fated to be their last. It was during the festive Christmas season of 1809, celebrated boisterously at Cassio's, that Mary Johnson gave birth to a second son on December 29, to the sounds of fiddles and jollity next door. Thomas writes, "This boy was as dark as the other was light, and he, too, gave the promise of being strong and hearty." The news spread to the revelers in the tavern, some of whom reportedly were from Tennessee and insisted the baby be named for Andrew Jackson. True or not, Johnson never used Jackson's full name — but he adopted his temperament.

Andrew Johnson would have no memory of his father. When the child was only three, Jacob was hired to accompany a party of prominent men on a fishing outing. His tasks were probably to clean the fish and to bring the food and drink. Some of these spirits may have been consumed a bit early because one of the men, Colonel Thomas Henderson, editor of the *Raleigh Star,* engaged in a bit of horseplay. He rocked the boat, and all three occupants fell overboard. One made his way to shore with little difficulty. The second, who could not swim, in a panic dragged Henderson down with him into the icy water. Jacob dived in, and with immense effort managed to get both men to safety. He never recovered from these exertions. A few months later, while ringing the town bell for another's funeral, he collapsed and died.

The only thing his heroics earned Jacob Johnson was an obituary of uncommon prominence for one of his station in the newspaper of the editor whose life he had saved. Henderson did try to help, taking on Andrew's older brother as a printer's apprentice, but soon the editor, too, was dead. Many of Jacob's admirers contributed to the family from time to time, but it did little to relieve the financial burden of a young widow with two growing sons to support. Polly's own earnings from weaving, spinning, and taking in washing were meager at best. It was hardly hyperbolic when the adult Andrew Johnson claimed to "have grappled with the gaunt and haggard monster called hunger."

Polly finally settled for the only solution readily available in those times to one in her circumstances. She married again. Had it been to someone like Jacob, there might have been at least some remote hope of educating her sons. Instead, she wed shiftless Turner Dougherty (or Doughtry), who possessed neither skills nor the inclination to use them. If anything, conditions got worse.

To relieve some of the pressure, both sons were apprenticed to a Raleigh tailor. When, having at least learned a trade, Andrew Johnson finally set out to establish his own tailoring shop in Tennessee, he still wasn't quite on his own. His mother and stepfather were by then in such dire financial straits that they accompanied him. As biographer Lloyd Stryker notes, young Andrew not only lacked schooling and influential friends, "his mother was wholly dependent on him for her support." His older brother had vanished by then to Texas. At eighteen, Andrew was already head of a household, and its sole breadwinner.

Johnson went on to one of the most improbable political careers in American history. Finally taught to write and compute by the devoted wife he met and wed in Tennessee, and immaculately attired in clothes of his own cut, he eventually ascended to a presidency of historical significance and turmoil — which culminated in his impeachment trial. His combative temperament did little to diminish controversy, although the issues he faced after the Civil War would have tried the talents of a Lincoln.

His mother, finally settled on a farm Andrew had purchased, figured in one of the most vituperative exchanges of Johnson's career. In a bitter reelection campaign for Congress, he was opposed by William "Parson" Brownlow, a man no more noted for rhetorical restraint than Johnson. How was it possible, Brownlow queried, for someone of such consequence as Andrew Johnson to have been the son of an "illiterate loafer" like Jacob Johnson? Was not Andrew in fact the spitting image of the nephew of a prominent Raleigh judge? Abraham Lincoln had not been dismayed by intimations of illegitimacy in his mother's family, but this charge was leveled publicly in a political campaign against Johnson's own mother.

Surprisingly, Johnson responded not by physically assaulting Brownlow, who had also accused him of plotting an assassination attempt. Instead, Johnson went back to North Carolina, gathered legal affidavits about his birth, and referred to them in an open letter to the voters. In it he also characterized Brownlow as a "hyena," "vandal," "devil," and "coward," as well as employing less moderate epithets. Political discourse was not notably more elevated in the nineteenth century than in the twenty-first.

Johnson went on to win. His mother lived long enough not only to see him a member of Congress but also governor of Tennessee. She died in 1856, at the age of seventy-two, almost a decade before the divisive bitterness of her son's presidency. Andrew provided for her to the end, and for his stepfather as well. Both were buried at his behest in a Baptist churchyard.

Johnson himself belonged to no denomination, but frequently attended Roman Catholic mass in Washington, finding in that church's egalitarian treatment of its parishioners less of the social stratification he so resented. He had all but taught himself to read the Bible and other books while he was still an apprentice, and his faith must have been strengthened through the lessons administered by his devoted wife, Eliza, in order to withstand years of stress in public life. Johnson's oratory was no less biblical than Lincoln's. Once he said on the floor of the Senate, "Sir, I do not forget that I am a mechanic, neither do I forget that Adam was a tailor . . . or that our Savior was the son of a carpenter."

Had Mary McDonough Johnson remarried a man of some merit she, too, might have been able to help her sons and take her place among the other supportive presidential mothers celebrated in these pages. But, failing such a connection, she had no farm to fall back on, no property of her own, and no other means to provide assistance. Despite these frustrations, her son achieved astonishing success, and that must have given her immense gratification.

IN THE chronicle of presidential mothers, Hannah Simpson Grant is not so much missing as silent. In this her oldest son, Ulysses, more than any of her other five children, was truly her child. After Ulysses became prominent, his garrulous, relentlessly ambitious father Jesse tried to explain his difficulty relating to so silent a son. Jesse stressed how much more Ulysses resembled his mother: "He rarely ever laughs, never sheds a tear or becomes excited . . . never says a profane word or indulges in jokes." As biographer Geoffrey Perret points out, however, the mutual restraint of Hannah and Ulysses Grant "didn't indicate the absence of feeling." Perhaps "it was the mute testimony of feelings too deep for words. . . . However distant they may have appeared in the eyes of strangers, Grant and his mother were emotionally close."

Hannah had been at least a bit more demonstrative with her own family, the Simpsons, but their devout Calvinism was not so somber as her version of it would become. Only a generation removed from Ulster, the Simpsons had prospered in America. They were a close-knit, warm family. Hannah was born on a bountiful farm in Berks County, Pennsylvania, near the end of the eighteenth century. Her mother died when she was three, but her stepmother Rebecca was devoted to Hannah and made certain she attended the local school. Like so many others after the War of 1812, even comfortably situated John Simpson determined there was greater opportunity to the west, and moved his family to Ohio. Here the Simpsons settled on a six-hundred-acre farm, not far from Cincinnati. Except for the loss of her mother, there is little account of any childhood trauma in Hannah's life. After the move, her family retained close ties with their relatives back in Pennsylvania. The Simpsons were earnest Presbyterians, a family not only of property and propriety but also dedicated to learning. Their personal library was constantly in use. As biographer William McFeely writes, "The Simpsons had let neither their gentility nor their deeply rooted piety lapse in the move to the Ohio Valley."

Into this household swept Jesse Root Grant, whose family background could hardly have been more different. On a business trip nearby, Jesse was also looking for a bride. At twenty-six, he was already a year late in his carefully calibrated timetable. Nearly twenty-three, Hannah was on the verge of potential spinsterhood. Jesse was not put off by her taciturnity. The little she said seemed sensible enough. Jesse could talk sufficiently for both of them. He later described Hannah as a "plain, unpretentious country girl," but even if she was neat rather than pretty, her brown hair and slender figure were striking. Hannah in later years was described by biographers Dwight and Nancy Anderson as "a well-groomed, smallish woman with an open face and smooth, dark hair." Despite Jesse's brashness, John Simpson was impressed by the young man's ambition and his interest in literature. For his part, Jesse found little fault with Hannah, but perhaps he was most engaged by the attractive stability he saw in her family.

The Grants had started in America promisingly enough, traveling to Plymouth, Massachusetts, from England in 1630 on the "John and Mary." They eventually settled in Connecticut, where they prospered. But with Jesse's father, Noah, the family's fortunes took a turn for the worse. Initially a successful farmer, Noah claimed to have fought extensively in the Revolutionary War. He was home sufficiently often, however, for his wife to bear two sons. She died before the conflict concluded. After this tragedy, Noah apparently went to pieces, drinking heavily, losing everything, and becoming something of a wanderer. He set out for Western Pennsylvania, taking one son with him and leaving the other with his wife's parents. In Greensburg, he followed the shoemaker's trade, started dealing in animal skins, and married a young widow. Together they had seven children; Jesse Root Grant was the fourth.

Jesse's mother, Rachel, died after the family had moved again, to Ohio. By then, his father had pretty much scattered his children to any available friends and had started a tannery. Jesse was apprenticed to another tanner and later joined his half brother in that rigorous business. With no mother, and all but abandoned by his father, at the age of eleven Jesse Grant finally found a benefactor. Judge George Tod, on whose farm Jesse had labored, taught him to read and encouraged him to pursue a career of his own choosing. Jesse devised a plan for his life, the foundation of which was to be as unlike his father as possible. When the time came, he would be a true father to his own children.

All Jesse knew was something of farming and the tannery business. There was nothing attractive about treating the hides of dead animals, but leather in all its forms was absolutely essential to western expansion. It represented potential wealth to an aspiring young man, as farming did not. In time, perhaps, sufficient affluence might even lead to social acceptance, despite the means of ascent. Adroitly avoiding military service in the War of 1812, Jesse learned everything he could about the business. He wound up in Kentucky, but because he hated slavery he moved to Ravenna, Ohio. Working his way into a partnership, he moved again to Point Pleasant. However unpleasant his profession, by twenty-five Jesse was prospering in it — on target with the timing of his life plan. Felled by an illness, it was another year before he met Hannah Simpson, but in 1821 they were married.

Starting with some of his in-laws' books, Jesse went about trying to improve himself. He took classes in English, wrote letters to newspapers on every conceivable subject, and became active in politics. He craved the sort of solid status enjoyed by his wife's family, but business always came first. As McFeely writes, "In one way or another . . . Jesse Grant was always struggling to establish himself." What his wife, removed to so different an environment, thought about all this has never been recorded. The Grants' neat frame home had only two rooms, but it was no log cabin. To Jesse it represented only a way station on his road to respectability.

On April 27, 1822, ten months after their marriage, Hannah gave birth to their first child, a large, healthy boy. For six weeks he had no name. To Jesse, his first son merited something special. Hannah's father, perhaps because of his interest in antiquity and Old Testament connections, was partial to the name Hiram. Hannah's mother, from her reading, admired the ancient Greek hero Ulysses. That was fine with Jesse Grant, affirming that he was also acquainted with history and mythology. So the name Hiram Ulysses Grant was settled on. Jesse never called the boy Hiram, preferring "Ulyss." His strong son, Ulysses, Jesse boasted from the very beginning to anyone who would listen, "is a most beautiful child." Perret writes that "With his russet hair, blue eyes, and pink complexion, Ulysses Grant looked in childhood like a glowing miniature of his robust, energetic father."

By the time the boy was eighteen months old, Jesse moved his family to a much larger, brick house in Georgetown, Ohio, the new county seat. It afforded enhanced opportunity for his now flourishing business. The tannery was adjacent to the home. In Georgetown, Jesse befriended prominent men, his library grew, and eventually he was even elected mayor. He and Hannah would have two more boys, and three girls, but his firstborn son remained his favorite. Surely he must be exceptional. He carried not only his father's expectations but also a unique, heroic name.

For any child, bearing such a name was challenging enough. For a sensitive child, balanced between a doting father and an apparently distant mother, adjacent to what was still the American frontier, it was doubly difficult. Ulysses didn't look or feel very heroic. Although devoted to the unpretentious verities of her faith, his mother dressed him in a most fastidious fashion, very different from other children in Georgetown. At least he didn't suffer the flowing hair and dresses that would later be favored by Franklin Roosevelt's mother, Sara.

Sent to school at five, Ulysses was also undersized. Even a decade later, he weighed only 115 pounds and was barely over five feet tall. One might think the rougher boys would have made him an object of ridicule, if not the target of their fists — but by and large, this didn't happen.

Something about young Ulysses seemed to intimidate, or at least inhibit, other children. He said little, but he appeared to be taking everything in. His steady gaze was just like his mother's. To Hannah it was the worldly who required words. The godly relied on reflection and revelation. Ulysses may not quite have inherited her pious Christian certainty, but he duplicated her demeanor. However quietly, they came to confide in each other. Like so many other mothers of presidents, Hannah probably harbored hopes that someday her son would be a minister of the gospel, but her face revealed as little to the outside world as her voice. Mother and son were stoical, a quality both Greek and Christian.

Even as a child, Ulysses preferred the company of adults. He was little interested in games or hunting. He couldn't abide vulgarity or violence of any kind. Like Lincoln, he abhorred cruelty to animals. He came to love being around horses, and other solitary pursuits. He longed to travel. He was a dutiful student, but hardly outstanding. He dreaded speaking in public, even in a classroom. Ulysses was also scrupulously honest and truthful, qualities Jesse bragged about, and which Hannah probably inspired. But in the hardheaded world of frontier commerce, honesty could also be taken for stupidity. In one notable instance, sent to buy a colt, young Ulyss was instructed by his father to offer twenty-two and a half dollars but was told that he could go as high as twenty-five if necessary. He revealed everything to the seller and paid the higher price.

Hannah's unique form of childrearing, the talk of Georgetown's mothers, could make her, as well, look a bit light-headed. Even when Ulysses was an infant, she let him crawl without supervision between the feet of horses tethered outside the tannery. When he was sick, she simply gave him castor oil, put him to bed, and trusted in the Lord. Every day was a gift from God, and his will would be done. In the absence of a Presbyterian church, she became a Methodist, her fundamental Christianity

Hannah Grant
Courtesy of the Ohio Historical Society

beyond denominational distinctions. The faith that sustained Hannah
Grant may have been devoid of the joy experienced by other mothers of
American presidents, but it provided the same comfort.

As the Andersons write, Hannah "seldom smiled and spoke only
when she had to. Ulysses said later he had never seen her cry, and no
one remembered her laughing. . . . No one played cards in Hannah
Grant's house and no one danced or played music there either." If so
somber a home depressed Jesse, there is no record of discord between

husband and wife. Perhaps, after the haphazard nature of his own childhood, Jesse valued the serenity and security Hannah provided. He came to appreciate his good fortune in having married such a woman. Jesse wrote of Hannah, "Her steadiness, firmness, and strength of character have been the stay of the family through life."

Apparently neither parent really scolded Ulysses or their other offspring, or offered very much in the way of direction, except by example. Yet the children were very well behaved. Jesse hoped they would carry on his business, and after school, all the children worked hard to help their parents. From the age of eight, Ulysses did everything for his father that involved horses, but he avoided as much of the bloody premises as possible. Eventually Jesse's daughters made good marriages, and his two other sons did indeed become tanners, but Ulysses early announced that as soon as he turned twenty-one, his days at the tannery were over.

Ulysses was the only child of Hannah and Jesse Grant who so thoroughly took after his mother. Since he was most intent on pursuing a different sort of life than his father's enterprise provided, it is not surprising that, as he grew, Ulysses's thoughts turned to traveling. Like many others who became president, he felt the urge to escape at a young age. One of his most enjoyable pursuits was to drive his neighbors on their trips out of town, in a coach with his own horses. Precisely where, his father wondered, was Ulysses himself heading? Had he worked so hard to see his oldest son become a struggling farmer or a marginal "down-the-river" trader? These were vague options the boy had mentioned.

Ulysses had been provided with the best education possible in the region. After the Georgetown school, he attended Marysville Academy in Kentucky, and later a well-regarded Presbyterian academy very much to Hannah's liking. Just as at home, Ulysses proved to be a competent but not exceptional student. Finally, Jesse decided to seek an appointment for his Ulyss to the United States Military Academy at West Point. The education was free, it was focused and disciplined, and it might direct his uncertain son toward a productive career.

Ulysses didn't want to go, apparently not so much because he hated the idea as because he questioned his own capacity to measure up. However he felt about his father, Ulysses was keenly aware of how thoroughly he had fallen short of Jesse's expectations. How Hannah viewed all this is unknown, although it is not likely she could have looked favorably at a potential military career for her son. The appointment went through, and Ulysses finally agreed to depart. The congressman involved, never having heard Ulysses's middle name "Hiram" used, assumed the new cadet's name was Ulysses S. (for Simpson) Grant. So it was submitted, and so it remained for the rest of Grant's life. Throughout his youth, he had remained close to his good-hearted Simpson grandparents and others in his mother's family. It was his Uncle Sam Simpson who monogrammed his trunk "UHG," feeling "HUG" might be an embarrassment. He didn't yet know about "U. S. Grant."

Grant's neighbors, who probably shared his apprehension about the departure for West Point, gave him a tearful sendoff. The farewell at his home was not so emotional. "They don't cry at our house," Ulysses explained. He grew much taller and broader at the Academy and did better than anyone had expected, but his first return home elicited little overt excitement from his parents. "How are you, son?" his father asked. His mother noted that he seemed to stand much straighter, and then went about her business. In subsequent years, his father's pride would resurface, as Ulyss achieved prominence beyond anything he could remotely have imagined. But always, when she heard praise for her son, Hannah would flee the room like a schoolgirl. Eventually she admitted that "he was always a good boy," but worldly renown was never a high priority to Hannah Grant. It seemed almost a reproach to the Lord.

Ulysses's letters home from West Point to his mother are surprisingly tender, the only tangible evidence of the depth of his feelings. "I seem alone in the world without my mother. . . . I cannot tell you how much I miss you. I was so often alone with you, and you so frequently spoke to me in private, that the solitude of my situation here . . . is all the more striking. It reminds me the more forcibly of home, and most of all, dear Mother, of you. . . . Your kindly instructions and admonitions are ever present with me." Some of these instructions and admonitions must have reflected Hannah Grant's firm Christian faith, the touchstone of her life.

Perhaps, like George Washington, Grant tried to compensate in his own married life for whatever he felt was lacking in his childhood, but any implied bitterness was directed toward Jesse. When Grant became a major-general, he wrote to his wife, "Is Father afraid yet that I will not be able to sustain myself?" There were never such reflections on his mother. Neither parent figured very prominently in Grant's extraordinary memoirs, completed when he was dying of throat cancer, but it was not Grant's style, any more than his mother's, to write publicly about matters so private. The most effusive comments ever written about the stern-visaged Hannah Grant were from Ulysses's wife, Julia, upon meeting her for the first time: "A handsome woman, a little below medium height, with soft brown eyes, glossy brown hair, and her cheer . . . like a rose in the sun." Her mother-in-law, Julia insisted, was "the most self-sacrificing, sweetest, kindest woman I ever met, except my own dear mother . . . altogether I was well satisfied with my dear husband's family."

There is some indication that the rather haughty Julia later revised her opinions, but approval and reproach were all the same to Hannah Grant. Unlike her husband, who predictably made a thorough pest of himself, Hannah neither visited the White House nor attended either of Ulysses's presidential inaugurations. One can only surmise why, but there was nothing obtrusive in her nature. She probably did not want to burden her son, and would have been less than comfortable at the lavish entertainments presided over by her daughter-in-law.

A reporter who visited Hannah during those days could not elicit a response from her to any questions. He thought perhaps she was harboring some terrible secret, or was simply slow-witted, a suspicion once directed at Ulysses. Perhaps his decade of failure, loneliness, and alcoholism between wars was viewed by his mother as the humbling balance for his later success, but no word escaped her lips. The soul of consistency, she died at the age of eighty-four in 1883, only two years before her son. In her stoical way, she may have supplied the strength to help him transcend the transitory triumphs and tragedies of this world. It must have been from personal experience that Grant concluded, "How much American soldiers are indebted to good American mothers! When they go to the front, what prayers go with them!" Hannah Simpson Grant's prayers were not silent to her son.

CHAPTER EIGHT

Pre-War Mothers, Post-War Sons

- ♨ Sophia Hayes
- ♨ Eliza Garfield
- ♨ Malvina Arthur

SOPHIA BIRCHARD HAYES is reminiscent of many other strong-willed presidential mothers. She too was pious, protective, and resolute. What makes her distinctive is the extremes to which she carried these qualities. She was so protective that it is a wonder her son Rutherford turned out to be as decisive as he was. As for Sophia's piety and resolution, the loss of so many loved ones would have tried anyone's faith. If, through it all, her methods seemed excessive, at least she retained her sanity.

Like so many other mothers of American presidents, she would have liked to see her surviving son in the ministry, but she was more preoccupied with what she didn't want. Next to outright vice, the one profession she definitely disdained was politics. All being elected to Congress had done for her husband's brother-in-law was turn him into an alcoholic. Rutherford B. Hayes was meant for something a good deal more elevated than the level to which public life had sunk.

As a child in Vermont, Sophia Birchard gave early evidence of what she would be like as an adult. Even at twelve, she was extremely lively, if not memorably lovely. Biographer Harry Barnard describes Sophia as "attractive in a clean and chaste way," with a trim figure. She had rather a long "Yankee face," tightly combed brown hair, and piercing blue eyes. Her other memorable feature was her extremely rosy cheeks, which caused her no end of embarrassment, implying artificial embellishment. She was devoutly religious and read endlessly — not frivolous books but instructive, weighty works like *Pilgrim's Progress*. At the district school, she excelled. Her personality already expressed its ambivalence: a preoccupation with death and redemption unique in a child, yet wedded to such vivacity that a relative would later exclaim, "She is grand company. . . . She talks a perfect hailstorm. . . . Oh, it did me good to hear her!"

Sophia was of English descent. The first American Birchard brought his family to Roxbury, Massachusetts, in 1635. There were Birchards at Bunker Hill, and Sophia's maternal grandfather, "Old Captain" Daniel Austin, lived long enough to regale her with stories of the Revolution. Sophia was born in Wilmington, Vermont, in 1792. Her father, a farmer and merchant, died when she was only thirteen. Her mother remarried and was then divorced, a scandalous occurrence in nineteenth-century Vermont. She died when Sophia was eighteen. Sophia thus had an early acquaintance with grief.

Meanwhile, fourteen miles away in Brattleboro, Vermont, red-haired Rutherford Hayes, known to all as "Ruddy," was also growing to maturity. From a Scottish family named "Haie," renowned for valor, the Hayeses came to Connecticut in the seventeenth century. They, too, took part in the Revolutionary War, but also in subsequent disputes between New York and Vermont. The first Rutherford Hayes had the multiple careers common to early America. He was a blacksmith, an innkeeper, and a farmer. His fourth child and second son, born in 1787, was truly the apple of his eye, not only named for him but also clearly the most promising of his children. While Sophia was reading her tomes by candlelight and was already mothering her siblings, handsome young Ruddy, four years her senior, was clerking for the retail firm of Noyes and Mann. When they decided to open a general store in Wilmington, he was sent to manage it. When Sophia glimpsed Ruddy behind the counter, the sparks — despite her aversion to crimson — were instantaneous.

They were married in 1813. Although Ruddy was a captain of militia, the War of 1812 was unpopular in Federalist-dominated New England, and he was not called upon to fight in it, to Sophia's immense relief. In 1814, their first child, who was to have been named Rutherford Birchard Hayes, in honor of both families, was born dead. For the first time in her married life Sophia demonstrated a distinctive quality that pulled her husband through the tragedy. Stemming her own tears, she managed to cheer him up. Years later, her daughter Fanny defined this as Sophia's "singular trait . . . of being rather disposed to look on the dark side when others are joyous, and rising as others are depressed . . . thus preserving the equilibrium of our family." Scripture confirms that there is a time for everything in its season. The next year should have been a time for joy. One partner in Ruddy's firm, John Noyes, was elected to Congress, and the other partner decided to pull out. Ruddy was named to take his place. The war ended, and the couple had another son. This one, thankfully, was healthy, as well as red-haired. They named the boy Lorenzo.

Always apprehensive when things were going too well, Sophia was not surprised when a severe economic depression followed the war. Retailing was as hard-hit as manufacturing and farming. Sophia loved Vermont, despite the fact that so many of her kin had been buried there, and she was reluctant to leave it. And even when friends brought tales of immense opportunity in Ohio, prudent Rutherford Hayes was not about to pull up stakes without seeing things for himself. After looking thoroughly throughout the region, however, he found a large tract of land to his liking near the town of Delaware. Here there was already a degree of settlement, with schools and churches. He knew how important such considerations were to his wife, who was pregnant again. When he returned home, she had already given birth to their daughter Sarah Sophia. Ruddy sold the business, and, with his wife's concurrence, the family set off for Ohio.

Unlike many pioneers, Ruddy had the means to invest not only in more farmland but also in a potentially lucrative whisky distilling business that Sophia could not have approved of. Although he provided capably enough for his family, somehow the immense wealth Ruddy had hoped for escaped his grasp. He became severely depressed. As usual, Sophia found a silver lining in disappointment. She induced her chastened husband to join the Presbyterian Church that had always been her rock and salvation. After five years in Ohio, Sophia had reason to feel some satisfaction. She had a handsome home, abundant fruit orchards, many transplanted friends from New England, fulfilling work in the church, a loving husband, and a growing family. Sophia had given birth to a second daughter, Fanny, a delightful child, and she was pregnant yet again. It was time for things to go bad.

In the summer of 1822 a pervasive fever gripped the region. First little Sarah Sophia died. Then her father was stricken. In three days Rutherford Hayes, too, was dead. He was only thirty-five. Everyone else was sick. On October 4, a still feverish Sophia gave birth to a frail little boy. With undaunted courage, she named him Rutherford Birchard Hayes for the father and older brother he would never know. While ministering to herself, Fanny, and Lorenzo, Sophia nursed little "Rud" to health. Like Elizabeth Jackson, she willed her son to survive, and he did. But her succession of tragedies was not yet at an end. Only three years later, while skating, Lorenzo fell thorough the ice and drowned. At home, young Rud would have only his surviving sister, Fanny, to be his childhood companion. Is it any wonder his mother cherished and protected him from every peril, real or imagined?

For a time, Sophia's bachelor brother, Sardis, stayed with them, a surrogate father figure. As biographer Charles Richard Williams writes, no widow or her son ever had a more faithful friend. But Sardis was restless by nature. In 1826 he returned to Vermont, then to New York, then to the South, his route followed avidly by Rud, anxious for his return, on a map. When he came back it was only for a day or two at a time, bringing books, gifts, and good cheer. Sardis would later come into money and become a valued counselor in Rud's life, but he never lived with the Hayes family again.

It was a little world of women, particularly after Sophia's spinster aunt, Arcena Smith, came to reside with them. She was congenial enough; indeed, there was almost an excess of affection in the childhood of Rutherford B. Hayes. Sometimes Sophia would hug him extra-hard, transmitting her own awareness of how transitory earthly happiness could be. Rud's mother was still youthful, and attractive to men. Suitors were abundant, but she would not hear of remarriage. It was not only because Ruddy had left her in relatively comfortable circumstances or because she possessed the capacity to manage things without masculine protection. She felt an enduring devotion to her dead husband, whom no one could replace, and she imparted it to her two surviving children. Live up to your heritage. We need no one else. Characteristically, she wrote to relatives, "My dear children are perfectly well, but I am filled with fear for them." It would never leave her.

Barnard observes that "She determined fiercely that Rud should survive. Most of her mistakes came from this single, understandable, rigid resolve. Inevitably . . . he became a mother's boy." First, she taught him to read, and then she read with him, not the stories of adventure he undoubtedly preferred, but from the same *Pilgrim's Progress* Sophia had treasured as a child. In her lyceum, it was second only to the Bible in significance. Rud's sister Fanny became not only a much-loved second mother but also a sort of older brother, as well. Even though, like her mother, she was small in stature, Fanny initially seemed more the boy, Rud the girl. She initiated and led all the games. She loved sports and excelled at them. Even when they wrestled, Fanny was much the stronger of the two.

Rud played at dolls long before he discovered toy soldiers. It was more than his early fragility that convinced Sophia that her son had to be kept away from other children; by the age of four he was healthy enough. It was simply her pervasive fear. The fewer outside contacts, the less likelihood of some inexplicable accident, like Lorenzo's. Rud was hardly ever out of his mother's sight. He was never permitted to do manual labor. Until he was seven, Fanny was virtually his sole playmate. Only at nine was he allowed to play carefully supervised games with other children. Barnard writes, "It was no wonder that neighbors . . . considered him 'timid as a girl' . . . and not even forty years later, when others would acclaim him for his manliness, could his mother really see him as other than a boy in need of sheltering."

Sophia, however, was an able teacher. She early taught Rutherford not only to read, write, and calculate, but also how to reason. She never quite trusted the little school in the village. Most of all, she stressed with Rud her religion and her morality. One had to live every day in awareness that there would be a final judgment. Sophia even considered taking her family back to Vermont, where the very air seemed healthier, but finally decided they were too settled in Ohio to be uprooted again. With some apprehension, she finally enrolled Rud in a local private grade school. He not only did well, he also had surprisingly little difficulty dealing with other children. But that was as far as his education could go in the little town of Delaware.

Rutherford was not really separated from Sophia until he was nearly fourteen. Sardis had recommended a boys' boarding school in Norwalk, Ohio — Norwalk Academy. Administered by Methodists, it was reputed to have a pervasive, positive Christian environment that would satisfy even Sophia, as well as high academic standards. Initially as reluctant as his mother, Rud found he loved the school, and again he excelled in his studies. In view of his sheltered childhood, it is remarkable how readily he adapted to the world outside his home. Oddly, Sophia was most concerned about her son's lack of manners. He'd had little opportunity to polish them, separated from the society of everyone except the three women he had lived with. She need not have worried.

At sixteen Rud went on to Kenyon College, then as now an excellent liberal arts institution affiliated with the Episcopal Church. There was far more emphasis on theology in 1838, but Sophia still wondered if a Presbyterian college might not have been preferable. Perhaps it was a form of mild rebellion against his mother's indoctrination that prevented Rud from openly affirming his Christian faith. He also questioned Kenyon's firm discipline, and talked of transferring to Yale, but eventually he buckled down. Repeating his earlier academic success, he graduated in 1842 as valedictorian. He also completed the transition from his excessively sheltered childhood, becoming the acknowledged leader of his class. For once, his mother's joy was unalloyed. She went proudly to his graduation and heard his oration. How much like his father he looked now. He was no longer a "feeble and fatherless child," but the culmination of everything she had labored for, the solace for so much suffering.

What would he do now? Fanny had married, and welcomed her brother to her new home in Columbus, where Rud had decided to read law. Surprisingly, Sophia was pleased. Law was a respectable profession. Not all lawyers went into politics. When a now-affluent Sardis paid Rud's tuition at Harvard Law School, she was not upset, only saddened by another separation. After graduating in 1846, Hayes returned to Ohio to set up his practice.

His mother was full of surprises. Rud discovered, if he hadn't known it before, how deeply she felt about political issues, even if her views were, of course, always couched in moral terms. Sophia approved of Sarah Polk's prohibition of liquor from the White House (Sophia's daughter-in-law "Lemonade Lucy" Hayes would ban even wine), but she was not so enthusiastic about President Polk's foreign policy. Sophia wrote Rutherford this timeless admonition: "If the time . . . wasted talking about Oregon had been spent in educating the ignorant or in improving the moral condition of the young of this land, instead of inflaming their minds about 'war and honor,' it would be better."

She could never quite keep from trying to guide Rud's life, however, and in this her logic was not always so reasoned. When Hayes decided to move his law office from Columbus to Cincinnati, Sophia insisted the latter was a city rife with sin, wickedness, and corruption, while Columbus, the state capital, was a model of morality. Perhaps she felt that way because she now lived in Columbus. Rud went anyway, after a month's visit with his mother and sister. At twenty-seven he was finally his own man. When, in 1858, he was elected by the Cincinnati city council to become city solicitor, his mother once more raised the flag of caution. "If you wish to be happy, never aspire to political honors," she warned, but she surely understood it was now too late.

The Civil War came to Sophia like a specter from the past. Her mind filled with new premonitions of death. She knew this conflict could not be avoided, as her husband had avoided service in the War of 1812, and that her son would seek no substitute. She hated the war, but viewed secession and slavery as "more wicked." She bravely wrote Rud, "If I had ten sons, I would rather they were all with you." This time, there was no looking on the bright side of disaster. With her daughter-in-law, Lucy, who was also deeply religious, she shared the ordeal. Somehow, Rud survived, despite being wounded four times. Once his wife brought him home to Ohio to recuperate. He would not take his seat in Congress while the conflict raged. He ended the war a brigadier-general and a genuine hero. Sophia felt relief, pride, and probably puzzlement. Was it possible he had not been taken from her?

Sophia Birchard Hayes died in 1866 at the age of seventy-four. A decade later, her son became president in the most controversial election since that of John Quincy Adams. Well, his mother had warned him of "the vile and frivolous company" that infested Washington. Even though he had never joined her church, however, Rud did not seem to have been corrupted by politics. Barnard writes that "From his tender attentions" to his mother, his "clean" look, his contentment with his wife and family, "the absence of any scandal in his affairs," Sophia would have concluded that he could not have been personally involved in any devious dealings. Her daughter Fanny had lived to be only thirty-five, the same age at which Rud's father had died. Sophia had written then to her sole surviving child, "My only comfort is that she is happy and free from care and pain in the mansions of the blessed." So much of what Sophia feared had come true, but her faith never faltered. The son she had sheltered had survived.

WHEN HE WAS twenty-one, James Garfield reflected, "In reviewing the varied scenes of my short yet eventful life, I can see the golden thread running through the whole — my mother's influence on me." Unlike Mary Johnson, Eliza Ballou Garfield did have a small farm, but her husband died just as suddenly as Jacob Johnson had, leaving her with four children to support. For sheer fortitude in the face of adversity, Eliza Garfield has no equal in the mothers of American presidents.

In her sixties she undertook to write "a brief sketch of my early life for the edification of my Children after I am laid in the Grave." It is fortunate she was able to get around to it; her early life had allowed little leisure for such pursuits. Her family, the Ballous, and her husband's, the Garfields, kept running into each other all the way from New York State to the Western Reserve of Ohio. The Ballous were of French Huguenot extraction, noted for their diminutive size and quick wit, described by a contemporary as a sort of "French pony breed." They settled in Rhode Island around the end of the seventeenth century. Many were creative and intellectual, educators and clergymen; a Ballou founded Universalism. Eliza's parents, however, were engaged in humbler pursuits, and she was born on a New Hampshire farm. "My father and mother," she wrote, "lived very happily," but her father died when she was only six. Her mother turned to her skill at weaving to support her family. "She was not ashamed to labor," Eliza wrote. "In those days it was no disgrace to work." Despite Eliza's high spirits, this tone of moralism was rarely absent from her reminiscences or her utterances.

The Garfields, as biographer Theodore Smith writes, were also "typical New England stock" — of Norman-English extraction, in other words. Edward Garfield was among the earliest settlers of Massachusetts, arriving in 1630. Unlike the Ballous, the Garfields tended to be tall and sturdy, evincing little in the way of intellectual curiosity. But they enjoyed a reputation for enterprise, warmhearted generosity, and great skill with tools. Abram Garfield and Elizabeth Ballou, born on farms in neighboring New England states as the nineteenth century dawned, were each the physical embodiment of their families.

At eighteen Eliza is described by biographer Allan Peskin as having "features perhaps already rather sharp and set," but also as having "inherited her mother's bright coloring as well as her clever hands. . . . [H]er fine singing voice made her welcome in any gathering. . . . She was small and quick . . . fond of company and chatter." Biographer Hendrick Booraem adds that although Eliza was short in stature, her wit, energy, and perception were already viewed as remarkable by her friends.

Abram Garfield was happy to be numbered among them. After both families had moved to Ohio, he set out to renew his acquaintance with the Ballous, especially their daughters. They had played together as children when they were neighbors in New York State. (After the War of 1812, such mobility became more prevalent in American life.) Abram was delighted with how the Ballou girls had grown. At first he courted Hitty, the prettiest, but it was her "saucy" younger sister Eliza whom he finally asked to marry him. It is little wonder she accepted. Eliza describes Abram at twenty as "five feet and eleven inches high, broad shoulders and chest, high fore-head, brown hair, blue eyes, light complexion . . . as beautiful a set of teeth as any man ever had . . . his bearing able and brave."

It was Abram's stepfather who had brought his vast brood, Garfields and Boyntons, to Ohio, seeking land and opportunity in a region only recently wrested from Chief Tecumseh and his Indian allies. Abram had no specific trade, but he knew farming and had demonstrated skill at woodworking. Moreover, even as a young man, he seemed to possess an instinctive ability to win the regard of others. He was handsome and blessed with prodigious strength — as renowned a wrestler as the young Abraham Lincoln — but it was also his cheerful Garfield demeanor that won Eliza over. Neither had much in the way of education, but Eliza, a true Ballou, loved books as much as Abram avoided them. Perhaps, she thought, she could do something about that.

They married in 1820 and set out with high spirits to seek their fortune in the Western Reserve, Ohio's northwestern frontier. They settled in what was still wilderness on the Cuyahoga River, near what is now Cleveland. Thousands of like-minded pioneers moved out in the same general direction, including a number of Boynton relatives. Starting with forty acres, Abram hoped to augment farming with woodworking. But almost as soon as he had settled his little wife in their snug log home, built with his own hands, both fell terribly ill. That common frontier ailment, the "ague," probably a form of malaria, felled even the hearty Abram. For parts of each of their first several years together, they were both so weak they had to live with some Boyntons who fortunately had moved nearby. Yet, despite everything, Eliza gave birth to four children in quick succession, two boys and two girls.

When Abram, anxious to quickly improve his circumstances, was finally up to working, he used some of his Garfield charm to talk two other men into taking on a contract to construct part of the new Ohio Canal. As Eliza recalled in 1868, "Then the Canal was all the vogue." Ohio hoped to emulate the success of the Erie Canal. Unfortunately, Abram's energy was no match for the laws of economics. A rise in costs wiped out his profits. After eight years of marriage, initiated with some promise, he was back where he started and bankrupt, with a family to support — his strength and his wife's undiminished confidence his only assets. While Abram pondered how to gain a fresh start, Eliza helped out by doing weaving for others. It was no disgrace to work.

Assistance, emotional and physical, also came from the Boyntons. Before long they helped Abram raise the roof of a larger log house, crafted with his customary skill. Just constructing it buoyed his spirits. He cleared new acres and planted wheat. Things seemed to be looking up. Eliza's certainty that she and her husband were well matched was borne out. Their strengths supplemented each other. Biographer John Taylor writes of Eliza, "It was she who was the great influence on her children, for she more than made up for her lack of formal education with self-reliance and imagination." By the third year in the new house, Eliza recalled in one of her writings, "We lived as well as our neighbors." Food of all kinds was abundant. "Your father would do as much work in one day as any man would do in two. . . . Our family circle was unbroken. We enjoyed ourselves with our little children."

Then tragedy struck, in the guise it so often did on the frontier, breaking their family circle suddenly and mysteriously. Their firstborn son, little Jimmy, his mother's favorite, collapsed and died in her arms. As close to despair as ever in her life, Eliza turned to religion to find some semblance of solace. A visiting preacher of the Disciples of Christ struck an empathetic chord. Derived from the Presbyterians, but less structured, the Disciples were missionary-minded and devoted directly to the authority of Scripture — "No creed but Christ, no book but the Bible, no law but Love, no name but the Divine." Calling itself simply the Christian Church, the Disciples were as much a fellowship as a denomination. A century later, Nelle Reagan, facing a different kind of challenge, also embraced the church's teachings. God did nothing without a reason. In time his purpose would be made plain. Eventually Eliza would also induce her husband to be baptized in her new faith, filling both with "perfect happiness," but before their immersion could be scheduled, she gave birth again, to her final child.

James Abram Garfield was born in a log cabin on a farm in Orange, Ohio, on November 19, 1831. Named for both his father and a departed brother, a not uncommon practice in those times, James was, in his mother's words, "the largest Babe I ever had." He "looked like a red Irishman, a very large Head and Shoulders. . . . He was a very good natured Child." James, physically so like his father must have been in infancy, seemed a gift from God. If the death of their first son was somehow a sort of judgment, might this not be a form of redemption? Unlike so many presidential parents who favored their oldest sons, the Garfields saw something special in their youngest.

James would know neither of those for whom he was named. In the dry, dangerous spring months of 1833, a fire broke out in the woods surrounding the Garfield home and the new acres Abram had cleared. To keep it from spreading, he fought the blaze all day. Coming home drenched and exhausted, Abram caught a violent cold, probably pneumonia. Misdiagnosed by an itinerant physician, he grew worse. In two days he was dead. Realizing the end was near, Abram is reputed to have said to his wife, "Eliza, I have brought you four young saplings into these woods. Take care of them." Abram Garfield was only thirty-three. His elder son, Thomas, was not yet eleven, baby James not yet two.

Many years later, in a campaign biography, James Garfield recalled with little exaggeration his mother's reaction: "She lost no time in irresolution, but plunged at once into the roughest sort of men's labor. The wheat field was only half-fenced. The precious harvest still ungathered." A slight woman of thirty-two, with four children to provide for, Eliza had little time to grieve. She had relatives willing to help, some nearby, but none were wealthy. The prospect of parceling out her children, even to kinfolk of her late husband, was unthinkable. They would stay together as a family, and survive. She took a mental inventory. She owned her house and fifty acres of land, only partially paid for. She was entitled by law to a year's support of a hundred and twenty dollars. Her neighbors would help her bring in the spring crop, but what then?

She and her son Tom, who grew up quickly under the circumstances, split rails, truly "man's labor," from timber Abram had cut for that purpose. Together they completed the fence enclosing their fields, protecting the ripening wheat from roaming cattle, who had been let loose during the forest fire. If the family were to remain intact, it must be self-sustaining. The only Garfield exempted from farm chores, of necessity, was baby James.

A skilled seamstress (the vocation of choice or necessity for so many presidential mothers), Eliza bartered her handiwork with the local cobbler for shoes. Wheat was traded for corn. From their few sheep Eliza and her daughters carded wool, wove cloth, and made all the family's garments. Eliza sold off twenty acres to her brother-in-law Amos Boynton, enabling her to pay off what was due on the remaining thirty. Still, property taxes had to be paid. No opportunity was overlooked. As new settlers moved into the area, Eliza used her spinning wheel and loom to make and sell finished garments from whole cloth. Nevertheless, the first winter without her husband was harsh indeed.

Nor was there much improvement in the next several years. Eliza insisted to her children that they were not a poor family. Poverty meant indigence, not paying one's debts, and accepting charity. Perhaps sustenance was not abundance, but the family and a loving God would provide. Smith writes, "The role played by the mother would be hard to over-emphasize," bolstered as it was by the enduring influence of her church. In the midst of the still rough backwoods of Ohio, no coarseness was tolerated in the Garfield household. Eliza viewed impurity of thought as tantamount to impurity of deed. Profanity and pride, she stressed, were no less to be avoided than gambling and drinking. Eliza led daily Bible readings, and the family walked together to the Christian meetinghouse every Sunday. Upon their return they reflected on everything they had heard. It was participatory religion, a sort of ongoing seminar, and as the children grew, it was by no means one-sided.

None of this was done, however, in a sanctimonious spirit. The young widow was recalled by her children as joyful, cheerful, and affectionate, as well as vigorous. With her beautiful singing voice she led them not only in hymns but also in sea chanteys, ballads of the day, and patriotic songs from the War of 1812. James later claimed that his mother knew so much music she could sing for forty-eight hours without repeating herself. She held them all spellbound with stories and song. Certainly Eliza loved all four of her children, but as biographers Margaret Leech and Harry Brown suggest, "She could see her handsome husband in the fair, strong-shouldered little man who frolicked at her knee." Even when he grew old enough to help out, picking berries, herding their few livestock and the like, James was always encouraged by his mother to take time to read. Not entirely because of age, he was the chosen one.

Eliza thus saw a further benefit in keeping her family together: James in particular might have the opportunity for more than a rudimentary, rural education. Nothing was of greater concern to Eliza. J. M. Bundy, one of the earliest biographers of James Garfield, observes, "The dynamic forces that were to take him out of the range of all previous Garfields lay coiled up in the fine, sensitive nature of his mother . . . a

Eliza Garfield
Courtesy of The Western Reserve Historical Society

woman of marked personality and . . . of courage and devotion. . . . Her son derived his intellectual attitudes from her." When the time came, it would take all her "courage and devotion," plus a degree of stealth, to induce James to accept these gifts.

Eliza's resourcefulness required little embellishment, but when her son's political career later began to take off, her legend escalated along with it. Understandably enough, even Eliza herself was caught up a bit in her own mythology as she aged. Her daughter-in-law Lucretia wrote in 1887 of the Garfields' lack of bitterness at their plight: "There was little complaining and the bright-spirited mother and merry-hearted children were a host against the demons of want. The day may be full of toil, but . . . the evening brought rest or reading, a visit to the cousins who lived just across the fields." It little diminishes Eliza's pivotal role in her imperiled family's recovery to give those cousins their due. The Boyntons clearly helped out to the limits of their resources.

If James owed his intellectual interests to his mother, he physically resembled his father, even as a child. The "red Irishman" at ten or twelve towered over other children, was immensely powerful, and had a great, unruly shock of brown hair. In skills and temperament, however, he was little like his father. James had no more love for farming than had Lincoln. Wielding an axe, he was a danger to himself or anyone else in the vicinity. It is a wonder he could hunt without hurting himself. Already a restless bundle of contradictions, he was clumsy yet hyperactive. He was "never still a moment at a time," his mother recalled, "always uneasy, very quick to learn, didn't like to work." James could be good-natured, fun-loving, and friendly one moment — then quickly turn moody and belligerent. Abram's temper had rarely been manifested at home. James could flare up at any time.

He cared little about his appearance, "overgrown, uncombed, unwashed," as his mother put it. Perhaps it was her own fault that he was growing up so wild and undisciplined. Unlike the other Garfield children, James had been indulged by his mother to the point where he later referred to his childhood as a sort of "chaos." As soon as his love for reading became apparent, his mother began bringing him every book she could find — history, the classics, adventure. An early indication of his restlessness was that he particularly loved stories of the sea. Clearly, James had potential. But how was it to be harnessed?

Fortunately, as the Western Reserve developed, Eliza was not alone in her love of learning. It was an inheritance shared with many other New England families who had emigrated. From the time he was three, James had been taken by his sisters to a district school a mile and a half away. In a matter of months he read so well he had been awarded a copy of the New Testament. When the township of Orange looked about to establish their own schoolhouse, the Widow Garfield was happy to oblige. However hard-pressed, she offered a corner of her own farm for the school's location.

While Tom, now quite definitely the man of the house, worked full-time on the farm, James and his sisters were able to attend school all winter in their own back yard. That was fine with Tom. He was no more interested in book-learning than his father had been. Eventually, after building his family a better frame home, confident they could manage, Tom went off to Michigan to make his own way. He would be a farmer all his life. Later Eliza's daughters would leave as well, for marriage and families of their own. Of course, Eliza had sought the school most of all for James, to whet his appetite for more formal education in the future.

All this was nearly sidetracked when James was ten. In a severe jolt to his emotional stability, his mother remarried. Her new husband, Alfred Belding, was ten years her junior. Their short-lived union is still shrouded in mystery and was hushed up during Garfield's political career. Perhaps Eliza sought financial stability to enhance her son's opportunities, but she had avoided matrimony earlier, when her situation was more desperate. All that is certain is that the marriage was brief, that Eliza caused the break, that Belding wanted her back (eventually being obliged to bring suit for divorce on grounds of desertion), and that James hated his stepfather. Even thirty years later, informed that Belding had died, Garfield could not reflect on him "without indignation." No one quite knows why.

Finally James and his mother were living alone, the glow of their hearth undiminished, their modest domain at least stabilized. Their region of Ohio had evolved from a wilderness to an abundant agricultural area with settled communities. Many of their neighbors enjoyed a prosperity in which even the thrifty Eliza Garfield was still unable to share. Despite his disdain for farming, James helped her diversify the property, raising corn and potatoes as well as wheat. He took on odd jobs, even farmed for neighbors, but his restlessness increased. All those books he had read of nautical adventure only fueled his wanderlust.

As an adult, although he never expressed less than unstinting admiration for his mother, Garfield had a rather ambivalent view of his childhood. He recalled carefree days at play "all around the little farm" of his "dear Old Home," but, as Peskin writes, "Not even the warmth of his mother's home could shield Garfield from the reality of his pinched circumstances." His campaign literature, like that of other presidential candidates, stressed that such adversity builds character, but Garfield was not so sure that was always the case. Even as the most favored of his mother's children, he had grown up aimless and uncertain, unacquainted with ease or security. True, it had eventually all worked out, but it had been a very close thing.

At sixteen, James announced to his incredulous mother that he, too, was leaving home to seek his fortune — if not on the seven seas, at least on a vessel plying the Great Lakes. She had the prescience not to protest excessively, taking what has come to be known as the long view. She had not forgotten her own youthful sense of adventure, however landlocked, setting out to start a new life with her husband. Rebuffed in his attempt on the Cleveland waterfront to be hired on a large vessel, James settled for a berth on a humble canal boat, following the route his father had helped construct. The next few months were the most harrowing of his life. He nearly drowned on at least three occasions. Yet, interestingly, at about the same time, in 1848, he started writing a personal journal, an act which implied that he would not follow this life on the water forever.

When he returned home from his first tour, intent on going back to the canal, his mother welcomed him without a word of reproach. James promptly fell terribly ill, probably of malaria. While his mother nursed his "haggard and forbidding" frame back to health, she prayed that he would never return to such an unsuitable vocation. She also adroitly offered at least a "short-term" alternative: why not consider going to school until he fully regained his strength? Even sailors could use some education. Eliza brought over a gifted young teacher named Samuel Bates. He taught advanced mathematics to students at Geauga Academy in nearby Chester. The two young men got on well. The mother watched, waited, and continued to pray.

Garfield later wrote, "My mother captured me. . . . She simply went about her duties quietly and permitted things to work themselves out." Of course, it wasn't quite that simple. She had known from the first that this special son was her "child of high destiny, born to be good and great." Channeling him from the canal to the classroom had to be done gradually. Eliza suggested that if James committed to only two semesters at Geauga, she would talk several of his friends into accompanying him there. She understood his apprehension at such an undertaking. This was no district school. Suppose he failed? Good as her word, Eliza sold the mothers of James's friends on Geauga, often over the objections of the boys' fathers.

Finally James agreed to go, at least until he felt stronger. Somehow, Eliza scraped together the necessary seventeen dollars for the first year's board and tuition. On the day her son departed, she was already certain her prayers had been answered. "Her plans for James were unfolding just as she had hoped," Booraem writes. As James progressed at Geauga, memories of his free life as a sailor receded, and his future spread out before him. He became very "industrious in his studies. . . . He was willing to work long hours just to get back" to school. He even labored as a custodian to earn the second year's tuition. Eventually embracing his mother's faith, Garfield began to see the hand of the Lord in his deliverance. He wrote his mother that "No greener boy ever started out in school," but by the age of eighteen he was already teaching others. He discovered he could speak forcefully in public, his favorite topic "The Era of Universal Peace." His journal began to reflect his mother's imagery as well as her hopes. "The ice is broken," he wrote, "I know without egotism that there is some . . . thunder in my soul, and it shall come out!"

The thunder led all the way to Williams College in Massachusetts, to heading a school in Ohio that became Hiram College, to becoming a lay preacher for the Disciples of Christ, to studying law, to the Ohio Senate, to a heroic career in the Civil War (where he would end up a major-general), to eighteen years in Congress, to nomination and election as president of the United States. It was only a little more than a decade after going off so reluctantly to Geauga that Garfield was leading troops into battle. His mother truly believed in "the era of universal peace," but she hated slavery more. Doris Faber writes that "By now James was married to a sweet and steadfast former teacher who might have been Eliza's own daughter, and together the two women trembled for him when he was away." They also prayed, and their prayers were answered.

In 1853 Eliza had finally sold the farm she had struggled so tenaciously to maintain. Her children returned for a last meal together at the old homestead, which their mother insisted on serving them personally. She probably also led them in a few songs. In later years, James was able to take her back to her childhood home in New Hampshire, gaining pleasure from her enjoyment at being "a girl once more."

After the Civil War, when her son went to Congress, Eliza accepted his invitation and that of his wife to live with them in Washington. Even as a young bride in her "golden times" and as a preoccupied young widow, Eliza freely shared her opinions of others. Only her piety curbed her tongue. Now, with little to occupy her time, she expressed herself without restraint. She was very fond of her son's wife, Lucretia, whom everyone called "Crete," and who treated her with the utmost deference. But Eliza could hardly approve of the Washington social scene, with its drinking and opulence, in which James and Lucretia played so prominent a part. Eliza's tart criticism of a life so foreign to her values and experience was bound to cause tensions. One of her granddaughters complained that their aged guest "nearly worried the life out of Papa and Momma."

To Leech and Brown, the irony of Eliza's relationship with James is that the very education she sought for him was bound, in time, to separate them. As his sophistication grew, although it was accompanied by his own deep religious convictions, he became "more indulgent than impressed by his mother's old time countrified ideas." Perhaps he still held her accountable for his undisciplined childhood, but James never doubted that it was also Eliza who enabled him to find his way. The emotional bond between them would always be strong, but it could not have been easy for Eliza to loosen her hold.

Although not the first presidential mother to experience the election of her son, she was the first to attend his inauguration. "From the tow path to the White House," the campaign literature had trumpeted, but it was really more from the schoolhouse to the White House. Nearing her eightieth year, Eliza was "proud and happy," but perhaps not all that surprised to see her son take the oath of office. As Peskin recounts, wearing the finery of "black silk, under her demure bonnet, her bright eyes . . . taking in everything," Eliza was a striking figure at the ceremonies. If, as Peskin adds, James Garfield "would be more remembered for what he was than for what he did," that only enhances the role his mother played in his life.

Only a few months later Garfield was shot by a deranged office-seeker. Unlike Lincoln, he lingered for another eighty days. At first the news was kept from his mother, but eventually she had to be told. She returned to Ohio and, probably on the advice of her son's doctors, stayed there as James's life ebbed away. His last view was of the Atlantic Ocean, from his retreat on the New Jersey shore. One of his last letters was to his mother, assuring her that he was on the way to recovery. When Garfield finally died, the nation's outpouring of grief rivaled that accorded to Lincoln.

Eliza's physical and emotional strength as a slight young widow had astonished her neighbors and sustained her children. Now even tinier, and enfeebled by age, her only desire was to join her youngest child. Instead, she was obliged to endure over six more years of sorrow. Her final prayer was finally answered in 1888, at the age of eighty-six. Like James Madison, she had "outlived" herself, but the last thoughts of Eliza Ballou Garfield were more likely those of Sarah Lincoln: "He was the best boy I ever saw." Eliza and James Garfield lie at rest side by side.

IT IS too bad that Malvina Stone Arthur did not, like Eliza Garfield, write a "brief sketch" of her life. It would have edified not only her children but also the public in general. In 1881, as her son, Vice President Chester A. Arthur, anxiously awaited news of Garfield's condition, there were still rumors that Arthur had been born in Canada, which would make him ineligible to ascend to the presidency.

These rumors were not true, or at least we don't think they were, but the limited light they shed on the story of Arthur's mother makes one regret that so little is known about her. Malvina Stone's English forebears settled in northern New Hampshire in the mid-1700s and moved throughout New England. Her grandfather, a veteran of the French and Indian War, lived an eventful life. He ran a ferry over the Connecticut River, developed a prosperous farm, and sired twelve children. His seventh son, George Washington Stone, the father of

Malvina, was ordained a Methodist minister. The family, writes biographer George Frederick Howe, were typical "frontier Yankees, frugal, god-fearing, and industrious." Her Uncle John, known as "Elder John," frequently preached at Baptist meetings and was greatly admired by Malvina. Despite such patriotic foundations and his own name, for some reason the Reverend George Washington Stone decided to move his family north, over the border, and settled in Dunham, Quebec. He lived there the rest of his life. Accordingly, his daughter enjoyed the heritage of two countries, although her own birth in Vermont is a matter of record.

Her husband-to-be, William Arthur, just as definitely was born in Ulster and is reputed to have been a graduate of the University of Belfast. An Anglican, he emigrated to Canada, became a teacher in Quebec, and in 1821 met and married Malvina Stone. Torn between teaching and the law, he moved south to Burlington, Vermont, in search of greater opportunities. Instead, at a Baptist revival, he was called, like Malvina's Uncle John, to preach the gospel. His eloquent sermons brought more converts than comfort, but as Pastor Arthur moved about in search of both, he managed to stay south of the border. He and Malvina had four girls, but finally, on October 5, 1830, she gave birth to Chester Alan Arthur. Reportedly, the boy's father was so carried away that he literally danced for joy — and named his son for the doctor who had delivered him, a cousin of Malvina's.

Where did that birth take place? Probably in Vermont, in North Fairfield or Waterville. Unfortunately, many of Chester Arthur's private papers were destroyed in a fire. As his political star ascended, some of his opponents found his Canadian connections too tempting to ignore. At least Andrew Johnson's enemies had limited themselves to accusations of illegitimacy; the most scurrilous rumor about the birth of Chester A. Arthur was that the first child of that name had died in infancy and his mother transferred the name to a second son, delivered while she was visiting her parents in Canada.

Finally a thorough investigative reporter for the *New York Sun* put all these rumors to rest, at least to the satisfaction of the United States government. But even the reporter's findings were based more on personal testimony than on actual records. When Garfield expired, Arthur was duly sworn in as president. Although previously something of a stalwart machine politician, he proved a creditable chief executive. Perhaps this was the result of his upbringing for, as William Judson Hampton writes, "In youth, there had been the training and influence of the Christian home; the start in life with no other endowment than health, character, courage, and honorable ambition." Indeed, Arthur's heritage encompassed three Protestant denominations.

William and Malvina would go on to have a total of nine children, but a later son died at two and a daughter at eighteen. Financial problems dogged the devout couple during their life together, and they denied themselves even some of the necessities of life to see Chester through Union College and launched on his career. What makes Malvina so appealing is the fortitude she demonstrated throughout all this trauma and her abiding faith — so much in the tradition of other presidential mothers. Chester and his brother William had both become rather skeptical of "literal Christianity," in the fashion of the times. Late in her life, Malvina appealed to William, in a letter meant for both her surviving sons, "Oh that God would answer my prayer, that before I am taken from life, you and Chester may come out publicly [and] confess Christ. . . . I know He will lead you to everlasting life and glory, if you are willing."

Alas, Chester was not quite willing. Yet before she died in 1869, at the age of sixty-seven, Malvina Stone Arthur at least had the satisfaction of knowing that, even if her prominent son could not fully affirm her faith, he had long accepted her values. As Howe testifies, habits of generosity and kindness "were included in his boyhood" and guided him throughout his life. His support of his parents helped ease their final years. Malvina Arthur's life may well have been as compelling as Eliza Garfield's, if only we knew more about it.

CHAPTER NINE

Family Values in the Nineteenth Century

ﹸ Ann Cleveland
ﹸ Elizabeth Harrison
ﹸ Nancy McKinley

AFTER HE WAS elected governor of New York, Grover Cleveland reflected in a letter to his brother, "Do you know that if Mother were alive, I should feel much safer. I had always thought her prayers had much to do with my success." The Bible on which Cleveland later took his oath of office as president had been a childhood gift from his "loving Mother." He kept it in the drawer of his massive desk, a gift from Queen Victoria, and extracted it again when he was sworn in a second time, the only president to serve two nonconsecutive terms. On that occasion, he inserted a bookmark at verse twelve of the ninety-first psalm, "They shall bear thee up in their hand. . . ."

To be borne up by the prayers of Ann Neal would have seemed most unlikely to those who knew her as a Baltimore belle. Her preoccupation was not with piety but possessions. Born in 1806 to a prosperous publisher of law books and his prominent wife, Ann loved luxury almost to the point of ostentation. Her collection of jewelry and her stylish wardrobe were the talk of her circle of friends. Lively and fun-loving, Ann might have enjoyed the attentions of a border-state Ashley Wilkes or even a Rhett Butler. What could she possibly see in that visiting Yankee divinity student, spare, serious, somber Richard Falley Cleveland?

True, the Cleavelands of New England were a family of weight, having produced prominent clergymen and intellectuals. Richard's grandfather had dropped the extra "a" from the family name in 1770. There

133

was nothing extraneous in Richard Cleveland's austere heritage. He had graduated with high honors from Yale and was attending Princeton Theological Seminary when he met Ann Neal. After completing his studies in 1828 he accepted, under the plan of union effected between Presbyterians and Congregationalists, a pastorate to the First Congregational Church in Windam, Connecticut. Surely he had the makings of a distinguished divine.

Perhaps it was his very difference that attracted Ann, how he contrasted with the callow young gallants of her acquaintance. What would it be like to join with someone so solid and motivated, elevated above those who wed for wealth and position? Whatever had stirred her affections, to the probable incredulity of her family and friends, Ann Neal became Mrs. Richard Cleveland in 1829. With her black personal maid and an abundance of trunks, she set off with her husband by coach and canal to New England. She was twenty-three.

That Richard did not prepare his wife for the inevitable reaction of the good women of Windam may have been due to his own blissful state at the time. His new parishioners were appalled to have a slave in their midst, particularly as the servant of their new parson's wife. They were equally aghast at the costly embellishments of Mrs. Cleveland's person. She seemed a pleasant enough young woman, but had she no knowledge of the scriptural admonitions against vanity and display? Quickly the maid was dispatched back to Maryland. Perhaps through necessity, perhaps through honest reflection — probably a bit of both — Ann Neal Cleveland determined to become more Puritan than the Puritans.

If it was not quite the instantaneous conversion of Paul on the road to Damascus, there is no doubt that in time Ann's faith became as sincere as it was firm. It gave her the strength to bolster her family through one disappointment after another. She had not only to endure the ceaseless toil of a country minister's wife, but also poverty beyond anything she could have imagined. Much as he tried, Richard never remotely fulfilled his potential. His calling was authentic enough, but he was more an ecclesiastical scholar than a forceful preacher. He would achieve no heightened recognition or responsibilities, have no collections of his sermons published. His family moved from one town to another with no improvement in status. The Clevelands went from Connecticut to Portsmouth, Virginia, to the Presbyterian pulpit of Caldwell, New Jersey, to a series of towns in New York State. Meanwhile, Ann was having babies, nine in all. Their fifth child and third boy, born in the manse in Caldwell in March 1837, they named Stephen Grover Cleveland in honor of his father's predecessor in the Caldwell pulpit, the Reverend Stephen Grover. This does not appear to have ingratiated Richard with his congregation, for soon the Clevelands were off again. When Grover came of age, he discarded his first name.

So often parents of presidents have favored their first sons. In this instance, from the very beginning, Ann Cleveland sensed there was something special about her third son. It can only be ascribed to a mother's instinct. As he grew — and he would always be large for his age — Ann saw her hopes justified. She loved all her children, but Grover indeed turned out to be the brightest, the most promising. Inevitably, he became her new focus, replacing his father not in affection but in expectations. Discipline was firm but loving in the Cleveland household, and it was administered by both parents. Time was viewed as a precious commodity, sinful to waste. Richard Cleveland admonished, "If we expect to become great or good . . . we must improve our time when we are young." Bible study at home was supplemented by local schools, but there was simply no money for higher education. This was particularly frustrating for Grover. In the 1840s the family lived in the central New York towns of Fayetteville and Clinton, with venerable Hamilton College close at hand. Years later, Cleveland recalled his mother's disappointment that he could not attend, but also her pervasive cheerfulness through it all. Ironically, Cleveland would eventually become chairman of Princeton's board of trustees, but even his cherished Sigma Chi badge was honorary.

What finally terminated any remote possibility of his going to college was the death of Richard Cleveland when Grover was only sixteen. His father was simply worn out, dead at the age of forty-nine. Through their grief, the bond between mother and son became even stronger. For the remaining thirty-seven years of her life, Ann Cleveland would rely on Grover for economic support, and he would rely on her for moral certitude. What Cleveland later said about his father applied equally to his mother: "Looking over my life nothing seems to me to have in it more both of pathos and interest than the spectacle of my father, a hard-working country clergyman, bringing up acceptably a family of nine children, educating each member so that, in after life, none suffered any deprivation in this respect."

The year his father died, Grover moved to New York City, where he taught at a school for the blind. From there he went to Buffalo, worked on an uncle's farm, became an apprentice clerk at a law firm, and by 1859 was chief clerk. Always he sent money home. Cleveland's hiring of a substitute during the Civil War, much criticized by his later political opponents, was motivated not by cowardice but by the necessity of financially assisting his mother and his unmarried sisters. As biographer Paul Jeffers points out, even as Cleveland's career in politics and law took off, he never ceased to rely on his mother's advice. In 1872, as sheriff of Buffalo, he asked her if it were morally justifiable to pay someone else to hang a man who had stabbed his own brother to death. She said yes, but in a rare instance of declining to accept her counsel, Cleveland decided he was officially obliged to spring the trap himself.

It is ironic that as scrupulously honest a man as Cleveland is so vividly remembered for an indiscretion. He did not marry until after his mother's death. That it was to his late law partner's lovely twenty-one-year-old daughter, Frances Folsom, nearly forty years his junior, created quite a stir. However, it paled by comparison with Cleveland's prior admission that, as a bachelor, he had fathered an illegitimate child. Although the young woman in question had other admirers, making Cleveland's paternity less than certain, he stepped forward openly to support both mother and child. Cleveland gave his campaign workers the eternally refreshing direction to simply "tell the truth." His admission did not deny him the presidency. The incident is captured in perpetuity, however, by a famous cartoon and bit of doggerel: "Ma! Ma! Where's my Pa? Gone to the White House, Ha! Ha! Ha!"

His mother did not live to either endure this scandal or enjoy her son's elevation to so exalted an office. When Ann Neal Cleveland died in Holland Patent, New York, in her seventy-sixth year, Grover had just been elected mayor of Buffalo. His mother was by then living in such obscurity that, according to historian Richard Welch, some of Cleveland's supporters insisted that she had been a poor Irish immigrant. Grover and her other surviving children stayed by her bedside until she was gone. This frivolous Southern belle, born to privilege, had metamorphosed into their revered figure of probity, the foundation of their own faith. "Her children arise and call her blessed," a grieving Grover Cleveland suggested for her memorial stone. From the day of her death to his own, Cleveland lamented "the desolation of a life without a mother's prayers."

IF Elizabeth Findley Irwin Harrison had only had more time. She was very much in the tradition of devoutly religious presidential mothers. When he made his own profession of faith in the Presbyterian Church while a student at Miami University of Ohio, Benjamin Harrison recalled his mother's habit of closing each evening with silent prayer. Her concerns became more vocal when her sons went off to school. In one letter to Benjamin and his older brother Archibald their mother wrote, "I pray for you daily that you may be kept from sinning and straying from the paths of duty. . . . I hope you will be prudent in your Diet . . . and abstain from cucumbers." It's sad so little of such colorful correspondence survives. Obviously Elizabeth Harrison had a wide range of interests. Unfortunately, she died at the age of forty, giving birth to her tenth child. Six of her children survived, and one, Benjamin, became president — some thirty-eight years after the death of his mother.

Of Scottish ancestry, Elizabeth Irwin was born in the lovely town of Mercersburg, Pennsylvania, home also of the Buchanan family. Her grandfather had established a prosperous flour mill. In the customary pattern after the War of 1812, her father, Captain Archibald Irwin, moved his family to Ohio. Here Elizabeth met and at the age of twenty-one married serious-minded lawyer John Scott Harrison. A widower, Harrison already had two or three children — accounts vary. His young wife would give him many more. It is a wonder she had any time for correspondence.

Although without the continuity of the Adamses, the Harrison family played a prominent role in American history. An earlier Benjamin Harrison signed the Declaration of Independence. Elizabeth's husband, who harbored no political ambitions, had the unique distinction of be-

Elizabeth Irwin Harrison
Courtesy of The President Benjamin Harrison Home

ing both the son and father of presidents of the United States. Both had unusual tenures. Doughty William Henry Harrison, his father, died only a month into his term. Young Benjamin Harrison, his son, served between the terms of Grover Cleveland, beating him in 1888, losing to him in 1892, and enjoying another decade of productive life. Accordingly, the clan could claim "Old Tippecanoe" and Benjamin, too.

Elizabeth Irwin Harrison died on August 15, 1850, when her son Benjamin was not yet seventeen. Harrison's sister decried his reputation, developed when he commanded troops in the Civil War, of having a rather "cold nature." His critics "did not know him," she insisted. "He told me once he felt the light in our home had gone out in our dear Mother's death." He proved as prudent a president and pious a churchman as she might have wished. Her light, though short-lived, had cast its reflection.

IN WILLIAM MCKINLEY'S celebrated and successful "front porch" campaign of 1896, his mother made a notable contribution simply by showing up. As her son greeted the multitudes who came to his home in Canton, Ohio, she rocked benignly on his front porch. In her venerable person, Nancy Campbell Allison McKinley exemplified her son's small-town, midwestern values. McKinley's wife was often ailing. His mother provided an appealing substitute. The nation was in transition, hoping to retain the verities she represented while becoming a world power and widening a middle class almost everyone sought to enter.

"Mother McKinley," as she came to be known, remained endearingly unpretentious throughout her eighty-eight years. When William was governor of Ohio and she traveled by train to see him, a fellow passenger asked if she had relatives in Columbus. "Yes, I have a son there," was all she replied. When William was inaugurated as president, the roses his ever-frugal mother had assembled for her bouquet came from another train's dining car.

Biographer H. Wayne Morgan notes that "on both sides of President McKinley's family there were ironworkers and tinkers." The McKinleys retained the independent and taciturn nature of their Scotch heritage. They had been fierce highland warriors. In America they not only fought for the Revolution, but cast bullets and cannon, a task even more crucial to its success than leveling a musket. Nancy Allison's English ancestors were Puritans who initially fled to Holland and then accompanied William Penn to Pennsylvania. Some were Quakers, but Nancy's branch of the family became staunch Methodists. The Allisons were inclined more to farming, the McKinleys more to tinkering, but the men of both families were obliged to undertake multiple tasks, whether forging iron and working wood or plowing fields and tending livestock. Their wives worked at least as hard, rearing large families and dealing with the heartbreak of inevitable loss, but providing for the welfare of all.

William McKinley may not have emerged from a log cabin, but his mother surely did. Her humble abode was just over the Ohio border from Pennsylvania, where she was born in 1809, the same year as Abraham Lincoln. Like the Allisons, the McKinleys had come to Ohio to seek greater opportunity. From the age of sixteen, the man who would come to be known as William McKinley Sr. worked the blast furnaces of his father's foundry, producing pig iron. Three books were always at his side — the Bible, the works of Shakespeare, and Dante. He met Nancy Allison in grammar school. Her eagerness to learn matched his own, but neither received very much in the way of formal education. Of William Sr., Morgan writes, "This man who was to father a president was not extraordinary except in the force of his character." Character, however, meant a great deal to Nancy Allison.

In 1829 she wed this strong, silent, kindly, and industrious young man, in a ceremony in which they symbolically pledged their troth by sharing a gourdful of water from an icy stream. Their life together would be harmonious but demanding. They settled in the small Ohio town of Niles, surrounded by hills containing deposits of coal and iron ore. Despite such promising possibilities and his energetic efforts, McKinley never quite found the success he sought. His family's fortunes ranged from just above to just below adequate, and he was constantly on the road seeking business for his foundry. That left his wife not only in charge of the household but also frequently alone in enforcing its discipline.

She would have nine children in all, the same number as her mother. There were four boys and five girls. Yet it was the seventh child, not the first male, who was named for his father. William McKinley Jr. was born on January 29, 1843, in a long, low, clapboard house that was attached to a general store. In later years, his mother insisted there was no special significance in waiting so long to name another William, and that she never doted on him. "I had six (other) children, and I had my own work to do. . . . I could not devote all my time to him." She did not raise him to be a president, she said; "I tried to bring up the boy to be a good man." Yet she early recognized special qualities in young William. He was as quiet as his father, "but he began to take notice of things when very young."

Nancy McKinley's family and faith were central to her life, to an extent unusual even for her time and place. She took the admonition that cleanliness is next to godliness with absolute literality. Not only was her home immaculate, she and her sister cleaned, swept, and tended the Niles Methodist Church as the second home it was to them. They kept the church going, and Nancy McKinley all but ran the town as well. Yet no one seems to have resented it. Not quite so quiet as her husband, she shouldered responsibilities so equitably and unobtrusively that she became a sort of one-woman self-help agency, tying the small town together. As Morgan relates, "She tended sick friends, helped with welfare cases, bore her share of community problems, and acted as peacemaker. . . . She boarded visiting ministers and teachers." She would have made a wonderful minister herself, had it been possible. Instead, she at least began to hope that her son William would one day be not only a minister but a bishop of the Methodist Episcopal Church. At the age of ten, young William made his personal commitment to Christ at the Niles church. He and his siblings had been enrolled in its Sunday school before they attended regular school.

Nancy McKinley's responsibilities to her church and her neighbors caused no neglect of her home or family. And there is no indication that she ever complained of her lot or expressed disappointment at her husband's inability to provide consistent financial security. She loved him no less. Even in affluence, she would have been just as thrifty, thorough, hardworking, and strong-willed. As biographer Eva Higgins points out, Mother McKinley's discipline was firm, evenhanded, and sometimes even harsh, but applied with an affection so evident that it did not need to be expressed by excessive hugging and kissing. There was no card playing, drinking, dancing, or very much levity in the McKinley household, but this did not prevent young William from enjoying a normal, happy childhood he would always recall fondly. He played games of all kinds and required no duress to attend either church or school. He looked forward to both. As his mother said, "He was just like other boys, except that he was of a more serious turn of mind." As he grew, William began more to resemble his mother, with dark hair and a piercing gaze.

Both parents had retained their preoccupation with education. In

1852 they moved to the larger town of Poland, Ohio, solely so that their children could attend a superior private academy, Union Seminary. It had been founded by New England Presbyterians, but was now administered by Methodists. As a result, William McKinley Sr., whose business kept him in Niles, ten miles away, for years could only see his family on weekends. His children's upbringing would now be even more in the hands of their mother. The inconvenience of this arrangement was balanced by living in a much more attractive house and by the superiority of the new school's instruction. Young William, who studied as hard as any mother might have wished, particularly prospered in this new environment. Debating became his passion, and opposition to slavery his fervent cause. The larger Methodist church in Poland supplemented his school at the center of William's life. He not only attended Sunday school but eventually taught it, and he reaffirmed his commitment to the church at the age of fourteen. Even clear-eyed Mother McKinley must have viewed the future with promise.

The financial panic of 1857 impelled more belt-tightening. The McKinley children worked any jobs that were available to help pay for tuition at the seminary. After his graduation in 1859 William enrolled in Allegheny College in Meadville, Pennsylvania, but ill health and financial problems forced him to leave after a year. Back in Poland, William taught school for a time and worked at the post office, but a more serious crisis was coming. With the advent of the Civil War in 1861, he joined up as a private in the Twenty-Third Ohio Volunteers. At the end of the war, he was a twenty-two-year-old major, and had been decorated for bravery.

Encouraged by another future president with whom he had served, Rutherford B. Hayes, McKinley turned to the study of law. When, little more than a decade later, Hayes was elected president, McKinley went to Washington with him, having won a seat in Congress. His mother must have felt understandable ambivalence. Throughout her long life, her demeanor changed remarkably little. More than anyone else, she had inspired her son to high achievement, but had he become no more than a dedicated country parson she would have felt satisfaction. Perhaps to pray for so much more had been too worldly. Yet McKinley's

Nancy McKinley
Courtesy of The Ohio Historical Society

chosen profession suited him. His father lived to see him serve as governor of Ohio; his mother lived to see him become president.

On the very evening of McKinley's election, excited supporters
found him and his wife kneeling beside his aged mother while she
prayed, "Oh, God, keep him humble." At the inauguration, another son
suggested to Nancy McKinley, "Mother, this is better than a bishopric."

There is no record of a response. As Morgan relates, she was now virtually the nation's mother, admired for her virtue and her common sense. "But the photographers, the smiling crowds to whom she waved, never turned her head. The spectacle and pageantry of power meant little to her. William was her dearest, but she cherished another dream for him that died hard." Asked if she were not proud of her son, when he was nominated for the presidency, she had replied, "No, I am thankful to the Great Giver that he has bestowed upon me such a blessing." Except for his new habit of smoking cigars, she could find little fault with her seventh child.

McKinley had not chosen the ministry, but his strong religious convictions lasted to the end of his life. As he told a committee of clergymen who visited the White House in 1899, "I am a Methodist, and nothing but a Methodist — a Christian, and nothing but a Christian . . . by the blessings of Heaven I mean to live and die, please God, in the faith of my mother." Each Sunday for many years he had taken her to church. Even as governor, he would return from Columbus to the home they had made in Canton to escort his mother on the Sabbath. In the summer of his first year as president, McKinley came back to Canton to see his now very frail mother, taking her to Sunday services one final time. Nancy Campbell Allison McKinley died on December 12, 1897. It was the only time the president's associates ever saw him break down in tears. By some exertion he had arrived in time to sit by her bedside before the end. He would die four years later at an assassin's hand.

Unlike Garfield's mother and Lincoln's stepmother, Nancy McKinley was spared the burden of outliving her son. But her comments reflecting on his election as president are very reminiscent of those of Sarah Lincoln. Mother McKinley said, "William has always been a good boy. He never gave me a cross word, and I do not believe he ever told me a lie. I am glad that he is president for his sake." To his own pastor, McKinley frequently reflected on the sheer goodness of his mother. In words reminiscent of Lincoln, he observed, "All that I am I owe to my mother."

CHAPTER TEN

"I Do Not Believe We Can Love Our Children Too Much"

❦ Martha Roosevelt
❦ Louisa Taft
❦ Jessie Wilson

THE MOTHER of Theodore Roosevelt was among the most devoted of all presidential mothers, irrespective of economic circumstances. More given to affection than to advice, Martha Bulloch Roosevelt lavished unconditional love on all four of her children in a fashion so public it would have offended many another society matron's sense of propriety. Martha called her family's hugging sessions "melts." Her second child and first son, Theodore — called "Teedie" by his parents — reveled in these displays of endearment. Unlike so many others who became president, young Theodore sought escape only from the limitations of his frail body. All his life he attempted to duplicate — if not exceed — every facet of his golden childhood. It represented more than the advantages of affluence. Teedie's letters from Harvard, his first extended separation from his parents, are extravagantly appreciative. To his "Darling, beloved little Motherling" he wrote that he "hardly knew a boy who is on as intimate . . . terms with his family as I am." To his father, also named Theodore, he wrote, "I do not think there is a fellow in College who has a family who love him as much as you all do me, and I am *sure* that there is no one who has a Father who is also his best . . . friend, as you are mine."

All this affection originated in Roswell, Georgia, in 1850. On his first trip south, nineteen-year-old Theodore Roosevelt Sr. came down from New York City to join a wedding party. The bride's fifteen-year-old half-sister was Martha Bulloch, called "Missy" throughout the region and "Mittie" by her friends. One inheritance that would be denied the younger Theodore Roosevelt was his parents' extraordinary good looks. Biographers describe Theodore Roosevelt Sr. as a strikingly handsome man. Doris Faber describes diminutive young Mittie Bulloch as altogether exquisite and bewitching. "She had the sort of silky black hair that takes a russet tinge under the glow of candles . . . her skin was the purest white . . . with a coral rather than a rose tint in her cheeks." Although often afflicted by ailments, Mittie embodied the less languid variety of Southern belle. In the same day she might read poetry under the wisteria but then tear about the expansive acreage of her father's estate on her favorite mount as recklessly as Mad Anthony Wayne. If, in later years, at least one diplomat would remark that her son Theodore had never really grown up, perhaps his beloved mother hadn't, either. She remained the quintessential Southern belle all her life, but she transcended self-indulgence in her devotion to the man she married and the children she raised.

The elder Theodore Roosevelt was understandably smitten on their first encounter, but so was Martha Bulloch. They were secretly engaged before his departure from Georgia. So quickly kindled, their affection never waned, an example of constancy that also would inspire their children. It took over two years, however, for their vows to be consummated. Mittie may have been more sprightly and Theodore more serious, but their letters during this period reveal a mutual passion and tenderness reminiscent of those of Abigail and John Adams. To her darling "Thee," Mittie wrote, "I only live in your being." Theirs was not a union so surprising as that of lively Ann Neal and dour divinity student Richard Cleveland, but the transition from Southern plantation to Northern brownstone could not be measured only in miles. Mittie understood that New York represented as much a new world as a different state.

There was nothing very dashing about the Dutch-derived Roosevelts, but they were a family of substance, prominent in the life of New York since it had been New Amsterdam. By 1850 Theodore Sr.'s father, Cornelius Van Schaack Roosevelt, was already a millionaire, having transformed the family firm from retailing to importing and real estate

Martha Roosevelt
Courtesy of the Theodore Roosevelt Collection, Harvard Library

investments. Eventually, it would become a private bank. The Bullochs, on the other hand, were a colorful clan, with Scottish roots. A Bulloch had served in the Continental Congress. A Bulloch had been governor of Georgia. And Bullochs, unlike the Roosevelts, had fought in both the Revolution and the War of 1812. Mittie's father, Major James Stephens Bulloch, although he died of a stroke while teaching Sunday school, had rather a rakish reputation. It was her much-loved mother, also named Martha, who had to approve her wedding to Theodore Roosevelt, which took place at the end of 1853.

Although she brought light and laughter to its gloomy corridors, eighteen-year-old Mittie had never undertaken such a responsibility as maintaining the great Roosevelt mansion in New York. Her new army of retainers was looking for direction, not merely to do her bidding. Soon, however, she was pregnant. Mittie's first child, named Anna after her favorite sister and nicknamed "Bamie" after the Italian "bambina," was a joy to both her parents, but also a challenge. The curvature of the baby's spine threatened to make her a cripple. She was laboriously nursed and exercised to eventual health through the patient efforts of both parents, even more than the care of physicians. This experience not only strengthened the ties between Mittie and Thee, it prepared them for even greater challenges to come. Moreover, it must have reassured her husband, were reassurance necessary, that Martha Bulloch Roosevelt could match his own resolve. This lovely, seemingly fragile creature had surprising strength.

In 1856 Mittie's mother sold the plantation, and with her daughter Anna moved to the Roosevelt mansion in New York. Another daughter lived nearby, in Philadelphia. With Thee often immersed in business, Mittie was bolstered by the presence of her kin and was better able to manage the household. Her mother was by her side when she endured the very difficult birth of her second child on October 27, 1858. It was a boy, whom they named Theodore after his father. Mittie thought him the homeliest baby she had ever seen, but loved him all the more. Theodore Roosevelt was the first American president to be born in a great city. (The Raleigh of Andrew Johnson's day did not yet qualify as a metropolis.) The Roosevelts would have two other children, a son named Elliott in 1860 and a daughter named Corinne in the momentous year of 1861.

Even the War Between the States failed to sever the ties that bound Mittie and Thee. Most of the heroism, not surprisingly, came from the Confederate Bulloch side of the family. One of few Roosevelt relatives to serve in the Union Army was Teedie's uncharacteristically colorful Uncle Robert Barnwell. A lawyer, politician, adventurer, and pioneering conservationist, he was also a scandalous philanderer. Most of his family cut him off, but he fascinated young Theodore, who would eventually read law in his office. For Thee, who firmly believed in the Union, the hostilities forced an agonizing decision. Ultimately, he could not bring himself to bear arms against his wife's family, and he hired a substitute. The Roosevelts were away during the bloody New York draft riots of 1863, but Mittie commented with incisive bias, "I do not wonder that the poor mechanics oppose conscription. . . . It certainly favors the rich at the expense of the poor." The Bulloch women were all but a secessionist cell on Twentieth Street, smuggling provisions south when Thee was away. Fortunately, he was home when they hung a Confederate flag from one of the windows to compete with Unionist bunting around the façade. Reportedly, he had to prevent a mob from storming the building.

Although he did not serve in the military, Thee risked his life repeatedly, traveling from battlefield to battlefield as the uncompensated head of the Allotment Commission he founded, enabling Union soldiers to set aside a portion of their pay for their families. It personified a second career of selfless service that made him seem even more admirable to his eldest son. His father's failure to fight, however, was probably the one lapse from perfection that Teedie would have difficulty justifying, although there is no record that he ever referred to it. His mother's brothers were among the foremost naval heroes of the Confederacy. Young Theodore's Uncle James Dunwoody Bulloch was the admiral who commissioned the lethally effective commerce raiders *Alabama* and *Florida*. His uncle Irwin Bulloch, a midshipman, fired the last shots from the *Alabama* and later served on the *Shenandoah*. Their service to the Confederacy was so conspicuous and costly to the Union that they were excluded from the general amnesty after the war. They settled permanently in Liverpool, England, and prospered as cotton merchants.

During one of several trips to Europe that helped round out his pre-Harvard education, eleven-year-old Theodore was "awestruck" when he met these legendary uncles. After he had found his initial fame as an author, Roosevelt induced his "Uncle Jimmy" to write his own memoirs. The old admiral's headstone would read, "American by birth, Englishman by choice." The influence of the martial heritage of his mother's family led to some conflicted values in Roosevelt's later life. He was a peacemaker who glorified war. As biographer Edward Renehan writes, Roosevelt developed a "Kiplingesque view of the battlefield as a place of honor, fulfillment, and robust democracy." There is a good deal of Darwin, as well, in his love of both conservation and hunting. Committed to a strenuous life "in the arena," Roosevelt was also the most prolific author who ever served in the presidency. None of our great presidents were simple men.

Perhaps the overwhelming nature of his parents' love, undiluted by excessive criticism, helps to account for Roosevelt's headstrong confidence in his own judgment as an adult, transcending so many seeming contradictions. His father's earnest admonitions tended to be of the uncomplicated onward-and-upward variety, more of action than reflection: "Seize the moment." "Get action." "Whatever you do, enjoy it." In later years Roosevelt wrote so glowingly of his father, the "ideal man," that his mother's complementary contributions are too easily overlooked. Her first task was simply to see that he survived. At the age of three, Teedie's asthma was already quite serious, and he was developing other debilitating ailments as well. Yet, despite his spindly legs, he didn't lack for energy. He simply couldn't sustain it. He learned to read early, impressed his tutors, and developed a lifelong love of the natural world.

When he was twelve, his father concluded, "You have the mind but you have not the body, and without the help of the body the mind cannot go as far as it should. You must *make* your body." From the age of thirteen, Roosevelt embarked on a rigorous physical regimen, starting with workouts in a private gym in his home, that rendered his energetic life possible. He was "self-made" in a more literal sense than less privileged presidents. He came to portray his father in almost mythic terms, and their midnight rides in an open carriage through the brisk wintry air were among Teedie's earliest memories. "I could breathe, I could sleep, when he had me in his arms. My father — he got me breath, he got me lungs, strength, life." However, as Faber stresses, it was also his mother who tirelessly comforted him. "Night after night, she sat up with him, cradling his dear funny old man's face in her lap while she soothed his asthmatic gasping with comic stories" from her Southern childhood.

It is hard to deny Roosevelt's conviction that his parents were an ideal couple, complementing each other. If Mittie had married someone other than Thee, her frivolous proclivities might well have become pervasive. Married to someone else, Thee might have become only an earnest prig. But the mother, too, could be serious; the father, too, could be fun-loving. They were, in fact, better together. When Teedie was sixteen, his parents rented a spacious house in Oyster Bay on Long Island's north shore. "There could be no healthier and pleasanter place to bring up children," Roosevelt recalled. After Teedie had become Teddy, he chose the location to build his rambling Sagamore Hill home and raise his own rambunctious family in the tradition of his parents.

Both his mother and his father were religious. Mittie prayed every night. A devout member of the Dutch Reformed Church, Thee started each day with family prayers, gathering his children around him. The coveted place was in the "cubbyhole" between their father and the sofa's arm. The elder Roosevelt's deep faith motivated his increasing interest in philanthropy, which ultimately supplanted business as his real vocation. He set an example some other millionaires came to emulate. Already one of New York's most respected citizens at the age of twenty-seven, when his namesake was born, Theodore Roosevelt Sr. resisted efforts to draft him as a reform candidate for public office. He believed in good government, but partisan politics were not his calling. He not only helped to found and fund major museums and hospitals, he financed such organizations as the Children's Aid Society and the Newsboys' Lodging House. Social workers found in him an influential ally. John Hay referred to his almost "maniacal benevolence." Roosevelt gave more than money. He spent every Sunday evening with the homeless boys he had all but adopted, and helped to shape their lives.

Young Theodore's ecumenism was patterned on his parents'. Although he was also born into the Dutch Reformed Church and had committed himself to the faith with his family pastor before leaving for Harvard, in Cambridge he taught Sunday school in both Episcopal and Congregational churches. As a youth, he composed nine reasons for regular church attendance. The ninth: "I advocate a boy's joining in Church work for the sake of showing his faith by his work." As president, Roosevelt frequently lauded the ministry "as the highest calling in the world." While he was capable in the First World War of interpreting Micah's admonition to "do justice" so that it justified fighting against the wicked Central Powers, "to love mercy and walk humbly with thy God" were deemed equally important.

In 1877, when Roosevelt was in his sophomore year at Harvard, his father died of stomach cancer. He was only forty-six. Renehan writes of the crowds that stood respectfully outside his home as his life ebbed away, and the more than two thousand who crowded into Fifth Avenue Presbyterian Church for the memorial service. Presumably there was no Dutch Reformed Church of sufficient size to accommodate them. Kerr describes young Theodore as "completely undone." He would heed his father's call to service and pass it on to his own children, even if in more martial tones. Mittie took the terrible loss well, at least publicly, feeling her task must be to cheer up others. She would not quite regain the buoyancy of her youth, but her example inspired her children. Young Theodore stayed at Harvard, graduated Phi Beta Kappa in 1880, abandoned natural science for politics, and married a lovely young lady named Alice Lee, who reminded him of his mother. "You must not feel melancholy, sweet Motherling," he wrote her, "I shall only love you all the more." She had no doubt of that, nor of her son's bright future.

Four years later, with Theodore already in the New York State Assembly, his wife gave birth to a girl they also named Alice. In less than forty-eight hours, at the age of only twenty-two, Alice Lee Roosevelt was dead. Her Bright's disease had not been diagnosed. On the same day, in the same house, viewed as "cursed" by Teddy's brother, Martha Bulloch Roosevelt died of typhoid fever. It was six years since her husband had passed away. Neither lived to the age of fifty. Theodore Roosevelt Jr. had lost both his wife and his parents by the time he was twenty-five. He would marry again, have six children in all, and prosper, but the tragedy was unspeakable. The joint funeral of his wife and mother was so poignant that even the minister was too moved to muster many words of solace.

In the autobiography Roosevelt wrote six years before his own death, he recalled his mother as "a sweet, gracious, beautiful Southern woman, a delightful companion, and beloved by everybody." His sister Corinne wrote that her brothers would carry their mother "up stairs as if she had been a baby, and they always said she was like a lovely Dresden china object of art. My brother Theodore delighted in the combination of wit, grace, and gentleness, which she possessed to an unusual degree." Half Northern, half Southern, perhaps Teddy Roosevelt's confidence came more from his father and his ebullience more from his mother, but he viewed both his parents as little short of perfection. Martha Bulloch Roosevelt's fragility was misleading. Indeed, it was her unsuspected reservoir of strength, no less than her husband's, that breathed the very gift of life into her son.

"I DO NOT believe we can love our children too much," Louisa Taft wrote to her mother in 1858. If Martha Roosevelt was one of the most devoted presidential mothers, so too was Louisa Torrey Taft. The child she referred to specifically was her already plump and pleasant one-year-old, William Howard. Perhaps the prior loss of her firstborn, Sammie, from whooping cough made William all the more precious to Louisa. She would have five children in all, three more boys and a girl, but there would always be a special attachment to her first surviving son. As Louisa wrote her older sister Delia, "I feel as if my hands and feet were tied to this baby." Although she delighted in large families, Louisa continued, "I am not afraid of having too many [children]. I began too late for that."

That Louisa began at all had been the severest shock of Delia's life. This was not the future either of them had envisioned. Raised in Massachusetts, they were to have gone off together like a less lethal version of Thelma and Louise — to enjoy independent lives of high adventure and travel. Marriage did not enter into their plans. Indeed, they had actually embarked on their joint venture, but sustaining it financially had proven so arduous that in 1853 Louisa Maria Torrey felt obliged to accept the matrimonial offer of kindly, mature Alphonso Taft. The solidarity of the Torrey sisters had also been sundered by the indisputable fact that Louisa was far the prettier and more congenial of the two. Still, they remained life-long best friends, and after the death of Alphonso in 1891 even lived together again in the old Torrey homestead in which they had been raised, and traveled more extensively than they had in their youth.

That two young women in staid New England in the middle of the nineteenth century had entertained expectations of a more fulfilling future than conventional matrimony or schoolmarm spinsterhood implies a good deal about their parents. The saga of the Torreys and Tafts is strikingly similar to that of the Smiths and Adamses — replete with letters and diaries glowing with enlightenment and originality, leading to generations of achievement in the nation's service. If these achievements were largely by men, the inspiration for them came mainly from women, many of whom longed to do more than inspire. As a young Delia Torrey wrote of her mother, "[She] is very ambitious and ambition in a woman is synonymous with unhappiness." An older Louisa Torrey Taft similarly wrote of herself, "I find that I shine by a reflected light. . . . I feel like asserting myself as having been *somebody* by my own account." Impressed by his mother's knowledge of the stock market, William Howard Taft, while at Yale, wrote jocularly to her, "When woman's field widens, Mother, you must become President of a Railroad Company. I am sure you would be a success." Even late in the nineteenth century, "woman's field" had not yet widened very far.

At least the Torrey sisters, unlike Abigail Adams, had the opportunity for a measure of formal education. The Torreys, on both sides, had been in Massachusetts since the mid-1600s. Samuel Davenport Torrey did so well as a Boston importer that he decided to retire to the more salubrious environment of the small town of Millbury, some forty miles away, when he was only forty-two. Always concerned about his health — as it turned out, unnecessarily — his major avocations for the next forty-six years were taking care of himself and expressing his progressive views without inhibition. These encompassed women's suffrage and their full legal rights. Torrey was viewed with bemusement by the town's leading citizens at least in part because so many of them were related to his wife, Susan. Both husband and wife were dedicated Unitarians, a faith they imparted to all four of their daughters. Emphasizing the universal humanity rather than the doctrinal divinity of Christ, Unitarianism framed Susan Torrey's conviction that every human life, male or female, should be encouraged to reach its fullest potential. Although, upon returning to Millbury, she at least officially rejoined the respectable Congregational Church of her family, that was one of her few concessions to conformity. As biographer Judith Anderson relates, Susan Torrey was viewed as "a kind of energetic eccentric," active in everything from painting to politics, intent that her daughters enjoy the educational opportunities she had been denied.

The two oldest, Delia and Louisa, divided by a decade from their other sisters, were particularly amenable. Already enlightened by visits to their home from every distinguished scholar who found his way to Millbury, Delia, at eighteen, and Louisa, at sixteen, were dispatched to the new Mount Holyoke Female Seminary. Unfortunately, its proprietor, Miss Mary Lyons, was not so advanced in her pedagogy as Susan Torrey might have expected. The daily regimen was stronger in home economics than intellectual enlightenment. Disillusioned, Delia returned home in less than a year. Louisa, called Louise by her family and friends, was more sensible, and at least finished what was to have been the first of a two-year course of study. Although Louise hoped to ultimately earn her living by writing, it was clear that the independent lifestyle so enticing to Delia meant that both sisters might be obliged to undertake at least a modicum of teaching. Even in the 1840s this respectably female profession required some form of certification. Susan Torrey now demonstrated her more practical side, supported by a husband who, however sympathetic, was pragmatic enough to appreciate the potential impact on his resources of four unmarried daughters.

Delia and Louise were sent to New Haven to board with their mother's sister, Harriet Dutton. They would not only take lessons from an experienced teacher, a relative of Harriet's — rather like "reading" law in an office — but would be permitted to round off their education by attending courses in natural science and philosophy at the all-male college of Yale. The implications of this were lost on no one, particularly Aunt Harriet. She had observed that, although Delia might be the brighter of the two sisters, Louise, "partly to her confidence in herself and partly to her musical gifts and also to her fine figure and manners," was more attractive to members of the opposite sex. As Doris Faber writes, "Louise was taller and handsomer . . . her glossy dark hair parted in the middle and drawn back into a quite elegant chignon." She was also not averse to flirting, but none of her male acquaintances seemed to suit her.

For several years she and Delia pursued their dream, teaching a semester or two at private academies and then venturing off to New York or Quebec. Income from writing articles was sporadic, at best, and teaching could not possibly support the sort of lifestyle they had envisioned. Too often they had to write home, chagrined, for money from their parents. It was never refused, but Louise eventually confided to Delia, "If Father finds us too expensive, I'm afraid we shall have to get married." It is likely that Delia was always the more intransigent of the two in this regard, the more intent on life-long independence. Their younger sisters both married. Delia never did.

Louise's conclusions coincided with a return visit to her Aunt Harriet in New Haven. There was another visitor, a Yale classmate of her Uncle Samuel's, named Alphonso Taft. He was an imposing six-footer, well over two hundred pounds, whose family had roots in New England as deep as the Torreys'. After Alphonso had graduated with honors from Yale in 1833, however, his parents moved to Ohio. In Cincinnati Taft had established a law practice, prospered, had expectations of becoming a judge, and had married a delicate young woman named Fanny. She bore him two sons before dying at the age of only twenty-nine. Alphonso was in New Haven for the express purpose of finding a second wife and a new mother for his boys. He was completely captivated by Louise Torrey, pronouncing her "a splendid woman" to her aunt and uncle.

For her part, Louise was coy, evasive, and teasing — her customary demeanor with admirers — so much so that Alphonso doubted his chances. For that matter, was she simply too lighthearted for him? However robust his appearance, Alphonso was forty-three, Louise only twenty-six. That might have placed her ominously on the cusp of spinsterhood in many minds, but there was still a substantial difference in age. And Alphonso's deadly serious demeanor made him seem even older. Still, Louise was intrigued. On a second visit to New Haven, Alphonso managed to capture her heart, in part by winning over her mind. Despite his seeming stolidity, Alphonso was genuinely in favor of women's rights, including their legal equality, and was sympathetic to Louise's varied interests. He would respect what today would be called her "space," and however restrained, there was no doubt about the depth of his love for her. The engagement was brief. Louise and Alphonso were married at the home of her parents on December 26, 1853. Susan Torrey was overjoyed to have such an imposing, enlightened son-in-law; Samuel Torrey, to finally have a married daughter. Only Delia was distraught, although even she must have recognized that Louise might have done a lot worse.

Indeed, the marriage was very successful. Louise's endless activities — her charities, book clubs, art lessons, musicales, and foreign language studies — somehow failed to interfere with either her contributions to her husband's career or her primary role as a devoted mother. Alphonso, whom she quite properly referred to as "Mr. Taft," was as loving a father to his newly evolving family as to his original two sons. His other children echoed William's conviction that "a man never had a . . . dearer, more considerate [father]." It sounds very much like Theodore Roosevelt's evaluation of his own father. The term used most often to describe Alphonso Taft is "kindly." After William married, his wife, Helen (whom he called Nellie), viewed her father-in-law as "gentle beyond anything I ever knew." Alphonso Taft hardly lacked ambition for his sons, but was less concerned with material success than with moral rectitude. He firmly believed, as Anderson points out, that "parents are judged by the character of their children." Sustained effort was more important than recognition. If any of his children failed to measure up in this singular regard, Alphonso could be stern.

Apparently he agreed with his wife's early assessment that "William is foremost and I am inclined to think he always will be." In Louise's case, this view may have originated with a sort of first-surviving-son syndrome, for jovial Bill Taft was surely not the brightest in a household full of achievement-oriented children. His methodical nature, much like his father's, could be mistaken for procrastination. All the Tafts felt pressure to excel, even long after their school years had ended. William's half-brother, Peter, for example, valedictorian of his class at Yale, had a nervous breakdown and died in an institution at a relatively young age. It may be unfair to ascribe this to an excess of parental pressure, but in the case of William's brother, Horace, there is a more positive example of rebellion. Horace, so slender he looked ascetic, abandoned the study of law, his father's preference, to found a boys' school in Connecticut, and disdained his father's politics to support reform Democrats. In such generational divergence one is reminded of the Adamses.

Alphonso Taft's ambitions for his own career were limited. He might have imagined becoming a justice of the Supreme Court of the United States, but he was not about to maneuver for consideration. As Anderson writes, "Alphonso Taft . . . had no driving ambition to rise in the political sphere. He was contented to enjoy a successful judicial career and even though he spent a few years in the political limelight, his goals did not extend beyond the law." He reached Ohio's supreme court, served in President Grant's cabinet as secretary of war and attorney general, and emerged unsullied by that administration's pervasive corruption. It is likely that Louise later interceded with President Chester Arthur to have her husband named to largely ceremonial ambassadorships in Austro-Hungary and Russia. She had found official Washington disappointing, its matronly hostesses no more sophisticated than Ohio's. In regal Vienna and St. Petersburg she blossomed, her grasp of languages and her enduring vivacity an immense asset in diplomatic circles. She finally presided over festive social events, her husband a rather bewildered appendage. How Delia would have loved it. Finally, Alphonso's health began to fail. He and Louise spent their final days together in a warm California cottage to make the end more bearable. "What a resource is a cultivated mind," she wrote her favored son. "What can people do when old and sick without intellectual resources?" They still had much to talk about, the hallmark of a good marriage. Alphonso Taft died at the age of eighty in 1891. He had cared for his family admirably, but in tangible terms he left little more for them to inherit than his good name.

Louise was now sixty-three, her children grown, William and his wife already expecting their second child. From her son's earliest days, Louise had been as intrusive in every aspect of his life as Abigail Adams had been in John Quincy's. Alphonso Taft looked for effort, Louise for results. All the details of family discipline were in her hands. She, who had been such a free spirit in her youth, carefully supervised all her children's studies, particularly young Bill's. Apparently Louise never quite appreciated the irony in all this. Eventually she came to a reluctant acceptance that her son was temperamentally very much like his father — a hardworking, deliberative man meant for the law, who neither enjoyed nor was intended for a political career. Louise never lacked affection for her children, but she could be harshly critical. As biographer Henry Pringle puts it, sometimes Bill tried too hard to achieve an impossible perfection. As he wrote his mother from Yale, "You expect great things from me, but you mustn't be disappointed if I don't come up to your expectations." He was a plodder, not a plunger. Like his siblings, he too excelled at school and even in athletics, but only by working harder than others. His immense weight, ultimately over three hundred pounds, may have had genetic causes, but it could also have been related to unending stress. In his earlier years, he had to please his parents; in later years, he had to please his ambitious wife, his dear friend Teddy Roosevelt, and all the others who urged him to aim for the presidency — eventually the American public itself. Perhaps he was too good-natured. Even in grammar school, where his great size dwarfed his classmates, he was more the object of their sympathy than their derision. Too often, when he craved reassurance from his parents, their response was to admonish him that true happiness resulted from working even harder. Yet his mother insisted that William's great fault lay in his craving for approval.

After Louise, widowed and in her mid-seventies, had unsuccessfully advised William against going on a delicate mission to Rome for President Roosevelt, she still could not resist going along. William's wife, Nellie, had been delayed from departing with him because of the illness of their oldest son, Robert. When Nellie finally arrived in Rome, she had to admire the sheer spunk of her mother-in-law, having the time of her life as once more a vivacious diplomatic hostess, the center of attention, still enticing to men. Taft, who had previously served in the Philippines, was to negotiate the sale of Vatican lands there to the United States. When the pope asked young Robert Taft what he hoped to be when he grew up, the boy replied that his ambition was to be chief justice of the United States.

This was, at least internationally, Louise's last stand. She never ceased, however, to send her son advice and to reassure him of her deep interest in his future. A Unitarian like his parents, William Howard

Taft called them his "guardian angels" and always felt that their prayers had guided his success. When he felt inadequate, which was frequently, he prayed all the more. Louise's social schedule as an ambassador's wife in Europe had never interfered with her presiding over religious services at each embassy every Sunday and forcefully leading every hymn. Her reasoned, universal faith could encompass the doctrinal divisions of others. She knew that her son must in the end find his own way, but expressing her opinions was by now too deeply ingrained for Louise to ever quite abandon it.

Nellie's own ambitions for William put her on a collision course with her mother-in-law. The two women were alike in craving influence, even recognition, for themselves, although, unlike Louise, Nellie had little interest in social diversions. Her father had been a judge, and she wanted more for her Bill, hoping for the presidency itself. Yet his father had counseled him that "to be chief justice is more than to be president." Perhaps a cabinet position might be a helpful stepping-stone, but William, like Alphonso, was too guileless to carefully plot his future. Near the end of her life, Louise sent her son this succinct observation: "Roosevelt is a good fighter and enjoys it, but the malice of politics would make you miserable." Later she even stated publicly, "I do not want my son to be president. . . . His is a judicial mind, and he loves the law." Still, when he was offered an around-the-world tour by Roosevelt to enhance his pre-presidential stature but hesitated to accept because of his mother's declining health, Louise told him firmly that he must go. "No Taft, to my knowledge, has ever yet neglected a public duty for the sake of gratifying a private desire." There was as much Torrey as Taft in that admirable sentiment.

Louisa Maria Torrey Taft did not live to see either her son's unhappy presidency or his subsequent career as a distinguished chief justice of the United States; he would be the only man in American history to hold both positions. She died on December 7, 1907, in her eightieth year, the same age her husband had been when he passed away. William was still at sea, anxious to return to see his mother at least once more. In a genealogical history of the Taft and Torrey families compiled by Louise and her sister Delia in their last years, they referred to William Howard Taft, then secretary of war, as having a "long and honorable public career." It would not be capped until 1921, fourteen years after Louise's death, when President Harding finally named her son chief justice.

In the next generation, the oldest son of William Howard Taft, renowned in the Senate as "Mr. Republican," three times vied unsuccessfully for his party's nomination for the presidency. Robert Alphonso Taft had been first in his class (without benefit of favoritism) at the Taft School, Yale, and at the Harvard Law School. His grandfather would have been proud. For Alphonso, the honor lay less in victory than in striving to do one's best. Louise, however, would have been disappointed. Such effort and achievement merited the highest level of success.

NEARLY thirty years after his mother's death, Woodrow Wilson paid her an affectionate tribute that also revealed a good deal about himself. "My mother," he recalled, "was one of the most remarkable persons I have ever met. She was so reserved that only those in her immediate family could have known how lovable she was. I seem to feel still the touch of her hand, and the sweet steadying influence of her wonderful character. I thank God to have had such a mother."

There was a similar gap between Wilson's public and private personas. He was generally considered to be not so much reserved as "cold," but the cerebral self-confidence he brought to the presidency masked inner turmoil and personal attachments as deeply emotional as his mother's. As president, he actually enjoyed it when people occasionally yelled "Woody" at him, since it was symbolic of at least a measure of affection, but he understood that he could never compete with "Teddy" Roosevelt in this regard. Of course, in this, Wilson was hardly unique. Few prominent Americans — indeed, few people — have been so effortlessly ebullient on and off the stage as Theodore Roosevelt. Nor was Wilson the only president whose public demeanor did not always match his inner emotional state. Story-telling Abraham Lincoln, for example, had periods of such deep depression that his friends hid sharp objects from him. "Give 'em hell" Harry Truman, on the other hand, was at home the gentlest and most considerate of men. Concern with image is not a recent phenomenon in American politics. But, for whatever combination of reasons, Wilson differs at least in degree from other presidents whose private demons overtook their public duties. The only professional academic ever to occupy the White House, his drive to excel came not only from his parents but from within. One cannot imagine him saying to his mother and father, as William Howard Taft had said to his, that they must not be disappointed if he failed to measure up. There have been presidents like Polk who all but worked themselves to death while in office, but the sturdy-looking Wilson seems to have had a breakdown of one kind or another at almost every pivotal juncture of his life. Yet he lacked little in emotional support. His father always encouraged him. His mother adored him.

Woodrow Wilson's family is the most thoroughly ecclesiastical in presidential history. His father, the Reverend Doctor Joseph Ruggles Wilson, was a powerful preacher who held major pulpits and became one of the most prominent figures of the Southern Presbyterian Church. Wilson's mother, Janet Woodrow, whom everyone called Jessie, was the daughter of the Reverend Thomas Woodrow, the scholarly pastor of an independent Congregational church in Ohio though of a family steeped in Presbyterianism. As biographer John Mulder writes, the Woodrows were a more distinguished family than the Wilsons, "tracing their ancestry to prominent Scottish divines across six generations." Jessie's close-knit family emigrated to New York in 1835 when she was five, then to Ontario, finally to Ohio. The fifth of eight children, Jessie's ties with her siblings became even stronger after the early death of her mother. Her brothers continued in the family tradition, becoming learned Presbyterian pastors in both the northern and southern United States.

At nineteen, Jessie was slender and shy, but her keen intelligence so impressed her father that he sent her to a female seminary in Steubenville, Ohio, to enhance her education. Described by Doris Faber as "whispy-haired" and possessing "an ethereal quality that substituted quite effectively for mere earthly beauty," Jessie made the acquaintance of a young theologian of reputed promise who hoped to combine preaching and teaching. Joseph Ruggles Wilson was also the handsomest man she had ever seen. She was utterly smitten. Even as his "incomparable father" aged, Woodrow Wilson would remark, "If I had my father's face and figure, it wouldn't make any difference what I said."

The Wilsons are thought of as a Southern family, but Woodrow's mother was born in England and raised in Ohio, and his father was both born and raised in Ohio. Joseph Wilson's parents were Scotch-Irish who emigrated together, married, and settled in Steubenville. His ambitious father worked his way up from printer to proprietor of a local newspaper, was elected a Whig member of the Ohio legislature, and had great plans for his ten children. Joseph, the youngest of his seven sons, and clearly the brightest, graduated as valedictorian of what is now Washington and Jefferson College and went on to excel at Princeton Theological Seminary. He was ordained by the Presbytery of Ohio in 1849 and within a matter of weeks, on June 7, was married to Jessie Woodrow by her delighted father. It may have appeared to the Woodrows as much a fortuitous merger as a marriage, but there is little doubt of the couple's devotion to each other. If Jessie's love for Joseph was perhaps tinged with a touch of adoration, well, that was fine with him.

Beginning his ministry in Pennsylvania while also teaching rhetoric at his old college, Joseph was able to merge his two career interests. Soon the Wilsons had their first child, a girl named Marion after the mother Jessie Woodrow had hardly known. Near the end of 1851 Joseph accepted a position at Hampden-Sydney College in Virginia. The Wilsons would be Southerners for the rest of their lives together, by preference as well as residence. In 1854 Joseph received a call from the First Presbyterian Church of Staunton, a lovely town nestled in the Shenandoah Valley. The couple now had a second daughter. In the spacious manse of the Staunton church their third child and first son was born on December 28, 1856. Oddly, he was not named Joseph Ruggles Wilson Jr., the name given to their second son almost ten years later, but Thomas Woodrow Wilson, after his mother's father. From the first, Jessie was especially effusive, at least within the family circle, about this "fine healthy fellow." He was "just as fat as he can be," she wrote relatives, and "as little trouble as it is possible for a baby to be." Had little Tommy been as homely as Theodore Roosevelt, it would have made no difference. As it turned out, the unique appearances of both men, the sons of strikingly handsome fathers, would become grist for cartoonists — Roosevelt with his bespectacled, owlish face; Wilson with his long professorial chin; both with such prominent teeth.

Jessie Wilson
Courtesy of the Woodrow Wilson Birthplace

"A boy never gets over his boyhood," Wilson would later write. His boyhood was dominated by the Civil War and its immediate aftermath. It delayed his formal education, but the conflict caused his family more emotional than physical upheaval. In 1857 Joseph Ruggles Wilson was called to the First Presbyterian Church of Augusta, Georgia, the same year he would receive his doctor of divinity degree. Despite the turmoil around him, the next decade would be his most productive. One of

Woodrow's earliest memories was hearing at the age of four that Lincoln's election meant there would be war. The First General Assembly of the Presbyterian Church of the Confederate States of America was held in his father's church in Augusta, and the Reverend Dr. Wilson was elected its permanent clerk. There seems to have been little doubt that the Wilsons would side with the South. Although later Joseph Wilson reasoned that his affection for the region made him rejoice in the final failure of secession, his fundamental belief in Scotch Presbyterian "Covenanter" theology could be construed to support the Confederacy and even the institution of slavery itself.

Established with both political and theological significance in Scotland in 1638, the Covenanter philosophy had come to imply an immutable compact not only in terms of worship but also as a guide to every aspect of human activity, a divine imprint on earthly affairs. In exchange for obedience to his will, God established a covenant of grace with believers and forgave their sins. The problem lay in discerning God's will. How were imperfect men, God's instruments in the world, to achieve absolute certainty? Revelation of the divine order of things could be interpreted to justify the continuation of a stratified society in terms of rich and poor, men and women, black and white. If happiness consisted of making the most of God's gift of life, it could lead to a gospel extolling material prosperity. In the Reverend Dr. Wilson's case, prayer and reflection reinforced in his mind that God's will *could* be known, and his grace received. Wilson did not always agree on specifics with other Presbyterian clergy, however. He supported education for women, for example, but neither he nor his son would question the social system prevailing in the South, either then or later.

The nature of his father's theology would have a profound effect on Woodrow Wilson's life and career until its very end. It was perhaps permissible to concede some pragmatic point, but never a question of morality. Like a loving parent, God could pardon delay, but not excuse compromise with the evil so prevalent in a world of unbelievers. There is no way to overemphasize the significance of the deep religious faith instilled in Wilson's childhood. Even during the war, daily family devotions continued uninterrupted, as did Bible readings and prayers. Sunday was given over entirely to worship — after Sunday school there was attendance at two church services and evening hymns at home. Young Tommy loved singing these hymns, and praying aloud. He always preferred the simplicity of the Presbyterian service to all others, but he also believed in being demonstrative in church.

Augusta was a major supply center for the Confederacy, and there was considerable fighting in the vicinity. The church building itself was at one time damaged, and its sanctuary served as an emergency hospital. Yet, as Mulder writes, Wilson's family suffered little in the Civil War. Relations with Northern relatives were strained, but only for a time. If anything, the family drew closer together. Jessie Wilson "in particular tried to shield her son from the world of violence and war by lavishing love and affection on him. To her friends she was known as reserved and sedate, but to her son she was warm, loving, solicitous of his health and welfare, and perhaps overprotective." She was also his first teacher, reading aloud to him before he learned to read on his own. Wilson was nine when the war ended.

That both mother and son suffered from a series of sometimes mysterious ailments may have helped cement their special bond. They were home together a great deal as Joseph Wilson's responsibilities heightened and his wife was pregnant with their last child. Young Woodrow was especially solicitous of his mother during this time, doing all manner of household chores for her. Later he would recall those days with his mother, saying, "I remember how I clung to her (a laughed at 'mama's boy') till I was a great big fellow; but love of the best of womanhood came to me and entered my heart through these apron-strings." Jessie Wilson was protective of all four of her children, but it was to her first son that she wrote, "You have never been anything but a comfort to me all your life! God bless you, darling boy."

Perhaps Jessie's reticence outside her family circle limited her effectiveness as a pastor's wife, but it did not seem to inhibit the career of her husband. After the war he went on to become stated clerk of the Southern Presbyterians, a post he maintained until after his wife's death. The family left Augusta to settle in Columbia, South Carolina, where Joseph continued to preach while holding a prestigious post at the Columbia Theological Seminary. He hoped to stay there until his retirement. Some historians believe that Jessie's influence on Woodrow was greatest while her son was at home, and his father's influence dominant thereafter. Certainly Jessie was physically closer to her son during the first decade of his life, but the pervasive role of both parents overlapped. It was simply different, and exercised differently, just as the Christian piety they shared could be seen more clearly through compassion on the mother's part, and certainty on the father's. As a family retainer said of young Wilson, "Outside, Mr. Tommy was his father's boy, but inside he was his mother all over." She was the foundation of his emotional life, and "Tommy" was her favorite name for him.

Both parents seemed to have decided rather early that their rather introspective son was destined to do exceptional things. Even in the intricate childhood armadas he constructed — an early nautical interest akin to the one Franklin Roosevelt would later have — Woodrow demonstrated advanced logistical skills. After the war, his father became more involved in instructing him. Outgoing and gregarious where his wife was reticent, the Reverend Dr. Wilson stressed the rhetoric he had once taught and now practiced every Sunday. He gave Woodrow regular reading and writing assignments and rigorously graded the results. Skill and confidence in self-expression were the keys to success. The tone of Woodrow's parents' relationship with him was set: his father's hallmark was pride, tempered by severe criticism and the highest expectations; his mother's, unconditional support and encouragement. As Joseph Wilson's own career seemed to stall, the pressures mounted on Woodrow.

Many presidential mothers hoped their sons might turn out to be ministers. It was a hope shared by Jessie Wilson, but it was more than a hope to her husband. Were there a Protestant pope, the Reverend Dr. Wilson would have envisioned his son as a candidate. At the advanced age of eighteen, Thomas Woodrow Wilson finally left the safe haven of his parents' parsonage for leafy Davidson College in North Carolina, then as now an outstanding liberal arts college in the South. Its close affiliation with the Presbyterian Church made it the ideal place to prepare for the ministry. Woodrow's Christian commitment was already strong, not alone through his parents. At the age of seventeen, he wrote in his diary that he had "professed Christ's name," coming forward to answer the call of an evangelical student at his father's seminary. Yet, he pondered in his diary, "I have increased very little in grace and have done almost nothing for the Savior's cause here below." Woodrow was finally on his own, and he was beginning to think for himself.

He had confirmed his commitment to faith, but he also had been nurtured to achieve his fullest potential in life. The question of what vocation to pursue became a concern of such intensity that it caused an agonizing reappraisal. There is little doubt that Wilson went to Davidson intent on studying for the ministry, but while there, he converted himself to serving Christ in a different calling. He would use his growing powers of expression, nourished by his father and marveled at by his mother, to become a great statesman. Academia would be only an intermediate career. Indirectly, his mother may have helped bring about this decision. Both parents had educated their son about his Scotch-Irish heritage, but it was his mother's English origins that most intrigued the youth. Great Britain's empire was approaching its zenith, but there were influences of social reform, as well. Wilson came so to admire Liberal Prime Minister William Gladstone that it was his example, not an American president's, that turned Wilson's path in a more temporal direction.

His father may have been disappointed, but not really discouraged. After all, his views of God's grace extended to its manifestations in this world. There was no limit to what his son might yet achieve. Both parents continued to pour out their thoughts in letters collected by the noted Wilson scholar, Arthur Link. Many are little short of love letters, but there is a contrast between letters from Jessie and letters from Joseph to their son — beyond the customary differences in concerns of mothers and fathers. Jessie sounds like a typical mother in this letter sent to Woodrow during his freshman year at Davidson: "My darling boy, I am so anxious about that cold of yours, how did you take it? Surely you have not laid aside your winter clothing? Another danger is in sitting without fire these cool nights." When her son finally decided to discard his first name as not quite mature enough, his mother wrote, probably through her tears, "My darling Woodrow, I am going to make a desperate effort to call you Woodrow from this time on. . . . I have learned to love the name we have called you ever since your baby-hood, that I have found it hard to resolve to give it up. But 'Tommy' is certainly an unsuitable name for a grown man."

His father's letters were equally supportive but more specific and a bit self-centered. This one, an 1879 letter from Joseph to his son, reveals Joseph's growing disappointment with the state of his own life: "So influential upon my life has been the belief that I had no special claims to superiority that I am anxious to see you escape this practical blunder — I would rather have you think too much than too little of yourself and your mental forces." Conflicts between his church and seminary in Columbia that a more flexible personality might have avoided or overcome were making Joseph's life miserable.

Woodrow had done well during his freshman year at Davidson, but before it ended, he had either a physical or emotional breakdown that required over a year of recuperation. When he returned to college, it was to Princeton, from which he graduated. His law studies at the University of Virginia were also interrupted by poor health, emotional distress, or both, and he finished with independent study. For a time he practiced law in Atlanta, but he gave it up to pursue a doctorate in history and government at the Johns Hopkins University. A remarkable academic career followed, culminating in his tumultuous presidency of Princeton. Wilson's tenure boasted many achievements but also included controversy over the role of elitist eating clubs and the location of the new graduate school, issues over which he clashed with board of trustees chairman Grover Cleveland. Wilson's even more meteoric political career was launched in 1910 when he ran successfully for governor of New Jersey.

Jessie's health began to consistently decline when Woodrow was away at school. Together they tried to keep their various ailments from distracting the Reverend Dr. Wilson, who had his own problems. Depression gripped the father as it would often afflict the son. Both fought it with tenacity and hard work, but neither would ever accept the sort of advice Jessie gave Woodrow: "Don't be too ambitious, dear — for that kind of ambition brings *only* worry and unhappiness." It was what Delia Torrey had said to her sister Louise about their mother, but to the Wilson men happiness, if attainable at all, could only result from high achievement. As the situation in Columbia turned into turmoil, Joseph Wilson decided to depart. He went on to a prestigious pulpit in Wilmington, North Carolina, but was embittered and discouraged. It showed in his detailed letters to Woodrow, who was now even more the focus of his hopes:

February 25, 1879

My dearest son —

I return to you the mss. containing your discussion of cabinet government. I have read it and re-read it, and have ventured to make a few verbal corrections. . . . It might, with advantage, be made to *glow* a little more. . . . What is most needed is clearness. . . . *You* have only to persevere. As it is, I feel proud of you and send you thanks for the pleasure this essay has given both your dear mother & myself.

Jessie's concerns remained more maternal. Not much later she wrote, "We received your last sweet letter today. We think just as *you* do as to the matter of clothing. . . . Get what you need for the coming season"; and a few weeks later, "I am glad that you were able to do your shopping satisfactorily. . . . I like to imagine how you look. . . . I am so thankful that you keep well & happy. . . . God bless you, my precious child."

Even when Woodrow's father expressed criticism or disappointment, his mother would soften the blow. Sometimes, as in 1879-1880, Joseph merged his own unhappiness with his son's circumstances. He wrote on November 19, 1879, "I am disposed that . . . half the battle of professional life . . . is won by first a manful declaration of independence as to surrounding circumstances, especially where . . . *duty* requires us to stand and fight." A letter from Jessie promptly followed, stressing that Joseph meant to imply no criticism of Woodrow. If their son thought so, "you were mistaken — as it is very far from the truth. I assured him that you would perfectly understand that he did not mean that."

The nearest to a crisis in their relationship came when Woodrow pondered the possibility of withdrawing or even being dismissed from his legal studies at the University of Virginia. From his aggrieved father:

June 5, 1880

My dear Son —

Your pain-giving letter has just been received. I have all along, had fear lest your frequent absences . . . end in grief, and tried to warn you . . . but then, I will add this — that come what may *you possess our confidence,* because we well know your character. . . . It is just because of my love that I have always tried to be faithful in telling you the truth about yourself. . . .

God bless and utterly reform you.

Your own father

On the same day his mother wrote:

My darling Son . . .

I need not try to tell you how distressed I am at the possibility of any disgrace coming upon *you.* Your father has written you. . . . I don't know what he wrote — for he is in one of his dark moods today — but whatever it was, you may be sure he loves and trusts you with all heart. . . . God bless my darling — and bring good out of this trouble.

Lovingly,
Mother

And yet it was Woodrow's father who wrote on a happier occasion, "My dearest boy — How much we all love you cannot be put into words, and we are proud of you besides." How was anyone to live up to such intimidating affections?

It was during his brief legal career that Woodrow met in Rome, Georgia, another minister's daughter, Ellen Louise Axson, the bright-eyed "Ellie Lou" he would marry two years later. Although she felt both Woodrow and Ellie Lou to be a bit young, Jessie approved of the choice and extended to the new Wilson all the warmth she had lavished on her son. She wrote Woodrow, "I feel assured that there does not live a sweeter or purer girl than she. . . . I am *sure* you will be happy." Perhaps Jessie, whose physical frailty now finally matched her appearance, understood that it was time to transfer the maternal care of her precious boy to another, no less devoted. With her husband still battling for the

Lord on lonelier ground, Jessie Woodrow Wilson died on April 15, 1888, in Clarksville, Tennessee, at the age of fifty-seven. Writing to his wife from his teaching assignment at Bryn Mawr College, Woodrow found his grief all but inexpressible. He later wrote, "As the first shock . . . of the irreparable blow passes off . . . my heart is filling up with the tenderest memories of my sweet mother." Just as Jessie would have wished, he added, "If I had not lived with such a mother, I could not have won and seemed to deserve . . . such a wife — the strength, the support, the human source of my life." Marriage, too, was a compact to Wilson. Characteristically, Woodrow again questioned whether he was fulfilling his own personal covenant with the Lord for "effectual public service." It would not be long.

With his wife gone, and his daughter Marian dead only two years later, the Reverend Dr. Joseph Ruggles Wilson finally retired from his preaching and teaching, his lifelong fight for faith, and in 1901 went to live with his son's family in Princeton. There he had granddaughters to tell what he had always known, that "Your father is a very great man." He lived to see Woodrow become a president, even if it was only of the university. Joseph died in 1903 and was buried next to Jessie in South Carolina. Wilson memorialized his father as "a master of serious eloquence, a thinker of singular power and penetration, a thoughtful student of life and God's purpose, a lover and servant of his fellow man, a man of God." Given his upbringing, it is not surprising that Woodrow Wilson would try so earnestly to redeem the world, and when he failed, turn from any semblance of policy to prophecy. Already when nominated by the Democratic party for the presidency in 1912, Wilson had proclaimed, "I am a Presbyterian and believe in predestination. . . . God ordained that I should be the next president of the United States." Perhaps Herbert Hoover, in characterizing Wilson as a typical "Scotch Presbyterian Covenanter," meant to refer to his inflexibility, but it was also his shield and strength.

If Wilson's force came from his father, the sentiment that humanized it was the legacy of his mother. It was to her that he dedicated his essay on the obligations of youth: "Your mother, who brought you forth, nourished you in your helplessness, loves you as only a mother can — who will trust you when all others forsake you, is ready to give her all to make you happy — are you to do nothing for her?" As Woodrow's younger brother wrote in 1919, "Our parents made companions and friends of their children, thus holding us to them in the bonds of strongest love and mutual confidence." There was a difference in the attitudes of the two parents, however. To Joseph Ruggles Wilson, it was necessary that Woodrow always strive to be the best. To Jessie Woodrow Wilson, her oldest son could not possibly be less.

CHAPTER ELEVEN

"It Always Seemed That the Boy I Lost Was Her Image"

- ⚹ Phoebe Harding
- ⚹ Victoria Coolidge
- ⚹ Hulda Hoover

AFTER THE DEATH of his mother, Warren Harding marveled at the certainty of her faith. Near the end, Phoebe Harding had been asked whether she was praying. "No, I am trusting," she replied. Warren continued, "She had the right to trust. . . . I could not speak for myself, but dear, dear Mother will wear a crown if ever a Christian woman does, and I believe in eternal compensations for such as her." Harding may have felt inadequate in the presidency, an appraisal shared by historians, but whatever he achieved in life was secured by this strong woman who kept her family intact. Had there been no Mother's Day, biographer Francis Russell suggests that Harding would have invented it. Every Sunday he brought or sent her flowers.

The families of Harding's parents, Phoebe Elizabeth Dickerson and the aristocratic-sounding George Tryon Harding II, are typical of presidential families. Both grew from immigrant roots, English or Dutch, in the seventeenth century. Puritan Richard Harding, "a mariner engaged in fishing," arrived in Braintree, Massachusetts, in 1623. Around forty years later, Phoebe's maternal forebears, the Van Kirks, came to Long Island. The Hardings, Dickersons, and Van Kirks replicate the familiar rise in status from farmers and blacksmiths to sea captains and frontier lawyers to doctors and legislators. Each family was active in the American Revolution — one of the Van Kirks reportedly supplying seven sons to the cause — and in the War of 1812. After that conflict, like so many others in New England and New York, Harding's forebears sensed greener prospects to the west and set off for Ohio.

So it was that barely a century before Harding's inauguration as president — the seventh chief executive from Ohio — his great-great-grandfather Amos built his log cabin on the frontier that was already America's breadbasket. Here Harding's father was born in 1844. In little more than a decade, the log cabin would be supplanted by a more substantial structure. Near the appropriately named town of Blooming Grove, the Hardings by now were secure enough to donate land, in the New England tradition, for a schoolhouse. On Sundays, it could be adapted to Baptist worship, their church of choice.

The preceding year, on the adjoining farm, Isaac and Charity Dickerson had a daughter they named Phoebe Elizabeth. She was the youngest of nine children, the eighth girl and reportedly the liveliest. Tryon, as he liked to be called, first noticed his new neighbor when they grew old enough to attend the subscription school together, although boys and girls entered through separate doors. From that time on, he could hardly take his eyes off her. The little girl in pigtails who excelled at recitations was becoming a slender, self-assured young woman.

Russell describes Tryon Harding as "dark complexioned and small, but alert." The swarthy complexion his handsome son Warren would inherit led to rumors of black blood in the family. These were exacerbated during Warren's political career, and the truth — if it matters — has never been ascertained. "How do I know?" Harding once told a friend. "One of my ancestors may have jumped the fence." One thing that Tryon knew is that he did not want to be a farmer. You could "read" any profession in the nineteenth century, particularly on the frontier — teaching, law, even medicine. Teaching was the easiest in which to get a start. Of course, a degree from any college provided a helpful foundation. At the age of fourteen, in 1858, Tryon entered Iberia, later Central Ohio College, a few miles from Blooming Grove. Administered by Free Presbyterians, it was really more like a high school. The small student body of both sexes from surrounding farms was taught grammar and the rudiments of math and science. In three years Tryon had his bachelor's degree and was able to teach at a rural school. Phoebe was never far from his mind. Now, however, the nation was embroiled in civil war. Despite his short stature, Tryon wanted to enlist. Despite his youth, he wanted to get married.

He was able to do both, but not until the spring of 1864. Coming by the Dickerson homestead, his wagon hitched to a team of horses, nineteen-year-old Tryon Harding asked to take two of their daughters out for a ride. They went directly to the Methodist preacher in the next town. He married Phoebe while her equally excited sister, Deborah, the only legal adult in the party, witnessed the swift ceremony. The elopement was kept from both families when Tryon went off rather musically to war, first as a fifer, later as a drummer, in units of the Ohio Volunteers. Returning ill but unscathed, he and Phoebe finally revealed their secret marriage to their less-than-distressed families. Tryon built another house on the site of the old Harding log cabin and went back to teaching school. He didn't intend to stay long. Like so many other fathers of American presidents, Harding hardly lacked for energy or ambition, but his nebulous plans would never quite work out. Like so many other mothers of American presidents, Phoebe Dickerson had grander dreams that would center on her first son.

On November 2, 1865, he was born — a large, healthy baby. The couple gave him the imposing name of Warren Gamaliel Harding. This was hardly Phoebe's choice, but was after a Methodist minister in Tryon's family. She would not lose many arguments in the future. Still, she soon started calling her boy "Winnie." Phoebe had always been deeply religious, and she was certain her son must be destined for greatness. When he was only ten days old, she took him to be blessed by the local Methodist preacher, and early began regaling relatives with stories of his exceptional temperament and talents. As Russell writes, "It was her belief, part of the American myth and common to many a farmer's wife, that he might grow up to be president of the United States." As it turned out, Harding would be the first president born after the Civil War. Warren was soon attending Methodist meetings with his mother, attired in a colorful, special dress and cap she made for him. She wrote her sister in 1866, "I have plenty of housework, sewing, knitting to do, besides taking care of the sweetest, dearest little brother you ever saw." Phoebe would have seven more children, but none who fueled her expectations as Winnie did.

Ever ambitious and restless, Tryon had tired of teaching. His aim was not to move outward so much as upward. He tried farming, since his family had property, but his real goal was to be a country doctor. He "read" medicine, poring over used texts and making the rounds with a local doctor who was also a Baptist preacher. He even went to a homeopathic medical college in Cleveland and received a degree. He became accepted throughout the region as a medical practitioner, but never achieved the wide recognition that led to financial security. Tryon also viewed himself as an entrepreneur, boldly exchanging one enterprise for another. He invested in real estate and livestock and ran a drugstore and a newspaper, all in Ohio, but sustained success escaped his grasp. Often his growing family was on the verge of destitution.

Despite her household chores and her babies, Phoebe became the family's salvation, especially after Tryon finally gave up aimless speculation and moved his brood to a forty-acre farm. Phoebe had always found time to help her neighbors, particularly in assisting with the birth of their children. She became a professional midwife — an essential occupation practiced by women, especially in rural areas. Her husband's medical degree had not led to security. Phoebe, who managed to find the time to take Cleveland courses of her own in obstetrics, began specializing not only in birthing but also in the treatment of women's ailments in their homes. Eventually she obtained a state license as a "homeopathic" and advertised herself as a doctor of obstetrics, treating women's and children's diseases. Offering the advantages of private sanitarium care at moderate cost, she was successful where her husband had failed. The support she supplied her family was not only financial but also emotional and moral. Tryon loved his children, but he was frequently distracted. By necessity, if not by inclination, Phoebe became the head of her household.

The Methodist church was her bulwark. She loved Scripture and poetry with equal ardor. Her Winnie, "bright beyond his years," whom she had personally taught to read and calculate at an early age, stood out at Sunday school. By the age of four, prepared by his proud mother, he was declaiming in public. As Russell points out, "Unlike the staid Baptist convictions of the Hardings, Phoebe's Methodism held something of the . . . glow of the Wesleyans of the previous century. Except for her religious zeal, she was a quiet, dark woman, always ready to help

Phoebe Harding
Courtesy of Brown Brothers

with self-acquired efficiency when any Blooming Grove woman was in labor." Biographer Charles Mee describes Phoebe at about thirty, "her hair pulled tightly back, her eyes calm and gentle . . . both austere and lovely." She particularly loved gardening and flowers, as the adult Warren Harding never forgot.

He spent several years in the local school that had been donated by his family, before moving to his father's farm near the larger town of Caledonia. Its Methodist church became Phoebe's second home, Bible quotations her daily discourse, hymns always on her lips. When his father acquired the local newspaper, young Warren had his first taste of printing, which he much preferred to farming. Of the many men who became president, proudly professing their ties to the soil, few seem to have really liked it very much at the time. Warren, more imposing than his father and very handsome, was invariably popular in school, despite occasional taunting about his dark complexion. He continued to be a good if not especially energetic student. At the age of fifteen he went on to Ohio Central College, where he blossomed. Building on his mother's early encouragement, Warren became an outstanding debater, edited the school newspaper, headed its literary society, and showed his first interest in politics. He also demonstrated his mother's influence by joining the local Methodist church, helping to earn his tuition by painting it and staining its pews.

His family, now settled in Marian, which Warren would always view as his home, had undergone a wrenching tragedy. A younger brother and sister died of complications from a severe form of jaundice. Phoebe's medical skills could not save them, and Tryon was away. In their anguish, each looked for answers. Tryon took his wife to a camp meeting held by Seventh Day Adventists, newly arrived in Ohio. Despite her firm Methodism, Phoebe began a Bible-study group in her home. Perhaps as a result of the inexplicable loss she had been powerless to prevent, Phoebe was drawn to the prophetic certainty of this new faith, which overcame even the constancy of her Wesleyan inheritance. Soon she was evangelizing with all the fervor of a convert. Warren always respected the sincerity of his mother's religious convictions, but after college, he became — at least formally — a Baptist, and was not particularly noted for his piety.

Marian was a city on the move, and Warren was no more anxious to depart from his roots than his parents had been. Like his father, he briefly tried a number of occupations — teaching, selling insurance, writing for a newspaper. In 1884 he and two friends bought a bankrupt paper, the *Marian Star*. It would never be truly profitable until Warren's hard-driving wife, Florence, whom he married in 1891, began managing its finances, but it helped launch his political career. An active Republican, Harding was finally elected, after as many defeats as victories, to the United States Senate in 1914. Utterly undistinguished but reliable and eminently amiable, he emerged as a surprising but successful candidate for the presidency in 1920. Perhaps his greatest asset was that he really looked the part. As the results proved, the nation was ready for a return to "normalcy," personified by this reassuring, friendly Midwesterner. If his talents were moderate, so was his rhetoric. Some writers have suggested that Harding coined the word "normalcy" himself in this context; if so, it was a rare act of originality.

Of course, looking back, there is little that seems normal in Warren Harding's presidency or in his personal life. He was as ill prepared for high office as the equally well-intentioned Ulysses S. Grant and was done in not by his enemies but by his friends. One of Harding's libidinous relationships led to an illegitimate daughter, and the rampant scandals in his administration drove him to his death in 1923. The medical cause of his death is believed to have been a blood clot after a massive heart attack. His wife, five years his senior, permitted no autopsy. She can't have been happy with his infidelity, but apparently there is no truth to the rumor that she hastened his demise. Harding called her "the Duchess," but it was his mother who always reigned in his heart.

Phoebe Elizabeth Dickerson Harding died on May 20, 1910, at the age of sixty-six, bedridden after a severe fall. She had lived long enough to see her son elected lieutenant governor of Ohio. Perhaps it is not too much to suggest that the best moments of Warren Harding's presidency were a reflection of his mother's ingrained Bible-based values. It was Harding's august secretary of state whose treaty reduced the navies of the great powers. It was Harding who expressed his belief in free speech by releasing the Socialist Eugene Debs from jail. Most of all, it was Harding, not the segregation-supporting Woodrow Wilson, who spoke in the South in favor of full legal equality for all the nation's citizens, black as well as white. This was not the result of Harding's complexion but of his convictions. He was not a strong man, but he had decent instincts. With his father and siblings, he had been by his mother's bedside when the end came. He later wrote, "She never complained, never feared before she lost consciousness. . . . Surely there are for her all the rewards in eternity God bestows on his very own." He could not speak for himself, he added, "but dear, dear Mother will wear a crown."

HARDING'S vice president, Calvin Coolidge, was visiting at his boyhood home of Plymouth Notch, Vermont, on August 2, 1923, when just after midnight a telegram messenger arrived with the news. The president had suddenly died in San Francisco. Coolidge's father, a notary public, administered a hastily typed oath of office. Calvin kissed the family Bible, grasped his father's hand, embraced his distraught wife, and dictated to his secretary — who had accompanied him — a brief public statement. Expressing continuity, it ended with the faith "that God will direct the destinies of our Nation." By the morning of August 3, neighbors and reporters from throughout the area had found their way to his door. The new president greeted everyone personally, his friends warmly, but said little. After breakfast, before returning to Washington, as biographer William Allen White writes, Coolidge "went across the field to the little family cemetery . . . where he paused for a time in front of the marble headstone where his mother lay buried." Her image had been with him every day since her death, and would be every day until his own.

Calvin Coolidge is still renowned for his extreme taciturnity, but his affection for his parents went beyond words. Coolidge did not require Theodore Roosevelt's exuberance. He so cherished his Vermont childhood that he wrote, "Even when I try to divest it of that halo which I know always surrounds the past, I am unable to create any other impression than that it was fresh and clean." Even after he became president, Coolidge continued to kiss his father whenever they met. Yet, as biographer Robert Sobel writes, "As close as Calvin was to his father, he was still closer to his mother, Victoria Moor Coolidge." Already an invalid when she bore him and his younger sister, Abigail, Coolidge's mother died when he was only twelve. "The greatest grief that can come to a boy came to me," he wrote in his autobiography, "Life was never to seem the same again."

"Vermont is my birthright," Coolidge wrote. "Here one gets close to nature. . . . Folks are happy and contented. They belong to themselves, live within their incomes, and fear no man." Coolidge was proud of his "English Puritan stock" and their "courageous pioneer spirit." The Coolidges went back to the Massachusetts Bay Colony, many achieving distinction. It was the grandfather of his grandfather, Captain John Coolidge, who founded the family's first farm in Vermont, near the town of Plymouth Notch on the eastern slope of the Green Mountains. The region was "an unbroken wilderness" until the French and Indian War, when a military road was cut through by Lord Jeffrey Amherst. Settlers began arriving in numbers only after the Revolution. Captain Coolidge's service entitled him and his five children to five homesteads. By 1840 the town and surrounding farms had over 1,400 inhabitants. Young Calvin's physical connection with all those Yankee forebears was his colorful grandfather, Calvin Galusha Coolidge, a cherished companion of his childhood who was never quite reconciled to *his* son's forsaking the soil to go into trade.

The family of Calvin's mother did not possess quite so diverse a heritage as her name suggests. Victoria Josephine Moor was apparently named after a queen and an empress, one English and one French, but her own mother, Abigail Franklin Moor, was as Puritan as the Coolidges, and her father, Hiram Dunlop Moor, was of Scotch, Irish, and Welsh descent. She was born on a Vermont farm in 1846 but moved at the age of two to the more populous hamlet of Plymouth Notch. Her parents had prospered, and they lived in the largest house in town. Here Victoria met and eventually attended a private academy with a sturdy youth named John Coolidge. On May 6, 1868, when she was twenty-two and he twenty-three, they were wed. They moved into a relatively spacious one-and-a-half-story five-room cottage, which was attached to the village post office Coolidge administered and to his general store. Virtually everything else that we know of Victoria Moor Coolidge is through the poignant memories of her son, the only time in his life he was moved to such eloquence. The terrible losses he suffered later, of his supportive sister and his beloved son, he mourned in language more spare and grief more silent.

John Calvin Coolidge was born on July 4, 1872. He always rejoiced in the patriotic nature of the date. Coolidge, meaning no disrespect but never given to anything extraneous, dropped the name John as soon as he could. His only sister, Abigail, called Abbie, was born three years later. She inherited something of her father's sturdy physique. Unfortunately, Calvin did not. His was more the delicate frame of his mother's family. He was small, frail, slender, and frequently ill with severe colds and asthma. "The only thing close to flamboyant about him," Sobel writes, "was his bright red hair, which contrasted with his pale, freckled face." He was also extremely shy. He would learn to love reading, sledding, and horseback riding, but even these favorite pursuits were solitary. He had no inclination for team sports. One day he would admit to his charming wife, Grace, "I am as much interested in human beings as one could possibly be, but it is desperately hard for me to show it." He would always be uncomfortable meeting new people, even as president. In that sense, as he admitted, "I've never really grown up."

It was not so much his lack of gregariousness that concerned his parents, however, as his perilous health. As Sobel points out, life expectancy, even in the fresh air of Vermont, was little more than forty years. Tuberculosis was especially feared, and many in the Moor family in particular had died of it. Before he went to school, with his mother ailing and his father already away at the state legislature, Calvin came under the influence of the other two people he felt most comfortable with — his grandfather, Galusha, and his grandmother, Almeda Coolidge. Calvin's mother loved novels and poetry, but his grandmother introduced him to biographies as well as the Bible she read a portion of daily. Their Congregational church was not based, Coolidge recalled, so much on "public profession" as on practical adherence to the gospel of faith, charity, and good works. While she was able, Almeda looked after the local church, a task in which she was succeeded by Calvin's father. Wed to such a deeply devout woman "who daily sought for divine guidance in prayer," Grandfather Galusha in his final illness had Calvin, already a veteran of Sunday school, read to him the first chapter of the Gospel of St. John. On taking the oath of office in 1925 after being elected president, Coolidge placed his hand on that portion of the gospel he best recalled from his childhood. His grandparents, no less than his parents, had taught him piety, honesty, and thrift, in addition to a bit about having fun. Galusha died when Calvin was only six, but not before taking him to the state capital in Montpelier and ceremoniously sitting him in the governor's chair.

John Coolidge was a good deal more than a country shopkeeper, postmaster, and sometime farmer. "My father," Calvin Coolidge wrote, "had qualities that were greater than any I possess. He was a man of untiring industry and great tenacity of purpose . . . decidedly a man of character. . . . I was exceedingly anxious to grow up like him." John was also a man of substance, who uncomplainingly supported his son well into his thirties and left a substantial estate when he died in 1926. He served as constable, justice of the peace, and member of the state legislature and senate; was a "colonel" on the staff of the governor; dabbled in real estate, insurance, and credit evaluations; was so handy with his hands and tools that he could fix almost anything; and possessed immense physical strength and a judgment respected by all. His father, Coolidge succinctly concluded, hated waste and "was successful." In short, he was a throwback to the fathers of presidents in the earliest days of the republic, who were invariably the first citizens of their communities, however modest those communities were. John Coolidge was so generous to Calvin that he could even be forgiven his remarriage seven years after the death of Calvin's mother. Carrie Brown Coolidge, whom John would also outlive, was in fact a loving stepmother to Calvin, but by then he was already in college.

In the autobiography Coolidge wrote almost a half-century after his mother's death, the shortest presidential autobiography ever written, it is extraordinary to see how vivid are his recollections of her:

> [My childhood home was] well shaded with maple trees and had a front yard enclosed by a picket fence. In summertime, Mother planted flower beds there. . . . While in theory I was always urged to work and to save, in practice I was permitted to do my share of playing and wasting. . . . It seems impossible that any man could describe his mother. I cannot describe mine . . . [but] She was of a very light and fair complexion with a rich growth of brown hair that had a glint of gold in it. Her hands and features were regular and finely modeled. The older people always told me how beautiful she was in her youth.
>
> Whatever was grand and beautiful in form and color attracted her.

Victoria Coolidge

Courtesy of the Calvin Coolidge Presidential Library and Museum

It seemed as if the rich green tints of the foliage and the blossoms of the flowers came for her in the springtime, and in the autumn it was for her that the mountainsides were struck with crimson and with gold.

When she knew that her end was near she called us children to her bedside, where we knelt down to receive her final parting blessing. In an hour she was gone. It was her thirty-ninth birthday. I was twelve years old. We laid her away in the blustering snows of March. . . . Five years and forty-one years later almost to a day my sister and my father followed her. It always seemed to me that the boy I lost was her image. . . . They all rest together on the sheltered hillside among five generations of Coolidge family.

So many stories were told of his father, but only Calvin seemed able to remember anything about his mother. "There was a touch of mysticism and poetry in her nature," he wrote, "which made her love to gaze at the purple sunsets and watch the evening stars." "I wish I could speak with her," he would still say decades after her death. "I wish that often." Her portrait was always in his office, on his dressing table at home, and in his breast pocket, inside the watch case next to his heart. Yet he never discussed his grief in public. White feels that both mother and son were probably repressed, but that does not really seem an accurate description. Coolidge so genuinely personified the careful, taciturn New Englander that eventually he began to enjoy, in contemporary parlance, putting people on. When he went up to Burlington to see his intended, a friend asked, "Got some business here?" "No," Coolidge replied, "came up to marry Grace." The memory of his ethereal mother was bound to evoke a personal tenderness he could not extend to others; her picture was like a religious icon. The fair creature Calvin recalled was not the stuff of anecdotes but of dreams. Yet she had loved most of all not her poetry and transitory flowers but the children she feared she would be denied knowing as adults.

Victoria would not see her son through his shy student days at Black River Academy, or at Amherst College, where he actually learned to enjoy public speaking and mingling with others. She could not offer solace during his long delay in getting settled as a Massachusetts lawyer who preferred trying cases to the back-slapping arena of politics, nor did she see his final ascent to a most unlikely career. His father witnessed it all, culminating in the near miracle of the arrival of "Silent Cal" in the White House. But the mother of Calvin Coolidge, too, was always with him. This is a book replete with the stories of dedicated mothers of American boys who became president. In the case of Coolidge, however, it is the son's enduring dedication to the memory of his mother that is celebrated — and equally remarkable.

ONE OF the most enjoyable aspects of assembling a book such as this is the surprises, not only about the mothers of American presidents but often about the presidents themselves. Who would have expected such eloquence of Calvin Coolidge, for example? The memoirs of Herbert Hoover are equally surprising, not so much for eloquence as for the forceful writing and the touch of humor they display. No other president underwent so thorough a metamorphosis in the public mind as Hoover, who turned in a few short years from one of the most admired Americans to one of the most vilified. Those who recall him in his final incarnation as a rather dour, crusty survivor — a reluctant national treasure intent on streamlining the federal government — might have difficulty imagining Hoover as ever having been young. Yet his youth was full of adventure and the sort of travel a young Richard Nixon or Lyndon Johnson could only dream of. His parents, had they lived longer, would have merited more than a mention in nurturing such ambitions.

Born on August 10, 1874, in a small frame cottage, Herbert Clark Hoover was the second of three children of Jesse Clark and Hulda Minthorn Hoover, Quakers who had settled in the rural town of West Branch, Iowa. Both, in their own way, were pioneers. Hoover's father, an ambitious blacksmith, was intent on becoming a successful farm implements dealer. Hoover's mother had been born on a farm in Ontario, Canada, of an old New England family, but moved with her parents to Iowa when she was only eleven. Remembered as "such a gifted girl" by her sister, Hulda attended the University of Iowa when higher education for women was still rare, taught school for several years, became a very active participant in Quaker meetings, and was deeply involved in promoting causes such as prohibition. She, more than Jesse, seemed destined to become a community leader. Hulda would have been a stalwart of the women's suffrage movement had she been born a little later. One of Herbert's earliest memories was of being taken to the polls by his mother, even though she could not vote. One can imagine Hulda as a fervent supporter of her son's humanitarian efforts, and of pacifism and world peace.

Hulda Hoover
Courtesy of Herbert Hoover Library

When Herbert was only six, his father died of typhoid fever. Hoover recalled, "My recollections of my mother are more vivid and are chiefly of a sweet-faced woman who for two years kept our little family of four together. She took in sewing to add to the family resources. It was only many years later that I learned of her careful saving of the $1,000 insurance upon my father's life in order that it might help in our education." To relieve some of the pressures on Hulda, kindly relatives took the children for months at a time to live with them. Herbert's childhood was brightened by a lengthy stay with his uncle, a U.S. Indian agent to the Osage Nation. Hulda had also earned a bit from the sale of her husband's business. It looked as if she might succeed in keeping her family intact.

Unfortunately, as Herbert continues, "Iowa [was] not all adventure or high life. Nor was Iowa of those days without its tragedy. Medical science was still almost powerless against the contagious diseases which swept the countryside. My own parents were among the victims." Hulda Minthorn Hoover died of pneumonia at the age of thirty-four on February 24, 1883, a promising life extinguished. Her son retained her high-minded Quaker ideals, manifested in his later emphasis on volunteerism and cooperative efforts to solve both national and international crises.

After his mother's death, a council of concerned relatives and friends took over the rearing of the three Hoover children. Hoover, raised by an uncle in Oregon, had nothing but praise for their compassionate efforts. Yet his true family was probably the Stanford University community, which he entered in 1891 as part of its first freshman class. Although a very quiet, self-contained youth, at Stanford he excelled as a student leader, met his future wife, found his vocation in engineering, and launched his career. By the age of forty he had managed mines on five continents, was more than a millionaire, and was just beginning his notable work in the nation's service.

This dry, didactic administrator of food relief hardly seemed a prospective politician, but his humanitarian efforts placed him among the most highly esteemed Americans — from the Great War through the 1920s. Why not "the Great Engineer" as president, keeping prosperity on track? Still, he retained the memory of more arduous times: "On leaving college I needed at once to find some person with a profit motive who needed me to help him earn a profit. At the risk of sounding counter-revolutionary or a defender of evil, I am going to suggest that this test for a job has some advantages." Hoover's writing, unaugmented by others, was so much more direct and colorful than his public speaking or his image. His ninety years of life, a span only equalled by

John Adams and Ronald Reagan among American presidents, encompassed extremes utterly at odds with his methodical, steady demeanor.

The neat, modest white Iowa cottage that was his first home must have always been close to Hoover's heart, but the memories of a mother who dies when a boy is only eight cannot be so vivid as, say, those of Calvin Coolidge, who had four more years to appreciate maternal devotion.

CHAPTER TWELVE

Smothering Mothering

✿ Sara Roosevelt

To MOST contemporary Americans, Theodore and Franklin Roosevelt seem to belong to separate eras. Their mothers, however, were born less than twenty years apart. If, as F. Scott Fitzgerald wrote, the very rich are different from the rest of us, they have also tended to differ from each other. Beyond enjoying immense wealth, Sara Delano Roosevelt had little in common with her predecessor Martha Bulloch Roosevelt. While Martha had been the radiant and pampered daughter of a landed Georgia squire, Sara was the strong-willed but circumspect product of a Hudson Valley hierarchy built on acquisitive commerce. While Martha was vigorous and outgoing but delicate, dying at the age of forty-nine, the physically robust Sara lived to be nearly eighty-seven. In their very different lives, each reflected something of the divergent mores of Northern and Southern gentry in nineteenth-century America.

There was one significant respect in which Sara and Martha Roosevelt were similar, however. Like Martha, Sara was a most devoted presidential mother, though this devotion was expressed very differently. Sara had only one child, and wanted only one. From virtually the day of his birth, Franklin Delano Roosevelt became the focus of all her considerable energies, to the exclusion of everything and everyone else. Her advice to him continued ceaselessly as long as she lived, even after the competing counsel of Franklin's wife, Eleanor, began to prevail.

There was nothing diminutive or delicate about Sara Delano. The word most often used to describe her is "formidable." One of eleven children, nine of whom made it into adulthood, she stood a full and very erect five feet ten inches tall. She was not only commanding but demanding, albeit in a ladylike way. Called "Sallie," Sara was not so comely as her sisters, who were celebrated for their beauty, but she had a good mind, a hearty constitution, a will so strong that it could be intimidating, and a zest for life just under the surface of her impeccable manners. She dressed faultlessly, traveled widely, took part in no shortage of diversions, and was handsome enough to attract her share of admirers, even suitors. But why settle for the sort of listless inheritors of family wealth who peopled her circle? In her mid-twenties, Sara was in no hurry to wed, if she got married at all. Nor was she pressured to do so by her father, whom she admired above all other men. He rather liked having this most spirited but still very respectful daughter at home.

Warren Delano was no bloodless specimen of the landed gentry. He was a bold, risk-taking entrepreneur, with more than a touch of the buccaneer. As biographer Frank Freidel writes, Delano prided himself on being a man of action capable of captaining his own sailing ships. He won, lost, and re-won fortunes in the China trade. This included importing opium, ostensibly for medicinal purposes. Later he invested in such domestic ventures as Appalachian coal mines. Delano's wheeling and dealing did not inhibit the social standing of his family. By Victorian times, to the English-aping denizens of the New York elite, heredity mattered more than enterprise. The Delano name had been anglicized not long after the 1621 arrival in Plymouth Colony of a young Huguenot émigré named Philippe de la Noye. As biographer Ted Morgan notes, the Delanos encompassed thirteen bloodlines that could be traced back to the Mayflower. They were at the top of carefully calibrated Eastern society. When Sara was born, in 1854, her father's fortunes were also at their height. Her family was ensconced in a spacious Newburgh mansion called Algonac, commanding a magnificent view of the Hudson River.

Only three years later, however, a financial panic wiped out her father's wealth, dissolving any semblance of security. Warren Delano

Sara Roosevelt
Courtesy of the Franklin D. Roosevelt Library

promptly sailed off to Hong Kong to seek a second fortune. Eventually his family, including eight-year-old Sara, followed him. Timidity was no part of her patrician heritage. During the years her adventurous father successfully turned things around, Sara's education was not limited to the lessons of proper governesses at Algonac. In Asia, and later in Europe, she was exposed to other cultures. Although she found most foreigners "horrid," at least she had seen them at firsthand.

At home her acquaintance encompassed the liveliest of those who were suitably placed socially. One of Sara's favorite people was young Theodore Roosevelt. Despite his unfortunate proclivity for politics, his zest for life was no less than her father's. At a dinner party given by Roosevelt's widowed mother at their Manhattan mansion, Sara was impressed by the attentions of another guest, a cousin of Theodore's named James Roosevelt. At fifty-two, tall, blue-eyed, whiskered, and widowed, James had a mature bearing that set him apart from Sara's younger admirers. He also reminded her, in a less dashing way, of her father. Indeed, although not intimates, Warren Delano and James Roosevelt sat on many boards together. Some of Roosevelt's railroad ventures and his attempts to finance a canal across Nicaragua had fallen victim to periodic financial depressions, but he still commanded sufficient capital to manage major investments. He also maintained a handsome home and farm called Springwood at Hyde Park, only twenty miles across the Hudson from the Delanos. James, who had attended Union College and Harvard Law School, had been rather a hell-raiser in his youth, but one wouldn't have known it from his dignified demeanor in middle age.

If not quite the Delanos, the Roosevelts had sufficient cachet to be counted among the leading Knickerbocker families. Although Franklin Delano Roosevelt, after entering politics, liked to dwell on his thrifty Dutch antecedents, his father James's branch of the family was at least as much English as Dutch. A common ancestor of Franklin and Theodore was Claes Martenszen Van Rosenvelt, who came to New York in the seventeenth century and established a prosperous mercantile business. By the time of the American Revolution, Roosevelts were both prominent sugar refiners in the West Indies and leading (if rather conservative) patriots in New York. The most prominent, Isaac Roosevelt, eventually presided over the Bank of New York, served in the state senate, and helped assure New York's ratification of the Constitution.

By the time he met Sara Delano, James Roosevelt was more interested in consolidating his holdings than in pursuing new commercial ventures. His pursuit was of Sara, who he sensed reciprocated his feelings. He invited her to a weeklong house party at Hyde Park. Doris Faber describes Sara's imposing appearance at the age of twenty-six;

"with her brown hair coiled into a dignified chignon, she looked rather regal already." It is hard to imagine what she might have been like as the little girl called "Sallie." By the time she visited Hyde Park, as Morgan adds, Sara "already had a matronly dignity." James Roosevelt may not have been looking for an empress, but he saw in Sara the perfect consort to help him preside over his compact domain. Like the English country gentlemen he emulated, he fancied himself the beneficent squire of at least the community around Hyde Park. When he asked Sara to arrange the flowers on his luncheon table, both appreciated the significance of such an invitation.

Warren Delano couldn't understand why Mr. Roosevelt started visiting him with such frequency. When Roosevelt finally came to the point, Delano was thunderstruck. He liked the fellow well enough, even though Roosevelt was a Democrat, an anomaly in the Hudson Valley aristocracy, and possessed financial assets only about a third of those Sara held in her own right. But Roosevelt was twice Sara's age, and his son "Rosy," by his first wife, was as old as Sara. Yet she, too, if not quite captivated, had been deeply impressed by Roosevelt. She prevailed on her reluctant father to grant his consent. The couple was married at Algonac in 1880, the same year Theodore Roosevelt married Alice Hathaway Lee.

Sara found in James the cheerful, considerate, and generous husband she had anticipated. Although not excessively ardent, he welcomed the prospect of another child. Perhaps an extension of the bloodlines of two notable families was in Sara's mind, as well, when she agreed to marry him. Franklin Delano Roosevelt was conceived in Paris during a ten-month honeymoon that was more like a grand tour. He was born at Hyde Park, a very difficult delivery, on January 30, 1882. His concerned father stayed by Sara's bedside all night. For whatever reasons, the arrival of this ten-pound, healthy, happy baby almost immediately transcended all her prior interests. "Giving birth was the one achievement of Sara's life," Morgan concludes. "She was a good, devoted, companionable wife, but she had no more physical relations with her husband for the remaining . . . years of her marriage. . . . All the rest of her days she fought a veiled but intense battle to retain possession of Franklin. This was her obsession, her purpose in life, her reason for being."

The obvious question is "Why?" Other dedicated mothers of future American presidents struggled to give their favored sons every advantage at least in part to redeem their own sacrifices, but Sara's son was born of privilege. Other intrusive and domineering parents of prominent men, such as the mother of Douglas MacArthur, had specific career goals in view, but Sara, who would always counsel Franklin to avoid consorting with unsuitable people, had no elevated responsibility in mind for him. Apparently he was special simply because he was her son and had Delano blood in his veins. His half-brother duplicated their father's career as a country gentleman of limited ambition. The irony is that, at least initially, Sara could see little more in Franklin's future.

Yet he was her life's work. James, as he eased into his role as paternalistic lord of the manor, also had a great deal of time to devote to his son. Together they rode around the estate and the surrounding countryside. Franklin developed an intense awareness of the natural world akin to Theodore Roosevelt's. He learned to love both the land and the sea. His father taught him to sail and ride, fish and skate, and he took him on the Roosevelts' private railroad car to business meetings. Sara was not the only doting parent. When James died of heart failure in 1900 at the age of seventy-two, Franklin was about the same age as his distant cousin Theodore Roosevelt had been when his own father died. Theodore's mother had lived for only another six years. Only half her husband's age when they married, Sara outlived James by forty-three years.

She despaired in her diary that "all is over" when he died, and her feelings for him were undoubtedly genuine. But how could all be over when the son they both cherished was not yet twenty? From the first, Sara had personally ordered every aspect of Franklin's life. Although servants and nursemaids were always at hand, as Freidel writes, Sara "herself bathed and dressed her baby, and breast-fed him for over a year. He was eight years old before he was able to take a bath alone. Until he was in his twenties, she kept the most minute diary of his activities. His upbringing absorbed her." Later, she would extend this involvement to his children and their children. Franklin wore dresses until he was five and had long blond curls his mother could not bear to have cut. When it finally became necessary, locks of his hair were placed in a satin-lined box that contained other mementos of Franklin's childhood. Sara saved everything.

Although she employed tutors to supervise his carefully structured education, Sara personally taught her son reading and geography. At the age of three, he made his first extended trip to Europe, and early developed a proficiency in foreign languages. Franklin's childhood lacked nothing except normalcy. Until he was fourteen, his only playmates were relatives and similarly privileged children from surrounding estates. Even his recreation was regulated by his mother. The closest young Franklin came to a customary classroom was, oddly enough, in Germany. When he was nine, during one of their many trips to Europe, his parents placed him in a German school while they took the waters in Bad Nauheim. For six weeks, Franklin had to relate to children he didn't know and receive instruction in a language other than his own. He relished the experience, although he didn't much like the Germans. His mother probably viewed most of them as "horrid," in any case. At home, she was so conscious of her son's feelings that if she felt obliged to reprimand him, it was always out of the hearing of the servants. There was a good deal of turnover in the Roosevelt household. Sara was neither the easiest employer nor the most generous.

As Morgan writes, there was nothing traumatic in Franklin's childhood. His parents, although not given to overt affection, never argued. All was ordered and predictable. They included their son in everything and took him almost everywhere, including their regular summer trips to Campobello Island in New Brunswick, Canada. Perhaps the only thing that saved Franklin from being smothered by all this attention was that his parents would occasionally take trips on their own, leaving their adored boy for a time in the care of governesses. He would be free to sail with little supervision, tend to his collections of ship models and stamps, and enjoy the stream of letters from his parents.

It would seem on the surface that the childhoods of Franklin and Theodore Roosevelt were similar. In fact, other than the endowments of wealth and privilege and the devotion of their parents, they were as different as the parents themselves. Franklin may have been their "special treasure," but the affection of Sara and James Roosevelt for their only son was more verbal than physical. In their very proper household, there were none of the emotional hugging "melts" of Theodore's family. Martha Bulloch Roosevelt was a joyous, guileless Southern belle, not bent on dominating anyone. Franklin Roosevelt's mother was a formidable figure intent on totally directing her son's life. Theodore Roosevelt's father was almost saintly, an exemplar of gilded-age philanthropy. It may be, as some historians have suggested, that he felt guilt over how his inherited millions had been accumulated, but whatever its motivations, his personal belief in direct social action was deep and devout. Franklin Roosevelt's father was a conventionally public-spirited, well-intentioned member of his class, but he was limited by parochialism and his Anglophile pretensions. What separates the two is the difference between authentic Christian charity and noblesse oblige. An unkind relative said of James's English affectations, "He tried to pattern himself on Lord Lansdowne, sideburns and all, but what he really looked like was Lansdowne's coachman." James Roosevelt did what was expected of one in his position. He cared for his employees, and the town of Hyde Park existed primarily to service his estate. He devoted time to community activities, charitable committees, and his church vestry. When President Cleveland wanted to name him an ambassador, he declined. His domain might be relatively modest, but it was his own. At his death, his estate went entirely to his wife.

However protected his family's mansion was from the turmoil of events outside, Theodore Roosevelt's Manhattan was a cosmopolitan world far removed from Franklin Roosevelt's idyllic Hyde Park. Moreover, Theodore had siblings, who at least competed for his parents' attentions. His critical health crisis had come early in his life, demanding the most strenuous response from both youthful parents. Franklin's health crisis came when he was almost thirty. His father was long deceased and his mother was in her sixties. Franklin Roosevelt's parents were products of their social environment to a greater extent than even their own parents had been. James Roosevelt had endearing qualities as a husband and father, but he was a terrible snob. When his far more affluent neighbors, the Vanderbilts, invited the Roosevelts to dinner, he insisted that Sara decline. He viewed them as parvenu. Accepting their invitation meant one would have to reciprocate. Both James and Sara attended church regularly, but it was more a matter of propriety than piety. To Sara, the Protestant Episcopal Church was the only socially acceptable denomination. She termed the church of many of her husband's relatives "Dutch Deformed."

Yet, in time, she must have wanted Franklin to be more than simply an exemplary son. It is said that she was not really surprised when he was elected governor, or even president. He was at least in part a Delano, after all, capable of any achievement, but could it possibly be worth having to deal with so many disagreeable people? To Theodore Roosevelt, public service had been an honored inheritance. Despite the similar insularity of their formative years, he was initially far better able than Franklin to deal as equals with those of humbler origins. Politics came naturally to Teddy. The experience that turned Franklin toward a commitment beyond the self-imposed limitations of his parents' world did not stem from their influence. When he was fourteen, his parents decided to send him to a remarkable New England boarding school called Groton. It had been established in the 1880s, too late for Theodore to attend. Even Franklin's parents understood that to become a truly self-confident adult, he had best learn to mingle with others before going off to college. Although Sara wrote in her diary, "It is hard to leave my darling boy," at least Groton was administered by Episcopalians.

Based on the Rugby School in England, Groton combined the concepts of Christian commitment and public service. It was the obligation of the well-educated sons of leading families to not only lead the nation but to devote their efforts to the less fortunate. Groton's founder and headmaster, Endicott Peabody, was to Franklin Roosevelt what Theodore Roosevelt Sr. had been to Theodore Roosevelt Jr. — the true father of his ambitions. The spartan regimen of Groton, combining physical and intellectual rigor, would have meshed well with Teddy Roosevelt's concept of a strenuous outgoing life. Indeed, he later wrote to a nephew at Groton who was lonely and homesick, "You must make good. . . . A boy with your ancestry *must* be worthy of his ancestry." At first Franklin had difficulty adjusting to this new environment. There was nothing lacking in his deportment. At home, adjudged to be a boy who could do no wrong, Franklin gave his parents little reason to complain. But he had no experience with meeting people, even young people, on his own. By his senior year, however, Roosevelt — who had entered a year late — had made fast friends and was active and well-liked. He had learned to cope.

He also affirmed his Christian faith not merely in form but in action, accompanying Groton masters and other students to pay charitable visits to the underprivileged in surrounding towns and at a summer camp. Freidel writes, "Roosevelt's religion, like that of Peabody, was simple and unquestioning. . . . As president, he was to hold private church services before his inauguration and on other momentous occasions." In one of his most memorable public services, he sang hymns "like the Methodists" with Winston Churchill on the HMS *Prince of Wales* in 1941. Perhaps Roosevelt attained too much self-confidence at Groton; when he went on to Harvard, his enthusiasm struck some of his more elitist classmates as excessive. Although elected editor of the *Crimson* and very popular on the campus, Roosevelt was not elected to Porcellian, the most prestigious club. In a residue of his patrician upbringing, Roosevelt long considered this the greatest disappointment of his life.

Sara missed Franklin so terribly that she visited Cambridge to be near him. She even considered taking courses at Harvard to "improve her mind." When her son turned eighteen, she had written him, "What a difference in our lives you have made and how I thank God daily for having given you to me." As she grew older and Franklin turned to a career in politics, Sara tried to transcend the limitations of her husband's world and her own bias. Their lives had been rooted in certainty. She had imparted to her son an appreciation of his lineage, but she understood that now he was looking more to the future than to the past. A letter from an uncle reinforced what Franklin had absorbed at Groton: "We are proud of our ancestors. Will our descendants be proud of us?"

Even with Franklin out of college, Sara's advice never slackened. Her continued influence was based on the pragmatic reality that she still controlled the family purse strings, but Franklin's streak of independence had long been apparent to her. His "Dearest Mama" letters from school always told her what she wanted to hear, but they were never so unguarded as Theodore Roosevelt's spontaneous outpourings to his "darling Motherling." Franklin had inherited something of his mother's strength and self-confidence. Perhaps in dealing with her he had also developed the calculation and avoidance of confrontation that would define his relationships in later life. Sara successfully urged him when he was twenty-one to delay announcing his engagement to his fifth cousin Eleanor, then only eighteen. After all, Sara had not wed until she was twenty-six, her father until he was thirty-three. But the marriage of Franklin to Eleanor was only postponed. When they wed in 1905, it moved Franklin even closer to the influence of Theodore Roosevelt, who gave the bride away and was inevitably the center of attention. Sara had to accommodate new realities.

Eleanor had initially viewed her handsome, fun-loving husband as something of an insubstantial "feather duster," and others considered him more than a bit arrogant, but his career moved inexorably toward public service. After Harvard, he studied law at Columbia. Although not taking a degree, he managed to pass the bar. By 1910 he was elected to the New York State senate as a reform Democrat. Reelected in 1912, he gave up his seat when asked by President Woodrow Wilson to serve as assistant secretary of the navy, a position previously held by his cousin Theodore.

As Franklin's career took off, Sara must have felt a mixture of pride and apprehension. She wrote him in much the same tone Abigail Adams had used to address her son, John Quincy. "Everything is so new," Sara commiserated, "that it will take time to fit *into* it. Try not to write your signature so small." Even years later, when Franklin was nominated by the Democratic Party to run for governor of New York, Sara continued to offer counsel as if he were still a schoolboy, reassuring him that, if need be, she would supplement his salary. The uncertainty in her own mind was not easily resolved. Her adored son might well be happier duplicating his father's comfortable life, but had she not raised him for something more elevated, some grand achievement? Yet politics led inevitably to associating with such unsuitable, unkempt characters as Franklin's new adviser, Louis Howe. It meant stress, controversy, publicity — the antithesis of a gentleman's values. Sara did not really want her

Sara Roosevelt with her son Franklin Delano Roosevelt
Courtesy of the Franklin D. Roosevelt Library

son to run for governor — or did she? Whatever her conflicted emotions, in the end the competitive fire of the daughter of Warren Delano won out. If her son was intent on running, she told him, "I do not want you to be defeated." She would always support him unreservedly, whether she agreed with all his decisions and positions or not. She might argue with him in private, but she uttered no discouraging words in public.

Sara Roosevelt has been portrayed in recent years as virtually the Wicked Witch of the East, in the prism of her difficult relationship with her daughter-in-law, Eleanor. Sara *was* domineering, and she could certainly be tactless, thoughtless, or even cruel, but her motivation was invariably whatever she thought would be best for Franklin. Her substantial wedding gift to the couple was a New York townhouse adjoining her own on Sixty-fifth Street, with a passageway between the two. Completely furnished to Sara's taste, the arrangement reduced Eleanor to tears. At Hyde Park, Sara continued to sit at the head of the table. She still presided over her son's domiciles even after his marriage, just as she continued to control his finances. Somehow, Franklin had difficulty understanding why his young wife, both of whose parents had died when she was very young, resented her subservient status. As children came, five in all, Sara undertook to direct their upbringing as well, increasingly disdaining her daughter-in-law's parenting skills. Eleanor came to feel, in the words of biographer Blanche Wiesen Cook, like "an outsider in a land of strangers." In time she would learn to assert both her independence and her own influence on her husband, but first two serious crises had to be overcome. Either could have wrecked Franklin Roosevelt's political career.

In the fall of 1918 Eleanor found a packet of love letters to Franklin from her vivacious social secretary, Lucy Mercer. The discovery of their affair, so devastating to Eleanor, nearly led to her divorce from Franklin. Sara simply forbade it, threatening — although it must have hurt her — to cut off all financial support. Her concern was likely far more with avoiding scandal and sustaining the code of her social class, but the result, in concert with a reconsideration by the parties involved, was to preserve both Franklin's marriage, at least formally, and his political career. It put Sara in uneasy alliance with Louis Howe, who had already envisioned Franklin as a future president of the United States. In the second, more sustained crisis, they would be at odds. In 1921, while vacationing at Campobello Island, Franklin contracted crippling poliomyelitis. After years of strenuous but fruitless attempts at recovery, he determined to continue his political career. In 1924 he nominated Al Smith for president at the Democratic National Convention, and in 1928, supported by Smith, Howe, and Eleanor, Roosevelt agreed to run for governor of New York. He would serve in political office for the rest of his life.

Almost from the first diagnosis of polio, Sara had remonstrated with her son to return to Hyde Park under her attentive care. Instead, from 1924 on, Franklin ventured from time to time to Warm Springs, Georgia, in the hope that its waters might have a curative effect on his immobile legs. Polio vaccines were still a quarter-century in the future. It has generally been assumed that Sara foresaw no possible future for her son but invalidism, that this hopeless illness had settled her mind about his future. Perhaps she even capitalized on his illness as a means of sustaining her ascendancy in his life. Sara had long since accepted her son's choice of a career, however, and may have even begun to enjoy it. It is possible that she believed a time of relative repose, away from the demands of public life, would hasten even the remote possibility of recovery. Nevertheless, whether she wished it or not, the practical effect had Sara prevailed would have been to end her son's political career. Yet there need not be sinister intent in a mother's concern for her son. As always, Sara wanted what she thought best for Franklin. It was at about this time, however, that Eleanor came into her own, and her view prevailed over her mother-in-law's. Eleanor would always believe that Franklin's more compassionate nature derived from his own suffering. However her personal relationship with her husband had changed, Eleanor ultimately become his eyes, ears, and legs — and a trusted, if sometimes overly persistent, sounding board. Often her ideas were in advance of his.

Sara, of course, remained intrusive — she could hardly be otherwise — but she accommodated her dignified demeanor to be as supportive of her son as possible. She endured interviews and managed to say nothing controversial. She appeared in newsreels, a striking figure in her long dresses. She even shook hands with cigar-chomping politicos. If not quite the endearing image of a Mother McKinley, Sara became a national celebrity of sorts, a reassuring reminder of nineteenth-century verities. When her son finally won the presidency, she issued a poignant plea: "I shall be glad if every mother will pray God to help and preserve him." As Anthony writes, Sara eventually came to relish "her public status, reigning over fund-raisers and balls, the grande dame of a historic era. She even wrote an eminently forgettable book, *My Boy Franklin*." In 1939, Sara very visibly helped Eleanor and Franklin host a historic visit from the king and queen of England, although the hot dogs that were served would not have been her choice of fare. Sara presented a rather regal figure herself, and even Eleanor came to admire her indomitable fortitude. She may not have been an easy person for anyone to live with, but she was constant and even cheerful. One of her favorite expressions was, "Every day is a good day."

Some historians have suggested that Sara's conservative influence induced her son to make less onerous the impact of his policies on the business and commercial interests of the nation. It is not true. This is not the venue in which to explore the changing configurations of the New Deal, or why many of those who shared Roosevelt's social background came to revere and revile him in turn. He was a most complex man — both charming and devious. His immense contribution in 1932, whatever his own doubts, was to impart hope to a nation on the verge of upheaval. Through this he saved both our political institutions and our free-enterprise system. It was only gearing up for war that hastened authentic economic recovery, however. Roosevelt's mother was neither an intellectual nor an ideologue. Her contribution was not in what he did, or tried to do, but in what he was: his air of confidence and his underlying tenacity. In the end, he was not so much smothered by her excessive devotion as sustained.

Nearing her eighty-seventh birthday, finally confined to a wheelchair like her son, Sara Delano Roosevelt came home from Campobello to Hyde Park to be with him. She died on September 7, 1941, and was buried on September 10. Eleanor later wrote to her daughter, Anna, that "Father has begun to forget all that was disagreeable in his relationship to Granny." He was not excessively emotional, she said, but Franklin cried uncontrollably when, alone, he looked through his mother's things and opened the box containing the locks of his baby hair she had cut. He wrote, "Those of us who enjoy the companionship of our mothers beyond the average number of years are indeed fortunate, for we know the good influence they exert. . . . The greatest pleasure we can get is to observe them rejoicing in our achievements." Rejoicing in his achievements was also his mother's greatest pleasure.

CHAPTER THIRTEEN

From the Heart of America

ಇ Martha Truman
ಇ Ida Eisenhower

SUPREME ALLIED COMMANDER Dwight David Eisenhower spoke not only for a nation but for himself as he launched the invasion that would liberate Western Europe. "I come from the heart of America," he said. A year later, when the war had been won, a reporter ventured into that heartland to the modest Kansas home of eighty-three-year-old Ida Stover Eisenhower and asked if she was proud of her son. "Which one?" she replied. On Mother's Day of that same momentous year, arriving at the White House from Missouri after her first airplane ride, ninety-three-year-old Martha Ellen Young Truman deplored the fuss over her visit, insisting, "I wouldn't have come if I'd known all these people were going to be here." Feisty or gentle, both mothers voiced the same unpretentious values. Take your work seriously, not yourself; keep your word. They imparted these values to all their children, not only the ones history would honor.

Of the extent of their mothers' contributions, Harry Truman and Dwight Eisenhower were always aware, and grateful. Speaking for his brothers as well as himself, Eisenhower said, "Mother was by far the greatest influence on our lives." Of his own upbringing, Truman recalled, "She was always a mother who did the right thing, and she taught us, my brother and sister and I, that too." One of the right things was to speak no ill of your kin. Truman never uttered a harsh word about his father, insisting that both his parents were "sentimentalists" who encouraged his ambitions. In old age, he urged oral biographer Merle Miller not to overlook his father, stressing that he had exercised "every bit as much influence" as his mother. It wasn't true, but saying so was characteristic of Truman's upbringing. Even when his relatives were in litigation with each other over the future of his maternal grandmother's farm, Truman lamented only their folly, which merely enriched the lawyers, rather than anyone's evil intent. In his memoirs, Truman, so renowned for plain speaking, recalled his resentment at how his sudden ascension to the presidency escalated "the intrusion of journalistic curiosity about my personal affairs and my family." It was nobody's business.

In later life Eisenhower admitted that his father "had the temper of a Pennsylvania Dutchman" and that it could "blaze with frightening suddenness," but he added that it had rarely flared up without justification. Unlike the equally quick temper of Truman's father, the elder Eisenhower's fury was most often directed at his own sons. But when his father died, Eisenhower expressed regret at how difficult it had been "to let him know the great depth of my affection for him . . . I'm proud he was my father." There is a kind of defensiveness here, akin to Truman's denial that his father had been a failure: "He was the father of a president of the United States, and I think that is success enough for any man."

After 1944, neither Truman nor Eisenhower would enjoy any semblance of the personal privacy they preferred, a residue of their plain Midwestern roots. So different in appearance, experience, demeanor, and even in their conduct of the presidency, they had much more in common — beyond growing up six years apart in neighboring states — than either might have cared to admit. Even the architecture of their ground-hugging presidential libraries would be similar — buildings of the heartland, less pretentious than those of their successors. Close collaborators in the 1940s, they became bitter adversaries in the 1950s. Their tentative reconciliation at the funeral of John F. Kennedy was largely for the sake of appearances. It was not only politics that divided them. To Truman, who cherished loyalty perhaps too indiscriminately, Eisenhower had by his silence betrayed his greatest benefactor, George C. Marshall. Whoever was more nearly in the right, neither had grown up in an environment of equivocation about right and wrong. Such clarity could be hard, but it was brightened in the childhood of each by the implacable optimism of their mothers.

IN RETIREMENT, Harry S. Truman would often tell groups of students who visited his presidential library that three experiences represented the ideal preparation for a career in public service: farming, finance, and the military. This must have seemed positively archaic to students in the 1960s, but it corresponded to Truman's own experiences. Farming was not a matter of choice. Truman, like Eisenhower, was a "Son of the Middle Border," to use biographer David McCullough's phrase, born in 1884 in the agricultural community of Lamar, Missouri. He was the first of three children of a family more Southern than Midwestern in its origins and outlook. His father, the feisty, restless, diminutive John Anderson Truman, both a livestock trader and a farmer, was a man of immense — and ultimately unrealized — ambition. His mother, the equally feisty Martha Ellen Young Truman, was not only a highly engaged participant in her children's lives, but also, until his marriage, Harry Truman's best friend. In addition, Truman had an advantage his successor Eisenhower would not; he was a first son. Sometimes it must have seemed to his younger brother and sister that in the eyes of their mother, Harry was the only son. Both the Trumans and the Youngs were in the second generation of families who had moved to western Missouri from Kentucky, with antecedents in North Carolina and Virginia. They derived from the "yeoman gentry" of England, mingled with Germanic and French origins.

When Truman finally married, his imperious mother-in-law, who never quite accepted him even after he became president, viewed his family as little more than dirt farmers. It was hardly the truth. Harry's paternal grandfather, Anderson Shippe Truman, was satisfied with being a successful farmer. A gentle, soft-spoken man, he loved the fertile farmland of the eastern end of Jackson County, Missouri, and never saw reason to leave. With his equally congenial wife, Mary Jane, who may have been related to President John Tyler, he established a modest but prosperous farm of two hundred acres and became a leader in his Baptist church and community. His second son, John Anderson, the father of Harry Truman, would not be so easily satisfied, or so soft-spoken. After his wife died, Anderson Shippe Truman lived for a time with his son's family and was reputed to be the first to predict that his young grandson, Harry, would be a future president of the United States. Harry never forgot the death of his grandfather, the first the child ever witnessed. He had pulled on the old man's beard to awaken him.

Harry Truman's maternal grandparents were very different and far more a presence in his life. His spirited grandmother Young would live into her ninety-first year, her unreconstructed Southern Democratic sentiments as much a part of Truman's inheritance as his Baptist faith. Like the Trumans, the Youngs came from Kentucky. They had married in a church on land once owned by Abraham Lincoln's grandfather. Unlike the Trumans, Solomon and Harriet Louisa Young, perhaps because both had been orphaned at an early age, possessed formidable ambitions. While Harriet Louisa administered a farm that grew to thousands of acres, near the appropriately named town of Grandview, Missouri, Solomon led cattle drives and wagon trains of pioneers and army provisions during much of the time between 1840 and 1870, all the way west to Utah, Oregon, and California. He was reputed to have purchased a good part of present-day Sacramento. Solomon Young was a man of prodigious energy, a risk-taker seemingly capable of almost anything, and was as often on the Santa Fe Trail as at home. Still, he and his wife managed to have nine children. Harry Truman's mother, Martha Ellen, was the next to last, born in 1852. Hers was anything but a humble rural childhood.

The Civil War, in Truman's Missouri and Eisenhower's Kansas, started long before 1861. Missouri had come into the Union as a slave state, and the Trumans and Youngs owned slaves. Kansas was seen by both sides as a place to settle the issue, and both the Trumans and Youngs lived near the border with Kansas. By the time Martha Ellen Young was four, "bushwhackers" and "redlegs" were already terrorizing communities throughout the region, violence that escalated into a particularly ferocious arena of the Civil War. It spared no one, not unlike the experiences of Andrew Jackson's family in the Revolutionary War. Although their sympathies were Southern, more by heritage than conviction, both Solomon Young and Anderson Truman felt it prudent to sign oaths of loyalty to the Union. The war largely bypassed the Trumans, but Solomon Young had relatives actually fighting for the Confederacy. While he was away — no conflict was going to interfere with business — Union forces, regulars and irregulars, repeatedly raided his farm, butchered his hogs, stole everything that could be moved, burned his barns, nearly hung his young son, and forced his wife to bake biscuits until her hands blistered. Until her dying day, Harriet Louisa Young harbored vivid memories of the war, its evil embodied in the Republican Party of the Union. When, late in her life, her grandson Harry came to visit, resplendent in his new National Guard uniform, she told him politely but firmly to leave. She never wanted to see a blue uniform again. Her sympathies were imparted to her children, and to their children. Harry may have had his earliest interest in history kindled by these stories. When his mother visited the White House in 1945 she would not sleep in the Lincoln Bedroom.

After the war, the Youngs' prosperity returned. Martha Ellen, called "Mattie," moved with her family to a new, much larger house. She never did farm chores, was attended by servants, learned both indoor and outdoor skills — to ride, shoot, play the piano, crochet, and cook — and gained an appreciation of art and literature at the Ladies' Baptist College. Although she invariably rose early and worked hard, helping her mother supervise some twenty hired hands, she was indulged by both her parents. Martha Ellen particularly loved to dance, later describing herself as "what you might call a lightfoot Baptist." She had very much a mind of her own, and no intention of marrying until she was good and ready. McCullough describes this lively young woman as being above average height — about five foot six — striking and slender, "with dark hair, a round bright face, and a way of looking directly at people with her clear, gray-blue eyes." She was very much a Young.

It may have been at one of the dances frequently held in the homes of neighboring farms that she first really noticed John Anderson Truman, although both families had come from the same part of Kentucky. Neighbors of the Trumans in Missouri, the Youngs had contributed the land for the Blue Ridge Baptist Church, which both families attended. Although a year older than Mattie, John was two inches

Martha Truman
Courtesy of the Harry S. Truman Library

shorter. The fact that he was known as "Peanut" may have contributed to his growing reputation for truculence. He was also very proud, a meticulous dresser, and tenacious in going after what he wanted. It was trim Mattie Young whom he wanted now. He found her captivating. It didn't matter that she was twenty-nine and not quite carried away by his attentions. John Anderson was helping his widowed father run their farm. He had proved to be a very competent farmer, but he had far bigger plans, and a role model before him — Solomon Young, the father of his intended. He would be an entrepreneur like Young, succeeding by instinct and grit, trading and investing until he, too, became rich.

Persistence finally paid off. John and Mattie were married in the Youngs' parlor at the end of 1881. Their wedding picture is instructive, the five-foot-four bridegroom seated, his hair slicked down, an intent look on his face, while his taller bride stood straight, with her hand on his shoulder. In a carriage borrowed from her father, they set out immediately for the small town of Lamar to embark on John's new career. Why it wasn't launched instead in burgeoning Kansas City, only fifteen miles away, is a mystery, as is why John Truman chose to speculate in mules rather than cattle, but both decisions imply that he lacked the judgment to be a successful trader. He also lacked the luck. His wife, however, was patient and supportive. Their first child was stillborn, but on May 8, 1884, in their tiny cottage, Mattie gave birth to a healthy son. They named him Harry, after Martha Ellen's favorite brother, Harrison. "Don't call him Harrison," John insisted. "They'll call him Harry anyway." For his middle name, they wanted to honor both fathers. Unable to decide between Shippe and Solomon, they simply settled on the letter "S."

John moved his family many times in pursuit of his elusive goal of prosperity. It was in Harrisonville only two years later that the Trumans' second son was born — John Vivian, named for his father and a Confederate cavalry officer. By the time their third child and only girl, Mary Jane, arrived three years later, the whole family was back on the spacious Grandview farm of Solomon Young. John Truman had reluctantly, if temporarily, returned to the only profession he was really suited for. On the farm his immense energy was an asset that could be contained and channeled. His own father died that year, and, by now, the legendary Solomon Young had slowed. His vast holdings, once over five thousand acres, were down to a more manageable six hundred. Still, he needed help in working the place. Harry Truman remembered his mother's father as a "gentle . . . great big man with a beard" who took him riding to county fairs and gave him gifts and candy, "the best time a kid ever had." His appreciation of both grandfathers would only grow with the years. Early in 1892, Solomon Young quietly died at the home from which he had so often departed in the past. His restless son-in-law, after setting things in order, moved his family again. This time, however, it was not entirely his idea.

From the start there was a special relationship between Martha Ellen Truman and her oldest son. As Harry Truman's daughter Margaret writes, "There was an enormously strong intellectual-emotional bond between Dad and his mother," which lasted until the end of her life. Harry Truman's favorite cousin, Ethel Noland, provides a more detailed, if idealized, depiction of Martha Ellen Truman, one which illuminates remarkable parallels with Eisenhower's mother: "[She] studied art and music. She played the piano, and she had a most remarkable idea of the proper values in life.... She never deviated from her idea of what was right, and she didn't let her children do that either.... Her discipline was so fine that greatness seemed to grow out of it."

Martha Ellen taught Harry to read before he was five. He was quick to learn, and actually enjoyed reading, as he genuinely enjoyed the piano lessons his brother would avoid. His mother could see potential, but she discerned that something was not quite right. Harry could readily read the large print of the family Bible but not the small print of a newspaper. At a Fourth of July celebration, as the fireworks exploded above Grandview, she learned what was wrong. Harry responded only to the noise, not the dazzling display overhead. He really couldn't quite see it. Her husband was away, but Martha Ellen didn't wait for his return. She put Harry in the family buggy and rode straight to an eye specialist in Kansas City, an unusual journey in those times even for the daughter of a wealthy farm family. The diagnosis was that Harry had a serious affliction called "flat eyeballs." It could only get worse. If he were ever to see clearly, he needed to wear very thick, very expensive glasses and keep them on all the time. He could not roughhouse or play competitive games with other boys for fear of damaging his glasses or himself. Mattie Truman was not about to have her promising son ridiculed as "four eyes" by rustic ruffians, and the local school was not very good, anyway. They would move to the county seat of Independence, with its superior schools, and at least a veneer of cultivation.

As it turned out, Harry's father was not averse to the move. Until his final experience with farming, John Anderson Truman would always view it as a temporary expedient. His prudent father had left him an inheritance of a few thousand dollars, and he was anxious to explore business ventures again. Perhaps he would return to livestock trading or invest in real estate or speculate in grain futures. Somehow, something had to succeed. Moreover, both parents looked forward to the amenities of life in Independence and to a more fulfilling existence for themselves as well as for their children.

In some ways, Independence was like a more sophisticated and moderately larger Abilene, to which the Eisenhowers would move the following year. It had a similarly eventful past. Both the Oregon and Santa Fe trails started in Independence, and it had witnessed raucous days as a jumping-off place for the 1849 California gold rush. It had been the Mormons' original Zion, although they were obliged to depart, and the James Boys had robbed banks in the vicinity, with somewhat greater success. Now it was an incorporated city of six thousand, settled and prosperous. Families who had arrived from places like Kentucky even a generation sooner than the Trumans viewed themselves as the local gentry and were none too hospitable to newcomers. At the top were the Wallaces, whose daughter, Elizabeth Virginia, was called "Bess" by her friends. From the time he met her at the nearest Sunday school, which happened to be Presbyterian, Harry Truman wanted to be her friend.

Except for his years in the army and in Washington, Truman lived his entire life within Jackson County, Missouri. A microcosm of American expansion, its western end was anchored by the metropolis of Kansas City, already boasting a population of 200,000 in 1900. The rural eastern end of the county, homogenous and Protestant, still included the established county seat of Independence, with more than 40,000 residents spread over twenty-five towns and villages and some three hundred farms in the bountiful Missouri River Valley. The Young spread at Grandview was still one of the largest. The diverse immigration that built Kansas City was more internal than foreign — poor whites and blacks moving up from the South. Politically, the whole state, including both sides of Jackson County, was predominately Democratic. But inevitably, with such increasing diversity, factions were emerging. They would affect both Harry Truman and his father.

Truman always insisted that he had enjoyed the happiest possible childhood. Whether that is true depends on how long childhood is considered to last. Certainly, the early years in Independence were happy. His father finally had a run of good luck and was actually making money on his investments. Although not quite considered the social elite, his family was ensconced in a spacious home on fashionable Crysler Street on an enormous lot that soon contained an extraordinary menagerie of cows, ponies, goats, chickens, and all varieties of household pets. On the property were a barn and hayloft, ideal for children's adventures. Whatever the neighbors may have thought, it is not surprising, as Truman recalled, that "we had wonderful times. . . . Our house soon became headquarters for all the boys and girls around."

Of course, some of those boys must have initially viewed Truman as something of a sissy, but by sheer effort, the shy newcomer won them over. Unlike his father, he never had a fight. If he could not participate in sports, he would become the impartial arbiter for others. There were inevitable frustrations. Umpiring baseball games is not the same as playing in them. Truman earned respect, but nothing approaching the popularity young Eisenhower would later enjoy. There was no shortage of chores on Crysler Street, and there were punishments, but discipline was not severe. Martha Ellen sometimes felt the need to spank a disobedient child, even Harry, but John, so quick to anger at any slight to his honor, never laid a hand on his children. A scolding or a stare sufficed, but it was quite a stare. His severity was not excessive — he even enjoyed singing — but John Anderson Truman did not have the warmest of personalities.

Harry Truman could not recall ever having had a bad teacher. He loved school. No one considered him brilliant, except perhaps his mother, but everyone was impressed by his conscientiousness. He never seemed to stop reading. He is reputed to have read every book in the Independence Public Library, although his daughter amended that to every book that might be of interest to a boy. The affliction that had cut him off from so many customary childhood pursuits opened an opportunity to learn, unencumbered by diversions. The gift he would most treasure was a four-volume set of Charles Francis Horne's *Great Men and Famous Women,* presented to him by his mother on his twelfth birthday. He particularly relished biography and history. Truman wrote in his memoirs, "My debt to history is one which cannot be calculated." Perhaps he ought to have added a reference to his corresponding debt to his mother for introducing him to the wonders of reading, and then saving that gift by preserving his vision. He was a mother's boy in the sense that, as Margaret Truman writes, "His world revolved around [her]." For one thing, he had a lot of time to be around his mother. She instilled in him "moral fiber," as well as an appreciation of music, books, and art — a widened world. She also, like Andrew Jackson's mother, once saved his life. As a child, Truman had a series of serious illnesses and seemed to be accident-prone. His diphtheria almost became paralysis, he broke his collarbone in a freak fall, and he nearly lost a toe. But when he choked on a peach pit that nearly strangled him, it was his ever-present mother who forced it down his throat with her fingers.

One has the feeling that John Anderson Truman hardly knew what to make of his bookish son. It is one thing to find pleasure in playing classical music on the piano but quite another to enjoy combing a little sister's hair and pushing her pram, which Harry did, almost like a miniature version of his mother. John adored his daughter and understood his sturdy son Vivian, a boy's boy, who wanted nothing more than to be a good farmer, but Harry was different. Harry Truman and his father did have one compelling interest in common, however. They both loved politics. Perhaps, in the son's case, it was derived from all that reading. From an early age, Harry traveled with his father to the endless picnics, barbeques, torchlight parades, and rallies that were staples of turn-of-the-century political campaigning — politics as entertainment.

John Truman's fists were prepared to pummel anyone of any size who found fault with his children, but most of his altercations were over political differences. He never ran for office, but he took the whole business very seriously. When Grover Cleveland returned to the presidency in 1892, bringing the Democrats back to power, John climbed to the top of his house to raise a banner, and later that night rode a gray horse in the local victory parade. Such partisan pugnacity was bound to attract attention. It came in the person of William Kemper, a prominent banker and investor from Kansas City. There he supported the emerging Pendergast political machine, and enlisted John Truman's aid to promote its candidates in the rural regions of Jackson County. Accordingly, when Harry Truman finally ran for political office, even his factional loyalties were inherited. Under Kemper's auspices, Harry was a page at the 1900 Democratic National Convention in Kansas City, saw William Jennings Bryan in the flesh, and may have envisioned his own future. Whether he was an accidental politician as well as initially an accidental president — he ascended to the presidency when Franklin Roosevelt died in office — will always be a subject for conjecture.

Kemper became the new role model for John Truman. Kemper's success, if not his encouragement, induced Truman to undertake larger risks. When Harry was still in high school, his father lost everything in commodities trading, even the small farm given to his wife by her parents. The family moved to a more modest house, followed by more serious sacrifices. Harry had finally managed to turn some of his acquaintances into fast friends. The brightest, such as Charlie Ross, were going off to college. Bess Wallace, who graduated in Harry's high school class, now seemed more unapproachable than ever. In an uncharacteristic waste of time, Harry had studied with a classmate to prepare for examinations for appointment to either service academy, until he finally realized that his eyesight rendered it impossible. Now college of any kind was out. Harry had worked part-time since the age of fourteen at a local drugstore, where he had observed the hypocrisy of the town's leading citizens, coming in to retrieve their hidden liquor bottles after church. His parents had agreed to terminate that employment so that Harry could study full-time in preparation for continuing his education. Now he would have to go back to work. Whatever Truman thought of his father at that juncture, there is no mention of it anywhere.

The family moved to Kansas City, where John Truman endured the indignity of laboring for wages as a night watchman. There Harry held a succession of jobs, ultimately working as a clerk and bookkeeper at major banks, where his industry and demeanor were much praised. It was not all grim. The bright lights of the city held an immense attraction for young Truman, especially its music halls and theatres. Settling in a lively boardinghouse he met, among others, Eisenhower's older brother Arthur, who was also working for a bank in the city. There also Harry overcame his shyness by playing the piano, although it was not the Chopin his mother would have preferred. He became more gregarious, and with his friends he joined a newly formed National Guard unit. If Truman had a plan for his life, Kansas City provided an introduction to both its financial and military components. He already had a taste of farming.

The three notable biographers of Truman in the 1990s, McCullough, Robert Ferrell, and Alonzo Hamby, all tend to view his youth as energetic but episodic. There is a notable dissenter, Richard Lawrence Miller, who, writing a few years earlier, portrayed a more calculating Truman, a young man who had his specific goals set by high school and who shared his dreams only with his mother, the one person who had inspired them. Whatever the truth may be, it is generally agreed that Truman really came of age in World War I. His mother was not a pacifist, but when Truman left for the army, he recalled, she "smiled . . . and told me to do my best for my country, but she cried all the way home." As an artillery captain in France, Truman finally discovered that he had the capacity to lead other men, even into battle. It is a discovery Eisenhower would make in high school, although his battles came much later.

Harry did experience a prior opportunity to come to terms with his father, even if it was in a calling neither Truman relished. After his own belated venture at growing corn was washed away in a flood, John heeded the call of his aging mother-in-law and her bachelor brother Harrison to return to Grandview and again take over management of the farm. His family joined him, Harry very reluctantly returning from Kansas City. Few of his new friends expected him to stay in the boondocks very long, but he worked side by side with his demanding father, developing a mutual regard, until the elder's death in 1914. These final Grandview years also reinforced in Harry the importance of deliberation. His father was a combative little man, but Harry respected him as the soul of reliability; his word was his bond. John Anderson Truman had held a number of part-time posts as a result of his work for the Pendergasts. The most notable was as a road overseer, keeping the roads clear for farmers who would rather contribute six dollars a year

Martha Truman
Courtesy of the Harry S. Truman Library

than do their own labor. Many of these political appointees simply pocketed the money. Truman took the responsibility seriously, setting an example for his son's future career. When his crew hesitated to lift a large boulder, John impatiently did it himself. The effort ultimately killed him. Harry was with his father when he died. He left farming shortly thereafter to follow some entrepreneurial ventures of his own —

including an oil-drilling business that nearly made him a millionaire — and then volunteered for the army service that eventually launched his political career. His brother Vivian claimed that Harry had to memorize the eye chart to be accepted into the active military on any level, but Harry was intent on serving. After the haberdashery Truman launched with an army buddy failed in the postwar recession, Truman was induced in 1922 to run for office. Through many highs and lows, politics became his profession.

Martha Ellen Young Truman outlived her husband by thirty-three years, and she never lost her intimate interest in her children. At eighty-two she campaigned for Harry's first Senate race, reportedly claiming as one qualification that he had "plowed the straightest furrow in Jackson County." She even chaired a meeting of women campaign workers in 1944. Harry wrote her constantly, his "Dear Mama" letters a testament to his continuing regard for her counsel. When Truman finally married Bess Wallace in 1919, one of his army friends told his mother, "Well now, Mrs. Truman, you've lost Harry." She replied, "Indeed, I haven't," and she meant it. He would visit her every Sunday for chicken dinners — and advice on everything — until he went to Washington. Then the letters began again, sometimes almost daily. For as Margaret Truman Daniel recalls, it was to his mother, more than to anyone else, that Harry Truman "turned again and again for the emotional support he needed."

THOUGH Dwight Eisenhower may have "come from the heart of America," the Eisenhower family had emigrated from a different heartland, the "Heimat" of the country their martial descendant would help to subjugate in the Second World War. Although related to respectable Lutherans, they were Mennonites, religious dissidents from the Rhineland, who had fled to Switzerland and then to Holland, finally embarking for America in the 1740s. The family name was originally Eisenhauer, for "iron hewer," but their vocation was farming. Settling in the rich agricultural region around Lancaster, Pennsylvania, they joined those who had come before, establishing their community of Brethren in Christ. Known as "River Brethren" for their practice of freshwater baptisms, these Pennsylvania Dutch, like their successors, were devout pacifists who feared only God, and were renowned for their self-supporting industriousness and the orderly fruitfulness of their farms. Here they had prospered for over a century when a war waged by others intruded into their insular haven. Confederate troops on their way to Gettysburg passed nearby, doing little damage but reminding a certain Jacob Eisenhower and his neighbors of their vulnerability to outsiders.

A minister as well as a farmer, Jacob had followed in the footsteps of earlier Eisenhowers as a community leader. And not only his fields were fertile. His wife, Rebecca, bore him fourteen children. One, named David, arrived shortly after the Battle of Gettysburg. He would be the father of another David, whose first name was later changed to Dwight. Even if their settlement survived the conflict, arable land was limited in Pennsylvania — and becoming costly. How, Jacob Eisenhower pondered, could he provide farms for so many offspring?

The war had come much closer to a community with similarly Germanic origins in the Shenandoah Valley of Virginia. It destroyed the farm of the Stover (originally Stoever) family. In its aftermath, Ida Stover, their only daughter amidst seven sons, believed that it also hastened the death of both her parents. The grim experience made her an even more fervent pacifist. Yet ironically she was to become the devoted mother of a general — Dwight Eisenhower.

Without questioning the foundations of their faith, at least until much later, there was a streak of stubborn nonconformity in both David Eisenhower and Ida Stover. As biographer Stephen Ambrose points out, the only thing David enjoyed about farming was tinkering with machinery. He had a knack for anything mechanical, and hoped to study engineering. Ida, a latter-day Abigail Adams, longed simply to learn, to use the English she had been taught in order to read more than the Bible. She particularly loved music. They would be a most unlikely couple: David stolid, stocky, silent, and darkly handsome; Ida cheerful, vivacious, outgoing, and fair — not so much beautiful as glowing, with a ready smile her sons, one in particular, would inherit. David and Ida would meet not in some great metropolis each might have dreamed of, but at an academic backwater on the plains of Kansas.

As the railroads pushed west after the Civil War, offering cheap, abundant land for settlers, Jacob Eisenhower took them up on it, inducing his whole community of River Brethren to move with him to Kansas, an extraordinary migration. His sturdy, thrifty folk adapted well, duplicating their prior abundance. Perhaps such success encouraged Jacob to indulge his son. Hoping David would ultimately come to his senses and return to farming, his father nonetheless allowed him to attend the nearby Brethren college, named Lane University for Kansas's first United States senator. Although it mixed mechanics with classics, the modest establishment was hardly a school of engineering. David learned how to read the Bible in Greek, but his career hopes were dashed.

Back in Virginia, after the death of Ida Stover's mother, her father, who would live only a few years longer, despaired of his ability to support his eight children. In better days he had saved enough to provide a modest inheritance for each when they turned twenty-one, but in the interim, they were given over to the care of his late wife's parents. The elderly couple's grim humorlessness was matched only by their harsh frugality. Ida couldn't wait for the darkness to lift and ran off at the age of sixteen to Staunton, the same town where Woodrow Wilson had been born. There she found a family willing to provide room and board in exchange for cooking and cleaning. Finally able to attend high school, Ida did so well that she was soon teaching children herself. At twenty-one, she invested the first $600 of her inheritance in a piano she would prize for the rest of her life. Then she joined an aunt heading west with another group of Brethren. Ida had heard that the sect had established a small college in Kansas, near the new homes of two of her brothers, and that — wonder of wonders — it accepted female students.

Here she met and fell in love with David Eisenhower, a sophomore sixteen months younger than herself. They were married in the college chapel in 1885. Neither would graduate. One imagines it mattered far less to Ida. She loved learning for its own sake. Despite all her privations, she exuded joy, and was more than ready to fulfill it in motherhood. She started by mothering her husband. But she could never contain his violent temper, which was not overtly directed toward her but later manifested itself in brutal beatings of their sons, beyond the norm of even traditionally authoritarian German fathers. Austere David Ei-

Mr. and Mrs. David Eisenhower on their wedding day,
September 23, 1885
Courtesy of the Dwight D. Eisenhower Library

senhower was the unquestioned head of his household, but Ida was its heart. She must have understood, too, as her children would, the unspoken truth that she was not only the more compassionate but also the stronger of the two parents.

Jacob Eisenhower would not give up easily. He gave the couple the same generous gift that had launched his other married children, $2,000 and a 160-acre farm. David promptly mortgaged the farm to a brother-in-law and opened a general store in a little Kansas town called Hope. Anything but farming. Not surprisingly, he demonstrated little talent for retailing, and enjoyed less luck. His temper surfaced, he took in a partner who turned out to be crooked, and he never fully appreciated the extended credit requirements of farmers. The venture was a disaster. A lawyer hired to clean up the mess took everything but Ida's piano. All her life, this gentle soul detested lawyers, as did her husband, although one of their sons became one. They also hated debt, as deeply as Harry Truman came to after his own store failed over thirty years later.

The Eisenhowers' first son had been born, and another was on the way. Desperate for any sort of work, David found a job as a railway mechanic. Unfortunately, it was in Texas. Ida, whose neighbors helped her pack, dutifully followed. So it was that in a small rented house in Denison, Texas, on October 14, 1890, their third son was born. They named him David Dwight, but soon decided to reverse the order to avoid confusion. By now it was clear even to Jacob Eisenhower that at least one of his sons was not cut out to be a farmer, but the Brethren looked after their own. David's sister was married to a man who helped manage a creamery in Abilene. They needed someone to take charge of their machinery, an ideal job for a man with David Eisenhower's skills, although his salary would still be modest. After only two years in Texas, the family returned home.

Abilene, Kansas, was a comfortable, placid, rather dull town of some four thousand people, surrounded by wheat fields, but it had a lurid past. Railroading and cattle drives had brought every variety of frontier roughneck and adventurer to this terminus — to drink, fight, gamble, consort with loose women, and raise hell generally, all under the watchful eye of Sheriff "Wild Bill" Hickok. Dwight Eisenhower's lifelong love of Western novels may have derived from this personal connection. By the 1890s, however, respectable folk already preferred to view Abilene's embarrassingly recent heyday as colorful mythology. The more affluent lived on the north side of town, separated by railroad tracks from the equally proud families of workingmen on the south side. That is where the Eisenhowers resided, in a tiny cottage. One of

Dwight's brothers died in infancy, but his five others survived to manhood. During her first seven years in Abilene, Ida's logistical talents emerged. Somehow, despite too many people jammed into too little space and supported by too little money, she created a reasonably harmonious family life, leavened with her own good cheer.

Ida's unquenchable optimism was finally rewarded when a relative offered an alternative of palatial proportions. The family could reside in a much larger house on a three-acre lot for a small rental, with an option to buy, if they would care for David's father. They accepted with alacrity. Dwight Eisenhower never deployed troops with more precision than his mother exercised in her new domain. Her goal was virtual self-sufficiency. To the barn and apple orchard she added a vegetable garden, a cow, chickens, ducks, pigs, and anything else that might contribute to the family larder. Her organizational talents were the equal of a Maria Van Buren's. Daily chores, indoors and out, were rotated to give every son equal experience at everything. Among Dwight Eisenhower's earliest memories was his avoidance of the most onerous tasks, to his parents' consternation. Of course, they were still poor, but as Dwight recalled, "We didn't know it then. All we knew is that our parents — of great courage — could say to us: 'Opportunity is all around you. Reach out and take it.'"

Ambrose describes Dwight at nine or ten as normal-sized, wearing clean but hand-me-down clothes, generally barefoot, "with a shock of light-brown hair, blue eyes, a friendly disposition, and his mother's grin." The most striking quality was his restless energy. He was never still, always on the go. He already loved sports and had inherited something of his father's temper. He would fight readily, no matter what the size of his opponent, as much to burn off energy as for any specific reason. He was already called "Little Ike"; his older brother, Edgar, "Big Ike." At elementary school, despite the monotony of "rote learning," Dwight liked arithmetic, spelling, and history — especially military history, which did not sit easily with his mother. Like Harry Truman in Missouri, he needed little encouragement to read history by the hour, even if it was a "great man" sort of history.

It must be said to the credit of both parents, David as well as Ida, that they encouraged their children to think for themselves, if not to act quite so independently. Their future lives, their professions, would be based entirely on their own preferences. There would be none of the coercion David had faced from his own father to stay close to the soil. They would have no limits placed on their goals or their mobility. Although two dissimilar personalities, David and Ida were of one accord in this aspect of childrearing, and in the example they set, although David was the more silent partner. Dwight Eisenhower was always certain that his parents genuinely loved each other, however undemonstrative they were in expressing their affection. He could never recall them arguing. Neither cursed in front of their children, despite David's temper, nor did they smoke, drink spirits, or gamble. They were pious, although David disdained the beard and Ida the bonnets of the more conspicuously devout of their neighbors. Her personal trinity was religion, family, and music; her litany, hard work and service to others, accompanied by hymns and endless aphorisms to inspire her sons. Right and wrong were clearly understood and nonnegotiable. Discipline was firm, but in its implementation came the point of departure.

All six sons were frightened to death of their father. Ida was capable of spanking her children, at least when they were young, if they were particularly recalcitrant, and she was not above threatening them with swift retaliation when their father returned from his long hours at the creamery, but it was David who was the harsh disciplinarian of the family. Even in 1954, Dwight put a tactfully benign face on this singular difference between his parents. His sullen father, who communicated with his strap, "had quick judicial instincts." His sensitive mother, "had, like a psychologist, insight into the fact that each son was a unique personality and she adapted to the methods of each." Dwight's youngest brother, Milton, who was to become a distinguished college president, recalled, "Father and Mother complemented each other. Mother had the personality. She had the joy. Dad had the authority." Ambrose adds, "David hardly ever smiled; Ida smiled as easily as she breathed. She was quick to laugh; quick to give sympathy. Like David, she demanded much of her sons; unlike him, she gave much."

Each son's memories were replete with examples. When he was deemed too young to go out trick-or-treating with his older brothers on Halloween, Dwight threw a fit. After the customary hiding from his father, he was visited in his room by his mother, who gently remonstrated, recounting verse after verse of biblical admonitions to restrain anger. Then she bathed and put salve and wrapping on his hands, injured in impotent rage when he had beaten his fists on a tree stump. In a television interview a half century later, Eisenhower recalled it as "one of the most important moments in my life, because since then . . . I've gotten angry many times, but I certainly have tried to keep from showing it." He was not always successful.

When he was twelve, Dwight tried to physically intervene when his father administered a particularly savage beating on Edgar because he had missed school. David finally stopped, and he must have harbored at least a grudging respect for the sheer courage of his young son. Characteristically, many years later, Dwight Eisenhower viewed the incident as only an extreme example of his father's firm resolve that his sons not stray from the path that led to success and accomplish more than he had achieved. (As it turned out, all the Eisenhower boys were successful. As president, Dwight had no equivalent of the brothers who embarrassed so many of his successors. Indeed, until the late 1930s, his might have been viewed as the least promising of the Eisenhower brothers' careers, particularly in terms of income.) His father even seemed to relish seeing his boys fight each other so long as they stood together against outsiders, especially those from the north side of town. Whether in terms of competition or solidarity, facing down confrontations was a preparation for the realities of adult life.

As that time approached for each son, even their father lessened the bonds of tradition. Bible readings and daily prayer sessions, while still important, became less frequent. Doris Faber writes that "Cards made their appearance, and in time cigarettes were allowed; music, secular as well as devotional, tinkled from Ida's still-prized piano in the parlor. All of this was in a real sense preparation for what lay ahead." It must have been a sort of liberation for Ida Eisenhower, as well, although her personal devotions never flagged.

There is no doubt that in high school Dwight David Eisenhower was one of the most popular young men in Abilene. Possessing his mother's outgoing personality, he made friends readily. He still loved roaming, hunting, and fishing, but sports were at the center of his life.

Despite weighing only 150 pounds, he excelled at football and baseball, and discovered through athletics a talent for leadership that others also began to recognize. He also discovered girls, but was as shy around them initially as the bespectacled Harry Truman had been over in Independence, Missouri. Truman learned to earn regard, but Eisenhower won it easily, in part because he was strikingly handsome. (Some years later, the woman who would become his wife called Dwight Eisenhower the best-looking man she had ever seen.) Where Truman had to work hard for everything, Eisenhower's studies improved with little apparent difficulty. In high school both boys still loved history and biography best, and expanded their reading on their own — Truman through the town library, Eisenhower through a local news office. Their high schools were about the same size, as were their graduating classes and the proportion of boys to girls. Dwight graduated with thirty-four classmates, twenty-five of them girls.

In rural towns at the turn of the century, only the brightest, most affluent, or most motivated young people finished high school, let alone college. Among the many boys who withdrew from Eisenhower's high school were his oldest brother, Arthur, who would leave to work in Kansas City, where he met the young Harry Truman. Eisenhower's other brothers, however, went on to college, including Edgar — "Big Ike" — who departed to the University of Michigan to study law. Now "Little Ike" became just "Ike." When Dwight was a fourteen-year-old freshman in high school, Edgar had stood guard by his bedside in a demonstration of the kind of loyalty both parents had instilled. Dwight had scraped his knee. It became infected, and the infection spread to the extent that doctors wanted to amputate the leg. While his mother prayed and specialists were called in, Dwight declared he would rather die than have the leg cut off and made Edgar promise to prevent it should he lose consciousness. His parents decided not to permit the surgery. Dwight very nearly did expire, but eventually recovered, saving more than his athletic career. He repeated a year and graduated in 1909. The high-school yearbook predicted that Dwight would eventually teach history at Yale. Edgar had been projected a potential president of the United States.

Of course, everyone in the family continued to work. However much David and Ida wanted each son to excel on his own terms, having one choose law was a bit much for the lawyer-loathing Eisenhowers. Edgar's father favored medicine as a profession, but almost anything other than the bar was acceptable. Edgar, who was only able to initiate his studies with the aid of an uncle's loan, made a pact with Dwight. They would take turns at college. During Edgar's first year, Dwight would work, and then the process would be reversed. It turned out to be an unworkable arrangement, but it gave young Ike time to think things out. He obtained a good, not very demanding job as night manager of the creamery. His friends noted a new seriousness, self-confidence, and focus. He had also bulked up physically.

Ike understood the financial realities. He had a friend who was applying for the Naval Academy. It provided a first-class education, it was free, and they played football. Ike decided to apply, too. He took cram courses to prepare for the entrance examinations, just as Harry Truman had in Missouri. Neither was looking for a naval or military career, only for a free education. Truman had realized his eyesight precluded any consideration for admission, but Eisenhower faced a different problem. At twenty he was already too old to enter the Naval Academy, and, in any case, the local appointments had already been made. He indicated his willingness to go to West Point instead, came in second in the exam, and gained the appointment. The train trip east would be by far the longest he had yet experienced but only the prelude to an unimaginable journey. His brothers were excited; his father revealed little emotion. His mother said only, "It is your choice." When he took his suitcase and walked the few blocks to the Union Pacific depot, she waved to her departing boy from the front porch. Then, Dwight's brother Milton recalled, she could no longer restrain her tears. It was the first time he had ever seen her cry. She ran to her room and did not leave it that day. Lawyers only cheated people; soldiers killed them. Yet in time Ida Eisenhower, whom Ike viewed as the most sincere pacifist he had ever known, learned to accept her son's career and even take pride in it. But, of course, she was proud of all her sons.

All the Eisenhower children returned, with their wives and families, in 1935 to celebrate David and Ida's golden wedding anniversary. David had taken a better paying job at the local utility company, and, even in the midst of a national depression, times for his family were better than

Ida Eisenhower with her son Dwight Eisenhower
Courtesy of the Dwight D. Eisenhower Library

they had ever been. David almost smiled. Had he not been right all along? When, in 1942, David Eisenhower passed away, Dwight could not attend his father's funeral, having pressing engagements elsewhere. But he composed a brief eulogy praising David Eisenhower's "sterling honesty, pride in his independence, his exemplary habits . . . [and his] undemonstrative, quiet, modest" manner, among other things. It was not the occasion to reflect on his father's complexity. In later years Ike's parents had taken to holding their own Bible study meetings in private homes. Their intensive contemplation of Scripture eventually led them, along with many of their friends, to join the Jehovah's Witnesses. Ida had never aggressively proselytized in the Brethren, nor did she now. Those intrusive reporters so repellent to Eisenhower, as to Truman, felt his mother's new sect might embarrass the general, but they met a frosty response from Ike. Her "happiness in her religion," Ike snapped, "means more to me than any damn wisecrack that a newspaperman can get published."

Inevitably, as she aged, Ida's memory lapsed, and she needed help getting about, but she readily recognized her soldier son when he paid her a surprise visit on a brief leave home in 1944. This time laughter mixed with the tears. Then in 1946, at the age of eighty-four, Ida Stover Eisenhower died. Ike praised "her serenity, her open smile, her gentleness with all and her tolerance of their ways." It was not so challenging, as it was with his father, to express his boundless affection for her, the light of all their lives.

THE PHENOMENON of "Trumania," the simplistic reinvention of Harry Truman that began about the time of Watergate, and the subsequent reappraisal of Eisenhower, says as much about us as it does about them. One often hears, "Wouldn't it be great to have a straight shooter like Truman again? Or a man who stood honestly above politics like Eisenhower?" It demeans the memory of neither man to recall that Ike in his "hidden hand" presidency once told his press secretary, "Don't worry, Jim. I'll confuse them," or that Truman in his "give 'em hell" 1948 campaign that would have delighted his father accused his lackluster opponents of being duped by Communists as well as Fascists. There is a good deal of truth behind the new mythology; there are real facts in much of the folklore. But to see, as Tom Wolfe might say, the men in full, is to acknowledge that there was nothing simple about either Truman or Eisenhower.

Whatever view one takes of these two men, however, one undeniable fact is the devotion of their mothers. Not long before Martha Ellen Young Truman passed away in 1947, she feared that her least favorite Republican, Senator Robert A. Taft, would be nominated the following year and that her son might not choose to contest the presidency in his own right and oppose him. "Don't you think it's about time you made up your mind?" she demanded of Harry Truman. Ida Stover Eisenhower would not have been so concerned about politics, but she also insisted that her boys make up their own minds. Both mothers had laid a strong foundation for their sons to do so.

CHAPTER FOURTEEN

Maternal Ambition

୬ Rose Kennedy
୬ Rebekah Johnson

IF ROSE ELIZABETH FITZGERALD KENNEDY came to believe as much in the forms of her Roman Catholic faith as in the substance, as some biographers suggest, it is surely understandable. There is solace to be found in repeating the familiar rituals of a religion so rich in tradition, however their meaning has been tested by tragedy and heartache. Rose lived with ambivalence all her life, both before and after her marriage. Her flamboyant father, her ambitious husband, and her most successful son were all blatantly unfaithful to their wives, yet they never ceased going to mass, even if not so constantly as Rose. In his fashion, each man was devoted to his family, but committed more to success than to morality. The lessons Rose's husband taught were about winning, winning at all costs. "We don't want losers around here," Joseph P. Kennedy barked out to his brood. There was more of Darwin than St. Francis in his view of life, and he even had Rosemary, his third child and eldest daughter, who suffered from retardation and mental illness, lobotomized and shut away. Born in 1918, she had been christened Rose Marie, her mother's "dainty daughter," but problems surfaced early in her life. Rosemary could never be a winner, like Joe's other eight children. How could she compete, as they were impelled to, or fit into her father's grand schemes?

Except for the scale of their strivings, the Kennedys have been a thoroughly American success story. Yet the source of their political

232

power lay in their also being Irish, another area of ambivalence. What strenthened them politically inhibited them socially. Joe Kennedy once exclaimed, "I was born in this country. My children were born in this country. What the hell does someone have to do to become an American?" Rose pondered plaintively when the "nice people" would finally welcome her family. Her husband craved power above everything; she, most of all, acceptance by the "Brahmin" Protestant aristocracy of Boston, and later even by the established Irish gentry of New York. All the money in the world couldn't buy it. When it finally came — her family elevated to little less than American royalty — it was too late to really matter to Rose. The price had been too high. By then her daily devotions meant so much more than the approval she had once yearned for.

Years before, Rose called her husband "the architect of our lives." Yet their second son, who became president, viewed his mother as the "glue" that held the whole family together. Whatever in his youth had helped prepare John F. Kennedy for the White House, he insisted, "I learned from my mother." Was this simply campaign rhetoric? If there was competition not only among the children but between Rose and Joe in influencing them, within it lay the foundations of success. Whether value-based or coldly pragmatic, both parents encouraged a commitment to service. Rose may have hoped that at least one child might become a priest or a nun, but public life would always be the main arena for the Kennedys. Rose herself, as a Fitzgerald, had been practically weaned on politics. The motivations were always a bit muddled. Power for its own sake and power to redress ancient grievances overlapped with the use of power to do good for others. "God's work must truly be our own," John F. Kennedy once said. Yet even his mother, who found solace in St. Augustine's confession that "our heart is restless till it finds its rest in Thee," could lapse from pure piety. When her son triumphed over Henry Cabot Lodge Jr. in the 1952 senatorial race Rose, too, was triumphant, proclaiming, despite herself, "At last the Fitzgeralds have evened the score with the Lodges."

She was always more a Fitzgerald than a Kennedy, even after her marriage merged the clans. Rivalry between the families went back a century or more, and was never entirely muted. In her eighties, at a Thanksgiving dinner, Rose reminded her children and grandchildren,

"I want you all to remember that you are not just Kennedys, you are Fitzgeralds, too." The Fitzgeralds, she continued, had come to America before the Kennedys and had risen to political influence sooner. "When the Irish Catholics had no one to speak for them, the Fitzgeralds did." The saga of the two families encapsulates the story of the Irish ascendancy in America, particularly in Boston. Both were drawn to these shores more by opportunity than by hunger. Almost neighbors in Ireland, as well, they came from County Wexford, an area less afflicted by the terrible potato famine than most of the Emerald Isle.

The first American census in 1790 counted only 44,000 Irish-born immigrants, and these were mainly from Ulster, in the north, largely Scotch-Irish and Protestant. After the great famine, that number multiplied over twenty-fold. By 1850 more than a third of the residents of Boston were Irish, with similarly immense migrations to New York, Philadelphia, and other major cities on the eastern seaboard. By 1890 there were more Irish than native-born Bostonians.

Biographer Thomas Reeves traces the Fitzgeralds back to an Italian clan who helped William the Conqueror become ruler of England. They had been in Ireland for eight centuries when Thomas Fitzgerald, Rose's grandfather, decided to emigrate to Massachusetts. Starting as a humble farmhand and street peddler, he worked his way up to ownership of a grocery store and invested profitably in Boston tenements. Married in 1857 to the daughter of another Irish immigrant, he sired twelve children. His wife was pregnant with the thirteenth when she died.

What is remarkable about the Fitzgeralds, as with the Kennedys, is how quickly they became established, at least economically, in contrast to the agonizingly gradual ascent of so many other immigrant families. Each generation of Fitzgeralds and Kennedys leapt a giant step beyond the one preceding it. Thomas's most promising son, John Francis, born in 1863 and known as "Little Fitzie," didn't attend neighborhood parish schools but instead gained admission to the elite Boston Latin School. He went on to Harvard Medical School before the death of his father obliged him to help support his eight surviving brothers. Of the "three Ps" that led to Irish Catholic influence in Boston, becoming a policeman or a priest held little attraction for the man who came to be known as "Honey Fitz" rather than "Little Fitzie." Politics was his natural vocation, the obvious outlet for his extroverted personality. Had he been able to continue his medical education, Fitzgerald's bedside manner would surely have featured what came to be called "Fitzblarney." As historian James Hilty writes, Fitzgerald was a tireless, "gregarious, back-slapping, quintessential Irish politician who knew every voter's name, attended every wake," and concluded most campaign appearances by leading the dedicated supporters he called his "dearos" in a stirring rendition of "Sweet Adeline."

Throughout his political career, Fitzgerald masked his keen intelligence by playing this sort of stage Irishman, patronizing his North End constituents and infuriating more circumspect Irish leaders in Boston. They believed political power could be obtained without confirming the crude ethnic stereotypes of their nativist detractors. Their criticism bothered Fitzgerald not at all, as he moved onward and upward. Starting as an aide to a ward leader, he soon held a patronage job at the Boston Custom House, gaining contacts that helped him launch a successful insurance business. He was elected to the Common Council, and before he was thirty headed the North End Democratic organization. He served in the state senate and for three terms in the United States Congress. By 1900, still only thirty-seven, he decided to finally relax for a bit, became the respectable publisher of a Catholic newspaper, and kept an eye on things from his palatial Boston residence.

In 1889 he had married his twenty-three-year-old second cousin, Mary Elizabeth Hannan. She was quite attractive, but so diffident, at least in public, that she seems rather an odd choice to be a politician's wife. Perhaps it was this very difference that Fitzgerald found appealing. As Reeves writes, Mary Elizabeth was a "shy, strong-willed, religious, thoroughly domestic daughter of Irish immigrants who had settled in a small town northeast of Boston." The first of their six children was born on July 22, 1890. Having grown up among so many males, Fitzgerald was delighted that she was a girl. He and his wife named her Rose Elizabeth. She would always be her father's shining star.

If in fact the Kennedys did arrive in America later than the Fitzgeralds, it was not by much. Patrick Joseph Kennedy emigrated in 1849, making the uncomfortable passage in steerage and bringing with him little more than his energy and ambition. A fine-looking, muscular fellow, Patrick met Bridget Murphy on board. Within a year, settled in East Boston, they were married by a priest who would one day become the city's archbishop. Patrick followed the cooper's trade, working wood into wagons and whiskey barrels. The couple had four children, the last named for his father. Unfortunately, hardworking Patrick Joseph Kennedy Sr. died of cholera soon after the birth of his namesake. As biographers Peter Collier and David Horowitz observe, "The first Kennedy to arrive in the New World, he was the last to die in anonymity."

Young Patrick, whom everyone called "P.J.," was obliged from an early age to help his hard-pressed mother, who clerked in a notions shop, and his sisters. He got what schooling he could from local nuns. As he grew — and became as strong as his father — he found work on the docks. He made friends as readily as John Fitzgerald, but P.J. had a very different temperament. He was sociable but no backslapper. His gift was for listening. Somehow his frugal mother and now-married sisters scraped up enough to enable teetotaling Patrick to open a saloon. It did so well that he opened others, his Haymarket Square location becoming a popular watering hole for local politicians. He launched a liquor-importing business, invested in a hotel, became a banker, and by the age of thirty was not only wealthy enough to have his own mansion in East Boston but also deeply immersed in politics. He had long been a member of the political and social clubs that enabled Irish families to lift one another from poverty. P.J.'s notable success, his thoughtful demeanor, and his reputation for good sense made him a natural community leader.

So did his striking looks, another inheritance from his father. As Hilty writes, "A large man with thick red hair, bushy eyebrows, and piercing blue eyes, P. J. Kennedy had about him an air of dignity and wisdom." He became a ward leader and was elected to the state legislature and state senate, where he served for a time with John Fitzgerald. But, although Kennedy didn't mind public speaking on occasion, his preference was for working behind the scenes. He became a mover and shaker rather than a professional officeholder, gaining a seat on the powerful Board of Strategy, which really ran Boston politics.

In 1887, following the pattern of upward mobility so prevalent in the families of the Founding Fathers, he married Mary Augusta Hickey, the bright, socially ambitious daughter of one of the most prominent Irish families. Mary longed to escape the insularity of her life, however luxurious her surroundings. She craved acceptance by the "best" Boston families, as would her daughter-in-law a generation later. In 1888, the same year her husband made a seconding speech for Grover Cleveland at the Democratic National Convention, and the first year Boston elected an Irish mayor, Mary gave birth to a boy. P.J. had wanted to name his first son Patrick Joseph Kennedy III, but his wife insisted that reversing the names sounded "less Irish." Joseph Patrick Kennedy would be an even more adept social climber than the mother who dominated his youth.

By 1905 Fitzgerald had had enough of repose and decided he wanted to run for mayor. Being mayor of Boston had, by this time, become almost the Irish equivalent of the presidency. Dutifully appearing before the four-member Board of Strategy to gain their endorsement, Fitzgerald again met P. J. Kennedy. The two men could hardly have been more different, in appearance as well as demeanor. John F. Fitzgerald was short, slight, energetic, and dapper, perpetually smiling, as quick in his movements as a vaudevillian, with nothing deliberate about him. Loud and pugnacious, he already had a reputation as a philanderer. His interest was less in issues than in the raw accumulation of power. Such a candidate was the last thing image-conscious leaders like Kennedy were looking for. Denied their approval, Fitzgerald ran anyway, adroitly turning the Board of Strategy itself into his major issue. From his North End base, he tirelessly canvassed every Boston neighborhood, proclaiming, "Down with the bosses!" and "The people, not the bosses, must rule." Offering little in the way of details, he promised "a bigger, better Boston." It was in this frenetic campaign that the larger-than-life image of "Honey Fitz" was born.

By his side was not his staid, reticent wife but his lovely, lively fifteen-year-old daughter Rose, already at ease in front of any audience. She was dark-haired, slender, and poised — her presence alone endowing her father with the image of a good family man. On occasion, she even played the piano when irrepressible Honey Fitz burst into song. In fact, it was she who had originally taught him "Sweet Adeline." He won

Rose Kennedy
Courtesy of the John F. Kennedy Library

the primary and breezed to victory in the general election. In a manner of speaking, Fitzgerald patched things up with P. J. Kennedy. Their families even vacationed together, but there would always remain a personal distance between them. It didn't matter to Rose. She was getting to know young Joe Kennedy, a lean, freckle-faced, red-haired, more genial version of his father. Although the Fitzgeralds had moved from the dear old neighborhood to a Dorchester mansion with its own tennis court, and the people's mayor was even playing polo, Rose went to public and Catholic schools rather than to tony private academies. Popular and bright, she graduated from Dorchester High at the age of fifteen. Joseph, at his mother's insistence, attended the establishment bastion of Boston Latin. Although also the alma mater of Honey Fitz, it had been renowned since the seventeenth century as the school of Boston's Protestant elite. Outgoing Joe Kennedy excelled at sports and was liked well enough to be elected president of his class, but that still didn't get him invited to all the parties given by his classmates' parents.

The teenage romance of Joe and Rose blossomed during a summer vacation their families shared at the not very chic Old Orchard Beach in Maine. Although with his glasses Joe looked a bit like the comedian Harold Lloyd, Rose glowingly recalled, "His face was open and expressive, yet with youthful dignity. . . . He neither drank nor smoked, nor did I. He was serious but with a quick wit and a spontaneous infectious grin. . . . Even then he had an aura of command." Joe was no less enamored, but it was over nine years from the day Mayor Fitzgerald proudly gave his daughter, voted "Boston's prettiest high school senior," her Dorchester diploma that she married Joe Kennedy. Part of the delay was the couple's own doing. He wanted to go to Harvard and she to Wellesley. However, the protracted postponement of their nuptials was most of all because of her father. Honey Fitz, so practical in politics, had visions of his own. He didn't feel that any Kennedy was quite up to his daughter. The Kennedys were hardly more than "lace curtain" Irish in his view. Might not Rose be the first to cross the divide and wed a scion of the Yankee establishment itself?

Yet when it came to college, Fitzgerald wasn't about to abandon his Irish-Catholic roots, nor would Boston's archbishop let him forget them. Rose must be an example to others. To her everlasting regret, she never went to Wellesley but to the Convent of the Sacred Heart in Boston, an education augmented by piano lessons at the New England Conservatory of Music. Perhaps to make it up to her, her parents took Rose and her sister on an extended trip to Europe. At a convent school in Holland, she learned to speak fluent French and German, and mingled with the daughters of Catholic aristocrats. Rose then went on to well-respected Manhattanville College, outside New York City, completing her higher education before she was twenty. Although a superb "finishing" for an accomplished young woman, it was within an insular world separated from the Protestant establishment.

Enjoying every amenity that those in the parallel Protestant society enjoyed, from vacation homes and luxurious travel to servants and grand fêtes, the most successful Irish families in Boston were still confined to an island of their own. As Rose wrote in her memoirs, newspapers had separate society columns, "one about them" and "one about us." Her debut, the most gala debutante ball on her friends' social calendar, was not attended by "proper Protestant Bostonians." The younger leaders of each set might, as with Joseph Kennedy, attend the same schools, but they did not mix socially. And, as Rose noted, their parents were still in "a state of chronic, mutual antagonism." The Irish had wrested much of the political power in Massachusetts. Now they sought to at least share the economic influence of old-line firms and finally gain entrance into venerable clubs and events that continued to exclude them.

Rose had gone from being her father's accompanist at political rallies to his all but official hostess as mayor. She was comfortable in the company of the most eminent visitors, often serving as translator for those from abroad, and continued to make the rounds of her father's enlarged domain with him. Honey Fitz was as energetic a mayor as he had been a candidate, but scandals in his administration cost him renomination in 1907. His residual popularity won him additional two-year terms in 1909 and 1911, and it looked as though he planned on serving for life. But in 1913 another colorful, ambitious, canny Irish politician of even more dubious morality, James Michael Curley, challenged for the mayoralty. He hoped Fitzgerald could be induced to run for the U.S. Senate instead. Honey Fitz had no such intention, but he was forced from the race by a combination of blackmail and exhaustion. Curley threatened to expose Fitzgerald's affair with a comely young "cigarette girl" named Elizabeth "Toodles" Ryan. And this was not Honey Fitz's sole indiscretion. Indeed, Curley was prepared to give public lectures on "Great Lovers of History," citing Fitzgerald as his prime example. Curley's own career would be the inspiration for Edwin

O'Connor's novel, *The Last Hurrah,* and for the memorable motion picture that followed. Honey Fitz subsequently ran for other offices. In 1916 he was removed from his House seat after the discovery of vote fraud. He lingered around the edges of later Kennedy campaigns, but he was never quite the same after 1913.

Rose was horrified by the Toodles affair, but whatever Rose's mother thought, she volunteered nothing. She must have known of her husband's infidelities, but she always looked the other way. As Rose would later, Mary also looked inward. "At the heart of Mary Fitzgerald's life," writes Reeves, "was the Roman Catholic church, and she instilled an intense devotion in her children." This included reciting the rosary in Lenten darkness, decorating a family shrine with flowers, daily lessons in the faith, and nightly prayers to the Blessed Virgin. As Rose recalled, "I'm sure my knees ached and that sometimes I wondered why I should be doing all the kneeling and studying and memorizing and contemplating and praying . . . but I became understanding and grateful." Could she also appreciate her mother's grace under marital pressures?

At Harvard, Joseph Kennedy had enjoyed success, yet not nearly enough to suit him. He cultivated the most outstanding of his classmates but made more acquaintances than close friends. He demonstrated business acumen by profitably investing in real estate and running a tour-bus operation while keeping up with his studies. He was admitted to Hasty Pudding and other clubs, although not to the most prestigious, Porcellian. It is a slight he shared with Franklin Roosevelt, but Roosevelt had anticipated admission to Porcellian as his due. That a social outsider such as Kennedy would aspire to such a bastion of exclusivity is a measure of his ambition. It was his father's surprising defeat for the lowly post of Boston street commissioner that, according to Hilty, solidified the path Joe Kennedy chose to follow. He "cynically concluded that partisan loyalty and political power could be bought. . . . Real power, lasting control . . . emanated from wealth." Elective office could wait. Making money came first.

In the private chapel of William Cardinal O'Connell, Joseph Patrick Kennedy and Rose Elizabeth Fitzgerald were finally married on October 7, 1914. In the two years following his graduation from Harvard,

Kennedy had manipulated his way to becoming the youngest bank president in the United States. True, it was a small bank, but such an achievement at the age of twenty-five impressed Honey Fitz. A bit chastened by the recent revelations of his own excesses, in any case, Fitzgerald had finally given his consent to the union. After a two-week honeymoon at White Sulphur Springs, West Virginia, the couple settled into a nine-room house in the comfortably middle-class, predominantly Protestant Boston suburb of Brookline. Rose was already pregnant. The first four Kennedy children were born here in less than five years. First came Joseph P. Kennedy Jr. in 1915; then, on May 29, 1917, John Fitzgerald Kennedy, named after Rose's father; followed by Rosemary and Kathleen.

Joe, who was now Joseph Sr., set about achieving his goal of making his first million within the next ten years, while Rose looked after the children and tried to make friends. Unfortunately, there was no parallel Irish-Catholic social whirl in Brookline. When the United States entered the Great War, Joe viewed it as essentially an intrusion into his private plans. He obtained a deferment and left his bank to help manage an immense shipbuilding facility in Quincy. While there he had a dispute with the youthful Assistant Secretary of the Navy, Franklin Roosevelt, over payment plans for a pair of battleships. At the end of the war, Joe joined a well-established Boston investment firm. His business acumen at least gained him admission to the higher strata of Boston's economic hierarchy. Patiently waiting for advancement wasn't his style, however. Before long, Joe took off on his own, and he would remain his own boss for the rest of his business life. Plunging into the stock market during its twenties heyday, he made his first million and more, well ahead of the time limit he had set.

In Boston, as Collier and Horowitz point out, the nature of Kennedy's success only increased the ambivalence he and his wife felt so keenly, having a foot in two still-separated social worlds. Joe "was a self-made man, even a self-created man. Yet those who knew him best saw Joseph P. Kennedy [Sr.] as Irish to the core. . . . [He] was a paradox. He wanted all the outward signs and perquisites of belonging, yet he didn't want to give up the freedom of being a lone wolf. He was his own future." That future would include importing whisky, mysterious machinations on Wall Street, becoming a Hollywood mogul, and eventually government service. Surely Rose, whom Joe had pursued so avidly and with whom he shared so much, would be an equal partner in his immense success.

She was living a relatively lonely life in Brookline, becoming at least in the early years of her marriage the dutiful mother her children would later praise, while her husband was increasingly away, sometimes on extended coast-to-coast trips. She ate with the children and nurtured them. She sewed, and supervised a veritable army of help. Governesses and servants came and went with disturbing regularity. Rose was an extremely frugal, demanding employer. Perhaps that reflected her growing anxieties. Despite her overtures, most of the "nice people" of Boston still did not welcome the Kennedys into their homes. There was also a far more disturbing development. Rose had not learned of her father's infidelities through her pious mother but on her own. Rumors of her husband's amorous affairs, not yet so blatant as they would become later, now reached her ears too frequently to be disregarded. That he continued to be devoted to her and to their children was clear, yet he also seemed to feel that adultery could be an accepted, even expected, supplement to a contemporary marriage. Joe Kennedy had become used to getting what he wanted. He was a generous provider, and when at home an involved parent, but apparently in his mind a strong man's freedom extended to the bedroom.

Rose, however, viewed the situation very differently. Marriage was a sacrament, sanctified by God. Discovery of her father's lapses had deeply saddened her. To find them not only repeated but exceeded by the husband she had so respected was unbearable. Yet, if all flesh were weak, might not the spirit offer at least some solace? Her mother had turned away from her husband's sins, outward to her children and inward to her church. Uncertain what to do, Rose left her family in 1920 and went alone to a religious retreat. She also returned to the home of her faulted father, who counseled that her responsibility lay with her children and in submission to the husband he had only reluctantly approved. Her vows had been committed. In effect, she had made her bed, and now must lie in it for a lifetime. But if she could not change her husband, how could she continue to live with him?

The resolution Rose made changed her own life instead. If alcohol was the "curse" of the indigent Irish, perhaps infidelity was the vice of the rich. After 1920, her view of her marriage became as compartmentalized as her husband's. They would retain a partnership of mutual interest, with regard replacing romance, not unlike the relationship between Franklin and Eleanor Roosevelt — and prefiguring that between John and Jacqueline Kennedy. It was an attachment built around their children. Childrearing, Rose later affirmed, was a calling "fully as interesting and challenging as any honorable profession in the world," but her relationship with her children, still very close, became more officious and less personal. She would never be like her martyred mother; she would pursue a vibrant, separate life of her own. Still, the church of her childhood turned even more into a refuge. She determined it would provide each of her children with a moral foundation, one, she hoped, firmer than their father's. Even as their parents became emotionally distanced, the family grew: Eunice in 1921, Patricia in 1924, Robert Francis, called "Bobby," in 1925, Jean in 1928, and finally Edward Moore, called "Ted," in 1932. Joe Jr., already the heir apparent, was godfather to the youngest two. If the church was to involve them all, it was up to Rose. She attended daily mass and held private devotions in her home. More than the priests, she supervised intensive religious training for each of her children. Faith, in her view, was the only immutable fount of character, and she must set the example.

The irony is that all this liturgical effort led only to a third generation of ambivalence. It was the girls who were most deeply affected by their mother's efforts. Rose's sons, except for Bobby, who was closest to her, largely observed the rituals and then went on to follow the conspicuous example of their father. "Each of the boys," Reeves relates, "would strongly identify with the church and always attend weekly mass, while doing what was to their advantage . . . with little or no regard to its moral content." There were no rules for men. The world was imperfect, but one had to win, and winners could do just about whatever they willed. The Roman Catholic Church was an integral part of their lives, marriage and fatherhood would be another important component, but neither was pervasive. As Reeves observes, "Humility was fine in church." Outside, they had the souls of Kennedys.

The Kennedys are thought of as a Boston family, but as the children were growing up they lived little in Boston. In 1920 they moved into a much larger house in Brookline, which, as Hilty notes, "afforded space for more live-in help — a maid, a nurse, and a nanny — and most importantly a room for Rose to withdraw to read, think, sew, and be away from the children." Although she continued to relentlessly impart not only Catholic piety but also "neatness, social grace, gentle behavior, proper grammar and diction, dutiful obedience . . . [all within] a prescribed and regulated family life," Rose's pursuit of her own life made her increasingly inaccessible. The Kennedys might have invented the concept of "quality time." As the oldest children moved into their teens, they were obliged, more and more, to rely on each other for emotional support, Joe Jr. becoming almost a surrogate father. Home was wherever Joe Sr. decided it was. He had just about given up on Boston and the impenetrable snobbery of its self-appointed elite. "You can go to Harvard and it still doesn't mean a damned thing," he concluded. Boston was "no place to raise children." He moved his family to Riverdale, outside Manhattan, and then to Bronxville, in Westchester County. He established vacation homes in 1928 at Hyannis Port, on Cape Cod, and later in Palm Beach, Florida. The locale made little difference to their lifestyle.

Still largely excluded by Yankee society, the Kennedys created an exacting world of their own. Each house became their private domain, visitors accepted only if they accommodated fully to the Kennedys' demands. Somehow Rose managed to be self-indulgent and intrusive at the same time, another experience in ambivalence — vitality without intimacy. She continued to try to regulate every aspect of her children's lives. She was everywhere, and yet nowhere. Life at the Kennedys' compounds was both frenetic and ordered, especially in Hyannis Port and later at Palm Beach, the nearest to real homes the family ever enjoyed.

Rose put notes everywhere, including pinning them on her own dresses, to remind the children of their commitments. She organized every activity, stressing promptness. Clocks were placed in every room. Outside the sprawling Hyannis Port home, calisthenics were mandatory at seven a.m., followed by competitive sports everyone had to participate in. Collier and Horowitz write, "It was a regimen that abhorred weakness and tolerated no slackers. The children learned that her apparent distraction was protective coloration for a character that was actually strong-willed and durable." In fact, Rose was a skilled athlete, particularly interested in golf. Yet this fragile-looking drillmaster must have seemed more than a bit eccentric to her children and their friends. Was she a mother or an activities director?

Competition also came in other forms, with Joe Sr., when he was home, the debating coach of the dinner table. When away, he called daily, grilling every child on the news of the day, and he wrote endless letters inquiring about their activities. As historian Arthur M. Schlesinger Jr. writes, money was never discussed. "Conversations turned, not on business, but on public affairs. No child could ever doubt the order of priority." John Kennedy recalled, "My father wasn't around as much as some fathers when I was young, but . . . he made his children feel that they were the most important things in the world to him." There were two seatings for dinner, separating the children by age — both presided over by Rose, in the frequent absence of her husband. Although interested in the progress of all his children, Joe Sr.'s focus was on the older four, particularly the two boys. Outgoing Joe Jr. was most like him, hard-driving but more handsome and robust, a natural leader with a political future his father was already plotting. Jack, more slender, both reflective and outspoken but just as competitive, wanted to be a journalist. He was often sick, which concerned his mother more than his father. Discipline at the Kennedys' was more verbal, or nonverbal, than physical. Rose spanked her children when they were little, but their father's stare of displeasure was far more feared. The organization may have been matriarchal, but the ruler was a man.

Joe Kennedy returned from his years in Hollywood far richer — and ready for a new challenge. His affair with glamorous actress Gloria Swanson, the most visible of many, was not only intense while it lasted but was flaunted as well. Was it simply cruelty that induced Kennedy to bring Swanson home and include her on trips with his wife? Perhaps he was simply overcome with a grand passion. Whatever it was, Rose could not quite look the other way, as her mother had done with Toodles, but she endured the indignity with an extraordinary display of her own dignity. Perhaps living well *is* the best revenge. During the first six years of the Great Depression, Rose went to Europe on her own seventeen times, buying everything in sight — particularly the latest creations of Paris's foremost couturiers. She still had her trim size-eight figure, which she would keep all her life. Gloria Swanson might have sex appeal; Rose had style, and she was not above flaunting it.

If Rose was particularly self-centered during this period, it was not without reason. Despite her insularity, her children missed her terribly when she was away. Reeves writes that young Jack was particularly upset by his mother's absences — and by her lack of warmth even when she was at home. Jack recalled, "My mother never really held and hugged us." If she wasn't in Paris, she was in church. He would never have a large, "institutional" family, Jack vowed, and he didn't, but he inherited his mother's difficulty with expressing true intimacy. In the early 1930s the Kennedy children actually saw more of their father than of their mother.

The Depression didn't hurt Joe Kennedy financially. By now he was virtually impervious to economic upheaval, and he had the foresight to sell most of his holdings before the crash. It set him to thinking, however. He had all the money he needed. He was still young, and ready for the next step, prominent government service. Moreover, Washington would be the active arena now with a more activist Democratic president likely to succeed Herbert Hoover. Elective office was certainly an eventuality, if not for himself then surely for Joe Jr., who at school was excelling in everything. Not only the oldest but also the biggest and strongest of the children, Joe could be something of a bully, but his ambitions matched his father's. In 1928 Al Smith had been simply too Irish, too unlettered, too urban, too "Sidewalks of New York" to be elected president. It would take someone more like himself, or polished Joe Jr., to be elected the first Catholic president of the United States. It was no more improbable a goal than earning your first million by the age of thirty-five.

Although young Joe was an exemplary student, athlete, and leader at Choate, the establishment school his father had chosen, Jack just plodded along there. "You have the goods," his father assured him. "Why not try to show it?" Yet even Joe Sr. could see the potential in Jack, so different from the Irish-American stereotype, still at least personified in part by Joe Jr.'s gregariousness. Although reticent, Jack would become, as Schlesinger writes, "patrician, bookish, urbane — much closer . . . [to a young] Lord Salisbury than to a young Al Smith or, for that matter, to a young John F. Fitzgerald." Despite their personal distance, Rose and Joe were unified in not only expecting the highest achievement from their children but in viewing them as more than capable of it. Initially it may have stemmed from the residue of resentment, but by now they genuinely believed the Kennedy boys to be *better* than the inbred Brahmins, and their spirited daughter Kathleen more beautiful than any Beacon Hill debutante.

A Democrat by inheritance, Joseph Kennedy Sr. early anticipated that Franklin Roosevelt, with whom he had argued in 1918, would win the party's nomination for president in 1932. He raised substantial money for Roosevelt's campaign and got as close to him as possible. Many in the candidate's camp, however, viewed Kennedy as arrogant, headstrong, and anything but a team player. After the election, although he was not named secretary of the treasury, as he had hoped, Kennedy was made the first chairman of the Securities and Exchange Commission, and later head of the Maritime Commission. The ambassadorship to Ireland he turned down as being a bit patronizing. Late in 1937, however, Kennedy, fulfilling his limitless self-confidence, gained an extraordinary appointment. A bemused Roosevelt named this son of an Irish saloonkeeper United States ambassador to the Court of Saint James.

Rose found it hard to believe. As her husband said to her while dressing for a dinner at Windsor Castle in 1938, "Well, Rose, this is a helluva long way from East Boston, isn't it?" In a peculiar way, his appointment brought the two closer together. This was not due so much to the honor itself as to how warmly the entire Kennedy family was received in Great Britain. Social acceptance finally arrived not in Boston or New York or Cape Cod or Palm Beach but in class-conscious London. From king and queen to commoners, this refreshingly photogenic American family was greeted with genuine enthusiasm. In the spotlight as never before in her life, Rose Kennedy — who with her lovely "agate" eyes, fine-featured face, and strong chin had in truth the look of a New England aristocrat — was in her glory. Attired as fashionably as any

Duchess, she became an acclaimed hostess. Hilty writes that "She described these . . . as 'by far the happiest years of my married life.' The family traveled throughout Europe, vacationed in Cannes, shopped in Paris, and attended the coronation of Pope Pius XII as honored guests."

Invitations flooded in from the cream of English society. The Kennedy children formed romantic attachments, some of which turned out to be more than temporary. Their parents were close to becoming Anglophiles, adopting much of the manner and lifestyle of their hosts. At home, all this attention engendered more pride than alarm from Irish-Americans. With war clouds threatening in Europe, Ambassador Kennedy also got off to a strong start. His confident ease hid his concerns. By 1938, however, he began reminding English audiences that Anglo-American solidarity did not imply a joint foreign policy.

It was not the way Kennedy really felt. He was an ardent isolationist who, fearful of Axis power, imprudently supported Neville Chamberlain's appeasement policy of Nazi Germany and hobnobbed with British aristocrats sympathetic to fascism. As his granddaughter Amanda Smith comments in her wonderful compilation of family letters, Joseph P. Kennedy Sr., although very energetic, "lacked both diplomatic experience and a diplomatic nature." Roosevelt was appalled by Kennedy's actions. As unobtrusively as possible, Kennedy was recalled to the United States and, after a confusing series of negotiations between the two, gave a radio address supporting FDR's third-term bid in 1940.

Kennedy had been considering making a run himself for the Democratic nomination, or at least doing so in 1944, and he hoped Joe Jr. would be slated to run for governor of Massachusetts. After he granted newspaper interviews that undercut Roosevelt and recklessly attacked others, any relationship between the two was sundered. At his own request, Kennedy resigned in 1940. His wife and children had already returned to the United States in the prior year in the wake of war. Kennedy realized that he would never have a political career, but he was finally free to devote all his considerable resources to developing that of his oldest son. Joe, indeed, was the one he intended to be president, John perhaps a university president, Bobby a distinguished lawyer, and they'd find something for little Teddy as well.

As for Rose, the few lovely years were over far too soon. And even her abiding faith would be sorely tried by what was to come in the next decade. Rosemary was sent to an institution in 1941, the beginning of her separation from the family. Kathleen, affectionately called "Kick," as bright and lovely as Rose had been in her youth — and far more independent — fell in love with and married a Protestant English nobleman. He was killed in the war, and Kathleen was killed in an airplane crash several years afterward. In the interim, she had fallen in love with another Protestant peer, who was in the process of obtaining a divorce. Anguished Rose, who had been initially disturbed and heartbroken by the prospect of either union, and vehemently opposed both, could not bring herself to attend her daughter's funeral. Kathleen had been her parents' favorite among the Kennedy girls. Only devastated Joe Sr. flew to London for the memorial service. Still, the prior exchange of letters between the two had a special poignance. Rose wrote Kick in 1944, in final resignation to the marriage, "As long as you love Billy [Hartington, Marquess of Cavendish] so dearly, you may be sure that we will all receive him with open arms," and later, "it is Lent and I am praying . . . do your duty, that is best; leave unto the Lord the rest." Kathleen responded to Rose, after Billy's death, "You have done more than enough to show me the gateway to heaven. Please God I can half as well for the little Cavendishes."

Even before the United States entered the war Joe Jr. predictably left Harvard and joined the naval aviation program, but it was Jack who first saw action. Despite his serious physical ailments, his father's influence got him admitted into the navy. He earned a commission and eventually served as commander of a PT boat in the Pacific. During his prior service in Washington, in the family tradition, his amorous adventures were widely noted and almost got him into trouble. One lovely partner was a suspected German spy. In August 1943 Jack was proclaimed a hero when he saved the life of a crewman after their PT boat had been rammed by a Japanese destroyer. Joe Jr. was as relieved as the rest of his family about the news that Jack had survived, but he wasn't about to be upstaged by his younger brother. In August 1944 Joe volunteered to fly a plane loaded with explosives to destroy a German rocket site in France. There could hardly be a more hazardous mission. He was to bail out, the plane continuing to its target under radio control. It exploded too soon. Joseph Patrick Kennedy Jr. was killed instantly.

His father would never get over it, blaming Roosevelt, who he felt had maneuvered the nation into war, in the most embittered and personal terms, virtually accusing him of murder. "All my plans for my own future were all tied up with young Joe," Kennedy said, "and the best part of . . . life is over." Even his grief couldn't mask the fact that at least a measure of the elder Kennedy's sorrow was for himself. He and young Joe had been as one in ambition. Were both lives now over? The tragedy brought out the best in Rose. "Then and later," Hilty writes, "Rose offered the strongest example to the children in time of mourning. Finding solace in her church, she grew more resolute. . . . She said that the best way to survive tragedy was 'to turn some part of the loss to a positive, affirmative use for the benefit of other people.'"

Her admiring husband wrote that Rose "is ten thousand percent better than I am. Her terrifically strong faith has been a great help to her, along with her very strong will and determination not to give way." Their letters to each other, from their time in Europe, had been especially affectionate, he proclaiming, "I love you devotedly . . . more every day," she signing hers with "All my love, Rosa." However short-lived, it was almost a sequel to their youthful years of courtship. As her children grew and scattered, Rose's "round robin" letters to all of them became more frequent; some were so compelling that a twenty-four-year-old Jack wrote his mother, "I'm saving them to publish — that style of yours will net us millions."

In 1946, the Joseph P. Kennedy Jr. Foundation was launched. By then Joe Sr. had recovered sufficiently to place Jack, the war hero, at its head, with all the attendant publicity. Jack had composed a poignant memorial tribute to his fallen brother, *As We Remember Joe*. Now he had to pick up the banner. Jack, too, was special, Rose was certain, not only because he was a Kennedy but because of his way with words. By now she knew that none of her children would take holy orders, but the religious instruction she had imparted must not be entirely in vain. Bobby, the "runt" of the family, who had been most anxious to please her, was still the most devout of her boys and the most serious of all her children. Paul Dever, the Massachusetts governor who labeled Jack "the first Irish Brahmin," also called Bobby "the last Irish Puritan." If Jack could fulfill his father's vision, and Bobby add his zeal to the effort, Rose would do everything in her power to help them both. Although her own expectations for her sons were not solely based on elective office, it was the life she had known growing up, and her political instincts were still very sound. Moreover, both she and her husband understood that he could not be out front. He still loved the limelight, and had been rehabilitated to some extent by working on government reorganization in Washington, but his pre-war views had been so discredited by events that he would be a liability on the campaign trail. His checkbook, however, remained an immense asset. Rose Kennedy, the pride of the Fitzgeralds, would be the visible parent.

When Jack first ran for Congress in 1946, Rose made charming little talks, at first a bit shyly, but with increasing confidence as she gained more practice. Accompanied by her daughters, she added a personal touch to the campaign, holding receptions and teas for over 1,500 star-struck ladies. When Jack ran for the Senate in 1952, Rose's efforts escalated to teas attended by 70,000, and the Kennedy women were augmented by Jack's lovely young bride, "Jackie." Rose began talking longer, sometimes so long that she would be gently chided by her son, tiring of stories of how she had brought him up and of his heroism in the war. Rose even did a "coffee with the Kennedys" appearance on television. There were few substantive differences between moderate Republican Lodge and moderate Democrat Kennedy, except for the impact of the Kennedy women. Kennedy won.

Throughout, Rose reminded everyone of their religious obligations, so easily lost sight of in the heat of political combat. The entirety of a communication to Jack in 1959 reads, "This is a note to remind you of church. Mother." The first of six reminders of a "few things to help you and to help me" from Rose to Jackie was, "Would you please remind Jack of his Easter duty; I am sure that he could go to confession some morning in Washington as the church is quite near." Still, politics was in her blood. As she would later write to Bobby (from, characteristically, Chez Balenciaga in Paris), "I think you should work hard and become president after Jack — it will be good for the country and for you. And especially for you know who. Ever your affectionate and peripatetic Mother."

Rose Kennedy with her son John F. Kennedy
Courtesy of the John F. Kennedy Library

In the early campaigns, Joe Kennedy plotted strategy behind the scenes, gradually giving way to Bobby. Rose used her own contacts with House members, such as minority whip John McCormack, to advance Jack's career in Congress and get him on major committees. As the presidential primary season dawned in 1960, young Kennedy, who had nearly won the Democratic vice-presidential nomination in 1956, vied for the presidential nomination. Adlai Stevenson expressed his fears of "not the Pope, but the Pop." Biographer Richard Reeves writes that after 1956, Jack finally understood, as his father always had, that to win at this level, one had to become a "total politician." In Protestant West Virginia, Kennedy money swamped the other major contender, Hubert Humphrey. Kennedy stressed, "No one asked me my religion in the South Pacific." Rose's magic was also at work. She wowed the crowds in the first primary state, New Hampshire, telling how she had rocked her son to "political lullabies," and insisting that his political education had begun when he was only "knee high." With such a background, how could any other candidate be better qualified to be president than her son?

In the fall campaign, Rose, at seventy, traveled to fourteen states. She trudged through the Bronx for twelve straight hours, at the end looking neither tired nor rumpled. Offstage she could be cranky and demanding, but the press never saw it, or at least never reported it. She was tough, they wrote, and they were right. She was warm, they wrote, but here there is more doubt. As Thomas Reeves points out, just as the media covered up Jack Kennedy's promiscuity, they also made Rose into a model mother. Perhaps if her husband had been more considerate and less libidinous, she might have been the sort of mother the press pictured, as she had started out to be. Jacqueline Kennedy, like her mother-in-law, would learn to seal things off, find a kind of therapy in spending lavishly, and finally live her own life, but she was ultimately a devoted mother.

At Jack's impromptu Hyannis Port appearance on the morning after his slender victory over Richard Nixon in 1960, not only his wife and his mother were by his side, but proud Ambassador Kennedy finally made a public appearance. He could hardly contain his glee. He had lived to see it, after all — a Kennedy the first Catholic president of the United States. Characteristically, as soon as he got Jack alone, he made demands. Bobby, the one person Jack could most fully trust, must be his attorney general, and Teddy next in line for the "Kennedy seat" in the Senate. Not unlike royalty, it would be a succession. The patriarch, who when they were children had quizzed them on world events and followed their every activity even if from afar, would inevitably become less of an influence. However limited the time he had spent with his sons in their earliest years, he had prepared them for power once they reached the age of understanding. Letting go would not be easy for anyone.

The end came suddenly. Late in 1961, playing cards with his niece, Joseph Kennedy suffered a massive stroke. He was so close to death that Rose bought a black dress for the funeral, and prayed even more than usual. Then her husband rallied, but he was incapacitated for life, paralyzed on one side, and unable to speak intelligibly. In this agonizing state he lingered for eight years. Rose's thoughts of her husband again turned more tender, as they had in London and during the War Years, and merged with empathy for her second son, who was now president. Memories of her youth, so bright with promise, mingled with expectations of Jack's future, now entwined with the nation's. When she witnessed Jack attending mass alone after an exhausting night of inaugural revelry in the frozen capital city, Rose was moved. Something of her faith had broken through, after all. Something remained of all the daily prayers, the Our Fathers, the recitations of the rosary. "I realized that he was there of his own volition," she wrote, "that he wanted to start his presidency by offering his mind and heart, and expressing his hopes and fears to Almighty God, and asking his blessing." Throughout the brief thousand days of the Kennedy presidency, and particularly during the Cuban missile crisis, Rose wished that her husband were still accessible. "My son, my poor son, so much to bear," she lamented, "and there is no way now for his father to help him." More than ever, she became deeply involved in philanthropic causes, particularly speaking out on mental retardation, perhaps in belated tribute to her stricken daughter.

When Jack was taken so suddenly from her and the nation, Rose was a figure no less stalwart than her daughter-in-law. Five years later, at the age of seventy-eight, she was out campaigning again, this time with Bobby, the son most like her. There was a sweetness between them, their bantering exchanges more personal than those between Rose and Jack, and yes, even warm. Bobby would ask his mother to admit that she had started campaigning during Lincoln's administration. She still did not dwell on partisan issues but on raising children and being proud of them, and she still tended to run on a bit, but the crowds loved it. She was more humorous, more spirited, and more skilled on the stump than ever. If she could somtimes be abrupt — as when snapping to reporters who questioned excessive campaign spending, "It's our money" — Rose frequently demonstrated her distinctive grace. She greeted Eugene McCarthy, her son's most direct rival in the primaries for the 1968 Democratice presidential nomination, with "Have fun in the campaign." And then Bobby, too, was gone.

Distinguished historians and contemporaries of John F. Kennedy have been generous in their appraisal of how the Kennedy children were raised. Schlesinger writes, "More than most families, the Kennedys were bound together by a love which gave all the children a fundamental confidence. With its subtle and disparate solidarity, the family nourished a capacity for competition, for individuality and for loyalty." They have also praised Rose Kennedy as a devoted mother. Theodore Sorenson notes that her piety endowed John Kennedy with "spiritual depth." James MacGregor Burns considers Rose "a very model mother for a big family." Herbert Parmet believes that "for warmth, attention, and satisfaction [John Kennedy] turned to his mother." There is little doubt that Rose's most enduring gift to each of her children was not material, but how deep was her own personal faith? Thomas Reeves concludes that "Rose Kennedy's principal contribution seems to have been a ritualistic and demanding form of Christianity she passed on to her children, in which form mattered more than substance, public performance more than private conviction."

Yet he goes on to quote Rose at Jack's inauguration: "I said to myself, drawing on Cardinal Newman's words, 'He will do good, he will do God's work.'" As de Tocqueville wrote, "Who can search the human heart?" Whatever the diminution of her capacity for intimacy, Rose Kennedy's Catholicism appears to have been a matter not only of ritual but of conviction. Unfortunately, she could transmit it to her children only in part. If she increasingly found solace in the familiar forms of her faith, as her mother had, that is not surprising. She lived with ambivalence all of her life, and with unbearable tragedy for almost the last third of it. Rose Elizabeth Fitzgerald Kennedy died on January 23, 1995, at the age of 104. Her extraordinary strength, and its source, can be no less than inspiring. Her joy was perhaps the first victim of her husband's insatiable ambition.

IF Joseph P. Kennedy had a counterpart among the mothers of American presidents, it was surely Rebekah Baines Johnson. Although she was a devout Baptist, her aim was not to see her first son follow in the footsteps of a succession of prominent preachers. She wanted Lyndon to succeed in politics. As with the Kennedys, Rebekah's goal was to fulfill the ambitions of her family, but she was thinking less in terms of the Johnsons than of the Baineses. Her adored paragon of a father, she was convinced, *should* have been at least a congressman. Her son *must* be. She may have lacked the resources of a Kennedy, but Rebekah prepared and inspired her son in every way possible, even calibrating her affection to the degree of his progress. Lyndon Baines Johnson became the cynosure of her life, as surely as Franklin Roosevelt dominated his mother's. Unlike Sara Roosevelt, however, Rebekah always had a specific goal in mind.

The Baines heritage of learning and piety originated in Scotland and was transported almost seamlessly to the New World. Rebekah's grandfather, the Reverend George Washington Baines, who brought his family from North Carolina to Texas, was a highly regarded Baptist minister who became president of Baylor University. Of his six sons, none excelled in so many areas as Joseph. A lay preacher and pillar of his church and community, he served in the Civil War, taught school, put out a newspaper, and by the 1870s was an immensely successful lawyer. He was named Texas secretary of state at least in part because of his writing talents. Democratic politicians wanted him to compose their campaign biographies. His loyalties joined inheritance to conviction. "I am a Baptist and a Democrat," he proclaimed, a combination that boded well in Texas. He had married the agreeable daughter of a country physician when she was not yet fifteen, which raised only a few eyebrows at that time and place.

It would be twelve years before they had their first child, on June 26, 1881, a girl who grew to look much like her mother. They named her Rebekah, after the wife of Isaac in the Old Testament. Although she was later joined by a brother and a sister, for the Baineses their first-born daughter would always be the favorite, a refreshing rejection of gender inequity. Joseph was enamored of the hill country of Texas and decided to move his family and his flourishing law practice from the small town of McKinney, near Dallas, to just outside the even smaller town of Blanco. It may be that he viewed the region as a more promising foundation for his eventual goal of being elected to Congress. Here he built a mansion, reflecting cultivated tastes, that — except for its stone construction — seemed better suited to a Virginia tidewater plantation. It might have looked at home surrounded by manicured green lawns and stately trees. Instead, its incongruous bulk, as biographer Robert Caro writes, "towered over the stunted mesquite around it, and over the spindly little fruit trees in the recently planted orchard on one side. It seemed very out of place near Blanco's rickety wooden stores and . . . log cabins."

But the residents in those cabins did not seem to mind. Perhaps they were proud of such an edifice in their midst. They elected Baines to represent them in the state legislature. Growing up, Rebekah cherished the residence more for what it contained than because of its surroundings, although in time the gardens and orchards would grow into a kind of oasis. She recalled late in her life, "Most of all I love to think of the gracious hospitality of that home, of the love and trust, the fear of God, and the beautiful ideals that made it a true home." Those were the ideals of her father. He taught her to read and master the works of noted English and American novelists and poets. He taught her to love the natural world down to its smallest component as a visible manifestation of the Lord's largesse. He taught her to abhor lying, to treasure beauty in sentiment or skill, and to pursue a life committed to Christian service and the welfare of others. Rebekah adored her father. With his encouragement she went on to Baylor, where she majored in literature, one of few Texas women in those days to pursue higher education. As biographer Doris Kearns writes, Rebekah would later proudly recount to her son Lyndon how her father had thrilled the legislative chamber "with eloquent speeches on the rights and duties of mankind and the evils of liquor, the importance of cleanliness in thought and deed, and the iniquity of speculation." Yet he lost in his bid to be elected to Congress.

Disaster followed defeat. Inexplicably, Joseph Wilson Baines had one serious lapse, a land speculation of his own that went bad. He lost everything. It may have resulted from a vain attempt to retain his acreage, much of which had been rented to tenant farmers to whom Baines had been characteristically over-generous. The droughts common to the Texas hill country had been particularly severe, and crops such as cotton were devastated. Crestfallen, Rebekah returned home to help out, but it was not the same home. Her family moved to a much smaller house in the thriving community of Fredericksburg, which had been settled by thrifty Germans. It seemed a suitable setting to reestablish Joseph's law practice, but — nearing sixty — he lacked the energy to begin all over again. Rebekah gave elocution lessons and wrote articles about hill country happenings as a "stringer" for newspapers in the major Texas cities. She hoped someday to make her living as a writer. Her immediate task was to encourage her failing father, as he had always encouraged her. Although she was twenty-five, other men weren't really in her mind. It was her father who finally mentioned one, suggesting she interview for a story Sam Ealy Johnson Jr., who had succeeded to Baines's seat in the Texas legislature.

The two men could hardly have been more different, except for their commitment to their constituents. Sam was rough and wiry, although he stood well over six feet in height. He grinned easily, but Rebekah found him "cagey" about answering any specific questions. His manners were crude, his language no more literate than his neighbors', although in fact he had received enough education to have taught school. Four or five years older than Rebekah, he was a small-scale yet ambitious entrepreneur who farmed, invested in real estate, and traded livestock. His political concerns were local and practical, not phrased in elevated rhetoric about ideal societies. He was renowned throughout the region for his storytelling, not always suitable for mixed company, and he drank. Sam's people had come up from Georgia, audacious men of action who led cattle drives from Texas to Kansas, and who built their first hill-country home in Stonewall, near what came to be called Johnson City. Almost despite herself, Rebekah found something appealing in Sam's forceful personality, although he volunteered little that made for a particularly interesting story.

As for Sam Johnson, while he wasn't about to show it straight off, he was absolutely bowled over by Rebekah Baines. She was not only bright and beautiful; she actually enjoyed talking about politics. Of

Rebekah Johnson
Courtesy of the Lyndon Baines Johnson Library

course, she was probably delicate, nurtured by her protective parents, but her slender body was shapely, her eyes a deep blue, her hair ash-blonde. Caro describes her as a "soft-spoken, gentle, dreamy-eyed young lady who wore crinolines, and lace, and lovely bonnets." Rebekah's daughter would recall her mother's "flawless, beautiful white skin, protected from the sun." Sam didn't need much encouragement. Soon he seemed to be showing up almost daily at the Baineses', some twenty miles from his isolated cabin on the banks of the Pedernales River, on one pretext or another. He took Rebekah to hear florid political speeches, and she didn't seem to mind. In fact, to her great surprise, her father actually liked Sam, viewing him as a young man with promise, and fostered the relationship.

In November 1906, Joseph Wilson Baines died. His widow had to sell their modest home in Fredericksburg and move to San Marcos, Texas, where she was reduced to taking in boarders. Rebekah, who had returned to Baylor and was working in its bookstore to pay her tuition, was desolate. She memorialized her father as "the dominant force in my life as well as my adored parent, reverenced mentor, and most interesting companion." On August 20, 1907, she married Sam Ealy Johnson Jr. Perhaps her distracted state after the death of her father made her more amenable, but during Sam's whirlwind courtship her curiosity about him had turned into something closer to love. It would be put to the test almost immediately.

Rebekah moved not so much to a different locality as to a different world. Her life, like a Cinderella in reverse, turned from one of refinement, even in its reduced state of material comfort, to one of abject drudgery. Perhaps she did not comprehend at first that it also meant the end of any independent career for herself as a writer. Everything around her on Sam's farm reflected desolation: the cabin in which he lived, hardly more than an extended shack, the landscape itself, her companions and neighbors, such as they were — raucous farmhands and sturdy farmwives, no less coarse. Worst of all, when Sam drank he could become uncontrollable. Perhaps he harbored some inner demon. She had never been so lonely in her life.

Somehow, delicate though she was, Rebekah tapped a source of strength even she had not suspected. She loved to cook. Although there was no electricity, she managed to prepare meals in harvest time for as many as twenty workers at a time. She hated housework but waged an unrelenting campaign to keep the cabin clean. Perhaps to retain some semblance of her sanity, she continued her habit of putting down her reflections in a journal. Looking out at a dusty vista so nearly flat it seemed a joke to call it "hill country," and at the nearby town with perhaps half a hundred hard-pressed inhabitants, she considered her bleak circumstances: "Normally the first year of marriage is a period of readjustment. I was confronted not only by the problems of adjusting to a completely opposite personality, but also a strange and new way of life. . . . At least I realized that life is real and earnest." It might represent her new reality, but could she ever learn to accept such a life?

Despite having seen him at his worst, she loved her "opposite" husband. Sam cursed and drank in a way that would have appalled her circumspect father, had he been aware of it, and, although he went to the Baptist church every Sunday, it was a boisterous, tub-thumping form of religion utterly alien to the serene, inspirational dignity of the Baptist worship services she had known as a girl. Her father had recognized and commended Sam's ambition to Rebekah, but she early came to understand that it was limited to this inhospitable locale. Sam was, however, tireless. He certainly wanted to make money, in real estate or other ventures, and was also sincerely committed to helping his people in the legislature. But he had no ambition to leave the land he felt to be the source of his strength. He might build a larger, more comfortable house here, become more securely its first citizen, but he was too circumscribed, even if granted the opportunity, to ever run for Congress.

Rebekah, nonetheless, never gave up hope. She tried to maintain her standards and raise her husband's. She kept her good china and linens in readiness should someone prominent come home with him from Austin. In her apron, she would stand by the front door for hours, awaiting Sam's return. For all his wife's pretensions, he understood that she, whose complaints had been limited to wistful looks and sighs, was the best thing that had ever happened to him. And, with all his faults, Sam was still the best company she had.

On an August morning little more than a year after they had married, as Doris Faber puts it, Rebekah "discerned the reason she had been brought forth on this earth." When she went into labor the local creeks were rising, and Sam was away. His father, who lived nearby, saddled up his horse to make the perilous journey to bring back a German midwife. It was hours before a doctor was able to make his way to the Johnson cabin. As Rebekah later wrote, in her rather overheated style, "It was daybreak, Thursday, August 27, 1908, on the Sam Johnson farm on the Pedernales River near Stonewall, Gillespie County. In the rambling old farmhouse . . . lamps had burned all night. Now the light came in from the east, bringing a deep stillness . . . and then there came a sharp compelling cry — the most awesome, happiest sound known to human ears — the cry of a newborn baby, the first child of Sam Ealy and Rebekah Johnson was 'discovering America.'"

There was also a discovery on the part of his mother. Rebekah looked into the infant's eyes and somehow saw at once "the deep purposefulness and true nobility" of her father. Surely this child, whose birth was described by his mother in terms akin to the Nativity, would redeem her dreams and those of her father. Others saw signs as well. Reportedly, shortly after learning the news, the white-haired patriarch of the Bunton family, who had married into the Johnson clan, mounted his steed and rode wildly from farm to farm throughout the vicinity, exclaiming, "A U.S. senator was born this morning!"

It was months before "the baby" was named. Rebekah, naturally, preferred Joseph for her father, but didn't like the plebian sound of "Joe Johnson." She finally settled on adopting the name of a lawyer friend of Sam's, W. C. Linden, which Rebekah changed to the more "euphonious" Lyndon. Baines would be the child's middle name.

By the time he was two, little Lyndon was learning the alphabet from his mother. At three, arithmetic was added, and he was already reciting from some of the works Joseph Baines had read to Rebekah. At four, in part because of his hyperactive proclivities, he entered school early, but his mother always remained at the heart of his education. She would have three other children — two girls, one named after her, and a son named Sam Houston, for his father and the notable Texas hero. When Lyndon was five, his father gave the family a most welcome gift. They moved into a far more spacious Victorian home in Johnson City itself, closer to Sam's business and legislative interests in Austin. As Caro describes it, the house featured gingerbread scrollwork on its gables, surrounded by mature shade trees and wisteria. One can imagine Rebekah relaxing with a book of poetry on the lawn, having chased Lyndon from tree to tree, drilling him on some new lesson.

Even though less isolated and primitive than their former home, there was no escaping the surroundings. The house had no indoor plumbing, the town few stores or amenities. With her husband's investments at least for a time flourishing, Rebekah set out on a sort of one-woman crusade to bring at least a measure of enlightenment to Johnson City. Perhaps other mothers resented the Johnson girls' lovely frocks, sewed from pattern books Rebekah sent away for. Yet they seem to have genuinely appreciated her patient and kindly efforts to enhance their children's lives. Rebekah was the driving force behind a local literary society. She directed plays and wrote articles, once again taught public speaking and the social graces to shy country children, held spelling bees and tutoring sessions, and instructed the offspring of German families on how to speak and write in English.

Of course, much of this was to improve the quality of the local school that her children, too, attended. Their education was augmented by lively discourse at the Johnsons' dinner table, with debates and discussions of politics and other issues and competitive contests between the children. Sam was very much a part of it. Lyndon recalled the atmosphere as warm and loving, unlike the emotional austerity experienced by some other presidents who had deeply religious mothers. "[If] I argue with them," Rebekah insisted, it is only "to keep their wits sharp." She was very much a "hands-on" parent, given to hugging and encouraging her children, although she always held Lyndon to a higher standard than the others. If disagreements developed between them, she would invariably conclude that Lyndon must be right.

In her efforts to raise funds and standards for schools and organizations, Rebekah never lost sight of the religious foundations of her enlightened Baines legacy. In a community divided between fundamentalist Baptists, Methodists, and Disciples of Christ, her Bible stories for children were apparently ecumenical enough to offend no one. She taught Bible studies and formed — whatever Sam might think — a temperance society, warmly welcomed by many local women. Perhaps their admiration for Rebekah was tinged with envy, but she was highly esteemed in the early Johnson City years. Her first stories to Lyndon had been from the Bible. In his mother's mind, he might be destined for a career in public life, but that only made Christian morality all the more essential.

If Rebekah was patient with others, she was less so with Lyndon. On the one hand, as he grew older, she began to confide in him, and only in him, her innermost feelings. She had never ceased loving her husband, but once his limitations became evident, her oldest son, willing or not, became her confidant. He even slept in his parents' bedroom when Sam was so frequently away. Lyndon and Rebekah read to each other the same Browning, Milton, Dickens, and Longfellow that she had once read with her dear father. As Johnson confided to Doris Kearns, his mother, who so vividly recalled her father's financial downfall, felt threatened by the uncertainty of Sam's fortunes, which she blamed on his drinking. She cried constantly, at least within the confines of her home. "I knew she needed me," Lyndon said. "With me she seemed less afraid. She . . . told me over and over how important it was that I never lose control of myself and disappoint her that way. . . . She never wanted to be alone." It is little wonder that Lyndon in the third grade wrote and recited, "I'd Rather Be Mama's Boy." Yet it is not hard to understand why he came to almost resent the weight of her expectations. Nor is it surprising that Sam began to prefer the company of his younger son.

There was another side of Rebekah's heightened hopes that hardly contributed to Lyndon's emotional security. As Kearns writes, "Lyndon never experienced his mother's love as a steady or reliable force, but as a conditional reward, alternately given or taken away. When he failed . . . he experienced not simply criticism but a complete withdrawal of affection." It happened when as a child he rebelled against completing violin and dancing lessons, and years later when he questioned why he must go to college. Rebekah's exhortations were not so much harsh as unrelenting. When Lyndon fell short of her standards, she would simply ignore him, sometimes for weeks, lavishing attention instead on her confused husband and her other children. When Lyndon did what his mother wanted, he was always right. When he disobeyed, he wasn't merely wrong, he was shut out of her sight until he came around.

At least when he was little, Lyndon had an alternate, unconditional source of affection, his colorful grandfather, Sam Ealy Johnson Sr. An authentic cowboy, Sam was a link to a fast-vanishing frontier. His vivid stories of cattle drives, stampedes, and fighting in the Confederate army were compelling to Lyndon, however abhorrent to his disapproving mother. Old Sam also predicted that one day this lively boy would be a United States senator. When still little more than an infant, Lyndon would crawl in the direction of his grandfather's cabin. The elder Sam's political views had a profound effect on his son and, by inheritance, on his grandson. A populist and a progressive, he saw the freewheeling West he knew and loved hemmed in by remote eastern interests: money men, middlemen, railroad barons, land speculators, lawyers, bankers, and their counting-house clerks. The good, plain people caught in the middle would need champions in legislative halls. The old man died in 1913, at the age of seventy-seven. His porch had been a refuge for Lyndon from the pressures that were already mounting on him at home.

Rebekah's health was never quite the equal of her energies. Particularly after the difficult birth of her final child, she felt the accumulated wear of her married life. She could only pray that the Lord would lengthen her days sufficiently to permit her to witness the ultimate political ascension of her first son. Perhaps as a result of all the attention he received, Lyndon was a friendly and inquisitive child but also tended to be very bossy with others his age. Even as an infant, he preferred not to play quietly by himself but crawled away in all directions. At eighteen months, as Caro writes, with his already "great ears flapping," Lyndon took off to visit neighbors two miles away. At four he found his way to the local store, after which outing his mother decided to put him in school a year early. She accompanied him, with a baby in her arms, and asked the teacher to please hold Lyndon in her lap when he recited, as Rebekah did at home.

By the time he was five, Lyndon preferred playing with much older children, but he still liked being the center of attention. By his teens, he was emulating his father, whom he often accompanied on the campaign trail. Sometimes the youth would even grasp others by their arms and overalls — as he would later grab suit lapels in the halls of Congress — exhorting them with the fixed gaze that came to be known as the "LBJ method." As Caro notes, Lyndon began to resemble his father in appearance as well as in manner — tall and gawky, big-eared, big-nosed, and aggressive on or off the stump. He ambled in giant strides, however, never quite duplicating his father's jaunty strut. Lyndon seemed to envelop people, Sam to dance around them. Eventually there developed almost a sort of competition between father and son. Lyndon absorbed many of Sam's ideas but began to wonder if the old man's brand of country populism wasn't a bit out of touch with the new realities in

Texas. Similarly, Lyndon absorbed Rebekah's examples, but not for their own sake. He leaned toward the pragmatic, examples that led to clear conclusions, and stories with a practical purpose. His mother seemed a bit dreamy.

Both of these impressions would soon be borne out by events. After two terms in the legislature, Sam had given it up to devote a decade to his real estate investments. He then returned to his seat in Austin from 1918 to 1924. At the height of his influence he might have run for the congressional seat Rebekah's father had failed to win, but he never really pursued it. Increasingly he was at odds with powerful political and economic interests. His son would later champion the New Deal when it was at its height, but Sam supported farm relief, the eight-hour-day, and regulation of lobbyists and utilities when such notions were less widely accepted. He had fervently favored Woodrow Wilson's New Freedom but later switched his allegiance to Theodore Roosevelt's "Bull Moose" brand of progressivism. Sam was also a civil libertarian, opposing the internal security measures that followed the Great War and the growing influence of the Ku Klux Klan. No one doubted his courage.

All this Lyndon witnessed, traveling in his father's Model T car, accompanying Sam to his rallies and on his rounds. It was great fun, this introduction to politics on the local level. To his mother, the good times meant live-in help to do the cleaning she had always disliked. She still made certain her children were immaculately dressed, but now she had more time to devote to her many voluntary activities. Her husband's fall was sudden. Sam Johnson's personal financial depression arrived a few years earlier than the nation's. When his investments, never very soundly based, went sour, no one bailed him out. There was no offer of a respectable government job to tide him over. With so many forces in Austin arrayed against him, old friends and former allies were loath to come to his aid. In the hill country, sympathy was tinged with a bit of venom. Sam's sprightly confidence could be taken for arrogance, and didn't always win him friends. He lost his home. He also lost, at least for a time, the respect of his son. Of what value were Sam's honest intentions now? Relatives had to bring them food to assure the family's very survival.

If her husband never fully recovered from this blow, Rebekah also suffered, emotionally and physically. But she was proud as well as pious. Appearances had to be maintained, although everyone in town surely knew the truth. She had been their Lady Bountiful, traipsing down from the manor to rescue the benighted village. Their sympathy, for Rebekah, too, was probably mixed with a certain satisfaction at her comeuppance. She had never really disciplined her children, feeling that setting the right example should be sufficient. She had withheld affection from Lyndon, of whom so much more was expected, only when he fell short. Now, she felt certain, was the time he needed her most. When, at fourteen, Lyndon was reduced to riding a donkey to school, creating as gangling an apparition as a young Abraham Lincoln, the jeering of his classmates was merciless. Although he told them he would be president of the United States someday, it was a humiliation he never forgot. His mother's reminder that even Jesus had ridden on an ass into Jerusalem did little to assuage his hurt. By now he was contemptuous of both his parents, his father's impracticality and his mother's pretensions. Her admonitions no longer motivated him, any more than her feigned indifference had.

Nor did her tears, no longer directed at Sam, soften Lyndon's stance. He perversely abandoned the table manners she had taught him and began to run with a crowd immersed in drinking, carousing, fast driving, and general indifference to anything serious. He graduated from high school in 1924, after a brief stay at a private school his mother had managed to pay for, and then informed his disconsolate parents that he had no intention of going on to college. By now his father had decided, in the pervasive gloom, that Lyndon would never amount to anything. His mother knew better, but she wasn't yet quite certain how to bring about his resurgence.

What he needed, after all the cumulative pressures she had placed on him, was simply an antidote — time to blow off steam. Asserting his independence, he took off with some friends for California, hitchhiking, for a carefree year of vagabond drifting. It also gave him time to think. On the long way home he had what Kearns describes as a sort of epiphany. He would regain his mother's love and his father's respect. But first, to prove his physical strength, he worked as a laborer on a road-building gang. Then he finally agreed to go to college.

If it wasn't quite Harvard, in 1927 inexpensive Southwest Texas State Teachers College in San Marcos, only thirty miles away, seemed a somewhat more viable alternative to the Johnsons. Rebekah had worked there as a housemother after the death of her father. Now, all her mental wheels were again set in motion. She helped Lyndon obtain a job in a criminal lawyer's office and borrowed money from a sympathetic banker to get him started. Then she personally prepared her son for his entrance examination. Working his way through college, Lyndon also worked his way up, developing the skills later to be demonstrated in public life. He would never abandon many of the convictions of his father and grandfather, but he was a clear-eyed realist, placing ambition above ideology. He cultivated older men who had the power to help him. Making himself invaluable to their success hastened his own.

The first was the president of his college. Lyndon became a special assistant to the president's personal secretary and wound up as all but a partner in running the school. Initially rebuffed by the secret society that had dominated student life, by the time he graduated Johnson had replaced their power with his own. Before gaining his degree, he taught for a year at a school attended largely by poverty-stricken Mexican-Americans, a job arranged by the college president. Lyndon enjoyed teaching but agreed with his mentor that he was meant for a faster-paced profession. Still, he never forgot the faces of those children, their longing for learning etched deep in his consciousness. Nor did he forget his rejection by the conservative father of the first young woman he had dated seriously, who didn't want the son of a failed dirt-farming politician in his house. Indeed, Lyndon Johnson never overlooked a favor or a slight.

College had been an unqualified success, even if many students viewed Johnson as a spineless sycophant of the administration. Yet he was still insecure, wracked by doubts about his future. His father hadn't quite forgiven Lyndon's disrespect, but Rebekah wrote her son supportive letters almost daily. From the moment he set foot on the San Marcos campus Lyndon was fully her son again. He had written back, "Dearest Mother . . . You can't realize the difference in atmosphere after one of your sweet letters. . . . There is no force that exerts the power over me your letters do." As Caro observes, when depressed or doubtful, Lyndon's mood "could be lightened only by the one person in the world of whose love he was sure." Rebekah urged him to write his father, as well. Perhaps the rapprochement of the two men really began in 1931, when Lyndon went to Washington as an aide to wealthy new congressman Richard Kleberg. He never looked back. Neither did Rebekah, except to think again of her father. Lyndon had begun stressing the Baines in his name, evidence that he carried in his veins the blood of a family of learning and distinction. At last Rebekah's tears were of joy. Their time was at hand.

In 1934 Lyndon found another gracious, refined lady to sustain him. He married Claudia Alta Taylor, nicknamed "Lady Bird" in infancy, only two months after they met. Rebekah approved, but her response to the union was like Abigail Adams's to the bride of her son, John Quincy. Rebekah wrote her daughter-in-law, "My dear Bird, I earnestly hope that you will love me as I do you. Lyndon has always held a very special place in my heart. Will you not share that place with him, dear child?" Such a wife could advance her son's career, and Lady Bird also brought some financial resources into the marriage. To her "sweet son," Rebekah wrote, "I am loving you and counting on you as never before." When Lady Bird first met Rebekah, she made this perceptive observation: "It was obvious that Lyndon just loved her greatly, and I felt drawn to her, and yet I felt like patting her on the shoulder and saying I wasn't going to harm this son on whom she had pinned so many hopes."

The following year, in 1935, Sam Johnson suffered his first heart attack, which was quite serious. He was still very weak in 1937, when Lyndon, only twenty-nine, announced for Congress. The incumbent had died, and a special, hotly contested election was being held to complete his term. Lyndon campaigned so tirelessly not only on his own behalf but also for the policies of Franklin Roosevelt and Sam Rayburn, the powerful men he now began cultivating, that he ignored severe stomach pains. His appendix was removed only forty-eight hours before Election Day. Sam wanted to help, reversing their roles when he had been the candidate. Energized, he summoned sufficient strength to launch his son's campaign before an audience including almost ev-

Rebekah Johnson
Courtesy of the Lyndon Baines Johnson Library

ery resident of Johnson City. Lyndon recalled, "There was something in his voice and in his face that completely captured the emotions of the crowd." The applause was sustained. "I looked over at my mother and saw that she, too, was clapping and smiling. It was a proud moment for the Johnson family."

Lyndon's narrow victory made it no less sweet. He would come to be derisively labeled "Landslide Lyndon" for an even closer (and questioned) triumph in a Democratic senatorial primary, but losing was never in his lexicon. He not only went further in politics than his father, but beyond anything even Rebekah had dreamed of. She was a great admirer of Eleanor Roosevelt, who wrote a newspaper column and enjoyed the sort of independent life Rebekah had hoped to have; but, as could nothing else, Lyndon's success justified the life she had settled for. A few weeks after the election, Sam had another heart attack. Although the campaign had been only a temporary tonic for him, at least he shared in its success. Sam Ealy Johnson Jr. died on October 23, 1937, at the age of sixty. He had come home from the hospital, wanting to spend his final days where, as his son often said, "People know when you're sick and care when you die." Fearing that heart trouble might be hereditary, Lyndon hastened to advance his career, even as he mourned.

Although concerned for her husband of thirty years, Rebekah could not contain her emotions at her son's victory. It might be only the beginning of his Washington achievements, but it finally fulfilled her own quest:

My darling Boy,

Beyond "Congratulations, Congressman," what can I say to my dear son in this hour of triumphant success? In this as in all the many letters I have written you there is the same theme: I love you; I believe in you; I expect great things of you.

　　To me your election alone gratifies my pride as a mother in a splendid and satisfying son . . . but it in a measure compensates for the heartache and disappointment I experienced as a child when my dear father lost the race you have just won. . . . Today my faith is restored. How happy it would have made my precious, noble father to know that the first born of his first born would achieve the position he desired! . . . I gave you his name. I commend to you his example. You have always justified my expectations, my hopes, my dreams. How dear to me you are you cannot know, my darling boy, my devoted son, my strength and comfort.

Rebekah lived another twenty years, settling into a small house in Austin, writing a family history, and continuing to send letters to Lyndon. She would witness his rise to majority leader of the Senate, but nothing — perhaps not even the presidency — could have exceeded her excitement at his first triumph, before the age of thirty . . . "Congratulations, Congressman." Rebekah Baines Johnson died on September 8, 1958, at the age of seventy-seven. Her son said of her, "She was quiet and shy, but she was the strongest person I ever knew." Not everyone considered her quiet or shy, but of her strength there is no doubt. She was buried next to her husband in the Johnson family cemetery on the grounds of what came to be called the LBJ Ranch. But in her heart she was always a Baines, the daughter of a great man whose dream was redeemed by her son.

CHAPTER FIFTEEN

"My Mother Was a Saint"

ॐ Hannah Nixon

ॐ Dorothy Ford

ON AUGUST 9, 1974, in an emotional, rambling farewell to his White House staff and cabinet, between references to the example of Theodore Roosevelt and the pluck of his father Frank Nixon, departing president Richard M. Nixon paid a tearful tribute to his mother. "My mother was a saint," he said, "and I think of her, two boys dying of tuberculosis, nursing four others . . . and when they died, it was like . . . her own. Yes, she will have no books written about her. But she was a saint."

Except for their lack of distinction, the families of Hannah Milhous and Frank Nixon had little in common, Hannah and Frank themselves even less. The mystery is what drew them to each other. In biographer Herbert Parmet's opinion, their son Richard would be the product, or victim, of this "schizophrenic existence." Wanting to be tough yet sensitive, Richard Nixon's fate was to be "split almost down the line between Hannah and Frank, to behave like the one while wishing the world to believe he was the other." Yet both his parents were tough. Unfortunately, his father's cranky, demonstrative truculence could be self-destructive. His mother's strength was couched in gentleness and gentility. She once admitted, "I can't think of a Nixon or a Milhous holding an office higher than that of sheriff." As biographer Stephen Ambrose points out, however, both families had "a penchant for taking risks." Otherwise neither would have found their way to the western edge of North America.

274

The Nixon journey began in the mid-1600s, when Oliver Cromwell had come to the conclusion that the Quakers were one sect he couldn't win over "either with gifts, honors, offices or places." They were simply different. The movement had begun as a form of radical Puritanism in an England racked by internal strife. As biographer Roger Morris writes, "The most Protestant of the Protestants," the Quakers were rooted "in a fierce individualism and democracy of faith, the innate conscience and grace of every believer's 'inner light' or 'the light of Christ within.'" Such personalized revelation required the intercession of no ordained clergy and implied little regard for kings or protectors, but a commitment to every form of social justice. Calling themselves the Society of Friends, some Quakers evinced a desire for separation, others an evangelical fervor that threatened more structured denominations or any established order.

Both paths were perilous and could lead to persecution, in the New World as well as the Old. When Quakers finally began to emigrate, the English authorities were relieved to be freed of such dangerous nonconformists. But the Friends only gained a secure haven in North America when William Penn established his "holy experiment" in 1682. The monarchy having been restored, King Charles II was more than willing to resolve a debt owed to Penn's father, an affluent admiral, by granting these vast tracts of land. As the American frontier moved westward, groups of Friends fanned out from Pennsylvania. Morris notes that by the time of the Revolution there were over fifty thousand Quakers on the North American continent. As they followed the frontier, Quakers split into several "separations." The dignified introspection of established "meetings" on the eastern seaboard was far removed from the preaching, singing, proselytizing, and public testimony of Quaker "churches" in the West — which were more akin to Methodism. Even belief in pacifism and a desire for the abolition of slavery were no longer universal.

The Milhous family became Quakers in a most roundabout (one might even say Roundhead) fashion. They were of German descent, originally named Melhausen, and went to England to fight *for* Cromwell. Their reward was land in Ireland, in Timahoe County. Somehow, there they were converted to Quakerism, renounced their military heritage, and in 1729 sailed to Pennsylvania, where they had obtained two hundred fertile acres to farm. In 1805 they moved to Ohio, and in 1854 to Indiana. They were not so much restless as open to new opportunities. Apparently one pervasive characteristic many retained, though it seems at odds with their faith, was a rather smug self-satisfaction. As one in-law remarked, "The Milhouses thought highly of the Milhouses." Morris describes the Milhous family as "intelligent, well off, reverent, but no more so than many diligent Quaker families . . . [and] without conspicuous achievement through the nineteenth century and well into the next."

Reflecting the schisms of the Quakers themselves, opinion differs on Milhous involvement in abolition and the Civil War. Ambrose writes, "The family was abolitionist, and the farm was a way station on the Underground Railroad." Morris writes, "Anti-slavery Friends had separated from the Indiana church in the 1840s. . . . The Milhouses never sided with the abolitionists." Nixon's maternal grandfather, Franklin, was too young to fight in the Civil War, had he so desired, and his father was too old, but at least one Quaker relative, from Ohio, was a captain in the Union Army. The turmoil of a Quaker family during these times was poignantly portrayed by Nixon's cousin Jessamyn West in her book *The Friendly Persuasion,* later made into a memorable motion picture. Taking a bit of chronological license, West based her stalwart heroine on Hannah Nixon.

By the time he was twenty-eight, Franklin Milhous was already a widower, with two young children, hardly a novelty given the rigors of the frontier. Within his community and his church, he found a worthy second wife. At the age of thirty, experienced schoolteacher Almira Park Burdg seemed destined for spinsterhood. She was plain but very bright, loved poetry, and fortunately was very fond of children. She would bear seven, six of them girls. The third of these daughters, born on March 7, 1885, Almira and Franklin named Hannah, after a Milhous aunt and the mother of Samuel in the Old Testament. At least in the eyes of most people, Hannah would be no more a beauty than her mother, but her equal in learning, piety, and charity. Although after the war social issues were championed far more by Eastern Friends, Almira had no patience with equivocation. She revered Abraham Lincoln and forcefully espoused racial and religious toleration. As Richard Nixon recalled, "My grandmother set the standards for the whole family." Franklin was more fun-loving, but in his own way equally religious. Together they established lifelong values for their nine children, to be perpetuated in following generations.

Hannah's childhood was greatly influenced by the Quaker way of life and yet was rather distinctive in its worldliness. The Milhouses lived next door to Frank's parents' relatively luxurious dwelling, replete with indoor plumbing, a telephone, a large library, and even an organ (featured in the funniest scene from the movie *Friendly Persuasion*). Hannah went to school, as the Garfield children had, in a compact building on her own parents' property. Almira and Franklin both loved music and literature. In the evenings Hannah's father read aloud not children's fables but stories from the most noted American authors. As in other Quaker households, there was little hugging or overt displays of affection, but discipline was more verbal than physical. It was anything but an insular life. The Milhouses went on family trips to places as distant as Niagara Falls, the major American cities, and down the Ohio River. With so many relatives nearby, family gatherings and picnics were frequent. Almira had live-in help but did more than her share in preparing for these festive occasions.

Most of all, Hannah's upbringing was steeped in faith. Morris writes that "Beyond the Sunday services, the family sang hymns after supper, had communal Bible readings and prayers. . . . Quakerism both tempered and confined the lives of the children." Hannah recalled, "Father and Mother were full of love, faith, and optimism." But as the older girls grew into their teens, they were discouraged from attending even innocent square dances. The Milhous home became a community center for both social and religious activities. Although a "peaceful and comfortable" religion devoid of doctrinaire authority, as Ambrose observes, Quakerism as a way of life was pervasive "in speech, in mannerisms, in daily prayer," and in its traditions. "Thee" and "thou" were still used in common conversation. Through a childhood serene and secure, Hannah inherited her mother's strength and her faith. More than Almira, she would have need of both.

When she was twelve, in 1897, her family moved to California.

Franklin had up to this time been taking care of and expanding the prosperous nursery he had inherited from his father, a business which provided seedlings to surrounding farmers, but he was always looking for wider opportunities. A college graduate, he was concerned, as was Almira, about the lack of Quaker schools in the vicinity to further the education of their children. They were intrigued by a new settlement almost a continent away in California, conceived, as Morris puts it, in "a dusty mix of piety and profiteering," and named for Quaker poet John Greenleaf Whittier. All would be welcome, the developers insisted, but the gentle, thrifty, progressive Friends were particularly encouraged to come. When his father died, Franklin felt free to move. The lure of abundant land at low prices, a beneficent climate, orange groves, and an expansive Quaker community already under way was irresistible. Almira shared his wanderlust. In a series of chartered railroad cars the Milhouses journeyed west in relative comfort, taking with them virtually all of their possessions — from a carriage, horses, and livestock to lumber and as much of their old house as could be disassembled.

What they found was not quite paradise, but a Quaker church was already in place, and an academy — eventually to become Whittier College — had been founded in 1891. The community, which was to become the largest Quaker settlement in the United States, was some twenty miles from Los Angeles, far enough away from the railroad to provide protection against intruders yet near enough to prevent total isolation. The Milhouses settled into a spacious Victorian house and established their new nursery behind it. In due course a stream of relatives came west to join them, recreating their Indiana community. There were neither dancehalls nor saloons in Whittier, but visitors were inevitable. Richard Nixon wrote of his grandmother, as he later would of his mother, "She was always taking care of every tramp who came along the road. At her house no servant ever ate at a separate table. They always ate with the family. There were Negroes, Indians, and people from Mexico — she was always taking somebody in." If they didn't mind listening to a Bible verse and solemn prayer, anyone could get a square meal at the Milhous homestead.

Her mother's egalitarian example had a profound effect on shy, dutiful, bright, and profoundly religious Hannah Milhous. She finished grammar school with high grades and went on to the Quaker academy. Ambrose describes the teenaged Hannah as having "a dark, brooding look. Of medium height (five feet, five inches). . . . She was exceedingly slender, bony in her shoulders and face. She usually did up her long black hair in a knot. Her eyes were dark and deep-set. . . . All the photographs taken of her during her adolescence show a serious, almost forbidding face, and the testimony of her childhood friends and family agrees that she was indeed a serious young lady." Morris's description of the same features is a bit brighter: "[a] gentle young lady of wasp waist and serious countenance, marked by thick raven hair and eyebrows above dark, limpid eyes."

Hannah loved to cook, and of all the Milhous children she was probably the greatest help to her mother. She preferred spending evenings at home to socializing with groups or individuals of her own age. At fifteen, exemplifying the difference between western and eastern Quakerism, Hannah made a public confession of her faith when an emotional evangelist visited her church, and — shy or not — she urged others to follow her example. Her dedication to her religion was extreme even by the standards of the Whittier community. Ambrose notes that at least one relative called her "the angel unaware." Graduating from secondary school in 1905, Hannah went on to two years at Whittier College, specializing in languages, and became a teacher. Her social life expanded a bit, although within the church, to picnics and gatherings of Christian Endeavor. Still, as Morris writes, "At nearly twenty-three, shy and sheltered, she had never had a date." All that would change with startling suddenness when she met a brash, ambitious young man, seven years her senior, with the look of a "black Irishman," named Francis Anthony Nixon. Everyone called him Frank.

Nixon's forebears, Scotch and English as well as Irish, had come to America in the 1730s, settling in Delaware only some twenty miles from the Pennsylvania farm of the Milhouses. Demonstrative Methodists, the Nixons had no Quakerly qualms about fighting. Nixons fought in the Revolutionary War and, as had the Milhouses, moved on to Ohio. Frank would be born there in 1878. Frank's grandfather, an Ohio volunteer, died at Gettysburg in the Civil War. Frank's father, Samuel, struggled to keep two generations of his family together. Sickness and poverty took their toll. By his teens, infuriated by an abusive stepmother and the taunts of his better-dressed schoolmates, Frank Nixon set off on his own. Combativeness would be his lifelong companion. If challenged, he would fight anyone of any size, not unlike Harry Truman's father. In his own way, Frank was as religious as Hannah, but his was a righteous God who rewarded tenacity, not a God of mercy.

Offering little more than his energy, Frank tried any number of jobs, eventually finding work as a streetcar motorman in Columbus, Ohio. Exposed to the elements, Frank came to hate both the bitter cold and the transit management's indifference to their workers' plight. Astonishingly, he managed to organize an informal union to put pressure on a candidate for the state senate to introduce legislation to improve conditions. This first Nixonian political campaign was more successful for the candidate and other motormen, who indeed did ultimately receive both heat and enclosure, than for Nixon himself. Realizing he would be fired, Frank set out in 1907, at the age of twenty-eight, for the perpetual warmth of southern California. He had little more than the train fare.

Once he arrived, he quickly found another job as a motorman, in "interurban transit," but it was a good deal more scenic and comfortable than his old route in Columbus. Going back and forth from the center of Los Angeles to the growing town of Whittier, Frank decided to room in a boardinghouse near the Whittier terminus. It was, not surprisingly, run and largely inhabited by Quakers, who extended to the lonely newcomer a friendliness he had not previously experienced. Probably more to be sociable than for religious reasons, Frank began attending Friends worship services. Even at their very proper parties, he became enamored of a number of young women, who reciprocated his interest. His circumstances might have been humble, but Frank Nixon was handsome, well-groomed, and lively. Ambrose describes him as not especially tall, but well-built, with a strong nose and jaw, his dark hair precisely parted, and his suit "very carefully pressed." In appearance, he seems rather like the Irish father of Ronald Reagan, but Frank neither smoked nor drank. On the other hand, the affable Reagan knew how to keep the friends he made. Frank Nixon's opinionated bantering could drive them away. His early foray into politics had reinforced his support for those who championed labor. Nixon believed in Democratic populism, but later converted to the "sound money" Republicanism of McKinley, a precursor of his own future as a small businessman. Frank also converted to Quakerism, though to the more animated western variety.

When he met Hannah Milhous at a Valentine's Day party in 1908, Frank was captivated. He claimed that he "immediately stopped going with five other girls." He did not view Hannah as plain. She *was* shy, but also warm, intelligent, and altogether wonderful. Or so we must assume he concluded, because he started seeing her virtually every night. Hannah must have been overwhelmed at such attention, however ingrained her modesty — and flattered despite herself. Her parents were appalled. This aggressive outsider offered nothing — no education, no culture, no profession, no family, no future. His enthusiasm seemed more bluster than audacity. He had even lost his transit job after an accident and was working as a foreman at a neighboring citrus orchard. Frank Nixon seemed little more than a common laborer. But Hannah could be stubborn, to everyone's surprise, and nothing would dissuade her. She had never been in love before, but she insisted that she knew what it was. The Milhouses would always consider that Hannah had married beneath herself and her family. Forty-four years later, Frank's opinion, too, remained equally unaltered. "I knew I had picked the very best. And I haven't changed my mind." After only four months of what was probably as much a campaign as a courtship, Hannah Milhous and Frank Nixon were married in a Friends ceremony. It was June 2, 1908. Four months later Hannah was pregnant.

Frank's modest cottage at the citrus grove would be a depressing place to have a child. The Milhouses relented sufficiently to invite Hannah home. Frank was even given a job by his father-in-law. In June 1909, after a lengthy period of labor, Hannah gave birth to a boy she and Frank named Harold Samuel Nixon. The acceptably biblical middle name was also after Frank's father. The first name revealed Hannah's fascination with English kings of the Middle Ages. At the end of 1911, always sensitive about living off the largesse of others, Frank decided to plant his own lemon grove in the nearby town of Yorba

Linda (although the land was owned by the Milhous family). Here he built a sturdy clapboard house that still stands. The Nixons became a popular young couple in the town, despite their contrasting personalities. Even with her baby to care for, Hannah was very active in the Women's Club. Frank taught Quaker Sunday school with moralistic Methodist fervor. Both worked endless hours in the grove. Neither ever lacked for energy. Unfortunately, although the family lived as frugally as possible, there was no way to make the enterprise profitable. The soil was simply too sandy, the lemons of poor quality. Stubbornly, they persisted.

Hannah became pregnant again. On January 13, 1913, after enduring another difficult, protracted labor, Hannah gave birth to the couple's second child, a noisy, healthy, eleven-pound boy with brown eyes and black hair. They named him Richard Milhous Nixon — Richard for another favorite monarch of Hannah's. Soon relatives were reflecting on the contrast between quiet Harold and raucous Richard. His Grandmother Milhous, who had done some teaching and preaching herself, hoped he might enter one of those two professions. Richard's father anticipated a strongly opinionated young man with whom he could debate. In 1914, a third son, Francis Donald, was born, unburdened by a regal name. The couple's fourth son, Arthur Burdg, at least echoed Camelot. The fifth and final son, born many years later and rather a surprise to both his parents, they named Edward Calvert Nixon. Richard was nine, and already toiling with his parents and older brother in the grove, before his father finally gave it up. Oddly, the years at Yorba Linda had given Frank Nixon a degree of stability he had never known before. Even though the hardscrabble venture ended in failure, life was, after all, meant to be a struggle. To Hannah Nixon, however, who had never complained, "The lemon grove only kept us poor."

In the same speech in which he canonized his mother, Richard Nixon recalled the ill luck of his "old man. . . . He was a streetcar motorman first, and then he was a farmer, and then he had a lemon ranch — it was the poorest lemon ranch in California, I can assure you. He sold it before they found oil on it." As a child, Nixon longed to escape the limitations of his life. He heard the train whistles and dreamed of the "far-off places I wanted to visit someday." He loved reading *National Geo-*

Hannah Nixon with her husband and three of her sons
Courtesy of the Richard Nixon Library

graphic and poring over its photographs. His parents were unable to even take their family on vacations. Yet he adored his mother, and he did not so much dislike his father as feel a sort of pity for him. Nixon knew that in their own way each of his parents loved him and would do anything for him within their power, but he also understood how much he must do for himself. Perhaps one reason the unlikely collaboration of Nixon and Henry Kissinger worked is that they shared many personal characteristics. Both men had very strong mothers, and fathers who could be an embarrassment.

Frank Nixon even labored in the oil fields for a time — although in fact no oil had been found under his old lemon grove — before opening a grocery store and gas station back in Whittier in 1925. For several years it was actually a success, reinforcing Frank's gospel of the efficacy of hard work. No one worked harder than Hannah, arising before dawn to bake dozens of pies for which the store became noted, then waiting on customers until dark. Harold, Richard, and Donald were also old enough to put in long hours. School became almost a refuge. Even in relative affluence, the family was unable to eat together. Only religion could not be compromised. Ambrose writes, "There were daily prayers and church services of one kind or another four times every Sunday. There [Nixon] learned tolerance, and the Quaker distaste for showing emotion or expressing feelings physically." These had not been the lessons of Frank Nixon's youth. He never overcame his instinctive physicality, loving to hug and touch people. Women could resent it, sensing something more than simple friendliness.

There was a darker side to Frank's emotionalism. Sometimes, even after the years of frustration had seemingly ended, he would suddenly strike out with little provocation, argue heatedly with his sons, and settle the issue with his strap. His anger then dissipated as quickly as it had arisen. Richard was rarely the victim of these outbursts. He had early learned the art of detachment. He hated much of what he had to do for the store, such as sorting vegetables, but he never argued with his father. He could often sense when to avoid him, when to be silent, when to simply vanish. His mother understood. When his father's moods turned dark, Richard might escape into reading or daydreaming or simply observing from a safe distance. Decades later Nixon reflected, "Perhaps my own aversion to personal confrontations dates back to these early recollections." When Frank's volatility would turn into arguments with customers, Hannah calmly intervened. She would tactfully induce her husband to prepare meats in the rear of the store and let her and the boys wait on the customers. Many of them were poor Mexicans working on nearby ranches whom Hannah carried on credit. She and Frank seemed to have arrived at a mutual understanding of when he had gone too far, without compromising his status as head of the household. A soft word turneth away wrath.

Hannah, whose strongest admonition was "hush," had a different approach, a sort of escalating nonviolence. Richard and his brothers feared their mother's tongue more than their father's hand. "It was never sharp," Nixon recalled, "but she would sit you down and she would talk very quietly. Then when you got through you had been through an emotional experience." There are few if any amusing anecdotes about Hannah Nixon, nor was there much joy in her life. Her very righteousness put some people off and could be misconstrued as a sort of austere snobbery. But even her penny-pinching was purposeful. She had ambition, not for herself or — after she sensed his limitations — for Frank, but solely for her sons. Higher education was absolutely vital. Richard did not view her as lacking in warmth. He always, as Ambrose writes, "turned instinctively to his mother." As a boy, he "liked to have her sit with him when he read, and otherwise be with her." Like the far more extreme example of U. S. Grant and his mother, their empathy went beyond words.

Richard started grade school in 1918, demonstrating ability and orderly effort from the very beginning. He loved sports but lacked the talent or size to really excel at them. Encouraged by his mother, he enjoyed reading, music, and the sort of poetry he heard from her. He was already fastidious in his habits and a bit withdrawn from his peers. "He was interested in things way beyond the grasp of a boy his age," Hannah recalled. "He was thoughtful and serious. He always carried such a weight." She might have been reflecting on herself as a child.

Most like Richard was her youngest son, Arthur, a reflective loner, reticent to show affection. As they grew, Harold and Don, spontaneous and gregarious, reflected their father's more attractive qualities. In the summer of 1925, Arthur suddenly fell ill, suffering headaches, indigestion, and exhaustion. His alarmed parents called in a physician to administer tests, but neither medical science nor their prayers could save their son. He was suffering from tubercular encephalitis. After a sustained bedside vigil, he died. Richard had never before seen his father cry. Utterly distraught, Frank Nixon viewed the tragedy as a form of divine judgment. He started frequenting revival meetings, exhorted others to do so, and never again opened his store or station on Sundays. Hannah, who could not possibly become more devout, sought solace in the unknowable certainty of God's plan but grieved for the rest of her life. Richard, in Hannah's words, "sat staring into space, silent and dry-eyed in the undemonstrative way in which . . . he was always to face tragedy." Yet after Arthur's funeral, Richard admitted, "For weeks . . . there was not a day I did not think about him and cry." Now, according to his mother, Richard's "need to succeed became even stronger." Perhaps she shared something of that need.

At his eighth grade graduation from East Whittier School, Nixon took the spotlight as class president, "most outstanding" student, and valedictorian. Asked to compose an autobiography, his response was prescient. "My plans for the future . . . are to finish Whittier High School and College and then to take postgraduate work at Columbia University, New York. I would also like to visit Europe [and] I would like to study law and enter politics for an occupation so that I might be of some good to the people." Substituting Duke Law School for Columbia, it would unfold in much that way. The previous year, after the Teapot Dome scandal broke, Richard had announced to his mother, "When I get big I'll be a lawyer they can't bribe." Not surprisingly, his proud mother's graduation gift to her son was a Bible.

Richard's formal involvement in his mother's faith had also grown. He was playing piano at meetings of the East Whittier Friends Church, leading the youth division at the Easter sunrise service, and continued to have perfect attendance at Sunday school. Although one of Richard's teachers from the East couldn't tell the difference between the local Quaker and Methodist services, and Whittier College now had more Methodists than Quaker students, Hannah Nixon still felt herself immersed in a throughly Quaker community, of one mind in matters of conscience. She would have been comfortable at *any* gathering of the Society of Friends anywhere. Music at the worship services she attended was only a joyful noise, not an intrusion into the inner light.

In 1926, light-hearted Harold Nixon was surprised to be withdrawn from Whittier Union High School and sent by his parents across the country to fundamentalist Dwight Moody's Mount Hermon School for Boys in Massachusetts. It was likely more Frank's doing than Hannah's. Because they felt Harold had formed dubious acquaintances at Whittier Union High, they sent his serious-minded brother, Richard, to the much larger and more cosmopolitan Fullerton High School. The two boys, so seemingly dissimilar, were not only brothers but best friends. Harold admired Richard's drive and achievements, the sheer courage of going out for football at five feet seven inches and less than 150 pounds. To Richard, Harold possessed all the qualities he lacked — an effortless ease in any company, a cheerful, generous, optimistic outlook on life. Harold particularly loved flying, the outdoors, and living for the moment.

Their separation would not last long. In 1927 Harold suddenly returned from boarding school. He was desperately ill. This time the prognosis was clear — tuberculosis. His parents took him to a series of private sanitariums, but his health declined. Hannah finally came to a hard decision. The younger sons would stay in Whittier with their father. She would take Harold to a mountain resort in the dry heat of Prescott, Arizona, over four hundred miles away, and try to nurse him back to health. To save money, she rented a small hillside cabin and took in as boarders other young men suffering from the same malady. She would clean, cook, and care for them all. The climate itself was considered as curative as medical treatment. The degree of contagion was uncertain, but for two summers Richard went out to join them. The rest of the family also made the long trip whenever they could. With the strain showing on everyone, Richard transferred back home to Whittier Union High School so that he could help his father. He missed his mother terribly, and worried that she might be sacrificing her own life.

Harold lived longer than anyone, including himself, honestly expected. Hannah made a surprise visit home at Christmas of 1929 to tell her incredulous husband that, at the age of forty-five, she was again pregnant, but she soon went back to Arizona. Finally, Harold insisted that they both go home for good. In 1933, despite the pleas of his parents, he returned to Whittier to pursue, for however long, as normal a life as he could sustain, around everything and everyone dear and familiar to him. He and his mother learned of the deaths, one by one, of each of the youths she had cared for. Richard was home from Whittier College on a day he took his brother downtown to buy their mother a cake mixer for her forty-eighth birthday; then he returned to school. The following morning, Harold felt very weak, much as Arthur had eight years before. Later, he asked his mother to hold him tight in her arms, telling her, "This is the last time I will see you until we meet in heaven." When Richard rushed home, both his parents were crying uncontrollably. Hannah witnessed her twenty-year-old son sink "into a deep, impenetrable silence. . . . From this time on, it seemed that Richard was trying to be *three* sons in one, striving even harder than before to make up to his father and me for our loss. . . . Unconsciously, too, I think Richard may have felt a kind of guilt that Harold and Arthur were dead and that he was alive."

The striving had started even before Harold's death. At high school, encouraged by his father at home and his mother from Arizona, Richard had continued to excel, particularly in debating and public speaking. He was an acknowledged student leader, although more admired for his competence than truly popular with his classmates. Some even viewed him as a bit devious, and he lost a coveted election for student body president. He would not lose again for the next thirty years. Gradually he began to unbend a bit, and began to date. The Christmas visit of his mother immensely cheered him. As graduation neared, he seemed almost genial and relaxed. He was third in his class, with invitations to apply for full tuition scholarships to Harvard and Yale. But he understood how badly he was needed at home. Harold's medical expenses had been staggering. A new brother had been born in May 1930, the Christmas surprise. Richard would go to Whittier College, just as he had planned. A scholarship fund bequeathed by his Milhous grandfather supplied Richard's tuition. No one complained about nepotism. If Nixon felt regret at missing out on the Ivy League, it was transcended by the excitement of simply going to college.

The Great Depression hurt Frank Nixon's business but it did little to soften his temperament. As Parmet notes, he kept a loaded revolver in the cash register of his store, even as his wife, duplicating her mother, welcomed one and all to the back door, however limited her larder. Like most other institutions, Whittier College was forced as a result of the Depression to cut back. As Ronald Reagan would at Eureka, Nixon managed to speak for the whole student body of Whittier. He even convinced the staid trustees to approve dances on campus, as a preferable alternative to unsupervised licentiousness away from it. This time he was elected president of the student body in a triumphant senior year, capped by the award of a full-tuition scholarship to Duke Law School. He would have to scrimp and work his way through to meet expenses, but that was nothing new. In the glow of graduation, he didn't even mind being addressed as "Nixie" by jocular classmates. He would be called "Nick" in the navy and "Gloomy Gus" in law school. The only nickname he disdained was "Dick." The president of Whittier College predicted that "Nixon will become one of America's important, if not greatest, leaders." Hannah marveled at her son's single-minded dedication, how little affected he had been by the Roaring Twenties or the Depression that now dominated most people's thoughts. It all just "passed him by."

In an essay written for his senior religion course, Nixon distanced himself a bit from his birthright Quakerism. Trying to reconcile the science he had learned at college with the religion of his heritage, Nixon affirmed that although he could no longer accept the Bible as literal fact, "I still believe that God is the creator . . . [and] the modern world will find a real resurrection in the life and teachings of Jesus." It seems a modest revision, but Ambrose concludes that "from this point on, religion was no longer important to him . . . not the center of his life. . . . Thereafter, there was nothing approaching a crisis of conscience or belief for Richard Nixon." Although by now she must have realized it was most unlikely, Hannah still hoped Richard would be a minister, and she was not alone. Western Quakerism valued preaching, and Richard had proven to be a powerful speaker. He would always be more comfortable with audiences than with individuals. But as far back as eighth grade he had announced his calling — law leading to politics.

Hannah saw her son through Duke, naval service in World War II (which made her uneasy as a pacifist and fearful as a mother), marriage, law, and politics — to the very cusp of his presidency. Although she had initially felt that young Pat Ryan "was chasing Dick," she was won over when her future daughter-in-law came by to help prepare the pies Hannah still baked. As it turned out, Pat Nixon demonstrated a stoicism and willpower Hannah came to admire.

Was the long marriage of Hannah and Frank Nixon happy? Some of their contemporaries suggested that they complemented each other with their different strengths, loud and soft compromising at a livable level. Morris believes that they remained "clearly in love," with Hannah's "serenity and devotion seeming to absorb her husband's volatile bent." Their marriage survived years of poverty, stress, and wrenching tragedy. Most of all, as Morris writes, "I think she probably had a decisive influence because he practically worshiped her." Frank was proud of Hannah, from the day she responded to his overtures. He felt fortunate, a sentiment with which his Milhous in-laws would have agreed. He never resented his neighbors' preference for Hannah's gentler, more generous nature, or the fact that she was the person everyone seemed to love, while even his sons sometimes feared him. He never expressed jealousy of his wife, or his most successful son — only pride — and he well understood his own faults, even if he was sometimes powerless to control them.

Perhaps the enigma of Richard Nixon is in some way bound up in having such differing parents. It may be that he wanted to be more like Hannah, while finding himself inevitably acting more like Frank — but in fact, he wasn't very much like either. Frank was loud, imprudent, and outspoken. Yet he was completely honest. What he said might not always stand up to logic or reason, but his emotions were on his sleeve. It was not in him to be devious. For example, he told reporters in the 1950s that he wished his son had remained a well-publicized senator and then mounted his own campaign for president — none of this vice-presidential nonsense. Richard may well have wished, as had others, that his father would just keep still. Once given, however, Frank Nixon's support was as unconditional and uncompromising as his opinions. Even when he was dying in 1956, he urged his son not to lin-

Hannah Nixon with her son Richard Nixon
Courtesy of the Richard Nixon Library

ger with him but to make certain his political enemies didn't pull a fast one and deny his renomination as vice president. Francis Anthony Nixon might have preferred something more lively than his simple Quaker funeral service, but his son permitted no photographers or intrusive press. Although neither the "common" nor the "great" man Richard later celebrated, Frank was, as Parmet writes, "the driving force" of his family.

Hannah, however, was its heart. To Richard, in the final analysis, she was more an inspiration than a determining influence. He admired almost everything about her, but he could do no more than try to emulate her example. She was simplicity itself, her son as complex a personality as ever served in the presidency.

As she aged, Hannah less stringently contained her emotions. When a tearful Julie Nixon rebelled at yet another departure by her parents to some formal event, Hannah swept her grandchild up in her arms to comfort her. She became the favorite babysitter of both her young granddaughters. When Richard and his wife were having problems, Hannah agreed "to go to Washington and say nothing. I just want to help out Pat in every way I can." Hannah feared for her son's health in the stresses of public life. "I don't think I could take it," she said of the crisis that resulted in his "Checkers" speech, but she added, "I drew courage from my faith. That carried me through." It had always carried her through. If her son couldn't fully share in it, at least he could appreciate it. He once wrote about the "need to be good to do good." But one must also have the capacity to discern good in others.

On the day of her son's second inauguration as vice president, Hannah pressed this personal note into his hand:

To Richard,

You have gone far and we are proud of you always — I know you will keep your relationship with your maker as it should be for after all that, as you must know, is the most important thing in this life.

With love, Mother.

Morris writes that "Nixon did not read it until he was alone later that night. Deeply moved, he put it in his wallet and carried it throughout his political life." Hannah Milhous Nixon did not live quite long enough to witness her son's supreme triumphs and his ultimate tragedy. She died in 1967 at the age of eighty-two. Richard Nixon was wrong: books would be written about his mother, at least in the context of trying to understand her son. But he was also right. Immensely gifted yet fatally flawed, he was nonetheless the son of a saint.

ALTHOUGH he never quite elevated his mother to sainthood, Gerald Ford did pay tribute to her as "the most selfless woman I have ever known." Proclaiming that he owed "everything" to his parents, Ford meant his mother and stepfather, Gerald Rudolph Ford Sr., not his birth father. The elder Ford was a "marvelous family man" but was often unavoidably immersed in community projects or in trying to keep his business afloat. It fell to Ford's mother, Dorothy Gardner Ford, to do most of the day-to-day child rearing. She was the font of Ford's moral framework and even of his temperament.

"As a child," Ford recalled, "I had a hot temper which Mother taught me to control — most of the time." Patient but a disciplinarian, not averse to twisting his ear or sending him to his room, Dorothy Ford preferred to use reason. A more enduring antidote to fits of rage might be to read and reflect on Kipling's "If." A devout Episcopalian, she had even more faith in the efficacy of her favorite excerpt from Proverbs, which later in his life Ford would recall whenever he wanted to turn away anger: "Trust in the Lord with all thine heart and lean not unto thine own understanding. In all thy ways acknowledge Him and He shall direct thy paths." It is due to his mother's influence more than any other that Ford's autobiography would be aptly named *A Time for Healing*. In his public life he had a few lapses, such as suggesting that Supreme Court Justice William O. Douglas be impeached for immorality, but Ford's reputation for reasoned even-handedness was responsible for placing him in line for the presidency in traumatic times. Always plainspoken, he would be "a Ford, not a Lincoln."

Dorothy Ford's neighbors and friends, in their oral history recollections, invariably describe her as "wonderful," "gracious," "tireless," and "vivacious," but her life was not always placid. Ford described his mother as tall and rather stout, "with an attractive face." She was probably more slender when, at the age of twenty, she caught the eye of a wealthy wool trader from Omaha named Leslie Lynch King. Dorothy Gardner had been born in 1892 to a family in Illinois prosperous enough to send her not only to high school and a girls' finishing school but also to college. She had completed only a year when King swept her off to the altar. On July 14, 1913, they had a son they named Leslie Lloyd King Jr. Dorothy composed a charming announcement: "We send this little card to say/That on the given month and day/To us a tiny stranger came/And just below you'll find the name."

Despite such sentiments, her precarious marriage had run into trouble almost immediately. Apparently the impetus for its dissolution came from a familiar cause, the intrusiveness of in-laws. King resented his wife's reliance on the advice of her meddling mother. Dorothy complained that, despite her husband's assurances to the contrary, they were living with his domineering parents. Although she was always loath to discuss the details, it is also clear that her husband physically abused her. All she would say is that the marriage simply hadn't worked out. After only sixteen months of matrimony she filed for divorce on grounds of "extreme cruelty," packed up her son, and took off for Grand Rapids, Michigan, where her parents now lived. Grand Rapids in 1915 was described by one historian as "America at its best, a community of great expectations." Developed by thrifty, enterprising Dutch and German immigrants, it boasted 70 furniture factories, 134 churches, and the highest rate of home ownership in the United States.

Living in her parents' comfortable home, Dorothy met an earnest young salesman whose expectations were also high. Gerald R. Ford was somewhat solemn but clearly ambitious, and he was immensely impressed with Dorothy. Once stung, however, she was not about to rush into anything. Only when she was convinced that Ford would be a good father for her boy did Dorothy agree to marry him. She never regretted that decision, nor would her son. Hard work was Ford's gospel. He had gone to school only through the eighth grade, but deeply valued education. His demeanor was deceptive. As Philip Buchen, President Ford's law partner and close friend put it, Gerald Ford Sr. was "a man of high principles, rather stern looking but not stern acting." Another friend of the family added that Ford, indeed, was "stern looking [but] very good hearted, friendly, and very much respected in the community . . . public spirited, a good churchman . . . [and a] moderately successful businessman." He had only three rules for the four sons he would have: Work hard to make something of yourselves, never under any circumstances

Dorothy Ford
Courtesy of the Gerald R. Ford Library

tell a lie, and come to dinner on time. Eventually Ford left his employer, to the latter's consternation, and started his own paint and varnish company. For a time the firm prospered. The Fords, living initially in a rented house, moved in 1919 to a larger home in a better section of town and joined the ranks of Grand Rapids' homeowners.

Ford was intent on legally adopting his stepson, giving him the security of a loving family. When Leslie L. King Jr. became Gerald R. Ford Jr. he may have lost a resounding presidential name, but he gained incomparably more. The relationship between Jerry and his stepfather flourished; young Jerry may even have been a bit spoiled by this stern-visaged man. Recalling the leaner times in the 1930s, Ford Jr. has said: "Neither of my parents could be described as 'secure' economically, but emotionally both were very secure, and if I retain that characteristic today, I owe it to them." For years Jerry didn't even know he had been adopted. His earliest childhood memories were of a neighbor's distinctive car, horse-drawn fire engines, and his parents. The Fords were to have three more sons, from five to fourteen years younger than Jerry. He became their natural leader and role model, particularly as his athletic exploits gained renown. Headstrong and possessive at first, Jerry developed into a thoughtful and protective older brother, Dorothy Ford's influence at work. He even helped her change diapers.

If his father's warmth lay within, his mother's was displayed for all to see. During the prosperous years, energetic Dorothy Ford was involved in everything: Saint Ann's Guild at Grace Episcopal Church, the Grand Rapids Garden Club, the country club, the Daughters of the American Revolution, the local symphony auxiliary, and so on. But she was more than simply a sociable clubwoman. She had a genuine commitment to helping others. As Ford recalled, "When she wasn't attending meetings, she was busy baking bread or sewing clothes for needy families. . . . If a relative or neighbor suffered in any way, she would be reduced to tears." Her good works were not limited to relatives and neighbors. She volunteered at the Well Baby Clinic, made dolls for poor children at Christmas, and helped form a center in the most deprived neighborhood in town to help what today would be called the disadvantaged. She was a member of the NAACP as well as the DAR. She welcomed all her son's friends, black or white, into her home. When Jerry attended the University of Michigan he saw nothing unusual about befriending and rooming on road trips with the football team's only African-American player. The Fords instilled family values by personifying them.

As a neighbor put it, "They didn't talk religion, they just lived it." Dorothy's faith motivated the involvement of every member of the household in Grace Episcopal Church. Her busy husband was a deacon, her sons acolytes, choir members, and weekly attendees of both services and Sunday school. All the boys went on to become Eagle Scouts as well. If life at the Fords' in the 1920s seems almost a midwestern version of Rockwellian America, that is not far from the reality. Of his mother, Ford fondly remembered, "Having the family together for major holidays like Thanksgiving and Christmas would fill her with joy and she wasn't shy about expressing it." A childhood playmate of Jerry's spoke for almost everyone acquainted with Dorothy Ford when he said, "Jerry's mother was a wonderful lady. She used to let me come in and set the table for lunch. She had lovely things, china and silver and glass. And she made cookies — wonderful molasses cookies." In Buchen's opinion, "Jerry's gregariousness and his attractive qualities and his way with people I think he got from his mother, who was a very sociable woman and loved people . . . was a great conversationalist . . . took a great interest in all Jerry's friends, girls and boys . . . and I'm sure gave him his warm, outgoing qualities."

As Jerry's brother Richard recalled, telling the truth was a two-way street at the Fords'. "It was a very frank, open kind of relationship and I personally have to believe it was at least partially the result of home environment. And certainly involvement with the church was a factor." When he was vice president, Ford affirmed that it was his mother who "instilled in me the values I have. She set a very high ethical tone — a high moral tone. . . . She was very considerate, always thinking of others. She would send out countless birthday notes and get-well cards and the like. And the fact she had so many friends was helpful to me when I first ran for Congress in 1948."

It was Ford's father, however, who whetted his interest in politics. The elder Ford never ran for office, but he helped to found the "Home Front" that mobilized "good government" forces against the locally entrenched political machine of Frank D. McKay. Republican politics were not the only avocation of Gerald Ford Sr. Like his wife, he was deeply involved in community activities — so much so that she gently remonstrated that if he spent as much time on his business, they would all be rich. Many of Jerry's friends viewed his family as more affluent than they actually were. One, who happened to be African-American, marveled at how such a "rich boy" could be such a "regular guy."

That all would change in 1929. Characteristically, Gerald Ford Sr. responded to the Great Depression by resolving, "I'll just have to work harder." His business was severely diminished, however, and the family lost their comfortable home. Yet Ford never laid off any of his ten employees, and he managed to survive. By now, Jerry was in high school, a solid, conscientious student, a star in three sports, unpretentious but friendly, and extremely popular. He was narrowly defeated for the student council presidency, the only election he would lose until 1976, by being out-promised by his opponent. Perhaps he had followed his parents' admonitions too literally. Throughout high school he worked to help them out, at a restaurant and in his father's factory. As always, his mother "was one of my staunchest supporters. She never missed a football game in which I played." Once Ford's birth father, remarried and living in Wyoming, made a surprise visit to him, inviting Jerry to come out west to live with them. Although wealthy, Leslie King had not even kept up his child support payments. Ford only documents his firm refusal, but he may have said more at the time.

His true father, the self-made Gerald Ford, was intent that his sons receive higher education, but now it would take some doing. Athletic scholarships were not so abundant then as they are today, but by a combination of grants and grit, Jerry entered the University of Michigan in 1931. He would graduate with a B average and go on to Yale Law School. At Michigan he was an all-American center, playing on two national championship football teams. An enduring irony is how this finest athlete to occupy the presidency could be satirized as clumsy. Professional teams were interested in Ford, but he chose to study law, helping to pay his way by coaching football. He joined the navy in World War II, saw action, and ended up a lieutenant commander. In deference to his mother, he never drank or smoked at home, although he had picked up his first pipe in the navy. In 1945 he returned to Grand Rapids to practice law, and entered politics. Like his father, who had fought entrenched power, Ford — a moderate internationalist — won his first uphill Republican primary against an incumbent isolationist. It was tantamount to election; there were relatively few Democrats in the district.

Dorothy Ford with her granddaughter Susan
Courtesy of the Gerald R. Ford Library

Hardly a political partisan, Dorothy Ford chaired only the Ford party. Her staunch support was not limited to athletics, although she later urged her son, so secure in the House, not to pursue the vice presidency. "It would be nothing but headaches," Ford quoted her as predicting. She may have been right. Still, a close friend wished "that his mother would have lived to see him president; it would have been a wonderful thing." That she died only seven years before, at the age of seventy-four, is in itself remarkable. Dorothy Ford had many serious health problems — high blood pressure, diabetes, and cataracts in both eyes. She had endured a double mastectomy and other major surgeries. Most persistent had been her heart trouble, resulting in two heart attacks. But she insisted, her spirits ever high, "I want to die with my boots on." When her son was thirty-four, she had asked him with characteristic directness, "When are you going to settle down?" Jerry married the effervescent Betty Bloomer not much later, and then went on to Congress. He was elected minority leader of the House in 1965. Two years later — as her son reconstructed the scene — Dorothy was "just sitting there in her pew" at Grace Episcopal Church waiting for the service to start when her heart condition finally took her life. Among the hundreds of letters of condolence was one from Congressman George H. W. Bush: "Like the Fords, we Bushes have a close family and I can perhaps understand to some degree how you must feel." On the day she died, Dorothy Ford's appointment book was full for months to come.

In the spring of 1932 Jerry had sent his mother an apologetic letter from his fraternity house at Michigan. It was close to Mother's Day. "I'd like to send you flowers or candy or something but my financial condition is dreadfully insecure. So this will have to do. . . . Have a fine time and maybe next year I'll be able to do something more." He did enough — by justifying the patience and pride of this immensely energetic, optimistic woman who was most of all quite literally a homemaker. Dorothy Gardner Ford died just where she would have wished, trusting in the Lord with all her heart.

CHAPTER SIXTEEN

Overcoming the Odds

- ❧ Lillian Carter
- ❧ Nelle Reagan
- ❧ Virginia Kelley

IN JUNE 1943, after seeing their eldest son off to Annapolis, his first trip outside of Georgia, James Earl Carter Sr. and Bessie Lillian Carter drove home silently together and then grieved separately, she sobbing and fishing in a small pond by their house, he fishing and drinking at a friend's house by a different pond. It was symbolic of the differences that had arisen between them after twenty years of marriage and four children, a separation reflected in the recollections of their children. The oldest, now launched on the path that would make him a midshipman, had been named, logically enough, James Earl Carter Jr. His father called him "Hot" (for "Hotshot") when he was happy with his son, "Jimmy" when he was not. His friends would call him "Jim," only turning to "Jimmy" when he came to prefer it. His parents, whom everyone knew by their middle names, he called "Daddy" and "Mother," a reflection of how differently he viewed them. His father was almost excessively demanding, but he was always around. His mother was more pliable, but she was rarely at home.

Jimmy Carter later wrote, "My daddy was the dominant person in our family and in my life," a conclusion undoubtedly shared by his two sisters and younger brother. Biographers have speculated that many of Carter's idiosyncrasies as an adult stemmed from his desire as a child to live up to his father's expectations. Yet the values that Carter took to the presidency and his more acclaimed post-presidential career derived from his often-absent mother. At least in his official life hers was the dominant parental influence.

Like her older son, Lillian Carter would be more appreciated later in her life. As "Miss Lillian," she seemed in her seventies almost the nation's good, gray grandmother, a bit eccentric and outspoken, but an irrepressible inspiration to everyone who affirmed civil and human rights. She could hardly be blamed for wishing she had been born at a different time and place. As a child, all Bessie Lillian Gordy wanted was to be a doctor, like two of her favorite uncles. Called "Lilly" by her parents, she might have achieved such a goal in a city like Atlanta only a decade or two later. However, as biographer Kenneth Morris writes, "[to] a young woman growing up in rural Georgia in the early twentieth century, such an aspiration was unimaginable." Other than marriage and motherhood, there were only two occupations open to respectable white women — teaching and nursing. Dedicated teachers were still generally expected to be spinsters. Nurses might marry, but their profession was viewed as just a bit less respectable, with implications of promiscuity not unlike those leveled at airline hostesses later in the century.

Lilly chose nursing, the closest she could come to her goal, but she still needed parental permission. Although her handsome, mustached father did have some qualms, he was inclined to be sympathetic to his favorite daughter. The Gordys of Richland in the southwestern part of Georgia had antecedents similar to the Carters of Plains, although they could not claim the distinction of one remote Virginia branch of the enormous Carter clan. Emigrating from Scotland and England in the seventeenth century, the Gordys settled originally in Maryland. Taking advantage of lotteries, as the Carters had, they obtained land in Georgia and moved there in the early 1800s. Successful farmers, they held such local posts as tax collectors, and fought for the Confederacy in the Civil War. In the wake of defeat and reconstruction, they moved in a different direction than the Carters. Lilly's father, James Jackson Gordy, known to all as "Jim Jack," believed in education and activism. He also had a highly independent streak. In his youth he had fled to Texas after leaving a young woman at the altar. Returning after two years, he settled down with stable, sensible Mary Ida Nicholson. Since they belonged to separate branches of the Baptist Church, they compromised on Methodism.

The couple had eight children. Lilly, born in 1898, was in the middle. In addition, they raised two others, orphaned when Mary Ida's sister had died, and housed Jim Jack's widowed mother. With thirteen at the table, Lilly recalled hectic mealtimes but a "nice, happy . . . very close family," with a great deal of conversation going back and forth through the chaos. "I was papa's favorite," she confirmed, "and he was my favorite." Unlike the Carters, who would eventually prosper through farming and business, the Gordys pursued the professions, preferring town life to the countryside. Not only were two of Jim Jack's brothers physicians, one became a state legislator. His own path led more to respectability than prosperity. Although for a time a farmer and a teacher, his real love was politics. His aim, however, was not elective but appointive office.

To attain and sustain it required a delicate balance between pragmatism and the idealism he would come to share with his favorite daughter. Like Lilly, Jim Jack Gordy might well have viewed himself as being in the wrong place and time. The values Miss Lillian would ultimately transmit to her son who became president were imparted to her by her father. Living in the midst of a thoroughly segregated society, Gordy believed in racial justice and equality of opportunity. He felt that government, on the local and national level, could be a positive force for improving the lives of all its citizens, black and white. He affirmed the Christianity of moral example, not merely formal worship. Many years later, Lillian Carter and her son Jimmy would be the only two members of the Plains Baptist Church to stand in support of its racial integration. She once said to an interviewer, "Did you know politics had religion?" She also shared her father's love of good books and music. He would have been an enlightened man in any locale, viewing his daughters as the intellectual equals of his sons.

Living where and when he did, however, Jim Jack Gordy had to be circumspect. It was already flaunting tradition to have the distinguished black bishop of the African Methodist Episcopal Church, William Decker Johnson, enter his home by the front door, and they were unlikely to travel together. When Johnson died, Lillian Carter took her son Jimmy to the funeral, unaccompanied by her husband. Despite his beliefs on racial equality, Jim Jack supported Populist leader Tom Watson, a virulent racist, because he believed in his program of social justice. Gordy even gave him the idea to promote free rural mail service. Later Gordy also supported popular, plain-talking governor Eugene Talmadge for largely the same reasons, although unlike Earl Carter, Gordy was embarrassed by Talmadge's crude racial rhetoric. Jim Jack may have been a secret Republican — as anathematizing an identification for a prominent white in Georgia in the first half of the twentieth century as "liberal Democrat" would be in the second — but he had to get along with all factions.

Not that the positions Jim Jack held were all that prominent. He was Richland's postmaster for twenty-one years, most of the time Lilly was growing up, through both Democratic and Republican administrations. For four years he was a revenue officer, followed by six as a United States deputy marshal, and, finally, he held a ceremonial position as doorkeeper at the Georgia State Capitol. All this gave him a reasonably steady income, but with so many mouths to feed, little in the way of security. The family moved when it had to with relatively little fuss, but Lilly later learned that her good-natured mother had found living with a man like Jim Jack just a bit more stressful than she let on. Gordy had one other talent greatly appreciated by his daughter's son; he could predict elections, Jimmy Carter would tell his own advisors, with astonishing accuracy, without benefit of polls.

Late in 1918, Jim Jack gave his daughter permission to apply for nurses' training, but the First World War ended on the very day Lilly was accepted. With America's involvement in the war, and the subsequent need for nurses, the prestige of the profession had been enhanced, but after the armistice, government programs to train nurses were phased out. At the same time, a flu epidemic, virtually a pandemic, raged through the country. It took the life of one of Lilly's sisters, so traumatizing the family that her career plans were put on hold. She helped her father at the post office for two years but finally was able to apply for nurses' training again, though not in a government program this time. Miraculously, the modest town of Plains, less than twenty miles away, was on its way to becoming something of a medical center.

It was not quite the Mayo Clinic, but three brothers, the Doctors Wise — Thadeus, Boman, and plain old Sam — had chosen to open their private hospital in Plains. Sam Wise was a good friend of Jim Jack Gordy's, and although openings for nurses' training at the new facility were already highly coveted, Dr. Sam looked favorably on Lilly's application. During her tenure at the Wise Clinic, it expanded from twelve to ninety beds. The "three Wise men" were the town's leading benefactors. Finally able to pursue her vocation, Lilly found the training very rigorous, but for the first time in her life she was able to cut loose a bit. Whether nurses were, indeed, "fast" or not, the work hard/play hard regimen of the medical staff at Wise was the closest Plains could offer to the Roaring Twenties. Lilly discovered that she enjoyed drinking, smoking, dancing, and partying in general. It was inevitable in so small a setting that she would run into stocky and shy but ambitious young Earl Carter, four years older than Lillian, who in his own way also enjoyed a good time. With her long, lean face, Lilly was by no means beautiful. Her son Jimmy would remember her, when young, as "very slender, almost gaunt . . . but pretty in her own way, with her dark hair parted in the middle and eyes that always seemed to sparkle." Most of all it was her free-spirited vivaciousness that made her popular. Dating someone else at the time, she had little use for Earl. His country manners were no more attractive than his country looks. Earl Carter, however, fell like a ton of peanuts. He had never met anyone like Lilly Gordy.

As biographers Bruce Mazlish and Edwin Diamond write, "The Carters of Sumter County were not just a family — they were a Southern, rural, middle-class family," neither the plantation elite of the Virginia Carters nor the "white trash" beneath. They were hardworking, unpretentious, substantial businessmen and farmers — but James Earl Carter Sr. was just starting out in both directions. Earl hadn't been to college, but he had finished the tenth grade at Riverside Academy, as much schooling as any Georgia Carter had received up to that time. He came back from the First World War a lieutenant and used his mustering-out pay to invest in land and crops. Some of his investments panned out, some did not, but he was already viewed as a young man on the move. Dr. Sam Wise, who had taken Lilly under his wing, certainly thought so, and he urged Lilly to take a second look: "He's a boy that has more ambition than anyone in this town, and he's going to be worth a lot someday." To Lilly's surprise, her family agreed. Perhaps Jim Jack was even more hard-pressed than usual.

For whatever combination of reasons, Lilly and Earl were engaged in 1923. Lilly still had to complete her nurses' training at another hospital, and it took six months in Atlanta to do it. Thoroughly enamored, Earl called her every Sunday and drove to see her twice. Finally, the two were married, on September 26, 1923, by the pastor of the Plains Baptist Church in a modest ceremony at his home. Earl was twenty-seven, Lillian twenty-five. There was neither a reception nor a honeymoon. Earl's potato crop had failed. It has been suggested that Lillian Gordy married Earl Carter for his money. More likely, it was for his potential to make money.

Initially, however, there was also an undeniable affection, and it appears to have been mutual. Something in Earl won Lillian over, at least for a time. Perhaps she brought him out. The boisterous social life at the clinic carried over into the early years of their marriage. They both smoked, and enjoyed drinking and partying with their circle of similarly inclined young couples, the up-and-comers of Plains. Their first child was born precisely nine months after their first New Year's together, at 7 a.m. on October 1, 1924, with Dr. Sam in attendance. When Lillian went into labor, Earl returned from a farm in time to rush her to the Wise Clinic. James Earl Carter Jr. would be the first president of the United States to be born in a hospital. On the first day in the life of this "bright, happy baby who needed no special care," as biographer Peter Bourne notes, the governor of Georgia addressed the annual convention of the Ku Klux Klan. Two years later a daughter, Gloria, was born to the Carters; two years after that, a second daughter, named Ruth. It would be another thirteen years until the birth of their fourth and final child, William Alton, nicknamed "Billy." Earl joked ruefully that the boy couldn't possibly be his. Lillian didn't find it at all funny.

It is hard to discern, as with many marriages, precisely when the magic went out of the Carters' union, but it would seem to have been after the birth of Ruth. She became her father's favorite, his lovely "Shirley Temple" he would show off to his friends and eventually take out in place of his wife. Lillian must have realized that beyond their in-

Lillian Carter with her two oldest children, Jimmy and Gloria
Courtesy of the Jimmy Carter Library

sular social life, which soon became tiring, she really shared few interests with her husband. The world of ideas and literature her father had
made come alive held little attraction for Earl. Even Lillian's fond recollections of her parents' marriage had been tarnished a bit by her

kindly mother's revelation that matrimony was sometimes so stressful that she had to set aside an hour each week just to scream out her frustrations. On the other hand, Lillian demonstrated little interest in learning more about Earl's activities, although she little hesitated to spend the revenue they yielded. She accepted Earl as the unquestioned head of their household. That was an established tradition beyond challenge, even though she didn't always like it. Her solution was to spend more time out of the household. She was, after all, a trained nurse. Just before her first pregnancy, she had won the respected position of surgical nurse at the clinic, and between having children she continued to work, either in the operating room or as a private duty nurse. Up to a point, she could live her own life and even make some of her own money.

In politics, the subject that most fascinated her father, Lillian found Earl's interests to be local and provincial. He had ambition, all right, but in everything it was limited to his state and region. The great issues of the day largely escaped his notice, beyond the threat of government interference in his affairs. Earl was a loyal Democrat, but beyond his support of rural electrification, he hated what he viewed as the New Deal's wasteful and intrusive agricultural policies. Near the end of his life, Earl was elected to the state legislature. Lillian was little concerned with the matters it administered. When Earl died in 1953, Morris writes, she declined an opportunity to finish out the remainder of his term. Then she called her son, Jimmy, home "because she didn't know anything about [Earl's] business either."

Lillian did make an effort to become more active in Plains, joining social clubs and taking part in women's activities at the church, but they provided minimal stimulation, and she never felt quite at home. While the quality of her daily reading had declined since she left Richland, it was still copious. She started bringing books to the dinner table to read while she ate and encouraged her children to do the same; after grace, there was simply no conversation. Earl stewed, and ate in silence. Jimmy, who remembered being awakened by the noise of his parents' parties when they were younger, and taking refuge in his tree house, now found the sounds of their silence even more disconcerting.

Lillian hated housework and limited her cooking to one day a week. Her Sunday chicken dinners were welcome, but the rest of the week the family ate the fare provided by others. Increasingly, they were also looked after by surrogate mothers of unvarying warmth — a succession of black nannies and housekeepers. That was not uncommon in the South, but not to this extent. "My childhood world was really shaped by black women," Jimmy Carter recalls. Nursing remained Lillian's outlet long after there was any financial necessity for her to pursue it. Sometimes she was gone for days, and eventually she all but became the country doctor she had dreamed of being. Even when they were very small, the children's care was not only in the hands of hired help but was supplemented by Lillian's younger relations. In one instance, Lillian's negligence almost cost Jimmy his life. At the age of two, he was left with a ten-year-old cousin. Jimmy wandered onto the railroad tracks, and only the whistle of an oncoming train alerted his cousin, who pulled Jimmy away just in time. Lillian blamed not herself, but the child who was to watch her son. She had a temper, although unlike her husband she found it difficult to physically discipline her children. It was Earl who, whatever his schedule, took them to church, school, and their own social events, and even helped them with their homework. There were few, if any, photographs taken of all of them together, and no reunions such as the Gordys and so many other Southern families enjoyed. The Carters rarely spent even Christmas Day together. Lillian protested, "I think all my children are individuals," but increasingly, their ties as a family seemed more economic than emotional.

Lillian's vocation became more relevant and less remunerative about the time of Jimmy's fourth birthday. The family moved to a larger house three miles outside of Plains, in the tiny rural community of Archery, over the Webster County line. The property, known as "the Plexico Place" for those who had built the house in 1922, was a world apart, much more spacious but also more primitive. It had no indoor plumbing, and water had to be pumped by hand. Yet Earl built a rough tennis court adjacent to the house, where he and Jimmy would play as the boy grew older, and there was at least a phone line, although it was a "party line" shared with others. Archery was closer to the railroad line, an important consideration to Earl, and perhaps he sought more direct supervision of his farmland, the richest in the area. Still, it must have been hard to move his home and his family from Plains at precisely that time. The town was bustling in the 1920s, its population now over six hundred, and enhanced by an enlarged hospital. Plains boasted a brand new school, a new hotel, and many new stores and homes. It was a veritable metropolis, or so Jimmy thought when he reluctantly ventured back to sell his father's boiled peanuts.

Earl Carter was prospering, just as Dr. Sam and Jim Jack Gordy had predicted, his enterprises expanding in many directions. His main focus, as cotton production moved west, was growing peanuts, but his diversified products encompassed everything from pecans to pork. He speculated, buying and selling other properties, rarely going into excessive debt. His holdings grew to over four thousand acres, worked by black tenant farmers. His office, which remained in Plains, brokered commodities, sold insurance, and arranged mortgages. His store in Archery sold just about everything, much of it produced on his own farms, eventually expanding into the immense Carter warehouse back in Plains. Unlike most farmers in the region, he had the means not only to diversify but to mechanize. He bought cattle, produced their feed, marketed their products, and provided staple goods for the whole community. As Jimmy Carter writes, "almost all our food was produced in our pasture, fields, garden, and yard." Earl Carter was becoming known as "Mr. Earl," the respectful equivalent of his wife's "Miz Lillian." Hardheaded but astute, he had a Midas touch already the stuff of local legend. Yet he also had established a reputation for fair dealing and even for generosity — so long as you didn't owe him money.

He loomed so large to his children that as adults they were surprised to find that their bespectacled father had been only five-foot-eight and weighed at most 175 pounds. He demanded much of his off-spring, especially Jimmy, and his discipline could be harsh. Unlike Lillian, he would readily take a switch to anyone who disobeyed. Yet he was a loving father who commiserated with his children, and a reliable friend. He smiled far more often than he frowned. Earl Carter embodied the contradictions of the Southern society in which he lived — and which he accepted without question. If he was exploitive of his powerless black tenants, he was also paternalistic, his private charity considerable. He would help anyone in need, including his wife — to whom he provided medicines and supplies for her daily rounds.

Life in Archery was a microcosm of the rural South, a reality that each member of the Carter family faced in his or her own way. There was only one other white family in the community, headed by the Seaboard Airline Railroad's section foreman, but there were some twenty-five black families, living in conditions Lillian found unimaginable. She became their doctor, even delivered their babies, and enlisted Dr. Sam's aid to battle malnutrition and disease. Dr. Thad Wise feared pellagra, the result of heavy labor, excessive use of tobacco, and inadequate diet. There were no overweight tenant farmers. Of course, there was little profit in any of these activities. Lillian's attentiveness to the needs of black families became the talk of the proper matrons of Plains, for whom she had little time and from whom she found little favor. "I am more like my father," Lillian insisted, "I like controversial people." But it was more than that. How could she so tenderly nurture others yet have so little time or affection for her own? It was a question also raised by the Carter children themselves. She communicated with them in her own fashion, through books and notes. For example, she gave Jimmy a treasured copy of *War and Peace*. They would come home from school and find reminders for each of them affixed to the little black table that had become her desk. Years later, Jimmy and Ruth, trying to come to terms with their childhood, saw this old desk and exclaimed together, laughing, "It's Mother." The separation from their mother had been as much emotional as physical.

Jimmy developed a stoicism that was useful to him in later life, rarely complaining of either his mother's absences or his father's demanding expectations. Bourne writes that Jimmy "grew up both obedient to and resentful of authority, happy to look for safe ways to thwart it." His escape would be the navy — a long way off, but already in his mind at the age of seven. His father's plans were probably different. Although Jimmy Carter writes in his autobiography that his parents made no effort to induce him to remain on the farm, and that "everyone agreed that a naval career should be my ultimate ambition," it is hard to believe that his father never had in mind grooming his oldest son to be his heir.

Jimmy's childhood summers were made up of the kind of Huckle-berry Finn idylls other presidents have recalled, but also included a bit of Charles Dickens. He was not discouraged by the primitive conditions of Archery. Generally without shoes or shirt, the slight, freckle-faced, tow-headed youngster even looked like Huck Finn as he climbed trees, fished, hunted, and explored to his heart's content. His playmates were almost all black, until he went to school in Plains at the age of six, with only white classmates. His father assigned him tasks not unlike those of the children of his tenants, but then the responsibilities increased. Jimmy was given an acre to cultivate productively on his own, and he was even dispatched to the center of Plains to sell peanuts. Jimmy Carter lived in Archery for fourteen years, his greatest ambition "to be valuable around the farm and to please my father." His sisters did not work in the fields, except perhaps at harvest time when all hands were needed. His mother's involvement in the farm was limited to supervision of its pecan orchard, although, even if from afar, she managed the details of the household. Jimmy Carter writes, "There is little doubt that I now recall those days with more fondness than they deserve."

It appears that his parents' marriage had turned from a sort of stand-off to a trade-off. Earl built Lillian her own secluded pond house by a fishing lake, where she could spend scarce leisure time playing cards with a few friends or reading and reflecting on her own. It was Lillian's equivalent of the Val-Kill cottage at Hyde Park where Eleanor Roosevelt pursued her own private life. Sometimes Lillian and Earl still did things together, vacationing to Chicago or New York, sharing, of all things, a love of baseball. By chance, they were in Brooklyn when Jackie Robinson made his major-league debut. Lillian stood and cheered. Earl did not.

With so much cash on hand, the Depression did not affect Earl directly. It enabled him to buy properties low, and wait. But it affected almost everything and everyone else around Plains. The hotel closed. The bank failed. The Wise brothers' clinic burned down, and they reestablished it in the larger town of Americus. Plains's population was cut in half, as the unemployed looked elsewhere for scarce opportunities. Like Hannah Nixon, Carter turned no one away who asked for food. Many reciprocated by helping out with farm chores.

Even in his new all-white world at the Plains school, Jimmy Carter was not shielded from the deprivation of others. At the age of eleven he was baptized into the Plains Baptist Church, where he had attended Sunday school. He had yet to travel beyond Georgia, but he became fascinated with the Holy Land. Although he attended church more regularly than his mother, he also began, like her, to stress its moral message over its forms. He remembered old Bishop Johnson's son visiting his mother in the front parlor, and his father absenting himself. Perhaps, as Jimmy came to understand it, accepting more of his mother's racial toleration was a form of rebellion against his father's rigidity, but it was a sincere rebellion. Emulating what he could recall of Grandfather Gordy, Jimmy tried to overcome his own shyness, sticking out his hand, smiling, and introducing himself to his classmates. He was encouraged when they didn't make fun of him. One can almost see him, with the same broad smile, forty-six years later, announcing, "I'm Jimmy Carter, and I'm running for president."

Carter was a favorite of his teachers. In the eighth grade, he encountered one, Julia Coleman, who made so strong an impression that he would recall her in his inaugural address as president. Only an uncharacteristic escapade in high school, when he cut class, prevented Carter from graduating as valedictorian. He did speak at graduation, however, on "The Building of a Community," a composite of what he had learned from "Miss Julia" and his own "Miss Lillian." His parents were not only there to hear it, together they hosted a graduation party for the entire class.

Unlike other presidents who sought to attend a service academy, with Carter the impetus was not a matter of money. His father could afford to send him anywhere, and perhaps he had once hoped Jimmy would use college as a prelude to taking over the business. If his son were intent on a service academy, however, West Point seemed more relevant than Annapolis to Earl, an old army man. Jimmy's unlikely fascination with the Naval Academy had been fueled by Lillian's family. His maternal uncle, Tom Watson Gordy (named for the Populist leader Lillian's father had supported), a naval radioman, had for years been sending him nautical gifts and colorful postcards of exotic places. After Pearl Harbor, Tom was captured on Guam and remained a Japanese prisoner until the end of the war, his peril in the minds of everyone in both families. Intent on a naval career, Jimmy undertook to build himself up and prepare for the academy's exacting requirements. As short as his father, and much thinner, he found that at least in this his disciplined childhood was an asset. Finally reconciled, Earl eased the path to an appointment by befriending the local congressman, but it took more years of preparation by Jimmy at a local two-year college and Georgia Tech before he was finally admitted to Annapolis in 1943. With the acceleration of wartime demands, he graduated in three rather than four years, well up in his class.

Why did his mother cry at his departure? Perhaps it was the normal reaction of any mother, particularly since the war was still going on. Had she also some residual regret at having spent so little time with her boy during his formative years, and was she only now beginning to appreciate his potential? It is impossible to know. Whatever the case, at Jimmy's graduation she was obliged to share pinning on his insignia, an honor normally accorded only to mothers, with his fiancée, Rosalynn Smith, who had grown up next door to the Carters in Plains. The first young woman he had ever seriously dated, Rosalynn was the best friend of his sister Ruth. Although his mother protested that they were terribly young, the couple married in 1946. Rosalynn was only eighteen; Jimmy was twenty-one.

The relationship of Jimmy Carter and his mother, inhibited earlier by the insecurities of both, blossomed as Carter became a responsible adult. The mother-substitutes of his childhood faded in the recognition of the values he shared with Lillian Carter. She felt keenly his disappointment at not being named a Rhodes Scholar, but also relished his success in a naval career, however brief, that brought him close to the brilliant nuclear pioneer, Hyman Rickover. Even Jimmy's politics quietly mirrored his mother's, supporting Harry Truman in 1948, despite Southern disaffection, and listening sympathetically to Progressive Henry Wallace. Both mother and son would be inspired by John F. Kennedy, and Miss Lillian would once more encounter hostility, only more overt than before, for helping run Lyndon Johnson's campaign in Plains in 1964. Across the years, the distance between Jimmy and his mother was finally being bridged.

The pivotal year was 1953, little more than a decade after Jimmy had left for Annapolis. Earl had agreed to run for the state legislature to contest a more liberal candidate, who of course was a close friend of Lillian's and who remained the family lawyer after he lost. While still serving in Atlanta, Earl was diagnosed with inoperable pancreatic cancer. After Lillian phoned Jimmy with the news, he and Rosalynn rushed back to Georgia. Sitting by Earl's bedside, his twenty-nine-year-old son became better acquainted with his complex father. He had known little of his father's understated charitable side. James Earl Carter Sr., although fondly called "Daddy," had always been a symbol of authority to his son. At the funeral, as Bourne writes, Jimmy "was astonished at the hundreds of people, of both races, who came to express their concerns with an unanticipated degree of warmth and sincerity." Despite Rosalynn's reluctance, Jimmy understood that he had to return, not only to take care of many of these mourners but also to provide for his whole family, most of all his mother.

Miss Lillian was so devastated by the death of Earl, a man whose ideas she may have denigrated but whom she had once loved, that she had to be medicated. Perhaps her problems had been psychological all along, never feeling entirely accepted anywhere, after she left the security of the Gordy home and the Wise Clinic. Her now attentive children could not bring her out of a deep depression. Lillian dwelled on the past, admitting that her husband "had been a more affectionate father than I was a mother." Yet the structured world of Earl Carter was slowly coming apart. As Morris writes, "Jimmy Carter, inheriting his father's business in the 1950s, yet the son of Lillian Carter, would be among the generation that dismantled the old system."

Looking about for something to do, rather than simply becoming a doting grandparent, Lillian still found it a bit easier to relate to the children of others. For over seven years she was a housemother at an Auburn fraternity. She arrived there in a Cadillac donated by her son "so they wouldn't think I was poor." When she returned to Plains in 1962, the old boredom reappeared. Joining some old friends at the "Stitch 'n' Chat" club, gardening, and babysitting didn't seem like a very fulfilling life, but as her grandchildren grew, she took an appreciative interest in them that her four children had never experienced.

Watching a television program in 1966, she saw a public service announcement about the Peace Corps. It had no limitations based on age. She was sixty-eight, but healthy, an experienced nurse, and had never lost her desire to help "black people." She told her children she was going to volunteer her services, expecting that they would try to dissuade her. Instead, to her immense surprise, they were encouraging. She later protested, "I had to go to keep from losing face," but one suspects she may have been heartened by their approval.

It lasted only two years, but it was the great adventure of her life. She would not be sent to a "black" country, but to India. First she went to Chicago to learn Hindi and how to teach nutrition. Then she also had to learn the Marathi language. Her ability to pick up such challenging material quickly astonished her instructors. The main thrust of her assignment was to teach and promote family planning. Sent to a town outside of Bombay, she witnessed such extreme deprivation that the life of Archery's sharecroppers looked luxurious by comparison. Still, she coped and contributed. In the summer of 1968, prior to her return to the United States, she wrote her family, "I didn't dream that in this remote corner of the world . . . I would discover what life is really all about. Sharing yourself with others and accepting their love for you is the most precious gift of all." Coming back exhausted and looking as malnourished as many of those she had left behind, Miss Lillian still said to her daughter Gloria, "If it weren't for leaving home again, I'd spend the rest of my life in India — I'm torn between this life and my life there." It may have been a bit of the Southern hyperbole her son, Jimmy, inherited, but the experience not only recharged her batteries, it made her an instant celebrity even before the ascension of her son.

Her irreverent, easygoing younger son, Billy, would later comment, "I got a mama who joined the Peace Corps when she was sixty-eight. I got a sister who's a Holy Roller preacher, another wears a helmet and rides a motorcycle, and my brother thinks he's going to be president. So that makes me the only sane one in the family." In terms of the presidency, when Jimmy told his mother he was planning to run, she asked quite innocently, although her son was already governor, "For what?" She would always insist Gloria was the brightest of her children. Still, she played the most significant role in Jimmy Carter's "Peanut Bri-

Lillian Carter
Courtesy of the Jimmy Carter Library

gade," making public appearances on behalf of all his campaigns for office and speaking in public with candor, assurance, and humor. In old age, she became the woman she always knew she could be. The latent charm of the now-legendary Miss Lillian — even her bluntness — prompted the press in 1976 to view her as a more authentic personality than her less-spontaneous son. As Carl Anthony writes, ". . . instantly recognizable in her snow white pixie haircut, Miss Lillian was an eager celebrity of the late 1970s — whether cheering heartily at the World Series, playing poker on the way back from the pope's funeral, or sounding off on everything. . . ." She even represented President Carter overseas. As for the Equal Rights Amendment, Miss Lillian proclaimed, "I've been liberated all my life."

Carter may have learned the lessons of business success — ambition, hard work, discipline, shrewdness, even charity — from his father. But from his mother came his political credo — the positive, universal, unstructured message of literal Christianity, affirmed in his uncompromising espousal of civil and human rights. Jimmy Carter was the first president to declare himself a born-again Christian. Unfortunately, ministering to the multitudes is not the same as governing. A viable presidency is more than preaching, and promising never to lie is laudable, but in terms of reality no more prudent than promising never to raise taxes. For Jimmy Carter, as for his mother, appreciation came late. In his post-presidential career, through the Carter Center, he has been better able to merge faith and practicality, promoting conflict resolution and programs to combat poverty, hunger, ignorance, and intolerance. For this reason, he is perhaps our most admired former president.

Bessie Lillian Gordy Carter died on October 30, 1983, in her eighty-fifth year, outliving by a month her daughter Ruth, her husband's favorite. Billy also died in his fifties, in 1988, and Gloria in 1990, all of pancreatic cancer. At least Lillian was spared the desolation of witnessing so much personal tragedy. She left a belated legacy transcending her earlier inability to comfort her children and ease their isolation: the enduring moral message of her first son.

RONALD REAGAN has become the bane of biographers. Even before his poignant farewell to the American people confirming his Alzheimer's disease, he was being described as an appealing enigma, possessed of a selective memory. Reagan himself has sometimes been cited in seeming support of such a view. So outwardly warm and congenial, he admitted in his 1990 autobiography to an inclination from childhood "to hold back a little of myself." His dedicated wife, Nancy, once said, "There's a wall around him. He lets me come closer than anyone else, but there are times when even I feel that barrier." His official biographer, Edmund Morris, perplexed by Reagan's "genial yet inscrutable" nature, emerged from a celebrated writer's block to find he could only grasp the essence of his subject by introducing an intrusively new biographical style.

It is not within our province to evaluate Reagan's achievements as president, or even his managerial style (reportedly, a similarly confounding combination of focus and passivity), but to consider what and who in his Midwestern childhood most influenced both what he became and the ideas and imagery he was capable of voicing with the simple eloquence of a Lincoln. His "gift of gab" certainly derived from the almost quintessentially Irish father he so outwardly resembled. But Ronald Reagan was far more the child of his mother.

Both parents were amateur actors of some ability, but for Nelle Clyde Wilson Reagan, performing was more than an outlet. Next to her sons, it was the enduring love of her life. Through her plays and dramatic readings, as biographer William Pemberton relates, she did not merely demonstrate "how to convey feeling, mood, and storyline." She radiated a contagious optimism that extended beyond the footlights. If Harry Truman's mother was a "lightfoot" Baptist, Reagan's mother was a lighthearted Disciple of Christ. Her religion and her art were not in conflict. Both enabled her to transcend the considerable trials of her life.

Fathers of other men who became president have been drunkards or failures. John Edward Reagan was both. Perhaps failure led to drink. But there was nothing in him, even when drunk, of the meanness of a David Eisenhower, Frank Nixon, or Roger Clinton. Jack Reagan was more like the lovably helpless father in *A Tree Grows in Brooklyn*. At least in part because of her husband's binges, Nelle became something of a religious zealot, but hers was a religion steeped in compassion. Despite separations occasioned by circumstance, she never abandoned her husband. She prayed constantly for him to be cured of his disease, understanding that it was more a sickness than a sin.

In his autobiography, Reagan describes how gently his mother revealed the truth about what seemed at first "a mysterious source of conflict" between his parents. When his brother Neil and he were deemed old enough to understand, "she sat us down and explained

Jack's absences." He had an addiction to alcohol that he fought but sometimes couldn't control, "and we shouldn't love him any less" because he sometimes lost control "and embarrassed us. . . . We should remember how kind and loving he was when he wasn't affected by drink." It was true enough, but it also illustrated the fundamental difference between his parents. Although they may by then have seemed to others to be mismatched, Nelle and Jack shared a great deal beyond their undeniable devotion to each other: a love of the bright lights, remarkably enlightened social values for that time and place, and ambition. But beneath Jack's easy patter lay a salesman's cynicism. Nelle genuinely, as Ronald recognized, "looked for and found the goodness in people." So would he.

The origins of Ronald Reagan's parents were equally humble. Like Lincoln, Reagan was for a long while unable to trace his orphaned father's roots beyond his Americanized grandparents. As he later learned, the O'Regans had lived in County Tipperary, Ireland, a long way from Illinois, for generations. Most of them had worked as tenant farmers, living in abject poverty, and were buried in paupers' graves. In 1852, Michael O'Regan decided he'd had enough, moved to London, and, when he married, chose to sign his name Reagan. In 1856, the family emigrated to America, homesteading on land in Illinois. Their son, also named Michael, settled nearby, married, and in 1883 had a son, John Edward, who would be Ronald Reagan's father. When the child was six, both his parents died of tuberculosis. John was raised by an elderly aunt in a strict Catholic home, with little recollection of his mother and father. In the tiny town of Ballyporeen, whence the family had derived, the O'Regans were renowned for their drinking, but that no more accounts for Jack's excesses than for Ronald's moderation.

During his European tour in 1984, Reagan made a memorable visit to Ballyporeen. He noted that the more highly regarded of his clan were reputed to still spell their names Regan, like his secretary of the treasury at the time. Then, reflecting on the poverty of his forebears, Reagan hit just the right note: "Perhaps this is God's way of reminding us that we must always treat every individual with dignity and respect." Who can tell whose child or grandchild will someday rise to eminence? When John Kennedy had returned to Ireland twenty-three years before, he was greeted as a sort of grand seigneur, with the aura of a rock star. Despite his inevitable entourage, Reagan seemed almost to belong in Ballyporeen, and was more genuinely at home. For this grace he had also to thank his mother, who was neither Irish nor Catholic.

Well, perhaps a bit Irish. On her father's side, Nelle Clyde Wilson was of Scotch ancestry, which is often mingled with Irish in origin. Her mother's people came from England. At least one of her maternal forebears was known to be a domestic servant. Nelle's family emigrated originally to Canada, and then to the heartland of Illinois. Unlike Jack Reagan, Nelle grew up surrounded by a large, warm, and close-knit family. She had five brothers and sisters, some of whom were to provide solace and refuge when Jack's drinking became excessive. Nelle was born in 1883, the same year as Jack Reagan, near the same rural community of Fulton, Illinois. Neither had more than an elementary-school education. They met by working in the same retail establishment. Nelle had learned the skills needed to become an accomplished seamstress, and, at twenty-three, Jack was already an experienced salesman, anxious to improve his circumstances.

It is not difficult to imagine what attracted Nelle Wilson and Jack Reagan to each other. He cut a figure far removed from any local competition. A husky "black" Irishman, he was a bard of the prairies, his gift for storytelling celebrated well beyond Fulton, and he at least evinced an optimism equal to Nelle's. He also possessed, as Morris writes, a sort of virile elegance: "One would never guess from Jack's urban manners and sartorial grace, that he came from a family of rural Irish immigrants. He was that rare type, the instinctive gentleman." Nelle, despite her sharp features, a too-strong chin, and thin lips, was striking, with beautiful auburn hair and blue eyes, a figure slender but very shapely, and a native intelligence that matched Jack's.

Jack and Nelle were married in Fulton's Catholic church in 1904. Reagan has described his father as having "burning ambition," but apparently the goal that drove Jack Reagan was relatively modest — to own the largest shoe store in Illinois. Even in this, he would be thwarted. Certainly his drinking inhibited any sustained success. How much of it derived from frustration or even from heredity is hard to say, but Jack's most protracted binges were when things were going relatively well. Perhaps he understood that he was meant for something better than selling shoes but simply lacked the means to bring it about. Unlike his wife, he could not transpose that heightened ambition to his sons.

In 1906 Jack and Nelle moved to the town of Tampico, Illinois. It contained barely a thousand inhabitants, but Jack had obtained what looked to be a better opportunity at the Pitney General Store. In an apartment above the town's bank, their two sons were born — John Neil in 1908, and Ronald Wilson on February 6, 1911. Ronald was to have been named Donald, but a relative used it first. Neil was nicknamed "Moon," from the early comic-strip character Moon Mullins. For Ronald, "Dutch" was the instant appellation of his father. When he saw and heard his loud ten-pound son, delivered after Nelle had endured a full day's labor, Jack could only exclaim, "He looks like a fat Dutchman." Ronald didn't sound very manly, in any case. Both nicknames stuck. The two boys were to know little stability, following their parents to a succession of Illinois towns and even to a suburb of Chicago, all in Jack Reagan's endless quest for the retail opportunity he had envisioned. Ronald recalled going to four different schools in four years. Building enduring friendships was all but impossible. After Galesburg, Monmouth, Hyde Park, and back to Tampico, the Reagans would finally move to Dixon after the First World War, and Ronald, at the age of nine, would finally find what he came to view as his home.

Meanwhile, his mother, as buffeted as an army wife by all the packing and unpacking, had found consolation in religion. She had agreed to have her first son baptized as a Catholic, although by that time her meandering husband had more than lapsed. Ron, she was determined, would be permitted to make up his own mind when he came of age. In 1910, on Easter Sunday, Nelle Wilson Reagan was baptized by immersion into the Disciples of Christ. Like many converts, she would exceed most birthright believers in her professions of piety — and in acting on them. When he returned to Tampico, a more easily satisfied man than Jack Reagan might have settled down. As Morris points out, he was well on his way to becoming a community leader. He had been a town councilman, assistant fire chief, baseball-team manager, finance chairman of the church he rarely attended, and even a member of the Knights of

Columbus. However, Reagan's benefactor, H. C. Pitney, had decided to open an upscale shoe store in the much larger town of Dixon, to be called the Fashion Boot Shop. Jack would be installed as his manager and partner. It was too good an opportunity to pass up. Moreover, Tampico was already "dry," anticipating the nation — Dixon was not.

Morris notes that when Nelle left Tampico, "her frown began to etch" into that quizzical "slight peaking of the forehead" her second son would inherit. Neil believed himself to be more the son of his father, while Dutch was "always Nelle's boy." In fact, Neil would grow up a bit more polished and considerably more cynical than Ron. A formal family photograph, taken in 1914 when Ron was perhaps three, bears this out. Jack stands on the left, handsome and immaculate as always, the picture of an Irish tenor. Beneath him is the older son, Neil, hair neatly parted in the middle, wearing a suit the miniature of his father's, looking more like the scion of a prominent banker than of a shoe salesman. Chunky Ron, with fat cheeks and a full head of hair, stands next to his mother. At this age, he is still garbed in something closer to a dress than to a suit. Nelle, directly above, is attired like a fashionable Roman matron, her abundant hair neatly coifed, her sharp features still quite attractive, a confident half-smile on her narrow lips.

Almost from the start, Ron required little inducement to learn. Watching his mother as she traced every line on the page with her finger, he seemed to absorb sight with sound, beginning to read, he said, "by a kind of osmosis." He could read fluently by the age of five. He also discovered that he had a very retentive memory, an immense asset in the professions he would pursue. He was a loner and a dreamer and for a time was preoccupied with collections of toy soldiers and butterflies. His imaginary world encompassed the adventures he read about — the Rover Boys, Tarzan, Frank Merriwell at Yale, and especially the stories of Mark Twain. Like many other poor boys who became president, Ronald Reagan insisted that he was not really aware of his family's dire circumstances. They seemed normal to him. Perhaps in part because of the length of time spent there, he recalled his youth in Dixon as "sweet and idyllic as it could be." Indeed, Dixon was a picturesque town, ten times larger than Tampico, with many more amenities, situated by the Rock River between wooded hills and limestone cliffs. Children could

Jack and Nelle Reagan with sons Neil *(left)* and Ronald *(right)*
Courtesy of the Ronald Reagan Library

skate on the frozen river in winter, swim and fish in it during the long summer, take canoe trips and explore the cliffs like latter-day Tom Sawyers. Reagan admitted to still being a bit "introverted" when he first went to Dixon, but he soon learned to enjoy the outdoors, with its abundant wildlife, and began his lifelong love of horses. Times were still perilous. The store was not doing so well as expected, and the rural-based economy was slowing down. Even after their arrival in Dixon, the

Reagans lived in five different homes. Only the last could be called relatively spacious.

Nelle never quite gave up on Jack, but in the loneliness of their succession of towns, it is natural that her sons supplanted him at the center of her life. The church gave her direction; drama gave her diversion. Still, the family remained so close that Ron and Neil started calling their parents by their first names. Unfortunately, the Great Depression came early to the American heartland. Farm prosperity in the Midwest faded before the collapse of Wall Street. By 1930, Jack's "grandest dream" was only a bitter memory. The last thing hard-pressed farm families and unemployed cement-plant workers were looking for was a costly pair of shoes. Pitney closed the store, and for some time the only job Jack could find was at a grimy establishment two hundred miles away. Nelle stayed in Dixon, finding work as a seamstress-clerk at a dress shop and taking in boarders. It was the worst of times. As the Depression deepened, Pemberton writes, "Nelle held the family together. . . . She stretched her limited budget to keep the family fed and well clothed, drilled into her sons the value of an education, read to them at night, and took the boys to church several times a week." In the eyes of his small but formidable mother, Reagan would write, "all things were part of God's plan, even the most disheartening setbacks, and in the end everything worked out for the best." Despite the hard times, Moon and Dutch would later enroll at Eureka College; Nelle determined that, come what may, they would stay there, graduate, and justify the dreams for the better life that had become her goal.

Nelle's devotion to her church increased as times became harder. With her logistical skills, she even organized the town's Easter sunrise services. Ron not only welcomed all the books his mother brought him, when he was twelve he embraced her religion as well. Agreeing to be baptized into the Disciples of Christ, he talked his brother Neil, a titular Catholic, into joining him, although Neil soon lapsed. In his teens Ron was teaching Sunday school and even leading adults in Bible study. Nelle was delighted when she induced her initially hesitant son to join her in the dramatic readings she so enjoyed. In those more innocent times, Nelle still provided most of Dixon's public entertainment, heading a local troupe that drew large audiences. Ron's first recitation was so successfully received that he viewed it as a turning point in his life. "I liked the applause," he later wrote; it was an ideal antidote for a child suffering "the pangs of insecurity."

Everything changed for Ron about the time he entered high school. On a Sunday drive with his family, he picked up and put on his mother's eyeglasses and made a startling discovery. Suddenly he could see things with a clarity he had never experienced before. It turned out he was nearsighted, and he was fitted with a thick pair of glasses of his own. Unlike the experience of young Harry Truman many years before, Ron's glasses did not cut him off from boys his own age. His new vision enhanced his ability to enjoy everything. At the new Northside campus of Dixon High School, Ron finally separated from his older (and at that time bigger) brother Neil, who stayed at the old Southside location. Ron grew not only physically but in every other dimension. A solid if not outstanding student, he excelled in football and in every dramatic production, under a particularly inspirational teacher, and he was elected senior class president.

He also fell in love — with lively Margaret Cleaver, the daughter of the new minister of his mother's First Christian Church. Small, pretty, auburn-haired, and bright, Margaret reminded Ron of his mother. Soon, she became known as "Miss Brains," he as "Mr. Congeniality." Margaret's father was one of a succession of mentors for Ron, reinforcing his parents' belief in racial and religious toleration. Certainly Nelle approved, particularly as the couple planned to attend Eureka College, only a hundred and ten miles away and owned by the denomination. No more than eight percent of his classmates were able to go to college. Ron had worked since he was fourteen, initially with a pick and shovel. His most cherished job, however, was his seven summers as a lifeguard at Lowell Park, adjacent to a particularly turbulent stretch of the river. The memory of the seventy-seven people he saved from drowning, encapsulated by a cherished photograph of himself as a young Adonis, stayed vivid in his mind long after much else had vanished.

When he visited Eureka it seemed almost like the image of Merriwell's Yale he retained from his youthful reading, but it took a scholarship, jobs as a dishwasher and lifeguard, and virtually every dollar the family had saved to see him through. By that time the Depression was on in earnest. The hard-pressed college was considering drastic reductions in every area, including faculty. As a freshman, Ron made his first public address. This was no recitation. He had been chosen by the more reluctant upperclassmen to present the students' demands. They threatened a strike if the school's president did not reverse his plans for retrenchment. The results were not quite a clear-cut victory, but the president resigned and more prudent policies were adopted. The heady experience, as Pemberton put it, "was a defining moment for Reagan. He experienced for the first time the thrill of moving an audience." It was his own triumph, to be sure, but he understood how well his mother had prepared him for it.

A respectable student, as in high school, Ron also played football, starred in campus productions (again encouraged by an outstanding teacher), and as a senior was elected student-body president. Unlike Richard Nixon at Whittier, whose election was based on competence, or Lyndon Johnson in Texas, whose election was based on aggressiveness, Reagan won largely because of his popularity. He graduated in 1932 with a degree in economics and sociology, and not the remotest idea of how to market himself. Should he teach or coach for a time? He already knew he wanted somehow to become a professional actor, but might not something, anything, in radio offer a more viable opportunity? In such bleak times, it took months to break in, but eventually Reagan found a job doing sports and spinning records for a station in Davenport, Iowa. He proudly sent part of his first and subsequent paychecks to help his parents and enable his brother Neil to continue at Eureka. There would be ups and downs, but Reagan's career path was set. Like so many other mothers of presidents, Nelle Reagan would have liked to see her son become a minister, but the main thing was that he was settling for nothing less than what he wanted for himself.

Jack Reagan had eventually returned to Dixon to work again, though with little in the way of heightened expectations. A rare Democrat in Dixon, he finally had a bit of luck when he was hired by the new administration to help implement local relief programs for the Works Progress Administration, an immense boost to his self-esteem. The New Deal was welcomed by all the Reagans. Although they believed in the self-help philosophy of voluntary community cooperation, the neighborly small-town values Reagan extolled as president, in 1932 it seemed the federal government had a legitimate role to play. Success might come through hard work and ambition, but sometimes everyone needed a helping hand. To Nelle Reagan, the new reforms seemed initially like the practical application of her religion. Reflecting his parents, Ronald Reagan's first vote was for Franklin Roosevelt.

When Jack Reagan died of a coronary thrombosis at the age of fifty-seven — after years of drinking, smoking, and frustration — the only surprise was that his heart hadn't failed sooner. Characteristically, Nelle made all the arrangements, urging Ron not to intrude on his busy schedule until the actual funeral. As a child, even before his mother's revelations, Ron must have known something of his father's problems with alcohol. The arguments between his parents that would stop when the boys entered the room, the days of separation when his father simply vanished or when his mother would hastily bundle up both children and escape to her sister's, were followed by awkward reconciliations, his father's stubble and breath when he tried to kiss his sons both pathetic and repellent. Jack never "took it out" on his children, except for the emotional toll. As for Ron, however he tried to avoid the problem, he was obliged to confront it directly on a snowy night when he was only eleven. He found his father sprawled on the front steps. Should he ignore him and simply go in, leaving the problem for his mother to resolve? Instead, he grabbed hold of his father's overcoat and laboriously dragged him inside the house, taking, in the words of Pemberton, "a turn towards responsibility and maturity."

It is also possible that this explains something of Reagan's detachment as an adult — a detachment that was not merely the artifice of an experienced actor. Reflecting on the funeral of the father he had never stopped loving, Reagan could hardly fail to feel conflicted memories. Perhaps to his son, Morris suggests, "morally . . . John Edward Reagan had 'died' two decades before on the snowy porch of the family house in Dixon. . . . Then, as now, Dutch felt tenderness mixed with more selfish sorrow." Jack was not only better than his faults but better than his limited dreams. Ronald himself understood Jack's dilemma, as he wrote many years later: "While my father was filled with dreams of making something of himself, [my mother] had a drive to help my brother and me make something of ourselves." Still, in 1988, Reagan paid tribute to his father as not only "the best storyteller I ever heard," but also "the strongest man of principle I've ever met."

It was the most significant quality shared by both parents. They detested bigotry and injustice. On the road, Jack slept in his car in the midst of a blizzard rather than patronize a hotel that excluded Jews. Nelle brought hot meals to the inmates of the local prison and turned no one away from her home, even in the midst of the Depression, when food was scarce enough for her own family. The Reagans warmly welcomed all Ron's playmates, whatever their color or creed, and housed his two African-American teammates when the Eureka College football team visited Dixon and no hotel would admit them — this at a time when the Ku Klux Klan was powerful, not only in the South. Jack would not even let his sons see "Birth of a Nation" because it glorified the Klan. Ronald Reagan would always view people as individuals.

It is unfortunate that Reagan was too young to see his parents act together, in their earlier, promising years in Tampico. Morris relates their brief tenure as the town's "reigning theatrical couple," appearing in three full-length plays in 1913, both likely finding in the applause some recognition of their yearning for a more fulfilling life. By the time they returned to Tampico, the local dramatic society was dormant, and "Nelle's extravagant histrionics were finding their outlet in religion." It was in Dixon that she began to star on her own, with dramatic readings and recitations in and out of church, ultimately finding her new leading man in her son, Ronald.

Reagan did not go on to marry Margaret Cleaver, his high school sweetheart. They were separated for so long as he pursued his career that she met and married a foreign service officer. Nelle may have been disappointed, but as always she applied the dictum that in God's good time everything will work out for the best. Reagan would later be wed twice, to cinema actresses, the first of whom enjoyed recognition in Hollywood exceeding his, the second of whom sacrificed her own budding career to devote herself to his success and welfare. His father had lived to see his "Dutch" become a "star," if not president or even governor. His mother, who proudly viewed his screen roles as generally "just the way he is at home," died at the age of seventy-nine in 1962, the year

Ronald Reagan and his mother Nelle receive the key to
the city of Dixon, Illinois, from Mayor J. Fred Hoffman
Courtesy of the Ronald Reagan Library

her son became a Republican. The cause of death was a cerebral hemor-
rhage, hastened by what is now called Alzheimer's disease.

In their declining years, both parents lived in California, courtesy
of Ronald Reagan's largesse. In his words, "Nothing has ever given me
as much satisfaction as when . . . I could bring my mother and father
out here and give them a home." Reagan's escape, however fondly he

recalled Dixon, was from the limitations of small-town America, not from his parents — and particularly not from his mother. Of Nelle he said, "She always expected to find the best in people . . . and often did. . . . From my mother I learned the value of prayer, how to have dreams and believe I could make them come true." It was on her venerable, Scotch-taped, and thoroughly indexed Bible that Reagan took his first oath of office as president. If the storytelling came from Jack, so much of Reagan's persona derived from Nelle — the ambition, the optimism, the presence, reportedly even the inflection of his voice. Some people considered her overbearing, her sharp features — more pronounced as she grew older — paralleled by sharp opinions. Many more, however, viewed Nelle as personifying the healing qualities espoused by her faith. To her relatives and neighbors, she seemed almost to have been created by God to care for others. Ronald Reagan was not alone in viewing his mother, just as Nixon had seen his, as "a saint."

It was about Abraham Lincoln, not Ronald Reagan, that a biographer wrote, "His closest friends were baffled by his reticence. . . . They confessed they never understood him" — but similar things have been written about Reagan. Few presidents have escaped such analysis. Perhaps Reagan's earliest biographers made him seem too inscrutable. He is best remembered for what he chose to affirm. In such moments as his extraordinary poise after a near-fatal assassination attempt, his eloquent talk to Moscow students, and the grace of his final communication to the American people, there was no contrivance. As the colors fade, perhaps we should simply appreciate Reagan for such gifts, his love of country, and unmatched ability to express it, for what his "City on a Hill" represents. That this very image derives from his mother's church is another indication of his — and our — debt to her.

BILL CLINTON could never find male role models of sufficient weight to emulate. His lovable grandfather, his childhood pastor, his high-school band director were little more than people he remembered fondly. He admired the political figures he worked for, Frank Holt and J. William Fulbright, but they eventually lost. Clinton didn't believe in losing. He never knew his birth father, and his stepfather was more pathetic than influential. In truth, he had no real father-figures. His mentors at Georgetown, Oxford, and Yale came too late. Young Clinton was shaped not by men but by three women — his enigmatic maternal grandmother, who taught him to read and challenged for his affections; his extraordinary high-school principal, a widow who saw him almost as her own son; and most of all, his high-spirited mother, Virginia Dell Cassidy Blythe Clinton Dwire Kelley. One should not be misled by her four marriages. William Jefferson Clinton was the only real man in her life.

Virginia Kelley seems at first glance an unlikely candidate for inclusion in this book, except for the undeniable fact that she gave birth to Bill Clinton. There is, however, no doubt of Virginia Kelley's faith in her son and encouragement of his aspirations, the single quality that most unites the mothers of American presidents. Biographer David Maraniss provides a vivid picture of the mother of Bill Clinton, at about the time he was maneuvering for his celebrated photograph with President Kennedy in 1963. She "layered her face with makeup, dyed her hair black with a bold white racing stripe, painted thick, sweeping eyebrows high above their original position, smoked two packs . . . a day . . . drank liquor, was an irresistible flirt, and enjoyed the underbelly of her resort town, with its racetrack and gambling parlors and night clubs." She has described herself in similar terms.

Many men who became president sought to escape the circumstances of their childhoods and were inspired by their mothers. Here it was the mother who sought to escape, and found her inspiration in her son, the stable center of her life. But he, too, could hardly have been unaffected by all they experienced together, living in the different worlds of Hope and Hot Springs, Arkansas.

As Virginia Dell Cassidy, Clinton's mother was a fresh-faced, spontaneous girl who only around the end of high school in Hope, Arkansas, began to emulate her mother's addiction to cosmetics. Edith Grisham Cassidy, when fully prepared to go out, looked like a cross between Clara Bow and a geisha. Yet she had attained, by little more than absorbing a correspondence course, a respected position as a private-duty nurse. Her patients appreciated her skill, her encouragement, and her caring nature, qualities rarely manifested at home. Nothing her daughter did seemed to please her, and her unpredictable tendency to whip her only child bordered on the sadistic. Edith's mild-mannered, easy-going husband, James Eldridge Cassidy, whom everyone knew by his middle name, was often the object of his wife's verbal abuse, and occasionally of a projectile thrown at his head. Inexcusably, he had no ambition. Although the two had met growing up on neighboring Arkansas farms, Eldridge had been raised by relatives after his father died, had only a limited education, and was happy to settle for a job as Hope's iceman. Hauling the frozen blocks, first by horse-drawn wagon and later by truck, he had made a host of friends. He must have known he was in for trouble with ambitious Edith. To add to the turmoil, each suspected the other of philandering. It is little wonder Eldridge turned to drink. In a later era, the two might have divorced, but perhaps Edith found in violence a suitable outlet. Eldridge secured some solace by doting on his daughter, whom he affectionately called "Ginger."

Virginia didn't take her domestic trauma to school, where she made friends easily, was an honor student, and was popular enough to be elected to positions in student government. To make extra money she worked as a waitress. She was already becoming something of an accomplished flirt, however, and in time began to dress more provocatively and wear what she might previously have viewed as excessive makeup. She couldn't help seeing the humor in things, she said. But despite her unstable relationship with her mother, light-hearted Virginia also couldn't help but admire Edith Cassidy's steely determination to better herself. Virginia's first goal at graduation from Hope High School, in the ominous year of 1941, was to escape to somewhere more exciting.

She got as far as Shreveport, where she was accepted to nursing school at the Tri-State Hospital. No correspondence-course nursing career would do for Virginia. She also began to shed her small-town inhibitions, but it was in the hospital that she met a strikingly handsome and engaging young man named William Jefferson Blythe Jr. That he had brought in a female friend for an emergency appendectomy didn't matter to Virginia. She could see a bright, independent future in Bill's deep blue eyes. He said he was on his way to enlist in the army. Of course, he said all sorts of things, some of which didn't quite add up, but none of that registered with the already smitten student nurse. When she took Bill home even her exacting mother, to Virginia's surprise, fell for his charm. Her father liked just about everybody.

Two months later, Virginia and Bill were married. Five weeks after that, he went overseas. Virginia returned to nursing school, graduated, and — perhaps to save money — went back to live with her parents. At least now she might be treated as an adult, with a profession of her own to pursue. Bill wrote frequently, from North Africa and Italy, and returned home safely at the end of 1945. He had seen the world and had no intention of settling in a hick Southern town of less than ten thousand. He took Virginia to Chicago, where he had worked before, securing a job selling heavy equipment, but it kept him on the road a good deal of the time. They settled high in an old hotel, awaiting — like so many other newly married couples — the construction of a modest house in the already-expanding suburbs. Virginia was lonely in the metropolis, but excited. Soon she was also pregnant. With her new home not yet ready, she returned to Hope to prepare for her child, where at least there was company. On a May weekend, Bill drove south to pick up his wife, intent on gunning straight through. Somewhere in Missouri, when one of his tires blew out, he was tossed from the car and killed. Ironically, Blythe was buried in Hope, in the plot of his new wife's family. His son, William Jefferson Blythe III, was born three months later.

All of this would have come as intriguing news to Blythe's four or five previous wives. Not a few residents of Hope wondered about the absent father and the timing of the birth, but there is little doubt the baby — delivered a month ahead of schedule by Caesarean section — was Blythe's. It may seem prescient to some, however, that even the birth of the child who would become Bill Clinton was shrouded in an aura of mystery and scandal.

Settling back into her parents' home must have seemed to Virginia like a step downward. The house was big enough to accommodate both the new mother and child, but was it of sufficient size to encompass two mothers? To Edith, only forty-five, the baby represented a fresh start. He seemed to her, almost from the beginning, to be someone possessed of special gifts. It was important that William not acquire the undisciplined habits of his mother as he grew. Edith ordered his schedule, eating and sleeping, to the minute. Virginia and her father would simply have to adjust. Sometimes, in anger and frustration, Virginia would flee the house, Bill in his stroller, just to find fresh air and relief. Inside, the domain was Edith's. She could be gentle as well as stern — and even funny. For the first time, that side of her nature was lavished on a member of her own family. As for Eldridge, predictably, he adored the child, just as he adored the child's mother.

Virginia soon understood that she had to get out, but concluded that her independence could only be secured by enhancing her professional qualifications. It was a wrenching decision, but in less than a year she ventured to New Orleans to train to become a nurse-anesthetist, leaving her baby back in Hope. The attractions of the Crescent City brought out both sides of Virginia's emerging duality. She managed to have a very good time while ardently pursuing her studies. Back in Hope, Edith was more than a dutiful surrogate. Perhaps relieved to be freed of distractions, she lavished attention on Bill. She taught him to read at two. She dressed him with more care than she had ever dressed Virginia, and when he was three, he was already enrolled in children's programs at the First Baptist Church. She insisted to Eldridge that Bill was clearly an exceptional child with limitless potential, but all her husband could see was a cheerful, chubby, lively little boy. Bronchial problems had ended Eldridge's career as Hope's iceman. He had opened a grocery in a poor neighborhood, frequented by blacks as well as whites. Whenever his wife was called away, Eldridge would bring little Bill down and sit him on the counter. It was here that he first experienced racial integration, a rarity in Hope.

Under that counter was stashed Eldridge's stock of bootleg liquor, regularly supplied by a dapper businessman named Roger Clinton. Known as "Dude," he lived in the nearby resort town of Hot Springs, but he also owned the Buick dealership in Hope. Virginia had been acquainted with Clinton before she left for New Orleans, and she ran into him again on her visits home. There was a lot to like about Roger Clinton; he was immaculately attired, apparently well-heeled, and a lover of the good life. On the other hand, his reputation as a womanizer was based on reality, as Virginia soon discovered. She did not know, however, that he had a wife in Hot Springs, or that his prosperity was an illusion propped up by his more prudent brother. Still, she fell again for the blandishments of a smooth-talking suitor. This time her mother was not taken in, as she had been by handsome Bill Blythe.

Despite what she already knew about Roger Clinton and what she may have suspected, Virginia hoped they might together provide a good home for her son. There was no way she would leave him to the rigid supervision of her mother. Edith was so distraught that she threatened to seek legal custody of four-year-old Billy, as she called him. Although the suit never materialized, neither she and her husband nor the boy attended the ceremony joining Virginia and Roger Clinton. For the first time, women were fighting over Bill Clinton, the focus of their own ambitions.

He moved with his parents to his new home, in a neighborhood of other young married couples. For a while, all went well. His new father managed the Buick agency. When Virginia pursued her work, which sometimes involved irregular hours, a nanny looked after Bill. He was not only bright, he welcomed the company of other children. Their memories may be a bit embellished, but some of those he played with recall that already as a child Bill enjoyed bossing other kids around and being the center of attention. The domestic idyll didn't last long. Precisely what, Roger demanded to know, was Virginia doing with those doctors after their late-night labors? It was her parents' situation all over again, only with the husband initiating the discord. Roger's own philandering was no secret, but now his alcoholism became more acute, and with it his accusations turned to violence. He not only started to hit Virginia, he once fired a shot that narrowly missed her head. She had to call the police and send her son to a neighbor's.

Invariably, after he sobered up, Roger begged for forgiveness and promised to reform. To Bill's surprise, his mother always took Roger back. What was the child to make of it? He called Roger "Daddy," but he was not yet legally a Clinton, and his new father, the first he had known, gave him little attention. Were only women capable of affection? As Bill grew older, Virginia would sit with him and explain that she, too, had always craved a normal home, a stable haven. Even so, he must block out the bad things and focus on the good. He early learned how to compartmentalize his life. Perhaps it is not too much to add that Bill Clinton also discerned how to shade the truth, to see only what he wanted to see, to understand equivocation. Virginia reinforced her message by telling Bill that she, like her mother, had always known he was special. He was intended to do great things. Nothing was to get in the way.

Ostensibly to get a new start, Roger sold the Buick agency and moved his family to Hot Springs. He tried farming for a while, which Virginia objected to as inhibiting for her son's opportunities. They moved to a larger home in town that Roger could ill afford. Now, when he worked at all, it was selling auto parts. Hot Springs was nothing like Hope. Even its hilly topography was more enticing than Hope's flatlands. But within the resort town, there was another, almost startling separation: on one side, palatial hotels, gambling palaces, and every sort of diversion; on the other, a settled community of neat homes, schools, and churches. Vice and virtue coexisted side by side — and sometimes overlapped. Among Roger's friends were men far higher on the ladder of respectability who also led double lives, who patronized prostitutes, drank excessively, and regularly beat their wives, uninhibited by anyone's intervention. Bill kept hearing from his mother that he was meant for better things than the seamy side of Hot Springs, but he could hardly blot out the testimony of his own eyes.

Given the inner conflicts of Virginia Clinton, there could hardly have been a worse place for her to settle. Hot Springs reflected her own duality. Anesthesiology was a profession in demand, and she was a capable practitioner. But the attraction of the bright lights was irresistible. She would tear around town at all hours in her flashy convertible, gambling, drinking, taking in the shows, and, of course, at least flirting with other men. The inevitable arguments at home didn't seem to inhibit Bill's progress. He did well everywhere, first in Catholic school, then in public school. At the age of ten he appeared before the astonished pastor of Park Place Baptist Church and announced his intention to attend services regularly, with or without his parents. Bill no longer needed his grandmother to order his life. He learned to study, whatever the disorder around him. He took almost a paternal interest in his younger half-brother, also named Roger, who lived with them, hoping

— as it turned out, unsuccessfully — to at least provide him with some semblance of stability.

By high school, Bill was the one fully functional member of an irretrievably dysfunctional family. He had finally taken his stepfather's name, largely to blunt awkward inquiries from his classmates. He already understood the importance of image. Finally, in 1963, his mother, emotionally exhausted by Roger's increased drinking, abuse, and instability, filed for divorce. Bill testified as an eyewitness in the proceedings. In one instance he had physically confronted his stepfather and warned him never to lay a hand on Virginia again. It was nothing like courageous twelve-year-old Dwight Eisenhower's attempted intervention with his own father — by his teens, Bill towered over Roger Clinton — but it was the boy's affirmation that he was now the man of the house. Despite everything, Virginia dropped the proceedings and yet again took her prodigal husband back. Whatever the bond between them, he represented her weakness, Bill her strength. This time, however, when Roger returned home, it was almost as a visitor. The largest bedroom was Bill's. He even had his own bath. The property was now clearly his domain, his launching pad.

Predictably, Bill excelled at everything at Hot Springs High School — except sports. He was still a bit chunky, and sensitive about it, but it hardly inhibited his popularity with girls. At high school Bill also came under the influence of his third mother figure, principal Johnnie Mae Mackey. The opposite of Virginia Clinton in every ostensible way, Mackey was a walking embodiment of propriety. The one thing these two women shared was a confidence in the unlimited future of Bill Clinton. "They were both optimists," Maraniss writes, "and they saw one bright boy as the embodiment of their hopes. They had lost husbands . . . both of them. Billy Clinton was their manchild." When Mackey had to tell Clinton that, having already headed so many other activities, he could not run for student body president, she uncharacteristically burst into tears. The disappointment did not prevent Bill from delivering the final address at his high school commencement, really more a prayer than a speech: "And Lord, once more, make us care that we will never know the misery and muddle of a life without purpose."

Virginia Kelley with her son Bill Clinton
Courtesy of Reuters/CORBIS

With that performance, Bill had done the impossible, reuniting his mother and grandmother. Virginia could not wait to share her joy with her onetime rival, Edith Cassidy. She wrote her mother, "I was so proud of him I nearly died: He was truly in all his glory." She had already started sending news clippings to Hope, as in the years ahead she would remind everyone of when Bill would be on television. Like a fan, she followed everything he did. Like a mother, she even wrote a note thanking a family who had put her son up in Prague, inviting them to come visit her. Even her husband was won over. When he was dying of cancer and Bill returned from college to see him, Roger Clinton's pride, too, was palpable. How could it be that such a promising young man would carry on his name? When he learned he would be a Rhodes Scholar, Bill shed tears of his own that Roger Clinton had not lived long enough to share this moment, too.

Only ten years after graduating from Georgetown, Bill Clinton, at the age of thirty-two, was elected governor of Arkansas. Fourteen years later he would be president. His mother shared it all. Yet, if her own perseverance and pluck had prepared her son to go from success to success, if her faith in him had justified her life, by her own example she also contributed to Bill Clinton in a less positive way. As Maraniss writes, "He had been reared by a mother who loved to flirt, who walked around in a tube top and short shorts and spent considerable time each day trying to make herself sexually alluring and he left home just as the country was entering a new age of sexual freedom." The ambivalent legacy of gifted Bill Clinton has its parallel in his mother's life. When she witnessed his announcement for the presidency, no longer surprised by anything he might accomplish, she knew she had breast cancer. But she would not tell him, not yet, not before he won. It was no time to divert his attention with private afflictions. Everything must be sublimated to the goal. In this too, Virginia Kelley, who died in 1994, was the mother of Bill Clinton.

CHAPTER SEVENTEEN

Continuity and Change

✶ Dorothy and Barbara Bush

ACCORDING TO Burke's Peerage, there is hardly a family of any American president, however humble its domestic origins, that is not related in some convoluted manner to British royalty. Of them all, however, the Bush family is unquestionably the most regal, tracing its ancestry back to crowned heads in the fourteenth century. As biographer J. H. Hatfield notes, George Herbert Walker Bush is a fourteenth cousin of Queen Elizabeth II. Securely rooted in America's Eastern establishment, merging ancestry with affluence, this inheritance has been more a challenge than a boon to the Bushes. In three generations of elected leadership, they have consistently downplayed their pedigree and their wealth. Although heritage is no bar to achievement, American voters tend to favor those who "made it" on their own. As then Governor Ann Richards of Texas said so memorably of Republican presidential candidate George H. W. Bush in 1988, "Poor George. He can't help it. He was born with a silver foot in his mouth."

What was this prototypical Connecticut WASP, so preppy that his nickname is "Poppy," doing in Texas in the first place? Perhaps there was an element of escape involved — although, unlike Richard Nixon's longing after train whistles or Bill Clinton's transcending of a dysfunctional family, Bush's desire was not so much to leave behind the circumstances of his childhood as to create his own new chapter. Although his father could sometimes be forbidding and his mother more than a bit blunt, Bush loved and respected both his parents and appreciated the foundation they had provided him. When his new life in Texas turned to politics, that, too, was a family tradition. His father, a model of moral rectitude, had left his lucrative Wall Street career to serve in the United States Senate. Public service is valued on both sides of the Bush family. It was a maternal Walker uncle who told a reluctant young George W. Bush that "politics [is] the only occupation worth pursuing." America has changed a lot since John Adams felt obliged to engage in politics so that his sons and their sons might be able to follow more elevated professions. Despite its aura of scandal and the bloodlust of an intrusive media, public life is still viewed by families like the Bushes as a worthy goal.

The parents of George H. W. Bush were not smug snobs or status-conscious clubwomen, but strong individuals intent on their own achievements. Although his mother, Dorothy Walker Bush, faced limitations of caste and gender, she was described by her admiring daughter-in-law Barbara as "the most competitive living human." Her ancestors, who were originally devout Catholics, arrived on the rugged coast of Maine in the seventeenth century. Moving to the more congenial colony of Maryland, they eventually settled in Missouri and intermingled with families of other denominations. One prominent Walker married a Presbyterian. Over time most of the family accepted the Episcopalian faith that would be so firmly espoused by Dorothy. The family's wealth originated in a dry-goods business in St. Louis. Longing to locate at the heart of commerce, Dorothy's grandfather, George Herbert Walker, put its profits into an investment-banking firm in New York, which eventually became one of the nation's largest private banks, Brown Brothers Harriman. An avid sportsman, he donated golf's Walker Cup.

The Bushes were equally enterprising and mobile, intertwined, as biographer Herbert Parmet writes, with "some of the great landholding families of New York and New England." George H. W. Bush's genial grandfather, Samuel, made his fortune not in Manhattan but as an industrialist in Columbus, Ohio. His son Prescott Bush, born in 1895, was sent east to school, to Phillips Academy in Andover, Massachusetts, and later to Yale, initiating a family tradition. Settling first in Milton, Massachusetts, Prescott made his own fortune as a Wall Street

banker. The words used most often to characterize him are "imposing," "stern," and "commanding." He grew to six feet, four inches, with
a full head of black hair. Parmet describes him as "austere, regal, dignified, and imperious" — a classic authority figure. He loved children,
however, and would have five, although most of the day-to-day
childrearing was always in the hands of his wife, Dorothy, whom he
would marry in 1921 at the Church of Saint Ann in Kennebunkport,
Maine. (Kennebunkport was near Dorothy's family's spacious summer
home at what came to be called Walker's Point, which is still a refuge
for the family.)

Had she been born a generation or two later, Dorothy Walker
might have had a dazzling career of her own. She was the fire to her
husband's ice — outgoing, amusing, outspoken, and adventuresome,
yet very much a lady. A proper marriage for her was the preoccupation
of Dorothy's protective parents, who still lived in St. Louis. After attending private schools, she was sent east for "finishing" at Miss Porter's School in Farmington, Connecticut, in preparation for her presen-
tation to society. Called "Dottie," she particularly excelled in athletics.
In 1918 she was runner-up in the girls' national tennis tournament.
She was so gifted an athlete that even at the age of thirty-nine, a mother
of five, she took a set from a lady who had lost in the national tennis fi-
nals to the legendary Alice Marble. Dottie could play more than tennis.
She was an excellent golfer. And in a family softball game when she was
twenty-three and heavily pregnant with her first child, she hit a home
run, and then, realizing she was going into labor, was rushed to the
hospital to give birth. For all-around athletic skills, Dorothy Walker
might have rivaled even "Babe" Didrikson Zaharias, and she was far
more attractive. Although proud of Dorothy's accomplishments, however, her parents viewed such spirited exertion as verging on the unlady-
like. They preferred that their young champion be photographed by the
press solely in the guise of a sedate debutante, a bride, or a hostess. She
was not to be put on public display, even as an icon.

They were a handsome couple, Dorothy and Prescott Bush, although she was the more cheerful and sociable. Their first son, named
for his father, was born after the frantic hospital ride in 1922. Two years
later, their second son was born, and named George Herbert Walker

Dorothy Bush
*(in photograph above,
back row, second from right)*

Both photographs courtesy of the
George Bush Presidential Library

Bush, representing both families. His grandfather Walker called him "Little Pop," which became "Poppy." There would be two more boys, and a welcome girl, Nancy. As Prescott's investment house prospered, merged, and moved to Manhattan, the family relocated to a larger, comfortably unostentatious home in Greenwich, Connecticut. Here their children were raised in an atmosphere equally devoid of pretension. As biographer Pamela Kilian writes, "Both Prescott and Dorothy Bush hewed to the Puritan ethic. They believed in hard work, temperate living, and daily Bible readings." Sustaining such unpretentiousness was not easy. "Even during the Great Depression," Kilian continues, "there were three full-time maids and a chauffeur who took the Bush boys" to school.

Prescott Bush could be intimidating, Dorothy more accommodating, but both were demanding, no-nonsense parents. Good manners and propriety were important. Any form of snobbery was abhorrent. As their second son put it, "Dad taught us about duty and service. . . . Mother taught us about dealing with life in an old-fashioned way of bringing up a family [with] generous measures of both love and discipline." Nancy recalled, "We were a close, happy family, but we had strict rules." Boys didn't come to dinner late at the Bush home, or without a coat and tie. The same could be said for the girls, except that they had to wear proper dresses. Conversation was initiated by the parents.

In such a traditional home, father knew best. When he was preoccupied with a project, Dorothy took the children up the back stairs so as not to disturb him. Prescott Bush would never compromise his standards. He took Dorothy home from a meeting where the host told an off-color joke, and cut off contact with his own brother when he left his wife. Prescott Jr., who like all his siblings genuinely loved his father, admitted that it could seem almost "like the Fourth of July" when he went away on a business trip. The more relaxed atmosphere was palpable. His children feared not his hand but his disapproval, yet he could also be tender and had an unpredictable sense of humor. If Prescott Sr. presented a "terrifying challenge" to his children, it was not to make more money but to make something of themselves, particularly in a commitment to serving others.

Prescott followed his own advice. He first ran for Congress in 1950, losing a close contest to former advertising man William Benton, who had made a similar transition to public service. In 1952, however, he won an equally tight race for the U.S. Senate, in which he served until 1963. A conscientious, "modern" Republican, along the lines of Nelson Rockefeller, Prescott Sr. pressed for civil rights legislation and anti-poverty measures and opposed excessive spending for the space program on the premise that the money might be better invested at home in such areas as medical research. His demeanor may have been conservative, but his politics were those of progressive moderation, which he viewed as the Republican mainstream.

His son George's interest in politics emerged just as his own career ended. Throughout his childhood, as a relative said, George "placated" his demanding father, never challenging his authority and always seeking his approval. Yet, by his teens, George pondered what it might be like to get out from under, to be truly on his own. If he felt insecurity or anxiety, it was contained, and rarely expressed in anger. Parmet writes that "Such circumstances nurtured the development of George Bush, of whom a cousin said there was a 'Christian innocence.' . . . Everything had come to him without any grappling of right or wrong." That was because Dottie Bush harbored no doubts about which was which. She was the family's "spiritual conscience," Parmet continues, "making certain that Sunday services at the Episcopal church were not neglected." The daily readings of Scripture were her domain. Like everything else in her life, Dorothy Bush's deep religious faith was imparted without artifice. In her children's memory, their mother is almost a figure of legend, a mix of common sense, candor, and remarkable strength. It was young George who most inherited her athletic skill — first at Greenwich Country Day School, then at Andover, and finally as captain of the Yale baseball team. Yet when, as a boy, he complained about losing a tennis match because his game was "off," his mother replied, "You don't have a game. Get out and work harder and maybe someday you will." She was supportive, but didn't believe in inflating egos.

At the family's summer compound in Kennebunkport, Dorothy led a physical regimen not unlike the Kennedys' in Hyannis Port, which receded little as she got older. She made sure that her children and grandchildren were ranked on their expertise in all activities. These ranged from tennis, golf, and baseball to fishing, checkers, and horse-shoes. Dottie continued to compete in everything with all comers, male or female, irrespective of age. Whether swimming in the turbulent Maine water or competing in tiddly-winks, she never lost her prodigious will to win and, more often than not, outlasted everyone else. Gloating, however, was no more permissible than cheating.

Even when her son was vice president, she admonished him for any perceived lapse in conduct or excessive garrulousness to gain the limelight. It was more important to be genuine, to be oneself, than to yield to opportunistic grandstanding. Dottie's daughter, Nancy, summed it up by saying, "Mother is not much on houses or decorating. She didn't care about all that. She wouldn't be in the *Social Register*." She became an excellent horsewoman, for example, simply because she loved riding, not for public display. Her formal education may have ended at a proper girls' school, but her learning did not. Like her husband, she was less interested in social prominence than in promoting social responsibility.

George had so outstanding a record at Andover — he was a fine student, an athlete, and president of his senior class — that it must have gratified even his demanding parents. The commencement speaker in that perilous spring of 1942 was Secretary of War Henry L. Stimson, a visible reminder of World War II, which was uppermost in everyone's mind. At a Christmas dance George had met a lively young woman from Rye, New York, who was attending Ashley Hall in distant South Carolina. She planned to go on to Smith, but admitted to being so excited by the attentions of tall, handsome George Bush that she could "hardly breathe." Through subsequent dates and correspondence, their acquaintance grew into affection, and by the time she came up to his senior prom they considered themselves engaged. To the incredulity of their children, popular Barbara would always insist that George was the first boy she had ever kissed. The war came first, however. Instead of going to Yale, as he had planned, or even to Annapolis, George joined the navy. Just eighteen, bidding farewell to his parents, he saw for the first time tears in his father's eyes. George was sent to pre-flight school in North Carolina and eventually became the youngest bomber pilot in the naval air service.

He wrote as often as he could, not only to Barbara but also to his parents. Assiduously tending her "victory garden" while her husband raised funds for the war effort, Dottie enjoyed a welcome meeting with her son and Barbara in Philadelphia at the end of 1943. The aircraft carrier on which Bush's torpedo bomber squadron was to be based was being commissioned. Prior to the ceremony, Dorothy, who had in her purse the star sapphire engagement ring George was waiting for, asked a very nervous Barbara Pierce about her preferences in this regard. It needn't be a diamond, she assured Dorothy. By the time the carrier was launched, Barbara wore the ring she would never remove.

Soon George was bound for the South Pacific. In only a matter of months, both women were to endure agonizing uncertainty. In September 1944, on a bombing mission in the Bonin Islands, Bush's plane was shot down by anti-aircraft fire. Parachuting into the Pacific, he found refuge on a raft and within three hours was picked up by an American submarine. For a month, however, there was no word from him. He was presumed missing. When he finally arrived in Pearl Harbor and telegraphed home, the joy in Greenwich matched the relief in Rye. Barbara had taken a leave of absence from Smith to plan for her wedding, scheduled for December 19. George, however, who was awarded the Distinguished Flying Cross, did not return home until Christmas Eve, when he was greeted with the sort of reception Frank Capra might have filmed.

On January 6, 1945, at the First Presbyterian Church in Rye, New York, Barbara Pierce became Mrs. George Herbert Walker Bush. Young Prescott, who had been married only a week earlier, interrupted his honeymoon to serve as his brother's best man. Their mother was happily involved in everything, including a dinner the night before in Greenwich. George was in uniform. Barbara wore her mother-in-law's old but still elegant long-sleeved white satin dress and veil. After a reception for 250 people at the Apawamis Club and a too-brief honeymoon in Sea Island, Georgia, the couple traveled in George's 1941 Plymouth to married housing on naval bases in a succession of states. Although now a flight-training instructor, George also prepared for the final assault on Japan. They were in Virginia Beach when word came that the second atomic bomb had rendered the expected invasion of the Japanese home islands unnecessary. True to their roots, Barbara and George Bush went to church to give thanks before joining celebrants in the streets. Two months after the war ended, George was already at Yale, and Barbara was keeping house. Only a few years later, they settled in neither Greenwich nor Rye but in the wilds of Odessa, Texas. "Settled" is not quite the word; they would be constantly on the move, with six children in thirteen years.

Dorothy Bush was no less outspoken as a grandmother than she had been as a mother, but as she aged her children perhaps came better to appreciate a tenderness that had sometimes been masked by her forceful personality. The deepest tragedy of George and Barbara's married life was the death from leukemia of their first daughter, Robin. It was to his mother that a despairing George wrote. After Dorothy died, George found in her belongings a response to him, reflecting on Robin, that she had either neglected or decided not to send. "This letter . . . is kind of like a confessional . . . between you and me, a mother and her little boy — now not so little but just as close, only when we are older, we hesitate to talk from our hearts quite as much. . . . We can't touch her and yet we can feel her."

Everyone appreciated Dorothy Bush's strength, but it was her sensitivity that shone through, as well, when her husband died in 1972 of lung cancer at the age of seventy-seven. She composed the eulogy that was delivered by the rector of Christ Episcopal Church in Greenwich. Prescott Bush was a family man, she wrote, "who believed in necessary discipline when the occasion demanded, but was always loving and understanding. As the children grew older . . . he respected each as an individual, ready to back any decision thoughtfully reached and giving advice only when sought." Then her words turned personal, thanking her husband for giving her "the most joyous life that any woman could experience," and describing Prescott's inspiring integrity, his "lack of pride in material possessions." George praised his mother in a later letter as "heroic," his father's life as an "inspiration."

Dorothy Bush lived for nearly another two decades, rejoicing in her son's success, in his loyal wife she viewed as so much like herself, in her other children and many grandchildren. When George headed the American Liaison Office to the People's Republic of China, she, at the age of seventy-three, characteristically traveled to Beijing to see what the place was like. Then, after taking a few minutes to "shape up," she bicycled to the Great Hall of the People with the whole Bush family, very probably in the lead. "You should have seen the people stare at old Momma on the bicycle," Bush marveled. Although aging and ailing, she would not miss his inauguration as vice president. It was George who consoled his feisty mother when he came in for his share of criticism during the Reagan years. He wrote in 1986,

> Dear Mum,
>
> These are not easy times here, but they are times when the things you and Dad taught are coming to the fore. Tell the truth. Don't blame people. Be strong. Do your best. Try hard. Forgive. Stay the course . . . all that kind of thing.
>
> Poppy

When her son was elected president, Dorothy would not be denied witnessing this inaugural, as well, although she had to arrive in Washington in an ambulance plane, attended by physicians. When Bush asked which inauguration had been the best, Anthony writes, she replied, "Well, of course, today, George. I am sitting here holding the hand of my son the president of the United States." Her will never weakened. Two weeks after he lost his bid for reelection in 1992, Bush visited his ninety-one-year-old mother in Greenwich. She'd had a stroke and was slipping in and out of consciousness, but she mustered the strength to tell him she expected to be in heaven in a few hours. Bush wrote in his journal on November 19, 1992, "I go up to see Mother this morning. . . . The memories of her teaching me about life, memories of her sweetness and her leading me by example, her great capacity for love and kindness." She died that evening. Bush made another entry: "Tonight she is at rest in God's loving arms, and with Dad."

To her second son, Dorothy Walker Bush was "the beacon of our family — the center, the candle around which all the moths fluttered. . . . She was there . . . the power, but never arrogance, just love was her strength, kindness her main virtue. She taught us to be kind to the other guy, never hurt feelings, love." The fact is, she might have hurt a few feelings, including George's, by her proclivity for speaking her mind, but hers was an honesty rooted in affection, and the character she nurtured was one of robust faith.

THE ADAMSES, Harrisons, Tafts, and Kennedys have not been the only American political dynasties. The Bushes have become yet another. Years after the defeat of George H. W. Bush in his reelection bid for the presidency in 1992, a friend of his oldest son remarked, "These Bushes have this duty thing. You give something back to the system." And give back to the system they would. In the year 2000, George H. W. Bush, himself the son of a senator, would see his own son George W. Bush defeat Albert Gore Jr. (also the son of a political family) in a breathtakingly close and contested election. It did not always seem likely that this ascendancy would happen. The younger Bush's most satisfying professional experience prior to running for governor of Texas in 1994 was as part owner of a baseball team. His earlier, unsuccessful race for the House of Representatives even he came to view as premature. It had long seemed his more serious-minded brother Jeb was destined to be the one who continued the family's political tradition. Yet it was George who made his way to the presidency.

Had the election gone the other way, Gore's mother Pauline would have provided an equally compelling yet very different presidential mother story. But, after the dust had settled, it was Barbara Pierce Bush who, though proud to call herself "just a Mom," was elevated to the role of "First Mom" at the age of seventy-five. A mother of six who did most of the parenting in the house, she has been described as straightforward and compassionate. Her second child, the first girl, died at the age of seven, a shared anguish that created a special bond between Barbara and her oldest son, George W. He recalls, "The thing about my mother is that she could let you have it and then five minutes later be the most loving person in the world." Barbara's was not the pioneering professional path; a lingering regret is her failure to finish college. But, without deprecating the immense challenges involved in raising children, it must be said that she has been — and continues to be — far more than "just a Mom."

Barbara Bush is the only woman in American history to have witnessed both her husband and her son in the presidency. John Adams lived long enough to see John Quincy as president, but Abigail Adams did not. That this makes Barbara feel more fortunate than exceptional is the essence of her appeal. She knows who she is, and she is entirely comfortable with it — an authenticity that transcends politics. Barbara admits to being fiercely loyal to both her husband and her children, to taking criticism of them "very badly," and to sometimes even responding unpredictably — but family loyalty is not a quality Americans tend to criticize. Barbara's style is anything but contrived. If she looks older than her husband, so be it. She admits to having once tried to color her gray hair, before giving it up as a bad job, and to wearing her trademark three strands of imitation pearls in part to hide her jowls. What woman of a certain age cannot identify with that? And she does not apologize for the good fortune of having been born and married within a world of privilege. It is what one does with gifts that endows them with meaning. If unexceptional qualities have made Barbara Bush seem special, perhaps it is because so few public figures inside the image-obsessed "Beltway" embody them. In many ways she is much like her late mother-in-law, to whom she felt much closer than to her own mother.

Barbara Pierce Bush was always popular; only its extent has changed. Her childhood was not without trauma, but it was hardly dominated by it, and her family was well off, although not nearly so rich as the Bushes. The Pierce iron foundry in Pennsylvania, the source of family wealth, declined in the Depression of 1893 and never fully recovered. As a result, Barbara's father, distantly related to President Franklin Pierce, had to make his own way. A superb athlete and excellent student at Miami University of Ohio, Marvin Pierce went on to earn engineering degrees at Harvard and M.I.T. But it was in publishing that he made his mark, working his way up to president of the McCall's Corporation in New York. He met lovely Pauline Robinson, the daughter of an Ohio Supreme Court justice, at college, and married her in 1918. They had four children, two boys and two girls. Barbara, born on June 8, 1925, was their third child. Settled in a handsome home in the upscale suburb of Rye, on Long Island Sound, their house was a bit crowded, with six Pierces and a live-in Chinese couple to wait on them.

It was only in later years that Barbara came to better appreciate her rather austere mother. Pauline Pierce gravitated to her older daughter, Martha, who was as attractive and well-mannered as herself. Barbara, five years younger, developed early weight problems. At twelve she was already 148 pounds. As Herbert Parmet writes, Barbara also resented her mother's preoccupation with her sickly younger son, Scott, her houseful of very fragile antiques, and her excessive social life outside the home. As far as Barbara was concerned, it all amounted to general indifference. Although she inherited her mother's love of gardening, needlepoint, and dogs, the two were never close. Her dynamic, fun-loving father, however, made up for it, roughhousing with all his children, welcoming their friends, and seeming particularly fond of Barbara. She, too, loved sports, especially swimming and tennis.

Barbara had a tight group of friends, of whom she was the leading mischief-maker. Already five foot eight by the time she was in her teens, "Porky Pig," as she called herself, blossomed seemingly overnight into — if not quite a swan — a slender, very attractive young woman with reddish-brown hair and large, arresting eyes. She had loved her public elementary school but became even more popular, with both sexes, at the Rye Country Day School. Pamela Kilian quotes childhood friends of Barbara as saying, "The boys were wild about her. . . . She had more beaus than anyone. She was extremely popular. She was just awfully good with people. She was like her father, who was a delightful man. She was confident, very confident."

Before her junior year, Barbara's mother intervened. Martha had been sent away to a finishing school for girls with high academic standards, Ashley Hall in Charleston, South Carolina. Surely her lively younger daughter could also benefit from such exposure. Barbara was terribly upset, but she not only made the best of it, she made lifelong friends at Ashley Hall, even in its rather circumscribed environment. She also won the coveted sportsmanship award at graduation.

At the same time, Barbara kept in touch with her old friends in Rye and accompanied some of them during Christmas break of her junior year to a formal dance in the similarly social community of Greenwich, Connecticut. Here she met the love of her life, "the handsomest looking man you ever laid eyes on, bar none," George Herbert Walker Bush.

Only three years elapsed from the time he graduated from Andover to the day he was discharged from the navy. And between those two events, George and Barbara got married. At Smith, which she left to get married, Barbara had retained her popularity, playing soccer and lacrosse and socializing effortlessly. So pretty that her photo graced a fashion magazine's collegiate issue, she devoted less effort to her studies than to sending a constant stream of letters to George. After his discharge, he wasted little time finally entering Yale, which accommodated veterans by offering an accelerated program to gain a degree in only two and a half years. Miraculously, they found a small apartment, adjacent to many other newly married couples. Barbara might have completed her education at Connecticut College, but with so much that was new, she simply didn't feel the urgency to pursue it. Soon she was pregnant. On July 6, 1946, the Bushes joined the baby boom. George Walker Bush, the first of their six children, had a lot of company in their New Haven apartment building. Although he lacked the full name of his father, many would call young George "Junior."

Graduating from Yale in 1948, George Sr. was a Phi Beta Kappa in economics, a presence on campus, baseball captain, and tapped for Skull and Bones. He might have made his mark in investment banking or a brokerage house, but he didn't want to simply duplicate an inherited lifestyle or even its locale. The old urge to escape from under his father's thumb — and his gaze — resurfaced. George knew his wife was strong and resilient. He was right to have written her from the South Pacific in 1943, "How lucky our children will be to have a mother like you." They discussed various options, even considering farming. George sought not merely a commodity to invest in, but something he could see and feel. Ultimately he settled on learning the oil business in Texas.

It was not quite so abrupt a departure as it may seem. His mentor, who headed Dresser Industries where Bush would work initially as an equipment clerk, was a friend of Prescott Bush Sr., who probably admired his son's spirit of independence. To people like Dorothy Bush and Marvin Pierce, although they would miss their children, such enterprise was admirable. Unlike many other young, adventurous couples heading west, however, the Bushes had the security of knowing that if

Barbara Bush with a young George W. Bush
Courtesy of the George Bush Presidential Library

things didn't work out, their parents were fully prepared to bail them out. Still, George was intent on making it on his own. His father had given him a Studebaker for graduation, and with money saved from his naval pay the family of three set out for the wilds of Odessa, Texas. Truth be told, Barbara didn't want to go, but she had determined to be a dutiful wife, expressing her thoughts as openly as Dorothy Bush but then supporting her husband's decisions. They had overcome other challenges. Of course, she had never seen Odessa.

It must have looked as utterly foreign and desolate to Barbara Bush as the Pedernales had appeared to Rebekah Baines Johnson. Before and after the pervasive oil boom, such Texas towns would be most celebrated for the frenzy of Friday night high-school football. Barbara may have abandoned all the comforts of home, but her sense of humor was intact. "Everything in life is relative," she said. "We had the only house with a bathroom, and a car." Surrounded by little more than sagebrush and drilling equipment, Barbara set out to create a real home and to make friends of everyone she met. Her son George, her only child born in the East, was already growing to be an authentic and rather unruly Texan. George Sr., from 1946 on, considered himself more than a transplanted Yankee, but it is George W. who, having lived most of his life in the Lone Star state, really *sounds* like a West Texan.

In less than a year, Dresser Industries made George Sr. a full-fledged salesman and sent him to Compton, California. In all, the family would live in twenty-eight homes in seventeen cities. In California they moved five times in a single year, George traveling over a thousand miles a week. Barbara was seven months pregnant with her second child when alarming word came from the East. Her mother had died in a freak auto accident in Westchester County. Her father, who had been injured in the crash, urged Barbara not to risk losing her child by making a cross-country trip to attend the funeral. She agreed but later deeply regretted her decision. Her second child, named Pauline Robinson Bush for her mother, was born at the end of 1949. They called her "Robin." Barbara would have four more children in the next decade: John Ellis, called "Jeb"; Neil Mellon; Marvin Pierce; and finally, in 1959, another girl, Dorothy Walker, called "Doro."

Sent back to Midland, Texas, George decided to go into the oil business himself. He formed an independent development company, financed by an uncle, Herbert Walker, trading in oil leases and mineral rights in partnership with a neighbor. The Bushes had a lot of neighbors in Midland, many of them young couples from the East with Ivied backgrounds much like their own and lots of children. It was almost like a foreign enclave except that these intruders earnestly wanted to assimilate with the natives. They also wanted to make millions in oil drilling and exploration — "black gold."

That meant working extremely hard, raising more capital, taking risks, getting dirty on oil rigs and in warehouses, and traveling considerable distances. Bush developed ulcers, but his business was profitable from the start. For Barbara the venture meant years of intensive parenting, often alone. J. H. Hatfield writes, "She nursed young Jeb, played with Robin, and watched Junior try to become the next Willie Mays." Although George Sr. was a presence on weekends, coaching Little League and hosting immense neighborhood barbecues, and both parents taught Sunday school at the Presbyterian church, during the week it was largely a one-parent household. Even good-natured Barbara, utterly devoted to her family, came to resent it. "While he was out building a business," she recalls, "I was at home changing diapers and driving carpools. I was the enforcer and he was the gentle father — sort of a bad cop/good cop routine. . . . I had moments where I was jealous of attractive young women out in a man's world. I would think . . . George is off on a trip doing all these exciting things and I'm sitting home with these absolutely brilliant children, who say one thing a week of interest."

She had many more moments, however, of satisfaction. She learned to be more than a disciplinarian — a superb organizer, she juggled all her children's events and requirements, and kept the house clean and cheerful before they could afford help. She even kept score at her son's baseball games, just as she had for her husband at Yale. Neighborhood children gravitated to the Bush home, where the action and fun seemed to be, just as Barbara's informal hospitality would later draw congressional wives into her circle. Her logistical skill was acquired, but her genuine interest in others had always been there.

It was Barbara who first noticed the bruises on Robin's legs, and her unaccustomed lethargy. She was a lovely child, and had always been so active. Their doctor gave her blood tests, then struggled to break the heartrending news. Robin had leukemia, in a state so advanced it could not be treated. Her parents tenderly took her home and told no one. An attempt was made, over the next seven months, to treat Robin with a new drug at a New York research hospital. Early every morning in Texas, George went to church to pray, while Barbara accompanied their daughter, rarely leaving her bedside. Later husband and wife prayed together, often with their minister. Sometimes Robin seemed to rally, but on October 11, 1953, the four-year-old died. Barbara had tried to stay positive while Robin was alive, but afterward she was overtaken by inconsolable grief. "I felt I could cry forever." George poured out his despair to his mother, Dorothy. "We need a girl," he wrote, "her peace made me feel strong." They would have another girl, their last child, in 1959, but Robin's loss would always be felt.

Jeb was still a baby, but young George, at seven, was deeply affected. His parents had believed that sharing the news of his sister's illness would be too great a burden for him. "Why didn't you tell me?" George demanded of them after his sister died. He had sensed something was terribly wrong. "A little of me died with Robin," he recalled, but he felt it his duty to try to pull his parents out of their sorrow. After Barbara heard her son tell friends that he couldn't play because he had to stay with her and cheer her up, she began her emotional recovery. If anything, her attention to young George and Jeb became even more constant and protective. Might not they, too, be vulnerable?

Junior and his mother developed remarkable similarities. A family friend has been quoted as saying, "It's like you cloned Barbara to get George." Writer Jodi Enda adds, "They have a way of communicating that sets them apart," and quotes another friend: "At some points . . . you can hear him laugh because he knows what his mother's going to say. . . . They have the same twinkle in their eyes. They don't take themselves too seriously." As George W. puts it, "I just feel a special relationship with my mother . . . [who] fostered, nurtured, and brought me up. . . . We're pretty much alike, people tell us. . . . I don't mind a battle. . . . I've got my father's eyes and my mother's mouth." It was spontaneous Barbara who would characterize her husband's vice-presidential opponent, Geraldine Ferraro, as a word that "rhymes with rich." She learned to curb such tendencies, at least in public, but it would be no less easy for her son to do so.

Sometimes others needed protection against the young George W. Hatfield writes, "As a child in Midland, Texas, Junior was the smart-alecky and hot-tempered one of the Bush clan. He was a curiously incorrigible youth, who was a bit of a bully." He was also the class clown, and Barbara made frequent trips to the principal's office at Sam Houston Elementary School to deal with her son's disruptiveness. It continued into his teenage years at San Jacinto Junior High, despite Barbara's attempts at discipline. Midland was a segregated town in those days. Barbara could not abide bigotry, and washed her son's mouth out with soap when she heard him repeating racial slurs. As he grew, Junior's in-dependence merged with a will to win at almost everything that would have done his Grandmother Bush proud. Unfortunately, he simply could not accept losing gracefully. He insisted on being captain in any group activity, and would become so intemperate that Barbara had to banish him from golf courses and tennis courts in mid-game. It was no game to Junior. Although she saw similarities in their generally light approach to life, even Barbara found it exasperating to deal with her son's excesses when things got too competitive. "It was always a prob-lem in handling him," his often-absent father recalled. Perhaps the pe-culiar combination of aggressiveness, sensitivity, and self-deprecating wit George still possesses reflects the loss of Robin. Hatfield believes that the younger Bush's style of campaigning, his "wisecracking, occa-sionally teasing" banter, especially with the media, was first developed at home, when his responsibility was to "try to lift his parents out of their grief." Only humor could lighten the load.

By 1958 his father's oil company was doing so well that its head-quarters were moved to Houston. After only twelve years in Texas, George and Barbara resumed a lifestyle more along the lines they had known before the war, and with the arrival of Doro their family was complete. In 1962 George H. W. Bush was ready for the transition to public service that his father's example had implanted. With the Re-publican Party tilting to the right, away from Prescott Bush's modera-tion, George ran for party chairman in Harris County. His wife, as al-ways, was supportive. Kilian writes, "After fifteen housebound years centered on children — with George away on business much of the time — she found it a pleasure to be at her husband's side in a fast-moving campaign." She might do needlepoint during some of his repetitious speeches, but her outgoing personality and retentive memory made her an immense asset "in the mix and mingle before and after the speeches." George won, but when he contested for the United States Senate two years later against incumbent Democratic liberal Ralph Yarborough, he was swept away in the anti-Goldwater tide. Undaunted, George would be in public life for thirty years.

It was during the 1964 race that Barbara tried a hair rinse called "Fabulous Fawn." Her hair had turned prematurely gray the year Robin died, when Barbara was only twenty-eight. The coloring may have been fabulous, but during a warm airplane ride, it ran over everything. There would be no subsequent attempt. When her husband won his race for a House seat in 1966, Barbara picked up and moved again, to Washington. They had lived in Houston for all of seven years. By now, George W. was at Yale and Jeb was preparing for Andover. Barbara put Doro into the National Cathedral School, and her two remaining sons into St. Albans. George would go on to serve two terms in the House of Representatives and then become ambassador to the United Nations, chairman of the Republican National Committee, chief of the United States Liaison Office to the People's Republic of China, director of the Central Intelligence Agency, vice president, and then president of the United States. Barbara did not always agree with George's job selection, or the positions he espoused. She opposed his taking on the GOP chairmanship during the Watergate period, and her support for women's choice and gun control is well-established, but her vigorous advice was given to her husband in private. In public, her unaccustomed silence spoke volumes. One on one she is a more natural campaigner than her husband, another way in which she resembles her son.

George W.'s own rambunctious behavior continued through college, although he managed to graduate, become president of his fraternity, and continue the family tradition of being tapped for Skull and Bones. Perhaps his father's expectations intimidated him, just as George Sr. had sometimes resented his father's pressures. As Gail Sheehy writes, "Poppy, son of Senator Prescott Bush, was heard to say on occasion, 'Just wait till I turn these Bush boys out,' but for years the eldest son broke his father's heart. Frivolous, unfocused, sometimes reckless, George didn't seem the slightest bit interested in politics." In a celebrated instance, at twenty-six, a very drunk Junior challenged George Sr. to go "mano a mano," and the two had to be separated by Barbara. Somehow young George managed to get a business degree from Harvard, but his wild partying, probably including drug use, did not recede until, "struck by lightning" in 1977, he met and married an attractive, sensible, and down-to-earth librarian from Midland named Laura Welsh. He also finally discovered a job he loved as managing partner of the Texas Rangers baseball team, and found faith as a born-again Christian.

As George W. would say in 2000, "I believe in grace, because I have seen it . . . in peace, because I have felt it . . . in forgiveness, because I have needed it." As the Texas oil and gas boom evaporated in the 1980s, denying him the business success of his father, Junior's protracted adolescence descended into depression. It was mild-mannered Laura who laid down the law. George W. wryly recounts, "It was either her or Jim Beam." Rededicated to their marriage and twin daughters, the Bushes have been sustained by a shared faith. As president-elect, George W. Bush first asked for the prayers of "every American" and then initiated his administration with a special service dedicated to prayer and national healing at his United Methodist church in Austin. Waving his white Stetson at his Midland farewell, Bush paid tribute to the childhood values imparted by his parents. "It is here . . . where I learned to respect people from different backgrounds," he proclaimed. "It is here . . . West Texas, where I learned to believe in God." His daughters, named for their grandmothers, give evidence of continuing family traditions: Fun-loving Barbara is the fourth generation to attend Yale; Jenna, at the University of Texas, was senior-class president at her high school. Perhaps politics is in their future, as it almost surely will be for Jeb's handsome son, George P. Bush.

From the first, Laura found a supportive mother-in-law in Barbara Bush, just as Barbara had in Dorothy Bush. Barbara noted that, although quiet, Laura "accomplishes a good deal with quietness." Barbara also realized that her first son might, indeed, do well in politics, given some time and space. He genuinely enjoyed pressing the flesh, mingling with people, and being accessible; although he only owned a 1.8 percent share of the Texas Rangers, he was understandably the partner out front, campaigning successfully for a new stadium (and then selling his stake at an immense profit). He was also deeply involved in his father's political campaigns, becoming a relentless Bobby-Kennedy-like operative, never forgetting the derisive rhetoric of Ann Richards, or, after 1992, his father's defeat by Bill Clinton.

Perhaps that helps to account for his own candidacies. As with her husband, Barbara became her son's unobtrusive but trusted political confidant, demonstrating acute instincts and judgment sharpened by years in the public eye. Tempted to run for governor in 1990, George W.

decided against it; it was too soon, Barbara insisted, and, having already lost a premature race for a House seat, he concurred. As for religion, although Barbara is, like her husband, an Episcopalian, and has also attended Presbyterian churches, she finds no fault in her son's Methodism or the Catholicism of her son Jeb's family. It is not the church one follows, she believes, but the life. Barbara and Junior occasionally debate the nature of salvation, but that is preferable to questioning whether Junior will achieve it. He was not always so religious, but matured spiritually as well as emotionally in his forties. When he finally was elected governor of Texas in 1994, defeating the ostensibly unbeatable Richards, Bush's thanks to both his parents were heartfelt. While they were in the White House, he may have introduced himself as the "black sheep" of the family, but no longer. As Bill Minutaglio points out, Junior, in a way he would not have preferred, was perhaps finally liberated by his father's defeat in 1992 to pursue his own path to extending the family legacy. Still, there is continuity. George W. Bush took his presidential oath of office in 2001 with his left hand on the same Bible his father had used. Laura held it, as Barbara Bush had in 1989. The silver cuff links Bush wore had belonged to his grandfather, Prescott Bush.

As first lady of the land, Barbara Bush became the most admired woman in America. In part it was because of what she is — an exemplar of family values and traditional virtues. Her children have had many problems, but they remain devoted to their parents and to each other. "Grandmother Barb" to her twenty-three grandchildren, she still seems happiest in their company. This admiration derives not only from what she is, however, but also from what she does. She has strong opinions, but determined early to avoid any public role in espousing policies. She could accomplish many more positive things "by just getting out and plugging away" for nonpartisan causes. Get out she did, this poised patrician with a common touch, plugging away particularly for education and literacy. Her charming book on the most famous family dog raised millions for the literacy programs she championed. Kilian notes that, despite her affluent childhood, Barbara only traveled outside the United States after her husband attained high office. She eventually visited sixty-eight countries during his presidency, but, from the first,

Barbara Bush
Courtesy of the George Bush Presidential Library

she seemed at ease with almost anyone — premier, potentate, prime minister, or plain citizen.

There is still something of the deviltry of young Barbara Pierce in this matronly grandmother. As first lady, she insisted on putting the top ornament on the national Christmas tree, even though she'd done it eight times as the vice president's wife, because "it's the only thing I've done more than anyone else." When they visited British Prime Minister Margaret Thatcher in London and George Bush kissed her hand, Barbara reciprocated by kissing a delighted Denis Thatcher's hand. After Bush's presidential inauguration, she didn't hesitate to poke him in the ribs when he seemed momentarily confused. On a public platform, an acquired skill, Barbara tends to be bland and brief, as if still concerned that off-the-cuff remarks will get her or one of the family office-holders in trouble. She is at her best in small groups, especially in such natural settings as reading stories to toddlers.

There was an eloquent exception, however, in a 1990 appearance that defines who she is. Asked to deliver the commencement address at Wellesley College, Barbara's invitation was opposed by about a quarter of the graduates. These career-minded young women viewed Mrs. Bush as someone whose prominence was only gained through the achievements of her husband. Barbara won them over, however, with dignity, poise, candor, and a bit of humor:

> At the end of your life, you will never regret not having passed one more test, winning one more verdict, or not closing one more deal. You will regret time not spent with a husband, a child, a friend, or a parent. . . .
>
> Who knows. Somewhere out in this audience may even be someone who one day will follow in my footsteps and preside over the White House as the president's spouse . . . and I wish him well.

Traveling with her husband to Saudi Arabia to spend Thanksgiving with American troops during the Gulf War, she recalled her anxious days during World War II. She advised naval families in Florida, "Keep life at home on an even keel. . . . Many years ago . . . my heart and thoughts were somewhere in the Pacific . . . with a wonderful young naval pilot to whom I happened to be engaged. So we do understand a little bit of what you've been going through." To schoolchildren in Washington who had given her a necklace of paper doves, she said that she and her husband were praying for peace "like everyone else in America. . . . You may think the president is all-powerful, but he is not. He needs a lot of help from the Lord." The Bushes prayed together the morning he dispatched American troops to Kuwait. And that evening, as William F. Buckley relates, was not devoid of tears at the White House.

When peace came, George Bush Sr. had the highest public approval rating of any president since George Gallup started taking polls. Sixteen months later, it had plummeted sixty points. "It's the economy, stupid," Bill Clinton's campaign manager stressed to his staff. The

Bushes retired with grace, equally at home in Houston, Kennebunk-port, or Washington, wherever there are children to see and grandchildren to hold. They will probably get back a bit more to Washington now that their son is in the White House. Both are prepared to offer advice, but only if requested. As George Bush wrote his governor sons George and Jeb in 1998, "Remember the old song, 'I'll be ready when you are.... If you need me, I'm here.'" Earlier he had told them, "Do not worry when you see the stories that compare you favorably to a dad for whom English was a second language and for whom the word destiny meant nothing.... I am content with how historians will judge my administration." Beyond any public achievements, he has always been most proud, his wife reminds us, that "his children still come home."

As for Barbara Pierce Bush, her popularity will likely continue unabated, impervious to the fluctuating fortunes of her son's presidential administration. Before the 2000 Republican National Convention, cartoonist Ben Sargent pictured in two panels a telephone conversation between George W. Bush and his mother. "But everybody says I should play it safe . . . pick somebody who's above controversy . . . somebody good and gray," he insists. "George, I don't *want* to be vice president," she replies. It is enough to be her husband's "gray fox," her children's confidant, her grandchildren's inspiration, and the nation's first mother.

The Better Angels of Their Nature

HOW HAVE American presidents described their mothers?

There is not a virtue that can abide in the human heart, but it was the ornament of hers.

JOHN QUINCY ADAMS

Gentle as a dove and brave as a lioness.

ANDREW JACKSON

She who nurtured us in our infancy . . . taught us to raise our little hands in prayer . . . such a mother is of priceless value.

JOHN TYLER

She was a most affectionate and tender mother.

FRANKLIN PIERCE

Under providence I attribute any little distinction which I may have acquired in this world to the blessings which He conferred on me by granting me such a mother.

JAMES BUCHANAN

All that I am or hope to be I owe to my angel mother.

ABRAHAM LINCOLN

I seem alone in the world without my mother.

ULYSSES GRANT

I can see the golden thread running through the whole — my mother's influence on me.

JAMES GARFIELD

Do you know that if Mother were alive, I should feel much safer? I had always thought her prayers had much to do with my success.

GROVER CLEVELAND

By the blessings of Heaven I mean to live and die, please God, in the faith of my mother.

WILLIAM MCKINLEY

A sweet, gracious, beautiful Southern woman, a delightful companion, and beloved by everybody.

THEODORE ROOSEVELT

I thank God to have had such a mother.

WOODROW WILSON

Dear, dear Mother will wear a crown.

WARREN HARDING

Whatever was grand and beautiful . . . attracted her.

CALVIN COOLIDGE

My recollections . . . are chiefly of a sweet-faced woman . . . who kept our little family together.

HERBERT HOOVER

Those of us who enjoy the companionship of our mothers beyond the average number of years are indeed fortunate.

FRANKLIN ROOSEVELT

She was always a mother who did the right thing, and she taught us . . . that too.

HARRY TRUMAN

Mother was by far the greatest influence on our lives.

DWIGHT EISENHOWER

The glue that held our family together.

JOHN KENNEDY

She was quiet and shy, but she was the strongest person I ever knew.

LYNDON JOHNSON

My mother was a saint.

RICHARD NIXON

The most selfless woman I have ever known.

GERALD FORD

From my mother I learned the value of prayer, how to have dreams and believe I could make them come true.

RONALD REAGAN

She was the beacon of our family — the center.

GEORGE HERBERT WALKER BUSH

Such representative sentiments are what this book has been about. Thirty-three years ago Doris Faber described the mothers of our presidents as "the heroines of true American success stories." Seventy-nine years ago, the Reverend Dr. William Judson Hampton announced his intention "to rescue from oblivion the names as well as the lives of the mothers of our Presidents." Alas, that is still a worthy objective; most of us know far too little about these women, many of whom were remarkable in their own right, even had their sons not achieved the presidency. Hampton added that most of the mothers were "Godly women." That, too, is still true. Through the years much of the inspiration they provided their favored sons has been faith-based. Despite their human failings, and ours, this is still largely a book about the virtuous.

Whatever the source of their strength, it provided sustenance. So many American presidents have said, in effect, "I wish I could be more like my mother." By and large, these mothers have been the better angels motivating their sons' finer moments. May they not also inspire *us*, and when better than now?

BIBLIOGRAPHY

THIS IS ONLY the fourth book devoted to the mothers of American presidents, yet it is the second published within the last year. Perhaps a *First Fathers* is next, but any scholarship in this area is welcome. The three prior books are:

First Mothers, by Bonnie Angelo (New York: William Morrow, 2000). Although dealing only with the mothers of the last eleven presidents, the author draws on extensive research and interviews to compose a thorough, fascinating account, replete with anecdotes.

The Mothers of American Presidents, by Doris Faber (New York: New American Library, 1968; [repr.] St. Martin's Press, 1978). Out of print, but still selectively available, this brief but vivid and highly personalized overview is dedicated to rectifying the general neglect by historians of this subject, and succeeds splendidly.

Our Presidents and Their Mothers, by William Judson Hampton, D.D. (Boston: Cornhill, 1922). Although based on glorified myth as well as verifiable sources, this earliest study persuasively propounds the premise that presidential mothers, at least through Phoebe Harding, tended to be "Godly women." This work is also out of print, but available through rare book sources.

Some books about the fascinating history of the White House deal more with its occupants than its architecture, and at least touch on presidential parents. The most relevant of these is *America's First Fam-*

ilies: An Inside View of 200 Years of Private Life in the White House by Carl Sferrazza Anthony (New York: Simon and Schuster, 2000). Included in this lavishly illustrated popular history are brief chapters on "The Parents" and "Faith." Also see *American Presidential Families* by Hugh Brown and Charles Mosley (New York: Macmillan, 1993), and *The Presidential Character* by David Barber (New York: Prentice Hall, 1992).

Accounts of presidential wives offer at least glimpses of their own and their husbands' parents. Among the most readable are *First Ladies: An Intimate Group Portrait of White House Wives* by Margaret Truman (New York: Random House, 1995); *First Ladies: The Saga of the Presidents' Wives and Their Power, 1789-1990,* 2 volumes, by Carl Sferrazza Anthony (New York: William Morrow, 1990, 1991); *Smithsonian Book of the First Ladies* by Doris Faber (New York: Henry Holt, 1996); *American First Ladies: Their Lives and Their Legacies,* edited by Lewis L. Gould (New York: Garland, 1996); and *Heart and Soul of the Nation: How the Spirituality of Our First Ladies Changed America* by Cheryl Heckler-Feltz (Garden City, N.Y.: Doubleday, 1997). By and large, the reminiscences of first ladies have focused more on their roles in the White House than on their formative years — or their husbands'.

With only a handful of exceptions, accounts of presidential mothers vary from the virtually nonexistent to the not quite adequate. They rarely wrote about themselves. Most of the information available, of course, comes from books devoted primarily to the lives of American presidents; their parents, and particularly their mothers, are incidental. There is nothing remotely exhaustive about this list, but these are sources I have found most helpful:

George Washington

Alden, John R. *George Washington: A Biography.* Baton Rouge: Louisiana State University Press, 1996.

Bourne, Miriam Anne. *First Family: George Washington and His Intimate Relations.* New York: W. W. Norton, 1982.

Brookhiser, Richard. *Founding Father: Rediscovering George Washington.* New York: The Free Press, 1996.

Ferling, John E. *The First of Men: A Life of George Washington.* Knoxville: University of Tennessee Press, 1988.

Flexner, James Thomas. *George Washington: The Forge of Experience, 1732-1775.* Boston: Little, Brown, 1965.

Freeman, Douglas Southall. *George Washington: A Biography,* Vol. I, *Young Washington.* New York: Charles Scribner's Sons, 1976.

Jackson, Donald, ed. *The Diaries of George Washington.* Vol. I, *1748-1765.* Charlottesville: University Press of Virginia, 1976.

John Adams

Butterfield, Lyman H., et al., ed. *The Adams Papers: The Earliest Diary of John Adams.* Cambridge: Harvard University Press, 1966.

Ellis, Joseph J. *Founding Brothers: The Revolutionary Generation.* New York: Alfred A. Knopf, 2000.

Levin, Phyllis Lee. *Abigail Adams: A Biography.* New York: St. Martin's Press, 1987.

Nagel, Paul C. *The Adams Women.* New York: Oxford University Press, 1987.

Shaw, Peter. *The Character of John Adams.* New York: W. W. Norton, 1977.

Shepherd, Jack. *The Adams Chronicles: Four Generations of Greatness.* Boston: Little, Brown, 1975.

Smith, Page. *John Adams.* Vol. I. Garden City, N.Y.: Doubleday, 1962.

Withey, Lynne, *Dearest Friend: A Life of Abigail Adams.* New York: The Free Press, 1981.

Thomas Jefferson

Boorstin, Daniel J. *The Lost Worlds of Thomas Jefferson.* Repr.; Chicago: University of Chicago Press, 1981.

Brodie, Fawn M. *Thomas Jefferson: An Intimate History.* New York: W. W. Norton, 1974.

Ellis, Joseph J. *American Sphinx: The Character of Thomas Jefferson.* New York: Alfred A. Knopf, 1997.

Gardner, Joseph L., and Julian P. Boyd, eds. *Thomas Jefferson: A Biography in His Own Words.* Vol. I. Princeton: Princeton University Press, 1974.

Hirst, Francis W. *Life and Letters of Thomas Jefferson.* New York: Macmillan, 1926.

Malone, Dumas. *Jefferson and His Time.* Vol. I of *Jefferson the Virginian.* Boston: Little, Brown, 1948.

Peterson, Merrill D. *Thomas Jefferson and the New Nation: A Biography.* New York: Oxford University Press, 1970.

Randall, Henry S. *Life of Thomas Jefferson.* Vol. I. Repr.; Reading, Mass.: Da Capo/Perseus Books, 1972.

Smith, Page. *Thomas Jefferson: A Revealing Biography.* New York: McGraw-Hill, 1976.

James Madison
Ketcham, Ralph. *James Madison: A Biography.* New York: Macmillan, 1971.
McCoy, Drew R. *The Last of the Fathers: James Madison and the Republican Legacy.* New York: Cambridge University Press, 1984.
Moore, Virginia. *The Madisons: A Biography.* New York: McGraw-Hill, 1979.
Peterson, Merrill D., ed. *James Madison: A Biography in His Own Words.* New York: Newsweek, 1974.

James Monroe
Ammon, Harry. *James Monroe: The Quest for National Identity.* Charlottesville: University Press of Virginia, 1990.
Butterfield, Lyman H., ed. *The Adams Papers.* Cambridge: Belknap Press of Harvard University, 1961.
Cresson, W. P. *James Monroe.* Chapel Hill: University of North Carolina Press, 1946.

John Quincy Adams
Adams, John Quincy. *Diary of John Quincy Adams.* Boston: Belknap Press of Harvard University, 1982.
Hecht, Marie B. *John Quincy Adams.* New York: Macmillan, 1972.
Nagel, Paul C. *Descent from Glory: Four Generations of the John Adams Family.* New York: Oxford University Press, 1983.
———. *John Quincy Adams: A Public Life, A Private Life.* New York: Alfred A. Knopf, 1997.
Parsons, Lynn H. *John Quincy Adams.* New York: Greenwood Press, 1993.
Shepherd, Jack. *Cannibals of the Heart: A Personal Biography of Louisa Catherine and John Quincy Adams.* New York: McGraw-Hill, 1980.

Andrew Jackson
Davis, Burke. *Old Hickory: A Life of Andrew Jackson.* New York: Dial Press, 1977.
James, Marquis. *The Life of Andrew Jackson.* New York: Bobbs-Merrill, 1938.
Johnson, Gerald W. *Andrew Jackson: An Epic in Homespun.* New York: Minton, Balch, 1927.
Remini, Robert V. *Andrew Jackson.* Westport, Conn.: Meckler, 1990.

————. *The Legacy of Andrew Jackson.* Baton Rouge: Louisiana State University Press, 1988.

————. *The Life of Andrew Jackson.* New York: Harper and Row, 1988.

Martin Van Buren

Curtis, James C. *Martin Van Buren and the Presidency, 1837-1841.* Lexington: University Press of Kentucky, 1970.

Fitzpatrick, John, ed. *The Autobiography of Martin Van Buren.* Vol. I. Repr.; Reading, Mass.: Da Capo/Perseus Books, 1973.

Niven, John. *Martin Van Buren: The Romantic Age of American Politics.* New York: Oxford University Press, 1983.

Wilson, Major L. *The Presidency of Martin Van Buren.* Lawrence: University Press of Kansas, 1984.

William Henry Harrison

Cleaves, Freeman. *Old Tippecanoe: William Henry Harrison and His Time.* New York: Scribners, 1939.

Eshrey, Logan, ed. *Messages and Letters of William Henry Harrison.* Repr.; North Stratford, N.H.: Ayer, 1975.

Gunderson, Robert G. *The Log-Cabin Campaign.* Repr.; New York: Greenwood Press, 1977.

Peterson, Norman L. *The Presidencies of William Henry Harrison and John Tyler.* Lawrence: University Press of Kansas, 1989.

John Tyler

Chitwood, Oliver Perry. *John Tyler: Champion of the Old South.* New York: Russell and Russell, 1964.

Ellett, Katherine Tyler. *Young John Tyler.* Petersburg, Va.: Dietz Press, 1976.

Seager, Robert. *And Tyler Too: A Biography of John and Julia Gardiner Tyler.* New York: McGraw-Hill, 1963.

Tyler, Lyon G. *The Letters and Times of the Tylers.* Repr.; Reading, Mass.: Da Capo/Perseus Books, 1970.

James Polk

Cutler, Wayne, ed. *North for Union.* Nashville: Vanderbilt University Press, 1986.

Morrel, Martha McBride. *Young Hickory: The Life and Times of President James K. Polk.* New York: E. P. Dutton, 1949.

Nevins, Allan, ed. *Polk: The Diary of a President, 1845-1849.* New York: Longmans, Green, 1929.

Sellers, Charles. *James K. Polk.* Vol. I. Repr.; Princeton: Princeton University Press, 1966.

Zachary Taylor

Bauer, K. Jack. *Zachary Taylor: Soldier, Planter, Statesman of the Old Southwest.* Baton Rouge: Louisiana State University Press, 1985.

Bent, Silas. *Old Rough and Ready.* New York: Vanguard, 1946.

Farrell, J. J. *Zachary Taylor, 1784-1850.* Dobbs Ferry, N.Y.: Oceana, 1971.

Hamilton, Joffman. *Zachary Taylor: Soldier in the White House.* Indianapolis: Bobbs-Merrill, 1951.

Smith, Elbert B. *The Presidencies of Zachary Taylor and Millard Fillmore.* Lawrence: University Press of Kansas, 1988.

Millard Fillmore

Farrell, J. J. *Millard Fillmore, 1800-1874.* Dobbs Ferry, N.Y.: Oceana, 1971.

Barre, W. L. *Life and Public Services of Millard Fillmore.* Repr.; New York: Franklin, 1971.

Crawford, John E. *Millard Fillmore.* Westport, Conn.: Meckler, 1988.

Severance, Frank H., ed. *Millard Fillmore Papers.* Vol. I. Buffalo, N.Y.: Buffalo Historical Society, 1907.

Franklin Pierce

Gara, Larry. *The Presidency of Franklin Pierce.* Lawrence: University Press of Kansas, 1991.

Hawthorne, Nathaniel. *Life of Franklin Pierce.* Boston: Somerset, 1972.

Nichols, Roy Franklin. *Franklin Pierce: Young Hickory of the Granite Hills.* Philadelphia: University of Pennsylvania Press, 1958.

James Buchanan

Curtis, George T. *The Life of James Buchanan.* Vol. I. North Stratford, N.H.: Ayer, 1883.

Klein, Philip Shriver. *James Buchanan: Bachelor Father and Family Man.* Lancaster, Penn.: James Buchanan Foundation, 1991.

Klein, Philip Shriver. *President James Buchanan: A Biography.* University Park: Pennsylvania State University Press, 1962.

McFarlane, I. D. *Buchanan.* New York: Biblio, 1981.

Moore, John Bassett. *The Works of James Buchanan.* Vol. XII. Repr.; New York: Antiquarian Press, 1960.

Abraham Lincoln

Anderson, Dwight G. *Abraham Lincoln: The Quest for Immortality.* New York: Alfred A. Knopf, 1982.

Beveridge, Albert J. *Abraham Lincoln, 1809-1858.* Vol. I. Boston: Houghton Mifflin, 1928.

Current, Richard N. *The Lincoln Nobody Knows.* Repr.; New York: Greenwood Press, 1980.

Donald, David Herbert. *Lincoln.* New York: Simon and Schuster, 1995.

Foner, Eric, and Olivia Mahoney. *A House Divided: America in the Age of Lincoln.* New York: W. W. Norton, 1990.

Guelzo, Allen C. *Abraham Lincoln: Redeemer President.* Grand Rapids: William B. Eerdmans, 1999.

Herndon, William H. *Life of Lincoln.* Repr.; Reading, Mass.: Da Capo/ Perseus Books, 1973.

McPherson, James M. *Abraham Lincoln and the Second American Revolution.* New York: Oxford University Press, 1991.

Peterson, Merrill D. *Lincoln in Modern Memory.* New York: Oxford University Press, 1994.

Sandburg, Carl. *Abraham Lincoln: The Prairie Years,* Vol. I. Repr.; New York: Harcourt, Brace, 1974.

Tarbell, Ida M. *The Life of Abraham Lincoln.* Vol. I. New York: Doubleday and McClure, 1900.

Thomas, Benjamin P. *Abraham Lincoln: A Biography.* New York: Alfred A. Knopf, 1952.

Andrew Johnson

Castel, Albert. *The Presidency of Andrew Johnson.* Lawrence: University Press of Kansas, 1979.

Graf, L. P., and P. H. Bergeron, eds. *Papers of Andrew Johnson.* Knoxville: University of Tennessee Press, 1967.

Stryker, Lloyd Paul. *Andrew Johnson: A Study in Courage.* New York: Macmillan, 1936.

Thomas, Lately. *The First President Johnson.* New York: William Morrow, 1968.

Trefousse, Hans L. *Andrew Johnson: A Biography.* New York: W. W. Norton, 1991.

Williams, Frank B. *Tennessee's Presidents.* Knoxville: University of Tennessee Press, 1981.

Ulysses Grant

Anderson, Nancy S., and Dwight C. Anderson. *The Generals: Ulysses S. Grant and Robert E. Lee.* New York: Alfred A. Knopf, 1988.

Barber, James G. *U. S. Grant: The Man and the Image.* Carbondale, Ill.: Southern Illinois University Press, 1986.

Catton, Bruce. *U. S. Grant and the American Military Tradition.* Repr.; Boston: Little, Brown, 1972.

McFeely, William S. *Grant: A Biography.* New York: W. W. Norton, 1981.

Perret, Geoffrey. *Ulysses S. Grant: Soldier and President.* New York: Random House, 1997.

Simon, John Y. *The Papers of Ulysses S. Grant,* Vol. I, *1837-1861.* Carbondale, Ill.: Southern Illinois University Press, 1967.

―――, ed. *The Personal Memoirs of Julia Dent Grant.* Carbondale, Ill.: Southern Illinois University Press, 1988.

Simon, John Y., and David L. Wilson, eds. *Ulysses S. Grant: Essays and Documents.* Carbondale, Ill.: Southern Illinois University Press, 1981.

Smith, Gene. *Lee and Grant: A Dual Biography.* New York: McGraw-Hill, 1984.

Rutherford Hayes

Barnard, Harry. *Rutherford B. Hayes and His America.* New York: Bobbs-Merrill, 1954.

Bishop, A., ed. *Rutherford B. Hayes, 1822-1893.* Dobbs Ferry, N.Y.: Oceana, 1964.

Fitzgerald, Carol B. *Rutherford B. Hayes.* Westport, Conn.: Meckler, 1991.

Williams, Charles Richard. *The Life of Rutherford Birchard Hayes: Nineteenth President of the United States.* Vol. I. Boston: Houghton Mifflin, 1914.

James Garfield

Booraem, Hendrik V. *The Road to Respectability: James A. Garfield and His World, 1844-1852.* Cranbury, N.J.: Bucknell University Press, 1988.

Brown, Harry J., and Frederick D. Williams, eds. *The Diary of James A. Garfield.* Vol. I. Lansing: Michigan State University Press, 1967.

Leech, Margaret, and Harry J. Brown, *The Garfield Orbit.* New York: Harper and Row, 1978.

McElroy, Richard L. *James A. Garfield: His Life and Times.* Canton, Ohio: Daring, 1986.

Peskin, Allan. *Garfield.* Kent: Kent State University Press, 1978.

Smith, Theodore Clarke. *The Life and Letters of James Abram Garfield.* New Haven: Yale University Press, 1925.

Taylor, John M. *Garfield of Ohio: The Available Man.* New York: W. W. Norton, 1970.

Chester Arthur

Doenecke, Justus D. *The Presidencies of James A. Garfield and Chester A. Arthur.* Lawrence: University Press of Kansas, 1981.

Howe, George F. *Chester A. Arthur.* Repr.; New York: Ungar, 1957.

———. *Chester A. Arthur: A Quarter Century of Machine Politics.* New York: Ungar, 1935.

Reeves, Thomas C. *Gentleman Boss: The Life of Chester Alan Arthur.* Repr.; New York: American Political Publications, 1991.

Grover Cleveland

Brodsky, Alyn. *Grover Cleveland: A Study in Character.* New York: St. Martin's Press, 2000.

Jeffers, H. Paul. *An Honest President: The Life and Presidencies of Grover Cleveland.* New York: William Morrow, 2000.

Nevins, Allan, ed. *Grover Cleveland: A Study in Courage.* New York: Dodd, Mead, 1938.

———. *Letters of Grover Cleveland, 1850-1908.* Boston: Houghton Mifflin, 1933.

Tugwell, Guy Rexford. *Grover Cleveland.* New York: Macmillan, 1968.

Benjamin Harrison

Sievers, H. J., ed. *Benjamin Harrison, 1833-1901.* Dobbs Ferry, N.Y.: Oceana, 1969.

Socolofsky, Homer E., and Allan Spetter. *The Presidency of Benjamin Harrison.* Lawrence: University Press of Kansas, 1987.

William McKinley

Glad, Paul W. *McKinley, Bryan, and the People.* Repr.; Chicago: Ivan R. Dee, 1991.

Gould, Louis L. *The Presidency of William McKinley.* Lawrence: University Press of Kansas, 1981.

Higgins, Eva. *William McKinley: An Inspiring Biography.* Canton, Ohio: Daring, 1989.

McElroy, Richard L. *William McKinley and Our America.* Canton, Ohio: Stark County Historical Society, 1996.

Morgan, H. Wayne. *William McKinley and His America.* Syracuse: Syracuse University Press, 1963.

Theodore Roosevelt

Burton, David H. *Theodore Roosevelt.* Thorndike, Me.: G. K. Hall, 1973.

Hagedorn, Hermann. *The Roosevelt Family of Sagamore Hill.* New York: Macmillan, 1954.

Markham, Lois. *Theodore Roosevelt.* Broomall, Penn.: Chelsea House, 1985.

Miller, Nathan. *Theodore Roosevelt: A Life.* New York: William Morrow, 1992.

Morris, Edmund. *The Rise of Theodore Roosevelt.* New York: Ballantine, 1980.

Morrison, Elting E., and John Blum, eds. *The Letters of Theodore Roosevelt.* Vol. I. Cambridge: Harvard University Press, 1951.

Pringle, Henry. *Theodore Roosevelt: A Biography.* New York: Harcourt, Brace, 1931.

Renehan, Edward J. Jr. *The Lion's Pride: Theodore Roosevelt and His Family in Peace and War.* New York: Oxford University Press, 1998.

Roosevelt, Theodore. *Autobiography of Theodore Roosevelt.* Repr.; Reading, Mass.: Da Capo/Perseus Books, 1985.

William Howard Taft

Anderson, Judith Icke. *William Howard Taft: An Intimate History.* New York: W. W. Norton, 1981.

Pringle, Henry. *The Life and Times of William Howard Taft.* Vol. I. New York: Farrar and Rinehart, 1939.

Ross, Ishbel. *The Tafts: An American Family.* Cleveland: World, 1964.

Woodrow Wilson

Clements, Kendrick A. *The Presidency of Woodrow Wilson.* Lawrence: University Press of Kansas, 1992.

——. *Woodrow Wilson: World Statesman.* Boston: Twayne, 1987.

Lathan, Earl, ed. *The Philosophy and Policies of Woodrow Wilson.* Chicago: University of Chicago Press, 1975.

Link, Arthur S. *Woodrow Wilson: Revolution, War, and Peace.* Wheeling, Ill.: Harlan Davidson, 1979.

———, ed. *The Papers of Woodrow Wilson.* Vol. I. Princeton: Princeton University Press, 1966.

Mulder, John M. *Woodrow Wilson: The Years of Preparation.* Princeton: Princeton University Press, 1978.

Warren Harding

Fitzgerald, Carol B., ed. *Warren G. Harding.* Westport, Conn.: Meckler, 1991.

Mee, Charles L., Jr. *The Ohio Gang: The World of Warren G. Harding.* New York: M. Evans, 1981.

Russell, Francis. *The Shadow of Blooming Grove: Warren G. Harding in His Times.* New York: McGraw-Hill, 1968.

Calvin Coolidge

Coolidge, Calvin. *The Autobiography of Calvin Coolidge.* New York: Cosmopolitan, 1929.

Fuess, Claude. *Calvin Coolidge: The Man from Vermont.* Boston: Little, Brown, 1940.

McCoy, Donald R. *Calvin Coolidge: The Quiet President.* Repr.; Lawrence: University Press of Kansas, 1988.

Murray, R. K. *The Politics of Normalcy.* New York: W. W. Norton, 1973.

Sobel, Robert. *Coolidge: An American Enigma.* Washington: Regnery, 1998.

White, William Allen. *A Puritan in Babylon: The Story of Calvin Coolidge.* New York: Macmillan, 1938.

Herbert Hoover

Burner, David. *Herbert Hoover: A Public Life.* New York: Atheneum, 1984.

Eckley, Wilton. *Herbert Hoover.* New York: Twayne, 1980.

Hoover, Herbert. *The Memoirs of Herbert Hoover,* Vol. I: *Years of Adventure, 1874-1920.* New York: Macmillan, 1951.

Lyons, Eugene. *Herbert Hoover.* Garden City, N.Y.: Doubleday, 1964.

Nash, George H. *The Life of Herbert Hoover.* Vol. I. New York: W. W. Norton, 1983.

Nash, Lee, ed. *Understanding Herbert Hoover: Ten Perspectives.* Stanford, Calif.: Hoover Institution Press, Stanford University, 1987.

Smith, Gene. *The Shattered Dream.* New York: William Morrow, 1970.

Franklin Roosevelt

Asbell, Bernard. *The FDR Memoirs.* New York: Doubleday, 1973.

Cook, Blanche Wiesen. *Eleanor Roosevelt,* Vol. I, *1884-1933.* New York: Viking Penguin, 1992.

Freidel, Frank. *Franklin D. Roosevelt: A Rendezvous with Destiny.* Boston: Little, Brown, 1990.

Goodwin, Doris Kearns. *No Ordinary Time: Franklin and Eleanor Roosevelt and the Home Front in World War II.* New York: Simon and Schuster, 1994.

Israel, Fred L. *Franklin D. Roosevelt.* Broomall, Penn.: Chelsea House, 1985.

Lash, Joseph P. *Eleanor and Franklin.* New York: W. W. Norton, 1971.

Morgan, Ted. *FDR: A Biography.* New York: Simon and Schuster, 1986.

Parks, Lillian R., and Frances S. Leighton. *The Roosevelts: A Family in Turmoil.* New York: Prentice Hall, 1981.

Roosevelt, Eleanor. *The Autobiography of Eleanor Roosevelt.* New York: Harper and Brothers, 1960.

Schlesinger, Arthur M., Jr. *The Crisis of the Old Order, 1919-1933.* Boston: Houghton Mifflin, 1957.

Ward, Geoffrey C. *A First-Class Temperament: The Emergence of Franklin Roosevelt.* New York: Harper and Row, 1989.

———. *Before the Trumpet: Young Franklin Roosevelt, 1882-1905.* New York: Harper and Row, 1986.

Harry Truman

Daniel, Margaret Truman. *Harry S. Truman.* New York: William Morrow, 1972.

Ferrell, Robert H. *Harry S. Truman: A Life.* Columbia: University of Missouri Press, 1994.

———, ed. *The Autobiography of Harry S. Truman.* Boulder: Colorado Associated University Press, 1980.

———, ed. *Dear Bess: The Letters from Harry to Bess Truman, 1910-1959.* New York: W. W. Norton, 1983.

Gullan, Harold I. *The Upset That Wasn't: Harry Truman and the Crucial Election of 1948.* Chicago: Ivan R. Dee, 1998.

Hamby, Alonzo L. *Man of the People: A Life of Harry S. Truman.* New York: Oxford University Press, 1995.

Kirkendall, Richard S., ed. *The Harry S. Truman Encyclopedia.* Boston: G. K. Hall, 1989.

McCullough, David. *Truman.* New York: Simon and Schuster, 1992.

Miller, Merle. *Plain Speaking: An Oral Biography of Harry S. Truman.* New York: G. P. Putnam's Sons, 1973.

Miller, Richard Lawrence. *Truman: The Rise to Power.* New York: McGraw-Hill, 1986.

Truman, Harry S. *Memoirs,* Vol. I: *Years of Decisions.* Garden City, N.Y.: Doubleday, 1955.

Dwight Eisenhower

Ambrose, Stephen E. *Eisenhower,* Vol. I: *Soldier, General of the Army, President-Elect, 1890-1952.* New York: Simon and Schuster, 1983.

Brendon, Peirse. *Ike: His Life and Times.* New York: Harper and Row, 1986.

Chandler, Alfred D., Jr., Stephen E. Ambrose, Louis Galambos, et al., eds. *The Papers of Dwight David Eisenhower.* Eleven vols. Baltimore: Johns Hopkins University Press, 1970-1980.

Eisenhower, Dwight D. *At Ease: Stories I Tell to Friends.* Garden City, N.Y.: Doubleday, 1967.

———. *Crusade in Europe.* Garden City, N.Y.: Doubleday, 1948.

Ferrell, Robert H., ed. *The Eisenhower Diaries.* New York: W. W. Norton, 1981.

Lee, R. Alton. *Dwight D. Eisenhower: Soldier and Statesman.* New York: Nelson-Hall, 1981.

Neal, Steve. *The Eisenhowers.* Garden City, N.Y.: Doubleday, 1978.

John Kennedy

Burns, James MacGregor. *John Kennedy: A Political Profile.* New York: Avon Books, 1960.

Cameron, Gail. *Rose: A Biography of Rose Fitzgerald Kennedy.* New York: Putnam, 1971.

Collier, Peter, and David Horowitz. *The Kennedys: An American Drama.* New York: Summit Books, 1984.

Davis, John H. *The Kennedys: Dynasty and Disaster, 1848-1948.* New York: McGraw-Hill, 1984.

Goodwin, Doris Kearns. *The Fitzgeralds and the Kennedys: An American Saga.* New York: St. Martin's Press, 1987.

Higham, Charles. *Rose: The Life and Times of Rose Fitzgerald Kennedy.* New York: Pocket Books, 1995.

Hilty, James W. *Robert Kennedy: Brother Protector.* Philadelphia: Temple University Press, 1997.

Kennedy, Rose Fitzgerald. *Times to Remember.* Garden City, N.Y.: Doubleday, 1974.

Parmet, Herbert S. *Jack: The Struggles of John F. Kennedy.* New York: The Dial Press, 1980.

Reeves, Richard. *President Kennedy: Profile of Power.* New York: Simon and Schuster, 1993.

Reeves, Thomas C. *A Question of Character: A Life of John F. Kennedy.* New York: The Free Press, 1991.

Schlesinger, Arthur M., Jr. *A Thousand Days: John F. Kennedy in the White House.* Boston: Houghton Mifflin, 1965.

Smith, Amanda, ed. *Hostage to Fortune: The Letters of Joseph P. Kennedy.* New York: Viking, 2001.

Sorensen, Theodore C. *Kennedy.* New York: Harper and Row, 1965.

Whalen, Richard J. *The Founding Father: The Story of Joseph P. Kennedy.* New York: New American Library, 1964.

Lyndon Johnson

Caro, Robert A. *The Years of Lyndon Johnson: The Path to Power.* New York: Alfred A. Knopf, 1982.

Dallek, Robert. *Lone Star Rising: Lyndon Johnson and His Times, 1908-1960.* New York: Oxford University Press, 1991.

Divine, Robert A., ed. *Exploring the Johnson Years.* Austin: University of Texas Press, 1981.

Dugger, Ronnie. *The Politician: The Life and Times of Lyndon Johnson.* New York: W. W. Norton, 1982.

Goldman, Eric F. *The Tragedy of Lyndon Johnson.* New York: Alfred A. Knopf, 1969.

Harwood, Richard, and Haynes Johnson. *Lyndon.* New York: Praeger, 1973.

Kearns, Doris. *Lyndon Johnson and the American Dream.* New York: Harper and Row, 1976.

Miller, Merle. *Lyndon: An Oral Biography.* New York: G. P. Putnam's Sons, 1980.

White, Theodore H. *The Making of the President.* New York: Atheneum, 1965.

Richard Nixon

Aitken, Jonathan. *Nixon: A Life.* London: Weidenfeld and Nicholson, 1993.

Ambrose, Stephen E. *Nixon: The Education of a Politician, 1913-1962.* New York: Simon and Schuster, 1987.

Brodie, Fawn M. *Richard Nixon: The Shaping of His Character.* Cambridge: Harvard University Press, 1983.

Hoyt, Edwin P. *The Nixons: An American Family.* New York: Random House, 1972.

Morris, Roger. *Richard Milhous Nixon: The Rise of an American Politician.* New York: Henry Holt, 1991.

Nixon, Richard. *RN: The Memoirs of Richard Nixon.* New York: Grosset and Dunlap, 1978.

Parmet, Herbert S. *Richard Nixon and His America.* Boston: Little, Brown, 1990.

Wills, Garry. *Nixon Agonistes: The Crisis of the Self-Made Man.* New York: Mentor Books, 1971.

Gerald Ford

Cannon, Jim. *Time and Chance: Gerald Ford's Appointment with History.* New York: Harper Collins, 1994.

Ford, Betty, with Chris Chase. *The Times of My Life.* New York: Harper and Row, 1978.

Ford, Gerald. *A Time to Heal: The Autobiography of Gerald R. Ford.* New York: Harper and Row, 1978.

Reeves, Richard. *A Ford Not a Lincoln.* New York: Harcourt Brace, 1975.

Jimmy Carter

Bourne, Peter G. *Jimmy Carter.* New York: Simon and Schuster, 1997.

Carter, Jimmy. *An Hour Before Daylight: Memories of a Rural Boyhood.* New York: Simon and Schuster, 2001.

————. *Keeping Faith: Memoirs of a President.* New York: Bantam Books, 1983.

Mazlish, Bruce, and Edwin Diamond. *Jimmy Carter: A Character Portrait.* New York: Simon and Schuster, 1979.

Morris, Kenneth E. *Jimmy Carter: American Moralist.* Athens: University of Georgia Press, 1996.

Ronald Reagan

Cannon, Lou. *President Reagan: The Role of a Lifetime.* New York: Simon and Schuster, 1991.

————. *Reagan.* New York: G. P. Putnam's Sons, 1982.

Cardigan, J. H. *Ronald Reagan: A Remarkable Life.* Kansas City: Andrews and McMeel, 1995.

Morris, Edmund. *Dutch: A Memoir of Ronald Reagan.* New York: Random House, 1999.

Pemberton, William E. *Exit with Honor: The Life and Presidency of Ronald Reagan.* Armonk, N.Y.: M. E. Sharpe, 1997.

Reagan, Ronald. *An American Life: An Autobiography.* New York: Simon and Schuster, 1990.

―――. *Speaking My Mind.* New York: Simon and Schuster, 1989.

George Herbert Walker Bush

Bush, Barbara. *Barbara Bush: A Memoir.* New York: Scribner, 1991.

Bush, George H. W. *All the Best, George Bush: My Life and Other Writings.* New York: Scribner, 1999.

Kilian, Pamela. *Barbara Bush: A Biography.* New York: St. Martin's Press, 1992.

King, Nicholas. *George Bush: A Biography.* New York: Dodd, Mead, 1980.

Parmet, Herbert S. *George Bush: The Life of a Lone Star Yankee.* New York: Simon and Schuster, 1997.

Bill Clinton

Kelley, Virginia. *Leading with My Heart.* New York: Simon and Schuster, 1994.

Maraniss, David. *The Clinton Enigma.* New York: Simon and Schuster, 1998.

―――. *First in His Class: The Biography of Bill Clinton.* New York: Simon and Schuster, 1995.

George Walker Bush

Bush, George W., with Karen Hughes. *A Charge to Keep.* New York: William Morrow, 1999.

Hatfield, J. H. *Fortunate Son.* New York: St. Martin's Press, 1992.

Minutaglio, Bill. *First Son: George W. Bush and the Bush Family Dynasty.* New York: Time Books, 1999.

INDEX